D1066019

2ND EDITION

THE HOME INSPECTION BOOK

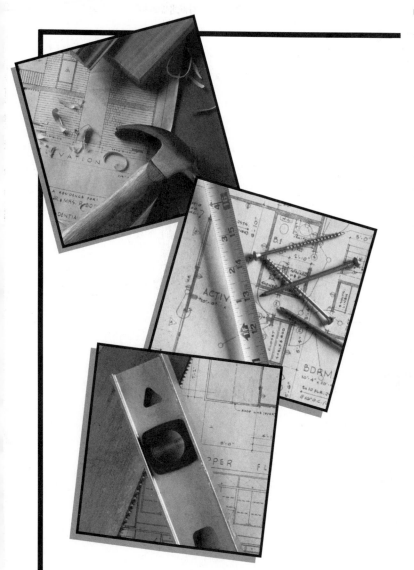

A GUIDE FOR PROFESSIONALS

WORKBOOK INCLUDED!

MARCIA DARVIN SPADA

Albany Center for Real Estate Education

www.albanycenter.com

THOMSON

SOUTH-WESTERN

Australia · Brazil · Canada · Mexico · Singapore · Spain · United Kingdom · United States

6.08

THOMSON

SOUTH-WESTERN

The Home Inspection Book: A Guide for Professionals, Second Edition
Marcia Darvin Spada

VP/Editor-in-Chief:
Dave Shaut

Executive Editor:
Scott Person

Associate Acquisitions Editor:
Sara Glassmeyer

Developmental Editor:
Jeanne Busemeyer,
Hyde Park Publishing Services LLC

Senior Editorial Assistant:
Adele Scholtz

Associate Content Project Manager:
Joanna Grote

Senior Marketing Manager:
Mark Linton

Manager, Editorial Media:
John Barans

Associate Technology Project Manager:
Bryan England

Marketing Communications Manager:
James Overly

Frontlist Buyer:
Kevin Kluck

Art Director:
Linda Helcher

Printer:
Globus Printing
Minster, OH

Library of Congress Control Number:
2007925594

For more information about our
products, contact us at:

Thomson Learning Academic
Resource Center

1-800-423-0563

Thomson Higher Education
5191 Natorp Boulevard
Mason, OH 45040
USA

CONTENTS

PART II   THE HOME INSPECTION PROCESS   41

Home Inspection Procedure and Reporting   43

Inspecting the Site   75

6   Inspecting the Exterior   95

Inspecting the Interior   137

Inspecting the Plumbing, Heating, and Air-Conditioning Systems   169

9 Inspecting the Electrical System   217

The *Home Inspection Book: A Guide for Professionals* offers a complete introduction to performing a home inspection. Although nothing can replace on-the-job experience, the basic tools are offered to you in a clear, easy-to-read format. The text is divided into three parts.

Part I, The Business of Home Inspection, answers frequently asked questions about home inspection as a profession. It also discusses the home inspection business and includes such topics as whether you should start your own business or work for others.

Part II, The Home Inspection Process, lists the tools you need and explores every component of the house exterior and interior. Moreover, the textbook includes an overview of environmental concerns. Numerous diagrams, photographs, and tables will help you better understand the material.

Part III, Workbook and Study Guide, will reinforce your learning with several different types of review activities. For more information about the Workbook, see "Instructions to the Student" on page xi and on page 267.

The textbook also includes appendices containing the Codes of Ethics and Standards of Practice from two home inspection organizations (ASHI and NAHI) and a list of home inspection organizations. A glossary of all key and other essential terms is included.

Many states are now requiring certification, licensure, or registration to practice home inspection. Because the number of states requiring licensure, or other types of certification, is expected to increase in the near future, many home inspection organizations offer accreditation. Field experience and an exam may be part of the application process. This text offers you many tools to reinforce and test your knowledge. They are:

- Learning Objectives
- Key Terms
- Putting It to Work
- You Should Know
- Illustrations and Diagrams
- Important Points
- Field Study Assignments
- Review Questions
- Workbook Activities

All of these items will assist you in preparing for a state exam or the exam for the organization of your choice.

ABOUT THE AUTHOR

Marcia Darvin Spada is the owner of the Albany Center for Real Estate Education, a New York–licensed proprietary school. A professional educator, Marcia teaches real estate and has developed curricula for numerous real estate courses used widely in colleges, real estate–related organizations, and proprietary schools throughout New York. In addition to *The Home Inspection Book*, she is author of *New York Real Estate for Brokers, New York Real Estate for Salespersons, New Jersey Real Estate for Salespersons and Brokers, Cram for the Exam: Your Guide to Passing the New York Real Estate Salesperson Exam, Cram for the Exam: Your Guide to Passing the New York Real Estate Broker Exam, Cram for the Exam: Your Guide to Passing the New Jersey Salesperson and Broker Exams,* and *Environmental Issues and the Real Estate Professional.*

Marcia holds a B.A. and an M.A. in English from the State University of New York at Albany and a B.S. in Real Estate Studies from Empire State College. She continues to update the material in this textbook and welcomes all comments. Her email address is cramforexam@hotmail.com. Visit her website: cramforexam.net for sample home inspection review exams and licensing information.

ACKNOWLEDGMENTS

Deep and grateful thanks to Anthony D'Agostino of Atlantic Home Inspection Service, Inc. for his technical expertise and the use of many helpful photographs. I am also indebted to Michael Casey, former ASHI President and Vice President and General Manager of Kaplan Professional Schools - Inspection Training Associates, for his review of the textbook. Also sincere appreciation to Vince Donnelley and Nick Chrysogelos; to Kim Spada, my daughter-in-law, and Vanessa Andrews, who are very capable editorial assistants; to the staff at Thomson/South-Western Publishing: Editors Scott Person, Jennifer Warner-Stephens, Sara Glassmeyer, Senior Marketing Director Mark Linton, Kara ZumBahlen, Chris Hudson, and Adele Scholtz; to Gay Pauley of Holcomb Hathaway; and to Elizabeth Sugg, who had the idea for this book. A special thank you to Dr. Bill Merrell of the Merrell Institute for all of his support and expertise. Finally, I appreciate the excellent work of Jeanne R. Busemeyer, Hyde Park Publishing Services, who produced the second edition of this textbook.

INSTRUCTIONS TO THE STUDENT

In each chapter, you will find a variety of features and activities to help you understand and learn the material. Refer to these instructions for using the features and completing the activities.

Key Terms. To prepare yourself for the information in the chapter, first look over the list of key terms at the beginning of each chapter. This will help focus your attention on important terminology throughout the chapter.

Learning Objectives. The course objectives tell you the focus of the chapter. You should be able to address all of the objectives once you read the chapter and complete the chapter review.

You Should Know. In most of the chapters, you will see small sections of boxed text highlighting important concepts. The topics for this feature are chosen because of their special importance to your home inspection career and the probability of these topics appearing on your exams. When studying for your exams, be sure to review this feature.

Putting It to Work. These boxed sections within the chapter offer you ways to apply your theory to practice.

Important Points. Each chapter contains a list of important points covered in the chapter. Use this list as a review and to help determine further study.

Chapter Review. The chapter review includes at least one field study assignment and review questions:

- *Field Study Assignments* allow you some hands-on experience. As you learn about the various components that make up the residential property, you will begin to investigate these components for yourself. You should choose a subject property or properties to investigate so that you can complete the field study assignments. You will find that you are observing in new and different ways the property components that you see all the time. Beginning today, you will begin to see with the eyes of the professional home inspector.

- *Review Questions* test your understanding of the information that you have studied, your retention of important points, and your ability to interpret the meaning of key terms. After studying the chapter carefully and completing all of the other learning activities, answer the questions. Upon completion, check the answer key at the end of the chapter.

Look over the questions before you begin reading the chapter to give you a focus on the topics contained in the chapter. Your completed review will serve as a useful study guide and will help you prepare for your course exam and any licensing exam you take.

In addition to these chapter-by-chapter tools, *The Home Inspection Book* includes:

Workbook and Study Guide. This comprehensive study tool will reinforce your learning with several different types of review activities: key term definitions and a key term matching exercise; an opportunity to meet chapter learning objectives; true–false questions; "How Would You Respond?" scenarios; and diagram reviews. Answers to all workbook questions appear in the Answer Key at the end of the Workbook.

50-Question Diagnostic Home Inspection Exam. Take this practice exam when you complete your coursework to test your mastery of the subject matter and to prepare for further home inspection licensure or accreditation exams.

Glossary. Don't forget about turning to the glossary. All key terms in the text together with other important home inspection terminology are contained in the glossary. Sometimes it is quicker to look up the meaning of a term in the glossary than to locate the term in the chapter.

A FINAL WORD

All of the activities are structured to help you learn and to test your understanding of the material. Don't feel uncomfortable if at first you are not doing as well as you think you should. For many, this is new material and it will take some time to absorb it. Don't hesitate to do the activities more than once if you feel you need the practice. You will be gratified to see your proficiency level increase as you progress through the course!

THE HOME INSPECTION BOOK

A GUIDE FOR PROFESSIONALS

PART I

THE BUSINESS

OF HOME

INSPECTION

1

CHAPTER 1

AN INTRODUCTION TO THE PROFESSIONAL HOME INSPECTION

D uring the last 15 years, home inspection has come into its own as a profession. The business of home inspection is a part of the multibillion dollar real estate industry. A home inspection has become as important to the buying and selling of houses as the actual real estate closing.

KEY TERMS

Home inspection

Home inspection report

Home inspector

Property condition
disclosure form

LEARNING OBJECTIVES

1. Summarize the purpose of and define a home inspection.

2. Explain the reasons why home inspection is a profitable, satisfying career now and in the long term.

3. Explain the purpose of the property condition disclosure form.

4. Summarize the present and future status of state regulation of the home inspection industry.

5. List home inspection organizations that can provide more information relative to a career in home inspection.

FIGURE 1.1

The home inspection industry: facts and figures.

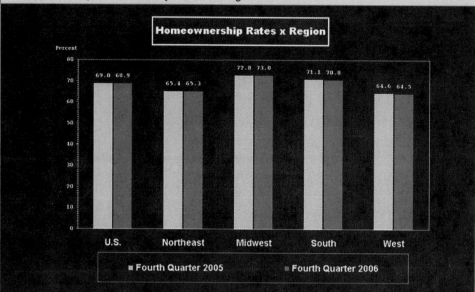

Source: U.S. Bureau of the Census.

As we enter the new millennium, we enjoy a very different society. Better technologies and information sources such as the Internet continue to give us more knowledgeable, demanding consumers. The home buyer is more sophisticated than ever and wants to maximize his value for the dollars spent on a home.

The future of the home inspection industry is bright (see Figure 1.1). Buyers want and need home inspections to support their purchase offers. Generally, buyers do not have sufficient knowledge of the various systems that make up the home. Real estate agents, lenders, relocation companies, and large employers that pay to relocate their personnel validate the need for a home inspection. Although buying and selling are the two main reasons why home inspection is in demand, there are other services offered by home inspectors.

HOME INSPECTION DEFINED

A **home inspection** *is an examination and observation of the exterior and interior of residential property including the grounds, the structure, and the mechanical systems to determine structural defects, broken or obsolete components, and damage due to water, wear and tear, and other conditions.*

A *qualified professional* **home inspector** *performs a home inspection.* The inspection may include, on request, extra services such as an examination of other property components including environmental concerns, swimming pools, or other buildings on the property. The **home inspection report** *is a written itemization and detailed summation of the findings of the home inspector with regard to a subject property.*

YOUR QUESTIONS ANSWERED

Home inspection is a challenging career choice because you are constantly faced with new problems to solve—all while you are helping others. The following are frequently asked questions that give an overview of the home inspection profession. Other sources of information include local home inspection offices, state licensing officials, and home inspection organizations (see Appendix D).

What are some of the advantages of a career in the home inspection business?

Home inspection offers a variety of career benefits. Here are some:

- There is increasing demand for the services of a professional home inspector.
- Part-time or full-time work is possible including working the hours you choose.
- If you decide to move, you can still practice home inspection.
- Long-term training, such as a college degree, is not required.
- The start-up expenses are low compared with other businesses. Generally, you realize immediate income and create a positive cash flow.

What are the reasons a home inspection is performed?

When a home is bought or sold, a professional home inspection is generally part of the transaction. The Department of Housing and Urban Development (HUD) has endorsed the need for a home inspection.

The request for a home inspection is generally made by the parties offering to purchase (contract of sale) a home. Built into the contract is a contingency clause that requires a home inspection prior to closing on the property (see Figure 1.2). The reasons are obvious. Lenders may require a professional home inspection as part of the mortgage application process because they want to protect their interest in the property by learning about any current or potential problems that may affect its value. The buyer wants a professional evaluation of the property so that detected problems may be considered prior to purchase. Should a home inspection reveal potential problems, the buyer may elect to void the contract or reduce the price offered.

Sellers may want to have an inspection performed before placing a property on the market. With a home inspection prior to placing the property on the market, the seller can better assess the property's value, correct any defects that might impair a sale, and avoid problems at closing or at some later time. Another relatively new service of the home inspector is the review of the seller's **property condition disclosure form**. Figure 1.3 is the New York form. This form is used in many states and may be mandatory in certain areas. *This form, generally furnished to the seller by a real estate agent, asks the seller to disclose detailed information*

FIGURE 1.2

Contingency clause from a purchase offer requiring a home inspection.

B. This Agreement is contingent upon a written determination, at Purchaser's expense, by a New York State registered architect or licensed engineer, by a third party who is _____, or other qualified person, that the premises are free from any substantial structural, mechanical, electrical, plumbing, roof covering, water or sewer defects. The term substantial to refer to any individual defect which will reasonably cost over $1,000.00 to correct. This contingency shall be deemed waived unless the Purchaser shall notify _____ no later than _____, as called for in paragraph 22, of such substantial defect(s), and furthermore supplies a written copy of the inspection report. If the Purchaser so notifies, then this Agreement shall be deemed cancelled, null and void and all deposits made hereunder shall be returned to Purchaser or, at Purchaser's option, said cancellation may be deferred for a period of ten (10) days in order to provide the parties an opportunity to otherwise agree in writing.

The following buildings on the subject property are to be included in this inspection: _____.

Source: Greater Capital Association of REALTORS®.

FIGURE 1.3 *Page 1 of the mandatory New York property condition disclosure form.*

NYS Department of State
Division of Licensing Services
P.O. Box 22001
Albany, NY 12201-2001
(518) 474-4429
www.dos.state.ny.us

Property Condition Disclosure Statement

Name of Seller or Sellers: _____

Property Address: _____
_____
_____

General Instructions:

The Property Condition Disclosure Act requires the seller of residential real property to cause this disclosure statement or a copy thereof to be delivered to a buyer or buyer's agent prior to the signing by the buyer of a binding contract of sale.

Purpose of Statement:

This is a statement of certain conditions and information concerning the property known to the seller. This Disclosure Statement is not a warranty of any kind by the seller or by any agent representing the seller in this transaction. It is not a substitute for any inspections or tests and the buyer is encouraged to obtain his or her own independent professional inspections and environmental tests and also is encouraged to check public records pertaining to the property.

A knowingly false or incomplete statement by the seller on this form may subject the seller to claims by the buyer prior to or after the transfer of title. In the event a seller fails to perform the duty prescribed in this article to deliver a Disclosure Statement prior to the signing by the buyer of a binding contract of sale, the buyer shall receive upon the transfer of title a credit of $500 against the agreed upon purchase price of the residential real property.

"Residential real property" means real property improved by a one to four family dwelling used or occupied, or intended to be used or occupied, wholly or partly, as the home or residence of one or more persons, but shall not refer to (a) unimproved real property upon which such dwellings are to be constructed or (b) condominium units or cooperative apartments or (c) property on a homeowners' association that is not owned in fee simple by the seller.

Instructions to the Seller:
a. Answer all questions based upon your actual knowledge.
b. Attach additional pages with your signature if additional space is required.
c. Complete this form yourself.
d. If some items do not apply to your property, check "NA" (Non-applicable). If you do not know the answer check "Unkn" (Unknown).

Seller's Statement:

The seller makes the following representations to the buyer based upon the seller's actual knowledge at the time of signing this document. The seller authorizes his or her agent, if any, to provide a copy of this statement to a prospective buyer of the residential real property. The following are representations made by the seller and are not the representations of the seller's agent.

GENERAL INFORMATION

1. How long have you owned the property? . . . .   _____

2. How long have you occupied the property? . . . .   _____

3. What is the age of the structure or structures? . . . .   _____
    Note to buyer – If the structure was built before 1978 you are encouraged to investigate for the presence of lead based paint..

4. Does anybody other than yourself have a lease, easement or any other right to use or occupy any part of your property other than those stated in documents available in the public record, such as rights to use a road or path or cut trees or crops? . . . .   ☐ Yes ☐ No ☐ Unkn ☐ NA

5. Does anybody else claim to own any part of your property? *If Yes, explain below* . . . .   ☐ Yes ☐ No ☐ Unkn ☐ NA
    _____
    _____

DOS-1614 (Rev. 8/06)   PAGE 1 OF 6 *regarding the property.* The home inspector reviews and compares this form to the inspection to arrive at a more accurate picture of the property's condition.

A home inspector may also be called on to provide extra services such as radon testing, an on-site sewage treatment analysis, a wood-eating insect inspection, and a water quality evaluation. For these tests and other environmental issues, the inspector may bring samples to certified labs for analysis or may recommend other professionals.

What background and attributes must a home inspector possess?

Some individuals who select home inspection as a career come from other sectors of the housing industry; this includes real estate appraisers, real estate agents, and home contractors such as builders, electricians, plumbers, and the like. A background in a related profession is helpful but not necessary. Many courses in the business of home inspection are available through colleges, home inspection organizations, real estate proprietary schools, and home study.

A successful home inspector is the type of person who pays attention to detail and has a willingness to learn. In addition, home inspectors must work well with people because they are in contact with home buyers and sellers; other individuals in the housing industry such as bankers, real estate agents, and local code enforcement officials; and people in related areas of expertise. Home inspectors must have a certain amount of stamina too because they inspect basements, crawl spaces, roofs (although standing on one is not a requirement), and the grounds surrounding a property.

Do I need to be a licensed professional engineer to be a home inspector?

A home inspector need not be a licensed professional engineer. To become a professional engineer, a state license is required. The license is based on the following requirements:

- Four years of college-level engineering that includes course work in aspects of structural, mechanical, and electrical engineering.
- Four years of professional engineering experience.
- Successful completion of a 16-hour written exam administered by the state board.

Although some home and building inspectors do have a professional engineer license, this type of licensure is not required to practice as a home inspector.

What are the state licensing or registration requirements?

Many states are currently formulating regulations to license, certify, or register home inspectors. Requirements vary from state to state and regulation does not exist in every state. Requirements may include field experience or the successful completion of a state exam, neither, or both. Table 1.1 lists states that participate in the home inspection regulatory process. Prior to embarking on a career in home inspection, investigate whether your state regulates home inspectors. Many home inspection organizations can guide you (see Appendix D) to the agency in your state government that regulates home inspection and provide information about any regulation in place.

TABLE 1.1	*State home inspector licensing/regulation (as of January 2007).*

Alabama *Licensure (Act 2002-517 enacted in 2002).* Requires individuals performing home inspections to become licensed by the Alabama Building Commission. The Alabama Standards of Practice and Code of Ethics (see Home Inspectors Rules and Applications) is adopted from the ASH Standards of Practice and Code of Ethics. The Alabama Building Commission gratefully acknowledges ASHI's consent. The Building Commission adopted the National Home Inspection Examination to assess minimum competence. The bill also outlines educational and experiential requirements to become licensed, sets license fees and insurance requirements, and defines penalties under which licensure may be suspended or revoked. This law replaces Act 96-574.

Alaska *Licensure (Chapter 134 SLA enacted in 2003).* In Alaska, home inspectors and associate home inspectors will be issued a certificate of registration by the Department of Community and Economic Development. To be a registered home inspector, an individual must: 1) pass the National Home Inspector Examination, 2) meet the educational and experience requirements as determined by the Department, 3) submit a complete application for registration within one year of passing the exam, 4) not have been convicted of specific crimes in the past seven years of the date of the application, 5) not have had the authority to perform home inspections revoked in the state or another jurisdiction, 6) not be the subject of an unresolved criminal complaint or unresolved disciplinary action in the state and 7) pay the appropriate fees. For the renewal of certificates, the Department will require at least eight hours of continuing competency activity in each licensing period. The Department will set the registration fees for home inspectors and associate home inspectors and determine the disciplinary actions and penalties for violating the terms of the certificate of registration. The law also sets home inspection requirements for residential loans purchased or approved by the Alaska Housing Finance Corporation. The law requires that a written report fulfilling certain requirements be submitted to the person requesting the inspection upon completion of an inspection that will remain valid for 180 days after the inspection and allows for civil action to be taken against home inspectors for one year after performing the inspection. The law requires the home inspector to carry insurance and a bond of $5,000. The law went into effect in 2003 and all home inspectors are required to have a license by July 1, 2004.

Arizona *Certification (Title 32, Chapter 1 enacted in 2002).* The Arizona State Board of Technical Registration (BTR) certifies and regulates the practice of home inspectors. The law requires 80 hours of education, successful completion of the National Home Inspector Examination, and evidence of successfully completed home inspections. In addition, the law requires that certified home inspectors have one of the following financial assurances: 1) Errors and Omissions Insurance in the amount of $200,000 in the aggregate and $100,000 per occurrence, 2) a $25,000 bond or proof of assets in that amount, or 3) an alternate financial assurance mechanism approved by the BTR with a value of at least $25,000. The law states that loss of or failure to obtain financial assurance is grounds for revocation of certification.

Arkansas *Registration* (Act 1328 of 2003) repealed and replaced **(Act 791 of 1997).** Under the "Arkansas Home Inspector Registration Act," all home inspectors in the state must register with the Secretary of State. Applicants must pass the National Home Inspector Examination. In addition, home inspectors must conduct all inspections in adherence to the Standards of Practice and Code of Ethics of ASH, the Arkansas Association of Real Estate Inspectors, or an equivalent professional home inspection association. The law also prohibits inspectors from performing repairs on a structure that he has inspected within the last 12 months. In order to register under the law, an applicant must procure general liability insurance of at least $100,000. These requirements, along with the duties and responsibilities of the Board, complaint and disciplinary procedures, continuing education requirements and more can be found In the Rules and Procedures of the Arkansas Home Inspector Registration Board.

California *Trade practice act* (Chapter 338) *enacted in 1996.* The law in California prohibits unethical home inspection practices, including repairing properties that home inspectors have inspected in the previous 12 months. The law encourages courts to consider the Standards of Practice and Code of Ethics of ASH and the California Real Estate Inspection Association when determining whether an inspection meets the required standard of care.

Connecticut *Licensure (Public Act No. 99-254 enacted in 2000).* Connecticut law requires home inspectors to be licensed under the "Home Inspection Licensing Board." In order to be eligible for a home inspector license, an applicant shall: 1) have successfully completed high school or its equivalent; 2) have either been engaged as a home inspector intern for not less than one year and not performed less than 200 home inspections for compensation **or** taken and successfully completed a board-approved training program, earned a home inspector intern permit, and performed not less than 100 home inspections under the direct supervision and in the presence of a licensed home inspector; 3) have passed an oral, written, or electronic competency examination; and 4) have paid a $200 fee. In order to receive a permit as a home inspector intern, an applicant shall: 1) have successfully completed high school or its equivalent; 2) have enrolled in and completed a board-approved training program; 3) have an identified supervisor who is licensed as a home inspector, is in good standing, and has agreed to perform the supervisory functions required; and 4) have paid a $100 fee.

Georgia *Trade practice act* (Chapter 3, Title 8) *enacted in 1994.* Georgia law requires home inspectors to provide written documents containing certain information with regard to inspections. This written document must include the scope of the inspection, including the structural elements and systems to be inspected, that the inspection is a visual inspection, and that the home inspector will notify, in writing, the person on whose behalf such inspection is being made of any defects noted during the inspection.

Illinois *Licensure* (225 ILSC 441 *enacted in 2001).* Illinois law creates the Illinois Home Inspector License Act and establishes a Home Inspector Advisory Board within the

Office of Banks and Real Estate (OBRE), which is charged with regulating home inspectors. To obtain a license, an applicant must: 1) be at least 21 years of age, 2) obtain a high school diploma or GED, 3) as a prerequisite for sitting for the examination, successfully complete 60 hours of pre-license education from an education provider approved and licensed by OBRE, and 4) take and successfully pass the Home Inspector Examination for Illinois, which consists of the National Home Inspector Examination and a section concerning Illinois statutes and regulations. Licensed home Inspectors are required to perform Inspections that meet the minimum standards of practice established by rule as adopted by the OBRE. The law also exempts certain professionals from licensure as a home inspector while acting under the scope of their licenses. The law became effective January 1, 2003.

Indiana *Licensure (P.L. 145 enacted In 2004).* P.L. 145 established the Home Inspectors Licensing Board to regulate home inspectors and associate home inspectors. The Board shall be responsible for setting the fees for licenses, investigating complaints concerning licensees and establishing continuing education requirements. The Board shall adopt a code of ethics, standards for competent performance of home inspections and standards for inspection reports. Under P.L. 145, licensing requires that a candidate: 1) be at least 18 years of age, 2) graduated from high school or earned a GED diploma, 3) not have been convicted of specific crimes, 4) complete a Board approved training program or course and pass an exam approved by the Board, 5) carry general liability insurance coverage of at least $100,000 and 6) pay a fee. The law also provides that a person who performs home inspections for compensation without a license commits a Class B Infraction. It also provides that any civil complaints based upon the professional services of a licensed home inspector must be filed within two years of the date the alleged Infraction occurred. This law takes effect July 1, 2004.

Kentucky *Licensure (KRS 198B.700) enacted in 2004.* (The Kentucky Home Inspector Licensing Law requires home inspectors to be licensed and defines the requirements of licensure. An inspector must be at least 18 years old, have a high school diploma or GED equivalent, complete a board-approved training program, pass an examination approved by the board, and submit a certificate of insurance. Inspections must be conducted in accordance with the standards of practice of ASH or NAHI or their equal. The law created the Kentucky Board of Home Inspectors, to which the Governor appointed eight members, including one member each from ASH, NAHI, and the Kentucky Real Estate Inspection Association. The law also establishes license renewal criteria, including continuing education of 30 hours for two years. Licensed inspectors must carry liability insurance in the amount of $250.000.

Louisiana *Licensure* (Chapter 17-A of Title37) *enacted in 1999.* Louisiana law creates the "Louisiana Home Inspectors Licensing Act." It creates the Louisiana State Board of Home Inspectors within the Department of Economic Development and requires the Board to establish minimum qualifications for licensing and allows the

Board to charge and collect fees. Applicants must be at least 18 years old and must have successfully completed high school or its equivalent, and passed the National Home Inspector Examination. Applicants must show evidence of successful completion of at least 120 hours of instruction, at least 30 hours but no more than 40 of which must be in course work containing actual practical home inspections. Home inspectors are required to provide a written report of the home inspection, and are prohibited from, at the time of inspection and for a reasonable time thereafter, advertising or soliciting to perform repair services on the home upon which the inspection was performed. As a condition of renewal of a license, a home inspector must show evidence of completion of 20 hours of continuing education. Active licensees are required to carry errors and omission insurance, and the Board must establish a group insurance program.

Maryland *Trade practice act enacted in 1992.* Maryland law requires home inspectors to disclose professional qualifications and the scope of the inspection within the home inspection contract. The law also requires home inspectors to conduct home inspections in accordance with the standards of practice set forth by a professional home inspection trade association such as ASH or the National Association of Home Inspectors.

Licensure (Chapter 470) *enacted in 2001. [Note: the following describes the law passed in 2001. However, this passage from the Maryland Web site makes clear that the law is not currently in effect for budgetary reason*

"The law for the licensing and regulation of Home Inspectors has been deferred until an appropriation to fund the program is allocated. Therefore, there will be no activity relative to the licensing, training or regulation of home inspectors. At this time, there is no date available as to when the licensing program will begin. Updates to the program will be posted on this site as they occur."]

Maryland law creates the State Commission of Real Estate Appraisers and Home Inspectors to regulate home inspectors in the state. Th e Commission is charged with establishing a code of ethics and standards of practice for licensed home inspectors, and providing a copy of such standards to each licensed home inspector. To qualify for licensure prior to July 1, 2002, an applicant must complete two of the following conditions: 1) complete a minimum of 48 hours of an on-site training course approved by a national home inspection organization of the Commission, 2) complete a minimum of 2 years of relevant work experience as determined by the Commission, 3) complete at least 100 home inspections for compensation, or 4) submit proof of full membership in or certification by ASH or NAHI. Effective July 1, 2002, an applicant for a home inspector license shall: 1) have completed a minimum of 48 hours of an off-site training course, 2) have a high school diploma or its equivalent, 3) have general liability insurance in an amount not less than $50,000, 4) submit an application sanctioned by the Commission, 5) pay the application fee of $50 to the Commission. The law also exempts certain professionals from licensure as a home inspector while acting under the scope of their licenses, and provides a reciprocity provision for licensed home inspectors from other states.

Massachusetts *Licensure* **(Chapter 146) enacted in 1999.** Massachusetts law requires home inspectors and associate home inspectors to be licensed under the Board of Registration of Home Inspectors. The Board is required to: 1) establish the requirements for licensure and for the standards of professional and ethical conduct; 2) establish standards for continuing education; 3) authorize and conduct examinations; 4) grant licenses to qualified applicants; and 5) establish penalties. The law also requires that the Director of the Office of Consumer Affairs and Business Regulation publish an informational brochure on home inspections which must be issued to home buyers at the signing of an offer to purchase. Licensed home inspectors must: 1) have successfully completed high school or its equivalent; 2) have been engaged as a licensed associate home inspector for not less than one year and have performed not less than 100 home inspections under the supervision of a licensed ho me inspector; 3) have passed the National Home Inspector Examination; and 4) paid the appropriate fee. A licensed associate home inspector must: 1) have successfully completed high school or its equivalent; 2) have performed not less than 25 home inspections in the presence of a licensed home inspector; 3) have passed the National Home Inspector Examination; 4) have an identified supervisor who is a person licensed in good standing as a home inspector; and 5) paid the appropriate fee. Licensed home inspectors and associate home inspectors must carry errors and omissions insurance in an amount not less than $250,000. Also, a home inspector or associate home inspector may not attempt to limit liability for negligent or wrongful errors or omissions by use of a clause within a performance contract that limits the cost of damages from negligent or wrongful errors or omissions.

Amendment to Current Law (Ch. 146 of 1999) **enacted in 2001.** The amended section of the law (Chapter 17 of 2001) extends the time period during which the Board may issue a temporary license to an applicant seeking licensure as a home inspector. The law moves the effective date back to November 1, 2001 from May 1, 2001 and establishes the criteria under which a temporary license may be issued. A temporary license may be issued if: 1) an individual has been engaged in home inspection for not less than three years prior to the effective date and has performed at least 100 inspections for compensation, or 2) an individual has been engaged in the practice of home inspection for not less than one year prior to the effective date, and has performed at least 125 inspections for compensation. Temporary licenses shall terminate in 90 days, or whenever the applicant furnishes proof of having passed a licensing examination approved by the Board, whichever occurs first.

Mississippi Licensure (Chapter 71) **enacted in 2001.** Mississippi law requires home inspectors to be licensed by the Mississippi Real Estate Commission (Commission) and is given the following powers: 1) receiving and approving applications for licensure and collecting fees, 2) implementing recommendations made by the Home Inspector Advisory Board, 3) adoption of a code of ethics

and standards of practice 4) developing a licensing exam (the Commission adopted the National Home Inspector Examination to assess minimum competence) which meets nationally recognized standards, as well as developing applications and licensing forms, 6) adopting rules and regulations for administering the law. The. The law also created a five person Home Inspector Regulatory Board (Board), members of which are to be licensed inspectors, and appointed by the Governor. The Board serves in an advisory capacity to the Commission, and was given the following duties and powers: 1) responsibility for matters relating to the code of ethics, standards and qualifications, 2) holding hearings and preparing examination specifications for licensure, 3) conducting investigations, 4) further defining regulation, educational and equivalent experience, and 5) recommending suspension or revocation of licenses. To qualify for a license under this act, a person must: 1) have successfully completed high school or attained an equivalency degree, 2) be at least 21 years old, 3) have successfully completed an approved course of study of at least 60 hours, which may include field work as required by the Commission, 4) pass the National Home Inspector Examination, and 5) provide a certificate of insurance for errors and omissions and general liability. Certain individuals acting under their profession or license are exempted from additional licensure by the Commission for "visual inspections"—specialty and general contractors, architects, engineers, financial institution employee, licensed real estate broker, appraiser or home builder. There is also a three-year limitation included for clients seeking to recover damages from an inspection, a reciprocity provision, and a grandfather clause included in the act.

Montana *Trade Practice Act* (Chapter 14, Title 30) *enacted in 1999.* Montana law, the Home Inspection Trade Practices Act, prescribes what elements must be identified in a home inspection and defines prohibited activities by a home inspector.

Nevada Certification (NRS 645D.120 **and** NAC 645D.210) **enacted in 1997.** Nevada law provides for the certification of home inspectors of structures by the Real Estate Division of the Department of Business and Industry. An applicant for certification as a certified residential Inspector : (a) must furnish proof to the Division that he has successfully completed 1) not less than 40 hours of academic Instruction In subjects related to structural Inspections In courses approved by the Division or equivalent experience as an Inspector, and 2) an examination approved by the Division, and (b) must possess a high school diploma or Its equivalent. Experience as an Inspector must demonstrate ability of the applicant to produce a credible Inspection report according to the standards and requirements set In the statute and codes. Applicants must submit to the Division a log of Inspections performed for a fee on a form supplied by the Division. Applicants must submit proof that they have errors and omissions insurance of at least $100,000 and general liability insurance of at least $100,000. The law also provides that a purchaser may not recover damages from a seller on the basis of an error or omission in the disclosure form that

(continued)

was caused by the seller's reliance upon information provided to the seller by a certified inspector of real estate.

New Jersey *Licensure* (Chapter 8, Title 45**) *enacted in 1998.*** New Jersey's "Home Inspection Professional Licensing Act," sets specific educational and experience requirements in order to become a licensed home inspector. All home inspectors are required to: 1) complete high school or its equivalent; 2) serve as a licensed associate inspector for at least one year; 3) perform at least 250 inspections; 4) carry $500,000 in insurance; and 5) pass the National Home Inspector Examination. Inspectors do not have to be a member or candidate of ASH in order to take the exam. In order to become a licensed associate home inspector under the law, an inspector must: 1) perform at least 50 inspections in the presence of a licensed inspector; and 2) pass the National Home Inspector Examination. Also, the law provides that, if home inspectors fail to disclose problems or accept payment from another party in the transaction, they can lose their license. Home inspectors are regulated by a five-member Home Inspection Advisory Committee, housed under the State Board of Professional Engineers and Land Surveyors.

In 2003, Public Law 2003, Chapter 77 was passed, amending the grandfathering requirements and extending the grandfathering window by one year, until June 30, 2004. Home Inspectors now have until December 31, 2005 to obtain their licenses.

In 2005, Public Law 2005, Chapter 201 was passed. The law states that to be eligible for home inspector licensure an applicant has two options: (1) successfully complete an approved course of study not less than 180 hours, as prescribed by the State Board of Professional Engineers and Land Surveyors, after consultation with the State Department of Education, which shall include not less than 40 hours of unpaid field-based inspections in the presence of and under the direct supervision of a licensed home inspector; or (2) perform not less than 250 fee-paid home inspections in the presence of and under the direct supervision of a licensed home inspector. The licensed home inspector who oversees these inspections must take full responsibility for the inspection and any report produced. In addition, the law stipulates that as a condition for home inspector biennial license renewal, an individual shall complete 40 credit hours of continuing education.

The law also changes current law, which states home inspector applicants must pass the examinations offered by ASH. The law instead will require applicants to pass an examination administered or approved by the Home Inspection Advisory Committee, which would not necessarily be ASHI's exam.

The law eliminates the classification of "Associate Home Inspector." During the first 180 days after the bill's enactment, the Home Inspection Advisory Committee shall, upon application, issue a home inspector license to any person whose application for an Associate Home Inspector license had been approved by the committee prior to December 30, 2005 or who satisfied certain requirements and had completed 40 hours of unpaid field-based inspections under the direct supervision of a licensed home inspector prior to December 30, 2005.

New York *Licensure* (Chapter 461 of the Laws of 2004). The "Home Inspector Professional Licensing Act" takes effect December 31, 2005 and requires that all home inspectors obtain a license. Home inspectors will be licensed for two years and must pay an initial fee of $250.00 and renewal fees of $100.00 thereafter. The basic provisions of the law include requirements for obtaining a license, including classroom education and on site inspection training, confirmation of an appropriate knowledge base via testing, the development of a required standard of practice and code of ethics, continuing education requirements for license renewal, and a duty of care of all license holders to the client. There are two routes to obtaining a license. An applicant must complete 140 hours of approved training, including 40 hours of unpaid inspection experience under the direct supervision of a licensed inspector, or have 100 hours of paid or unpaid inspection experience under the direct supervision of a licensed inspector. The applicant must also pass an approved written exam. Additionally, there are grandfathering provisions in the law that recognize the value of prior experience. To receive a license under this provision, an inspector must have inspected at least 100 homes within the last two years and pass an approved exam, or have inspected at least 250 homes for compensation and have been a practicing inspector for at least three years, prior to the enforcement of this law.

There is an advisory Council consisting of 4 inspectors and 2 public members, that must meet to advise the Secretary regarding the appropriate rules and regulations, education requirements, examination, standards of practice and code of ethics. The Council will suggest the number of hours needed to meet continuing education requirements.

The law requires that a licensed home inspector maintain appropriate general liability insurance.

Finally, Under the Duty of Care provisions, every home inspector must provide a written report to the client, indicating what components and systems were observed, and must maintain the client's wishes for confidentiality. The inspector may not do repairs on a home he/she has inspected for real estate sales purposes, inspect homes in which the inspector may have a financial interest, pay referral fees to agents or sellers, or inspect homes when payment is contingent upon closing, or pre-established or prescribed findings.

North Carolina *Licensure* (Chapter 143, Article 9F) *enacted in 1993.* The North Carolina "Home Inspection Licensure Act" provides for the licensing and regulation of home inspectors through the creation of a Home Inspector Licensure Board within the Department of Insurance. In order to become licensed as a home inspector, an individual must pass the licensing examination prescribed by the Board, have minimum net assets or a bond in an amount determined by the Board (not less than $5,000 nor more than $10,000) and meet certain educational conditions, including: 1) have a high school diploma or its equivalent, have been engaged as a licensed associate home inspector for at least one year, and have completed 100 home inspections for compensation; 2) have education and experience the Board considers to be equivalent to that in subpart 1. above; or 3) be licensed as a general contractor,

(continued)

TABLE 1.1   *State home inspector licensing/regulation (as of January 2007), continued.*

architect, or professional engineer. In order to become licensed as an associate home inspector, an individual must pass a licensing examination prescribed by the Board, have a high school diploma or its equivalent, and be affiliated with or intend to be affiliated with a licensed home inspector and submit a sworn statement by the licensed home inspector with whom the applicant is or intends to be affiliated certifying that the licensed home inspector will actively supervise and train the applicant.

The General Statutes and the Administrative Code are meant to be used together.

North Dakota *Registration (HB 1507 enacted in 2005)* states the requirements for home inspector registration and license renewal procedures. Applicants must be at least 18 years old, have submitted proof of errors and omissions insurance coverage in the amount of $100,000, and have paid a $200 fee. The law exempts applicants that perform home inspections for residential buildings located outside the corporate limits of any city or located in a city with a population under three thousand from being required to carry errors and omissions insurance in the amount of $100,000. The bill provides a penalty for home inspectors that fail to register, making any individual that provides a home inspection without registration guilty of a class B misdemeanor. Also states that an applicant shall submit proof of completion of an examination offered by the American Society of Home Inspectors, the National Association of Certified Home Inspectors, the Examination Board of Professional Home Inspectors, the National Association of Home Inspectors, or the International Code Council. For more information, including registration forms, go to the Home Inspector page at the North Dakota Secretary of State Web site or call 701-328-2900 or e-mail sos@state.nd.us.

Oklahoma *Licensure (*Section 858-622 of Title 59*) enacted in 2001.* The "Oklahoma Home Inspection Licensing Act" provides for the licensing of home inspectors through the State Board of Health, and a newly created Committee of Home Inspector Examiners (Committee). The Committee is charged with advising the Board of Health in establishing rules relating to: 1) qualifications and examinations for licensure (the committee has adopted the National Home Inspector Examination as the test for minimum competence), 2) renewal requirements, 3) reinstatement of licenses, 4) continuing education, 5) standards of practice and prohibitions, 6) approval of schools and educational course content for home inspection, 7) standards for schools to remain approved to provide courses of instruction, 8) reciprocity agreements, and 9) investigative procedures. These Rules have been established in Title 310, Chapter 276. In order to take an examination for licensure, an applicant must be at least 18 years of age, and successfully complete eighty (80) hours of home inspection training, or its equivalent, as determined by the Committee. Renewal of licenses will be granted provided home inspectors attend five hours of continuing education within the preceding 12 months. A grandfather clause is included as well, with a sunset date of January 1, 2002. Under the law, licensed home inspectors will be required to carry no less than $50,000 of general liability insurance.

Oregon *Certification* (ORS 701.350, 355) *enacted in 1997.* The Oregon Home Inspection Certification Law requires individuals who perform home inspections of two or more components to be certified by the Oregon Construction Contractors Board (CCB). An individual must meet minimum training and/or experience requirements to take a comprehensive test, pass the test and complete continuing education courses to renew certification. The Oregon Standards of Practice, Standards of Behavior and Definitions are adopted from the ASH Standards with Oregon amendments; Oregon acknowledges the assistance of ASH in developing its standards and definitions. Each certified home inspector must be an owner or employee of a business licensed with the CCB. Businesses that perform home inspections must be licensed with the CCB in categories that require either a $10,000 or $15,000 bond and either a $300,000 or $500,000 liability insurance policy. **Amendment to current law** (ORS 710.35, Chapter 812). The amendment to current law provides an exemption for a home inspector acting within the scope of his/her certification or licensure, from licensure as a real estate appraiser.

Pennsylvania *Trade Practice Act (*Act 114 of 2000, Title 68 *enacted in 2000).* The law in Pennsylvania provides a uniform definition for the term "home inspection" and for a national home inspection association. It establishes that a home inspector shall conduct their inspection in accordance with the standards of practice set forth by a professional home inspection trade association such as ASH or the National Association of Home Inspectors. It further outlines consumer remedies as they relate to a home inspection, and establishes penalties for misrepresentations of fact in an inspection report. Under the law, home inspectors are required to maintain errors and omissions and general liability insurance with coverage of not less than $100,000 per occurrence and $500,000 in the aggregate. The law is scheduled to take effect in December 2001.

Rhode Island Trade practice act enacted in 1996. The law in Rhode Island forbids home inspectors, pest control inspectors, and contractors from doing work on property that is inspected prior to real estate sales. The law was passed to help eliminate activities that could present a conflict of interest.

Licensure (**Chapter 65.1**) *enacted in 2000.* Rhode Island law creates a home inspector licensing law and requires that all home inspectors be licensed. Home inspectors would be required to maintain $250,000 of liability insurance, pass the National Home Inspector Examination, and abide by standards of practice and a code of ethics. NOTE: This law is currently not funded.

South Carolina *Licensure* (Title 40, Chapter 59, Article 3) *enacted in 1996.* South Carolina law requires any person desiring to be a licensed home inspector to file with the South Carolina Residential Builders Commission. A home inspector must show to the satisfaction of the Commission that he is currently certified as a home inspector by an organization recognized by the Commission, that he has a minimum of one year of experience as a home inspector

(continued)

under the supervision of a licensed inspector, and that he has performed a minimum of fifty residential inspections.

South Dakota Licensure (Chapter 36-21C**) enacted in 2000.** The South Dakota law provides for the regulation of home inspectors. The South Dakota Real Estate Commission shall issue and renew certificates to licensed and registered home inspectors pursuant to the provisions of this law. No person may provide a home inspection for compensation unless registered or licensed in the State of South Dakota. Applicants for a license as a home inspector shall meet the following requirements; 1) Good moral character; 2) Completion of high school or equivalency; 3) Employment as a registered home inspector for no less than one year and performance of not less than one hundred home inspections for compensation; 4) Successful completion of the National Home Inspector Examination to assess minimum competence. Applicants for registration as a home inspector shall meet the following requirements; 1) Good moral character; 2) Completion of high school or equivalency; 3) Successful completion of an approved course of study; 4) Successful completion of registration exam.

Tennessee *Licensure (2005 Public Act Chapter 65 enacted in 2006).* Any person who applies for licensure as a home inspector must submit an application on a form as prescribed by the commissioner. The application shall be accompanied by the fee specified in Section 4. Applicants shall furnish evidence satisfactory to the commissioner that the applicant: 1) is at least 18 years old, 2) has graduated from high school or earned a general education development certificate, 3) has not been convicted of a crime that has a direct bearing on the applicant's ability to perform competently and fully as a licensed inspector, 4) is not the subject of a disciplinary or enforcement action by another state or a local jurisdiction in connection with the performance of home inspections or the licensing or certification of home inspectors, 5) has successfully completed 90 hours of a commissioner-approved training program or course of study involving the performance of home inspections and the preparation of home inspection reports, 6) has passed a commissioner-approved competency examination administered by the state or an entity selected by the state, and 7) has obtained a certificate of insurance in an amount required by the commissioner for general liability as well as errors and omission to cover all activities contemplated under this chapter.

During the first 180 days after the effective date of this act (July 1, 2006), the commissioner may issue a license to an applicant who meets the requirements stipulated in the law if the applicant furnishes evidence satisfactory to the commissioner that the applicant: 1) has been principally engaged in the performance of home inspections in this state for at least two years, and 2) has complete at least 150 home inspections for compensation in the applicant's career.

Texas *Licensure* (Title 113A, Article 6573a, Section 23) *enacted in 1991.* The Texas licensure law, the Real Estate License Act, provides for the examination of home inspectors and established continuing education requirements. These and other requirements are contained in the Texas Administrative Code, Subchapter R, Rules. The law also requires home inspector applicants to work as apprentice inspectors under the supervision of a professional licensed home inspector. If an applicant is unable to obtain an apprenticeship, educational course work and an examination can be substituted. Home inspectors are regulated by the Texas Real Estate Licensing Board.

Virginia Certification (Virginia Certified Home Inspectors Regulations**) enacted in 2001.** The Virginia certification law provides a voluntary certification program for home inspectors in the state. However, no person may hold him/herself out as a "certified home inspector" without meeting the certification requirement s prescribed b y the Board. The Board may issue a certificate to practice home inspection to any applicant who has successfully completed: 1) any educational requirements as required by the Board, 2) any experience requirements as required by the Board, and 3) passed the National Home Inspector Examination. The Board may issue a certificate to practice as a certified home inspector to any applicant who is a member of a national or state professional home inspector association approved by the Board, provided that the requirements for the class of membership in such association are equal to or exceed the requirements established by the Board for all applicants. Because the law was enacted recently, the language does not include specific requirements. The Board is undoubtedly working on creating those rules and requirements, in preparation for the law's July 1, 2003 effective date.

West Virginia *Certification* (Title 87-05) *enacted in 2006.* West Virginia law, "Certification of Home Inspectors," establishes procedures to be followed to assure that consumers of home inspection services can rely on the competence of inspectors, as determined by educational and experience requirements and testing. As an initial requirement and qualification for certification as a home inspector, every applicant: 1) shall have passed the National Home Inspector Examination; 2) shall either present proof of having conducted business as an inspector for three years prior to August 1, 2006, or proof of satisfactory completion of at least 80 hours of instruction; 3) must have successfully completed high school or its equivalent; and 4) shall present proof of, and shall maintain, general liability insurance in the amount of not less than $250,000.00.

Wisconsin Certification (Chapter 440.97**)** *enacted in 1998.* Under Wisconsin's law, home inspectors must register with the State and pass an examination approved by the Department of Regulation and Licensing. The law instructs the Department to consider the use of an examination modeled after the National Home Inspector Examination. The law also requires that a home inspector perform a "reasonably competent and diligent" inspection; however, the inspection is not required to be technically exhaustive. Home inspectors are prohibited from limiting their liability from damages resulting in a failure to conduct a "reasonably competent and diligent" inspection. Also, inspectors are prohibited from performing repairs, maintenance, or improvements to a structure that they have inspected within the last two years.

Source: American Society of Home Inspectors (ASHI), www.ashi.org/customers/state.asp. April, 2007. Reprinted by permission.

Should I work independently or for another home inspection company?

The decision to have your own business or to seek employment with a home inspection company depends on a number of factors. Foremost might be whether there is a company in your community willing to hire you. Gaining experience by working with people who are in the business of home inspection is time well spent for the beginner. More experienced individuals may opt to set out on their own. Now is the time to talk to other established home inspectors in your community. See if they are willing to take you on as an apprentice.

What are the start-up costs to open a business?

Start-up costs vary depending on whether you work as a one-person operation or choose to employ others to work for you. Chapter 2 more fully discusses types of business arrangements. Generally, for a one-person operation, minimal start-up costs include office space and equipment—computer, software, printer, copier, cell phone, office telephones and installation, tools and equipment, a car or van, and errors and omissions insurance. You might also have to pay licensing or registration fees depending on where you live. You must figure in the cost of any course work you have taken as well. Depending on what resources you already have, your start-up costs may be $2,000 to $5,000 or more.

What must I do to start a home inspection company and have others work for me?

Chapter 2 more fully discusses the types of business arrangements available when you hire others to work for you. Do you want to become a sole proprietor, a partnership, or a corporation? Should you choose to have others work for you, a consultation with an attorney and an accountant will help clarify your choices. Any time people work for you, the cost of operating the business is much greater than working independently. Do you have the money to invest in office space, equipment and supplies, telephones, and all of the other necessities to operate a business? The necessary capital and the advice of other professionals are two of the most important items needed for any business start-up, but greater capital and increased professional assistance are required for a larger-scale operation.

Do I need to know how to repair or replace defects?

A home inspector is not responsible for making repairs to a property, for replacing any items that are defective, or for correcting code violations.

How much can a home inspector earn?

Home inspectors generally charge $275 to $500 for a typical inspection. Fees vary from place to place throughout the country. If licensure is in effect, the fees may be higher. The size of the property sometimes determines the fee schedule. Extra services such as a swimming pool inspection or an environmental concern may be charged separately. A part-time home inspector can earn about $10,000 a year, while a full-time inspector can earn $60,000 to $75,000.

Should I join a home inspection organization?

A number of excellent home inspection organizations offer a variety of services such as accreditation, education including course materials and home study, conferences and conventions, current information (often in the form of a newsletter), networking, and referrals. Many of these organizations also have state affiliates. See Appendix D for a list of some of these organizations. Most can be accessed through the Internet.

How much time does a typical home inspection take?

Generally, a thorough inspection takes at least three hours. Again, this depends on the size of the property and any extra services requested.

What other types of inspections are performed besides the single-family home?

Inspections are not limited to the single-family home. Inspections are performed on multifamily dwellings (e.g., apartment buildings), office buildings, industrial space, condominiums, and shopping centers. Inspections are also used for insurance purposes to assess property damage and to examine construction in progress. A home inspector is often used in the litigation process as an expert witness. Sometimes, inspectors may enter civil service as a code inspector. (If this work is something that interests you, check with your municipality to research the required credentials.)

The inspector who gains some experience in the single-family residential inspection business might consider branching out into one or more of these other career choices in the future.

Home inspection is big business and promises a stable income for the future. As buyers, sellers, and lenders seek further information about the residential structure, demand and income will continually increase.

IMPORTANT POINTS

1. Every time a home is bought or sold, a home inspection is generally a part of the transaction.

2. A home inspection is a thorough examination of the exterior and interior of a residential property to determine structural defects, broken or obsolete components, and damage due to water, wear and tear, and other conditions.

3. The home inspection report is an itemization and summation of the findings of the home inspector with regard to the specific property.

4. The most frequent request for a home inspection is generally made by the parties offering to purchase (contract of sale) a home. Built into the contract is a contingency clause that requires a home inspection prior to closing on the property.

5. Property condition disclosure forms are generally furnished to the seller by real estate agents and ask the seller to disclose detailed information regarding the property. The home inspector reviews and compares this form to the inspection to arrive at a more accurate picture of the property's condition.

6. A home inspector need not be a licensed professional engineer.

7. Many states are currently formulating regulations to license, certify, or register home inspectors. Requirements vary from state to state and regulation does not exist in every state.

8. To practice home inspection, start-up costs vary depending on whether you work as a one-person operation or choose to employ others to work for you. For a one-person operation, depending on what resources you already have, your start-up costs may be $2,000 to $5,000 or more.

9. Any time people work for you, the cost of operating the business is much greater than working independently.

10. The necessary capital and the advice of other professionals are two of the most important items needed for any business start-up, but greater capital and more professional assistance are required for a larger-scale operation.

11. A home inspector is not responsible for making repairs to a property, for replacing items that are defective, or for correcting code violations.

12. Home inspectors generally charge $185 to $500 for a typical inspection. Fees vary from place to place throughout the country. The size of the property sometimes determines the fee schedule. Part-time inspectors can earn about $10,000 per year and full-time inspectors can realize $60,000 to $75,000 per year.

13. Home inspection organizations offer accreditation, education including course materials and home study, conferences and conventions, current information, networking, and referrals.

14. In addition to single-family home inspections, inspections are performed on multifamily dwellings, office buildings, industrial space, condominiums, and shopping centers.

CHAPTER REVIEW

Field Study Assignment

Now is the time to explore career possibilities. Consult with the home inspectors and home inspection companies in your community. A quick method of finding some of these individuals is through the member directories of various home inspection organizations. This information is easily accessed on the Internet (see Appendix D). Consider offering yourself as an apprentice or accompanying a home inspector during an inspection. There is no better way to decide if home inspection is for you than to observe an actual inspection. Ask the home inspectors you meet to answer some of the questions that are presented in this chapter. How do the inspectors' responses compare with the answers given in the textbook?

1. A home inspection is most often required by the:
   A. seller
   B. buyer
   C. real estate broker
   D. either buyer or seller

2. The property condition disclosure form is completed by the:
   A. seller
   B. buyer
   C. lender
   D. real estate agent

3. Which of the following is required to become a home inspector?
   A. a professional engineering license
   B. membership in a home inspection organization
   C. a four-year degree
   D. a registration or license in states that require one

4. Harvey was in the process of inspecting a home when the owners asked him to fix the leak under the kitchen sink that he had detected. Which of the following is TRUE?
   A. It is part of Harvey's job as a home inspector to make repairs to items that he finds broken.
   B. Harvey is under no obligation as a home inspector to make any repairs.
   C. It is part of Harvey's job to repair only those items he feels confident about fixing.
   D. Although Harvey can refuse to fix the water leak, home inspectors must know how to fix all items that they inspect.

5. The compensation for an inspection of a typical residential property is:
   A. $150–$300
   B. $185–$500
   C. $500–$750
   D. $750–$1,000

6. A thorough inspection of a typical property should take about:
   A. one hour
   B. two hours
   C. three hours
   D. five hours

7. Which of the following is NOT offered by home inspection organizations?
   A. accreditation
   B. referrals
   C. licensure
   D. home study

8. Betty and Bobby Buyer ask that their home inspector climb onto the roof of the home they are purchasing to more fully investigate its condition. Which of the following applies?
   A. The home inspector should always comply with the wishes of the client.
   B. The home inspector must climb onto the roof to make an accurate evaluation of its condition.
   C. Only the bank can demand that the home inspector climb onto the roof.
   D. The home inspector is not required to climb onto the roof to make an evaluation of its condition.

9. Which of the following is NOT a type of business organization?
   A. bondsmanship
   B. partnership
   C. sole proprietorship
   D. corporation

10. What is one of the key differences between working by yourself or having others work for you?

   A. You have more overhead if you work independently.

   B. You always make less money if you work independently.

   C. Home inspectors who work by themselves do not have to obtain a license in states that require licensure.

   D. The cost of doing business is higher when you employ others.

ANSWER KEY

1. B	4. B	7. C	10. D
2. A	5. B	8. D	
3. D	6. C	9. A	

CHAPTER 2

THE HOME INSPECTION BUSINESS

As you explore home inspection as a career option, first think about how you would like to do business. Many people prefer to work for others and leave the business responsibility and operation to them. Some individuals, however, prefer to own and operate their own business. This chapter provides you with some of the information you must know to own and operate a home inspection business. It also explores the option of working for others.

LEARNING OBJECTIVES

1. Identify the advantages and disadvantages of opening a home inspection business.

2. Define the various types of business organizations.

3. List what constitutes appropriate insurance coverage.

4. Differentiate between the employee and independent contractor employment arrangement and define the advantages and disadvantages of each.

5. List the items to be considered when opening a home inspection business.

6. Summarize the issues that should be discussed with a prospective home inspection employer.

KEY TERMS

Corporation

Doing business as (d/b/a)

Errors and omissions insurance

Independent contractor

Latent defect

Limited liability company

Partnership

Professional liability insurance

Sole proprietorship

OWNING YOUR OWN BUSINESS

T he decision to own your own business may be made out of necessity. Perhaps there are no multiemployee home inspection businesses in your community. If there are such businesses, they may not be hiring new, perhaps inexperienced, people. Although no one can discount the advantage of gaining experience by working with other home inspectors, this might not be an option for everyone. One of the reasons why the home inspection business attracts so many is that it is relatively easy to start a one-person operation. You may eventually hire others to work for you as your business grows. In the meantime, you can work as an independent contractor (discussed later) for other inspector firms while servicing your own customers.

There is a great deal of satisfaction in owning your own business. At the top of the list is making your own decisions and moving the business forward according to your own dictates. A disadvantage is that you may not have a dependable income—especially at first. Nonetheless, individuals entering the home inspection business should consider operating independently—either at the outset or in the future.

Types of Business Organizations

Prior to opening your business, you should decide on the form of its organization. A business may be structured as a sole proprietorship, partnership, corporation, or limited liability company. There are advantages and disadvantages to each. Explore all possibilities with an accountant and attorney because there are different tax consequences and liability issues for each (see Table 2.1).

Sole Proprietorship

A **sole proprietorship** *is the simplest form of business organization and is owned by one individual and may use a name other than the owner's personal name.* For example, the business title of a sole proprietorship could be, Wally Wonder **doing business as (d/b/a)** Reliable Home Inspection. When required by state law, individuals who operate under a d/b/a must file the appropriate forms in the county where they do business. There is generally a small fee for the filing.

TABLE 2.1	TYPE	TAXATION
Tax consequences of various business organizations.	Sole proprietorship	Taxed as individual
	C corporation	Double tax at corporate and shareholder level
	S corporation	Taxed as a partnership
	General partnership	Taxed as a partnership
	Limited partnership	Taxed as a partnership
	Limited liability company	Taxed as a partnership
	Limited liability partnership	Taxed as a partnership

> The disadvantage of the sole proprietorship form of business is that you are personally liable for judgments that may be awarded against you or your company.
>
> **You Should Know**

Partnership

A **partnership** is *a form of business organization that is owned by two or more partners and created by a contract between the partners.* The partners do not have to have the same degree of interest in the partnership or the same degree of management authority. The partnership contract should contain the procedure for disposing of the ownership interest on the withdrawal, death, or removal of a partner.

Corporation

A **corporation** is *a legal entity recognized by law with tax rates separate from individual income tax rates.* Although it is unlikely that a home inspection corporation will have shareholders as do many corporations, the corporate form of ownership offers certain tax advantages and protects the business owner from personal liability for corporate acts.

Limited Liability Company

Two or more people may form a **limited liability company** (LLC), *which is a business that combines the most favorable attributes of a partnership and a corporation.* Owners of an LLC (called members) are not personally liable for the LLC's acts. An LLC is taxed as a partnership.

Protecting Yourself and Your Business

Any business, no matter how well run, may become involved in litigation. Today's society is *not* afraid to commence a lawsuit. For example, although an inspector does a thorough job of inspecting a property, certain latent defects may go undetected. A **latent defect** is *a hidden or concealed defect that cannot be discovered by ordinary observation or inspection.* The defect may be known to the property owner, but is hidden so that it is not easily discovered during an inspection of the property. Problems hidden inside Sheetrock or behind wallpaper or paint may cause a buyer to bring a civil action against the home inspector at a later date. A latent defect is a cracked sewer pipe hidden underneath a concrete floor. Eventually, the leak causes water and structural damage to the floor, footing, and even the foundation wall as erosion occurs (see Figure 2.1). Another example is a kitchen ventilation hood duct or bathroom fan duct vented to the attic instead of outdoors. This eventually causes moisture problems.

Problems that arise after an inspection may cause the buyer to accuse the inspector of failing to notice the problem. A buyer might begin an action against a seller for failing to disclose a latent defect. The seller, then, may file an action against the home inspector. The home inspector must purchase professional liability insurance in order to provide protection for his business.

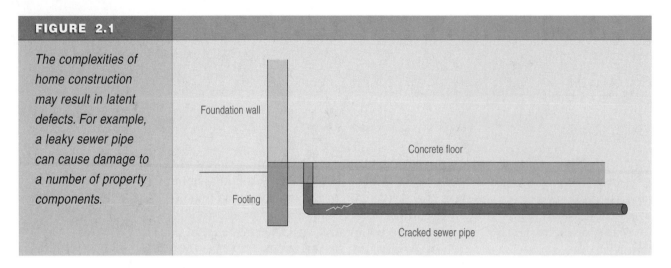

FIGURE 2.1

The complexities of home construction may result in latent defects. For example, a leaky sewer pipe can cause damage to a number of property components.

Foundation wall

Concrete floor

Footing

Cracked sewer pipe

Professional Liability Insurance

Professional liability insurance *covers individuals and business organizations* (dis-cussed previously) *for claims made by third parties; for example, the home owner or lender alleging negligence in the performance of a professional service.* Negligence, put simply, is the failure to use a certain degree of care, skill, diligence, or knowl-edge that is the industry standard for a professional in similar circumstances. Professional liability insurance is referred to most commonly as errors and omis-sions (E&O) insurance.

Errors and Omissions Insurance

Generally, individuals and businesses that practice in a professional field and receive compensation for services may be subject to a claim based on an error or omission. Defending yourself without insurance is very expensive. You are responsible for retaining an attorney, financing the cost of defending the action, and paying any judgment that is awarded.

Errors and omissions insurance (known as E&O) *is a form of professional lia-bility insurance that covers claims of negligence that occur while rendering a professional service and generally is billed annually.* The insurance company pays the cost of litigation and any judgment, up to the policy's limits, that is awarded. Have your insurance coverage in place prior to the first inspection.

Employing Others

As a business owner, you decide whether or not you want your workers to be employees or *independent contractors.* The most important distinctions between an employee and an independent contractor employment arrangement are that **inde-pendent contractors** *do not receive a set salary on a regular basis, do not work set hours, and must provide their own tools and equipment.* This is a decided advantage for the business owner because the independent contractor receives pay only for hours worked; an employee on a fixed salary must be paid whether on assignment or not. An employee receives certain benefits not given to an independent contractor. This increases the cost of workers' services over that of independent contractors.

In your business, however, you can have a combination of employment arrangements for different jobs. For example, hire the clerical staff as full- or part-time employees and hire the home inspectors as independent contractors. Generally, independent contractors are paid a set fee per job or on a commission basis. Ultimately, the payment arrangement and employment status are decided by the business owner and the person seeking employment.

OPERATING A HOME INSPECTION OFFICE

As you begin to organize your office, many of your system requirements grow naturally out of need. Certain items should be taken care of, however, prior to opening. As you read, think about other systems or purchases necessary to begin operation.

1. Check on licensure requirements and make sure you are in compliance. States license individual inspectors, not companies (see Table 1.1).

2. Take a close look at the financial picture. Itemize the monies needed to open a business. Decide how much you will charge for the various services rendered. Discuss an income and expense projection with your accountant. Consider initial costs such as equipment purchases, insurance, and advertising. Do not forget to investigate the competition. Are they successful or not and why?

3. Open a bank account. If you decide to have employees, two accounts are necessary: one for payroll and one for operating expenses. Now is the time to consider accepting credit cards. Although credit card companies charge a small fee on each transaction, they provide for the timely receipt of payments from your clients.

4. Decide on a business name. It is best to include the words "home inspection" or "home inspector" in the title. In those states that require the filing of a d/b/a, your name is checked to ensure that there are no duplicates in your county. If you form a partnership or incorporate, the Secretary of State's office checks the business name.

5. Assemble your furniture, equipment, and tools. A quality phone and message retrieval system can make or break a business—especially if you are a one-person operation.

6. Have stationary and business cards printed.

7. Have your attorney prepare contract forms for your clients, including a pre-inspection agreement form. Purchase or create inspection report forms (discussed in Chapter 4).

8. Investigate referral possibilities. Speak to other home inspection companies, real estate companies, lenders, attorneys, accountants, and building contractors. Send an announcement card, flyer, booklet, or business card to prospective customers. Join one or more home inspection organizations that will list you in their referral directory. These directories are available to the public as well as home inspectors in other localities.

WORKING FOR OTHERS

If you have made the choice to work for a home inspection company, evaluate your short- and long-term goals. If you know what you are looking for, it is much easier to find it. For example, do you want full- or part-time work? While you are getting started, part-time work is an excellent option; you work chosen hours and earn income from your home inspection work and another endeavor. As you become experienced and have more work, you can move into full time. A part-time business works well for people who are beginning a home inspection business.

Home inspection firms differ regarding employment terms and what they offer employees. The differences are due to the size of the firm (number of employees), the types of properties inspected (e.g., single-family homes, multifamily dwellings, rural, city), and other factors. The following are helpful questions to ask when seeking work with a particular home inspection firm:

1. What types of properties does the firm target? Will you work primarily in an urban, suburban, or rural area? Is the firm local, a part of a franchise, or international? Are there many offices or just one?

2. Is travel an issue? Where are the properties that the firm services? Perhaps you are not the type who likes to travel 50 or more miles to perform an inspection.

3. Are you an employee or independent contractor? An employee discusses salary and benefits; an independent contractor discusses the fee per job or the commission split. Does the compensation vary according to the size or type of property inspected? Ask if there are bonuses or extra compensation for services performed outside the scope of the general inspection.

4. Are you compensated for out-of-pocket expenses (e.g., gas, mileage, or monies spent for lab tests)?

5. Are you responsible for purchasing tools or are they supplied?

6. Is there a company van to use or do you use your own transportation?

7. Is there work space available on a daily basis for writing reports and making phone calls? Do you have clerical assistance or is the typing, computer entry, and appointment making your responsibility?

8. What type of computer system is used and is any needed training available? Does the company offer training on home inspection techniques and report writing?

9. If you are an independent contractor, how much work is available and are leads provided by the company?

10. What assistance does the company provide should questions or problems arise?

These are only a few of the topics that should be discussed with the company owner or manager before agreeing to employment as an independent contractor or employee. It is a good idea to meet and talk to other home inspectors who work with the firm for further feedback. Don't hesitate to have an attorney review the independent contractor agreement.

IMPORTANT POINTS

1. One of the reasons why the home inspection business attracts so many is that it is relatively easy to open a business as a one-person operation. You may eventually hire others to work for you as your business grows.

2. A business may be structured as a sole proprietorship, partnership, corporation, or limited liability corporation.

3. A sole proprietorship is the simplest form of business organization and is owned by one individual and may use a name other than the owner's personal name.

4. A partnership is a form of business organization that is owned by two or more partners and created by a contract between the partners.

5. A corporation is a legal entity recognized by law with tax rates separate from individual income tax rates.

6. A latent defect is a hidden or concealed defect that cannot be discovered by ordinary observation or inspection. The defect may be known to the property owner, but is hidden so that it is not easily discovered during an inspection of the property.

7. The home inspector must purchase professional liability insurance to protect against claims made by third parties. Professional liability insurance is referred to most commonly as errors and omissions (E&O) insurance.

8. The most important distinction between an employee and an independent contractor employment arrangement is that independent contractors do not receive a set salary on a regular basis. Generally, independent contractors are paid a set fee per job or on a commission basis.

9. An employee costs an employer more than an independent contractor because the employee receives benefits that an independent contractor does not.

10. Individuals thinking about opening a home inspection business must consider licensure requirements, finances, insurance, advertising, and the competition.

11. Prior to opening a home inspection business, open a bank account. If employees are hired, open two accounts: one for payroll and one for operating expenses.

12. Other business start-up considerations include deciding on a location and business name, and purchasing furniture, equipment, and tools. An attorney should prepare required contracts and may assist with creating report forms.

13. Continually investigate referral possibilities. Join one or more home inspection organizations.

14. New business owners and those employed in other fields might consider part-time work. You choose the number of hours to work and earn income from your home inspection work and another endeavor.

15. Home inspection firms differ regarding employment terms and what they offer employees. The differences are due to the size of the firm (number of employees), the types of properties inspected, and other factors.

16. Other considerations when choosing to work for a company include the firm's territory, travel requirements, salary, fee or commission split, reimbursement of out-of-pocket expenses, tool and equipment purchases, transportation, company support and training, and work availability.

17. Before taking a position with a home inspection firm, meet with other home inspectors for further feedback. Have an attorney review any independent contractor agreement.

CHAPTER REVIEW

Field Study Assignment 1

If you are considering opening your own home inspection business, consult an attorney and an accountant. Ask about their consultation fees and, at the consultation, ask what the fees are for any services rendered.

Field Study Assignment 2

If you are opening your own business, inform the chamber of commerce of your intentions. It has useful information for small businesses and can help you find local, state, and federal resources. For qualified applicants, the Small Business Administration (SBA) may assist with loan money, advice, and information about other federal and state resources.

Field Study Assignment 3

Using what you read in this chapter and obtained from Field Study Assignments 1 and 2, prepare an income and expense analysis. Determine the start-up costs and the amount needed to keep the business afloat. It helps to make some projections of future income over a specified period of time (e.g., one year).

Field Study Assignment 4

Visit local banks to assess the variety of services offered.

Field Study Assignment 5

If you plan to work for others, create a resume. Even if you have no prior home inspection experience, employers want to know about your professional background. Most communities have resume preparation services if needed.

REVIEW QUESTIONS

1. Vanya filed her business documents with the county clerk in the name of Vanya Black d/b/a VanBlack Home Inspections. Vanya's company is which type of business organization?
   A. sole proprietorship
   B. S corporation
   C. C corporation
   D. limited liability company

2. A latent defect in a structure is generally:
   A. one that cannot be fixed
   B. not visible on inspection
   C. easily visible on inspection
   D. found only in older homes

3. A type of professional liability insurance appropriate for the home inspector is known as:
   A. errors and omissions
   B. an umbrella policy
   C. limited liability coverage
   D. accident and property

4. Barry is planning to open a small one-person home inspection business and will work from home. Because he does not intend to employ others, which of the following should he do about insurance coverage?
   A. not concern himself about it
   B. buy professional liability insurance before his first inspection
   C. buy professional liability insurance only if he does not have a home-owner's policy
   D. buy professional liability insurance only if he works full time because part-time work does not justify the cost

5. Renee is performing a home inspection and finds that the upstairs bathroom is locked and she cannot get in. The property owner is not home. Because the home has an identical bathroom in the master bedroom, Renee does not record this omission on her inspection report. Renee's decision may constitute:
   A. an acceptable practice
   B. poor report writing and nothing more
   C. nothing more than circumstances beyond her control
   D. negligence

6. Juan decided to open a home inspection business and although he doesn't know much about house construction or systems, he is a welder and feels that is enough background knowledge to properly inspect a residential property. Based on his credentials, if Juan makes a mistake during an inspection, which of the following is likely to be the primary reason for his error?
   A. lack of care
   B. lack of knowledge
   C. lack of diligence
   D. insufficient number of years in the business

7. The main difference between an independent contractor and an employee is that an independent contractor is:
   A. generally less experienced than an employee
   B. does not need a home inspection license in a state that requires one
   C. compensated on a fee or commission basis per job
   D. compensated by a weekly salary

8. Which of the following is NOT necessarily required to open a home inspection office?
   A. compliance with licensure requirements in states that have licensure
   B. completing income and expense projections
   C. a full-time operation
   D. developing a marketing plan

9. In the operation of a home inspection business, two separate bank accounts are necessary if you have:
   A. a payroll
   B. an income over $25,000
   C. a full-time operation
   D. a business located in an urban center

10. Jamie opened a business and named it JDL's Home Inspection Service, Inc. Once the name of the business is chosen, what must Jamie do to have the name approved?
    A. nothing
    B. check with the clerk of the county where the business is located
    C. have the name cleared with the state agency that approves corporations
    D. change the name because states do not allow initials as part of a corporate name

11. Which of the following is NEVER a difference between home inspection companies in a particular state?
    A. size of the firm
    B. types of properties inspected
    C. number of employees
    D. licensure requirements

12. Which of the following is most likely to lessen liability problems for a home inspection company?
    A. a large workforce
    B. employee education and training
    C. boosting employee morale with a reliable bonus system
    D. taking only those jobs in close proximity to the office

13. Mariah is hired as an independent contractor by Perfect Home Inspections and is asked to sign an agreement. Mariah does not fully understand all of the clauses in the contract. Her employer tells her not to worry because all independent contractor agreements are standard. What should Mariah do?
    A. sign the agreement
    B. talk to some of the other employees in the company to find out what they did
    C. consult a competent attorney
    D. ask her boyfriend his opinion because he has signed many contracts in the past

ANSWER KEY

1. A	5. D	9. A	13. C
2. B	6. B	10. C	
3. A	7. C	11. D	
4. B	8. C	12. B	

CHAPTER 3

LAND USE REGULATIONS

K nowledge of public and private land use controls in the community where you inspect properties is essential. It is impossible to inspect property responsibly and competently without a basic understanding of the factors that affect land use. This chapter covers public and private control of land and federal, state, and local building codes.

LEARNING OBJECTIVES

1. Distinguish between public and private control of land.
2. Define each type of public land control: police power, taxation, eminent domain, and escheat.
3. Describe how land use regulations, such as master plans that include zoning, affect a particular parcel, neighborhood, or community.
4. Explain how land use relates to building codes, building permits, and certificates of occupancy.

KEY TERMS

Building code

Building permit

Certificate of occupancy

Condemnation

Deed restrictions

Easement

Eminent domain

Escheat

Nonconforming use

Plat

Police power

Setback requirements

Special use permit

Spot zoning

Subdivision

Taxation

Variance

PRIVATE LAND USE CONTROLS: DEED RESTRICTIONS

L andowners have the right to place private controls on their own real estate. These restrictions may exist on individual deeds or may take the form of restrictions effecting an entire subdivision. **Deed restrictions** *are in the form of covenants or conditions. These restrictions, or covenants, run with the land (move with the title in any subsequent deed).* Figure 3.1 lists sample deed restrictions.

The Residential Subdivision

A **subdivision** *is land that is divided into lots for development. A recorded subdivision map that shows the lots, their sizes, and where they are situated in the subdivision is called a* **plat**. During the planning stages, subdivisions are divided into lots and regulations (restrictions) are placed by developers. These restrictions address issues that maintain the quality and consistency of the subdivision and together with the plat, create a plan as to how the completed subdivision will look. A typical restriction might set forth **setback requirements** for dwellings; that is, *specified distances from the front and interior property lines to the building.* Subdivision property owners enforce restrictions by taking appropriate court action (see Figure 3.2).

PUBLIC LAND USE CONTROLS

 ublic control of land by the government covers a broader range than does private control. Figure 3.3 summarizes the public control of land.

Police Power

Police power *empowers government to fulfill its responsibility to provide for the public health, safety, and welfare of its citizens.* Government may exercise this power even if it restricts the fundamental freedoms of its citizens. Police power, however, must be exercised in the best interest of the public.

FIGURE 3.1	*Sample deed restrictions.*
	Restrictions such as the following typically are found on a subdivision deed. The conditions are enforced through legal action by the subdivision property owners.
	1. House trailers, boats, all-terrain vehicles, and any vehicles on blocks may not be parked on or adjacent to the driveway or in any location on the property that is visible to Sunny View Road.
	2. Backyard storage sheds must be situated on the property so that they are not visible from Sunny View Road.
	3. Fences may not be constructed from the street line (Sunny View Road) to the front line of the house.
	4. The house must be set back a minimum of 30 feet from Sunny View Road.

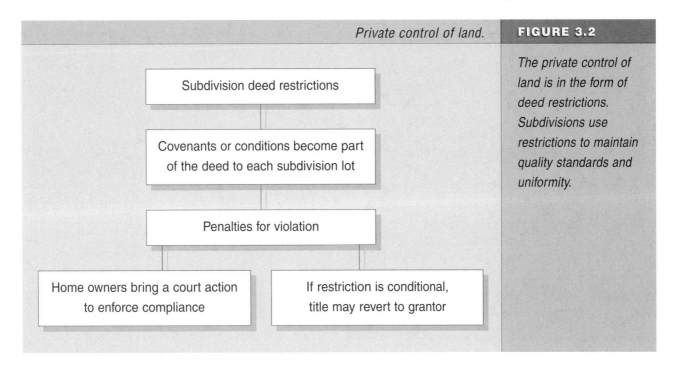

Private control of land.

FIGURE 3.2

The private control of land is in the form of deed restrictions. Subdivisions use restrictions to maintain quality standards and uniformity.

Taxation

The power of **taxation** *is one of the inherent burdens on private ownership of land. Property taxes constitute a specific lien against the real estate.* Even if there is no mortgage on a property, taxes must be paid continuously throughout the term of property ownership.

Eminent Domain

The right or power of **eminent domain** *is the power of a government or its agencies to take private property for public use. The actual taking of property under the power of eminent domain is called* **condemnation**. The condemning authority may be the state itself, authorized state agencies and departments, municipalities, school districts, public utilities, railroads, or the federal government.

Someone who holds an **easement** *does not own or possess the land where the easement lies. The easement holder merely has the right to use or have access to the land.* The right of ingress and egress (entry and exit) to and from the real estate is one of the primary purposes of easements. The most common type of easement is an easement in gross that is usually held by the government, an agency of the government, or a public utility. Examples are the water and electric lines that run underground in subdivisions. It is commonly stated that an easement grants a *right-of-way.*

You Should Know

Power of Escheat

If a property owner dies intestate (without having a valid will), the decedent's property is distributed to any legal heirs in accordance with state law. If there

FIGURE 3.3	*Public control of land.*

Public land use controls are based on the four powers of government: police power, taxation, eminent domain, and escheat.

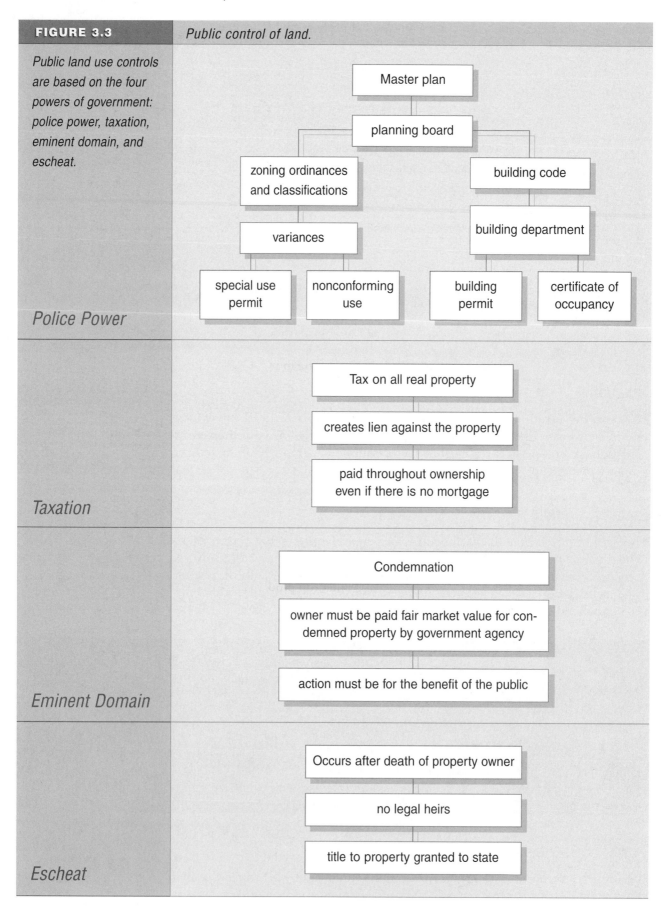

Police Power

Master plan

planning board

zoning ordinances and classifications

building code

variances

building department

special use permit

nonconforming use

building permit

certificate of occupancy

Taxation

Tax on all real property

creates lien against the property

paid throughout ownership even if there is no mortgage

Eminent Domain

Condemnation

owner must be paid fair market value for condemned property by government agency

action must be for the benefit of the public

Escheat

Occurs after death of property owner

no legal heirs

title to property granted to state

are no legal heirs, the state exercises its power of **escheat** *and the property goes to the state.*

LOCAL AUTHORITY

Although each state has control over certain public lands and open spaces, planning and zoning are the province of local governments and their respective planning boards. The community and its leaders create the master plan for the community. Local governments create planning boards that oversee zoning ordinances, subdivision development, budgets, site plan review, and building codes. A referendum of the community decides these issues.

Zoning Classifications

Areas in a community are divided into various classifications or zones; within these classifications there may be different uses. For example, within a residential zone, other subclassifications might be R-1 for prime single-family residential properties; R-2 for a mix of single-family and multifamily residences up to four units; and R-3 for a mix of high-rise apartment buildings, other rental properties, and privately owned single-family homes. Certain zones are more restrictive than others.

- *Residential zones* are subdivided into single-family homes and various levels of multifamily dwellings.

- *Commercial zones* include retail stores, restaurants, hotels, service businesses, and other similar businesses.

- *Industrial zones* are composed of light or heavy manufacturing companies and warehouses.

- *Vacant land* is land without buildings or "unimproved." This includes land in its natural state and land that does not possess improvements that serve a purpose.

- *Agricultural zones* are used for animal grazing and crop production. Zoning ordinances favor agricultural use, which is rarely prohibited or limited.

- Public *open space* is land that is not expressly developed for residential, commercial, industrial, or institutional use. Open space can be owned by private individuals or by the public (government ownership). Open space can include agricultural and forest land, undeveloped shorelines, public parks, and lakes and bays.

Local Land Use Planning

Local planning boards make recommendations about the general layout of a specific area in a city, town, or village and map the zones and uses allowed within each zone. Zoning boards of appeal grant or deny requests for zoning variances and special use permits within a particular municipality. The purpose of planning is to provide for the orderly growth of a community that results in the greatest social and economic benefits to the people living there. Together with the plan, the community agrees on certain zoning requirements. The proposals are presented by referendum to all property owners.

Zoning Board of Appeals

The zoning board of appeals has the power to review administrative rulings made by the planning board or other legislative body, and grant or deny variances and special use permits. It also ensures the fair application of zoning regulations and serves as a safety valve for the zoning system.

Variance. A **variance** *is a permitted deviation from specific requirements of a zoning ordinance.* For example, if an owner's lot is slightly smaller than the minimum lot-size requirement set by a zoning ordinance, the owner may be granted a variance by petitioning the appropriate authorities.

Special use permit. A **special use permit** *allows a use that is otherwise not permitted in a zone.* A special use permit cannot be granted without a public hearing. Unlike a variance request, special use permits do not require the property owner to demonstrate undue hardship because of the current zoning. Generally, a special use permit is authorized if the proposed use is in harmony with local zoning ordinances and laws, does not adversely affect the neighborhood, and is beneficial in some way to the community.

Spot zoning. With **spot zoning,** *a specific property within a zoned area is rezoned to permit a use different from the zoning requirements for that area.* Spot zoning is illegal in many states. A property owner may try to rezone her land from residential to commercial or industrial use because this type of land is often more valuable. The rezoning of a property solely for the benefit of the property owner without a corresponding benefit to the entire neighborhood or a rezoning that decreases the value of neighborhood properties constitutes spot zoning.

Nonconforming use. When zoning is first imposed on an area or when an area is rezoned, the zoning authority generally cannot require that the property owners discontinue a current use that does not now conform to the new zoning ordinance. A **nonconforming use** *is an authorized preexisting use of property in a zoned area that is different from the use specified by the zoning code.* This is called a preexisting nonconforming or "grandfathered" use. Figure 3.4 illustrates the various zoning issues.

STANDARDS, LAWS, AND REGULATIONS

 ities, counties, and other local governing units may impose land use regulations and building codes. These laws may not contravene federal and state laws but may be more restrictive.

Building Codes

Building codes *are another form of land use control to protect the public by regulating construction.* Uniform codes for building construction, electrical, and plumbing exist on federal, state, and local levels. A main source for state building codes is the International Code Council (ICC). The ICC is a nonprofit organization that develops a single set of comprehensive and coordinated national model construction codes. The founders of the ICC are the

■ Building Officials and Code Administrators International, Inc. (BOCA).

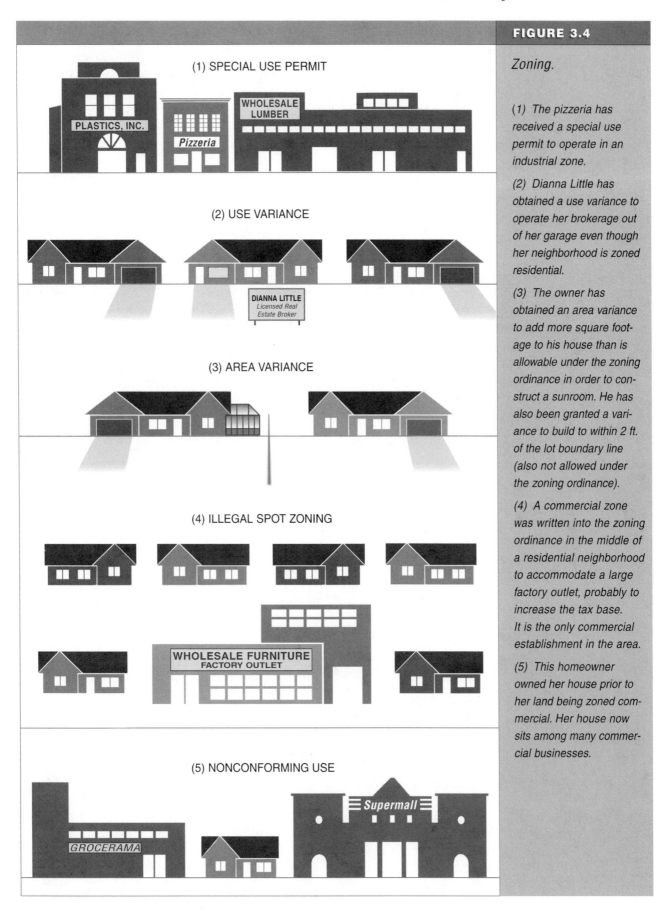

FIGURE 3.4

Zoning.

(1) The pizzeria has received a special use permit to operate in an industrial zone.

(2) Dianna Little has obtained a use variance to operate her brokerage out of her garage even though her neighborhood is zoned residential.

(3) The owner has obtained an area variance to add more square footage to his house than is allowable under the zoning ordinance in order to construct a sunroom. He has also been granted a variance to build to within 2 ft. of the lot boundary line (also not allowed under the zoning ordinance).

(4) A commercial zone was written into the zoning ordinance in the middle of a residential neighborhood to accommodate a large factory outlet, probably to increase the tax base. It is the only commercial establishment in the area.

(5) This homeowner owned her house prior to her land being zoned commercial. Her house now sits among many commercial businesses.

■ International Conference of Building Officials (ICBO).

■ Southern Building Code Congress International, Inc. (SBCCI).

Since the early part of the last century, these organizations developed three separate sets of model codes used throughout the United States. Although regional codes had been effective, a single set of codes was needed. The nation's three model code groups then created the International Code Council and developed codes without regional limitations. BOCA, ICBO, and SBCCI formed the ICC in 1944. The ICC website is www.iccsafe.org.

State and local codes are modeled after these federal standards. If a local building code is more restrictive than the federal or state code, the more restrictive regulations apply. If a municipality does not have a specific code, the state code applies. Table 3.1 sets forth the building code authority.

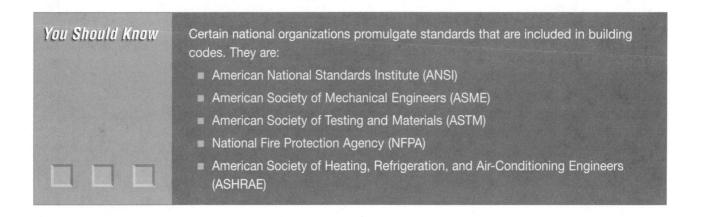

You Should Know

Certain national organizations promulgate standards that are included in building codes. They are:

■ American National Standards Institute (ANSI)

■ American Society of Mechanical Engineers (ASME)

■ American Society of Testing and Materials (ASTM)

■ National Fire Protection Agency (NFPA)

■ American Society of Heating, Refrigeration, and Air-Conditioning Engineers (ASHRAE)

Building Permits and Certificates of Occupancy

Building codes require that a property owner obtain a **building permit** *from the appropriate local government authority before constructing or renovating a commercial building or residential property.* While construction is in progress, local government inspectors perform frequent inspections to make certain that code

TABLE 3.1	CODE	AUTHORITY
Building code authority.	Federal building codes	Sets national standards
Local building codes, if more restrictive than the federal or state codes, set forth the building standards for a particular municipality.	State building codes	Sets state standards and is generally based on federal codes
	Local building codes	Sets local standards and is generally based on state and federal codes
	No local code	State code applies
	No state code	Federal code applies

requirements are being met. After a satisfactory final inspection, a **certificate of occupancy** *is issued, permitting occupation of the structure by tenants or the owner.* Some cities require a certificate of occupancy based on a satisfactory inspection of the property, and prior to occupancy by a new owner or tenant, of any structure even though it is not new construction or has not been renovated. The inspection is done to reveal any deficiencies in the structure that require correction in order to protect the new purchaser or tenant.

Building departments enforce the building code. Their role is to protect the public by ensuring that code restrictions are adhered to and that duly licensed and insured contractors perform any needed work.

You Should Know

As you will notice throughout your home inspection career, multiple and "creative" violations of building codes are possible. Home inspectors are *not* code inspectors. Each locality has trained code inspectors. As a home inspector, it is not your responsibility to investigate or have knowledge of every potential code violation. Nonetheless, home inspectors should possess or have access to the code manual for their area and refer to it when a possible code violation is suspected. You can and must raise code violation issues that you detect with your clients.

IMPORTANT POINTS

1. Land owners have the right to place private controls on their own real estate. These restrictions may exist on individual deeds or may take the form of restrictions affecting an entire subdivision.

2. Public land use controls include police power, taxation, eminent domain, and escheat.

3. Eminent domain is the power of a government to take private land for public use.

4. If an individual dies without any legal heirs, his property reverts to the state through the power of escheat.

5. Types of zoning include residential, commercial, industrial, vacant land, agricultural, and public open space.

6. The planning board establishes zoning regulations, creates a capital budget, and reviews site plans for new development.

7. The zoning board of appeals has the power to review administrative rulings made by the planning board.

8. A variance is a permitted deviation from specific requirements of a zoning ordinance. A special use permit allows a use that is not otherwise permitted in a zone. With spot zoning, a specific property within a zoned area is rezoned to permit a use different from the zoning requirements for that area. A nonconforming use is an authorized preexisting use of property in a zoned area that is different from the use specified by the zoning code.

9. Local support and enforcement of zoning ordinances and other legislation include building codes and the local court system.

10. Building codes are another form of land use control to protect the public. Uniform codes for building construction, electrical, and plumbing exist on federal, state, and local levels.

11. Building codes require that a property owner obtain a building permit from the appropriate local government authority before constructing or renovating a commercial building or residential property.

12. Home inspectors are not code inspectors. Each locality has individuals who are trained code inspectors. It is not the responsibility of the home inspector to investigate every code violation although a knowledge of and reference to local codes is essential.

13. Building departments enforce the building code and issue a certificate of occupancy that authorizes occupation of a structure.

CHAPTER REVIEW

Field Study Assignment 1

Go to your local library or town hall and obtain code manuals for your locality. Familiarize yourself with the code manuals for construction, electrical, plumbing, energy, and other standards.

Field Study Assignment 2

Start thinking about your home inspection library. If affordable, consider purchasing local code manual(s) for quick reference. Other basic reference materials include detailed information on plumbing, electrical, structural, and other construction issues and a map book of your market area.

Field Study Assignment 3

Find out when your local planning board or zoning board meets. Attend a meeting, or several meetings, to discover the land use issues under consideration in your area.

REVIEW QUESTIONS   *Choose the letter that best answers the question.*

1. Which of the following is NOT a public land use control?
   A. escheat
   B. eminent domain
   C. setback requirements
   D. master planning

2. Deed restrictions that run with the land are:
   A. nonconforming
   B. variances
   C. declarations
   D. covenants

3. Restrictive covenants are:
   A. statements of record
   B. public land use controls
   C. variances
   D. private land use controls

4. The Dorights live in an upscale subdivision and according to their deed, they are prohibited from constructing a tool shed in their backyard that is visible from the street. This prohibition is an example of a:
   A. deed restriction
   B. zoning ordinance
   C. variance
   D. nonconforming use

5. A recorded map that illustrates the streets, lots, and general layout of a subdivision is known as a:
   A. plat
   B. site plan
   C. zoning map
   D. topographical rendering

6. If a municipality determines that the construction of a highway is in the best interests of its citizens, this is an example of which government power?
   A. eminent domain
   B. police power
   C. escheat
   D. caveat emptor

7. The power of a government to take land for the benefit of the public is known as:
   A. escheat
   B. spot zoning
   C. eminent domain
   D. governmental covenant

8. Aunt Em died without any legal heirs. Her mansion on the hill and her considerable savings account became the property of the state where she resided. This power of the state government is an example of:
   A. condemnation
   B. eminent domain
   C. escheat
   D. police power

9. An easement is a type of:
   A. variance
   B. right-of-way
   C. special use permit
   D. nonconforming use

10. Which of the following create zoning ordinances?
    A. federal government
    B. local governments
    C. tax assessors
    D. state legislature

11. Which of the following is NOT authorized to impose public land use controls?
    A. building department
    B. planning board
    C. subdivision developer
    D. zoning board of appeals

12. An authorized deviation from a zoning ordinance is known as:
    A. an easement
    B. a deed restriction
    C. escheat
    D. a variance

13. What is the difference between a variance and a special use permit?
    A. No difference.
    B. A variance applies only to residential properties, whereas a special use permit applies to both residential and commercial properties.
    C. A special use permit does not require the property owner to demonstrate hardship as a result of the zoning ordinance, whereas a variance does.
    D. A special use permit requires that a special fee be paid to the municipality, whereas a variance does not.

14. Spot zoning is illegal in many states because it is generally:
    A. beneficial only to the property owner
    B. beneficial only to the municipality
    C. an illegal use of the power of eminent domain
    D. an illegal use of police power

15. Damon and his family owned and operated a tomato farm long before the area was rezoned from agricultural to commercial. They continue to operate their farm next to the shopping mall to this day. The farm best describes a:

A. variance

B. spot zone

C. special use permit

D. nonconforming use

16. If a local building code is more restrictive than an existing state code, which of the following is TRUE?

A. The state code applies.

B. Either the state or local code applies interchangeably.

C. The local code applies.

D. The code applied is decided by the developer on a case-by-case basis.

17. Before constructing or renovating a commercial property, which of the following must be obtained from the local government authority?

A. certificate of occupancy

B. proposed assessment

C. building permit

D. inspector's certificate

18. Before a tenant or owner can move into a new or renovated structure, or in some cases an existing structure, which of the following documents must be issued by the municipality?

A. certificate of occupancy

B. building permit

C. approved building plans and specifications

D. certificate of relief from disabilities

19. On inspection of the electrical wiring in an older two-family home, Eugene found several code violations. Which of the following should he do?

A. Immediately report his findings to the local building department.

B. Report his findings to the party who hired him and on the inspection report.

C. Call in an electrician to correct the code violation.

D. Refuse to complete the inspection report unless the home owner agrees in writing to correct the violations.

20. The purpose of the Council of American Building Officials (CABO) is to:

A. incorporate and unify the standards of the major building code organizations into one unified source

B. function as a watchdog organization for the federal government

C. oversee the standards of practice for home inspectors

D. develop new technology

ANSWER KEY			
1. C	6. B	11. C	16. C
2. D	7. C	12. D	17. C
3. D	8. C	13. C	18. A
4. A	9. B	14. A	19. B
5. A	10. B	15. D	20. A

PART II

THE HOME

INSPECTION

PROCESS

CHAPTER 4

HOME INSPECTION PROCEDURE AND REPORTING

This chapter first discusses how to obtain preliminary experience before you perform your first fee-paid inspection. In addition, it reviews the basic tools and equipment needed for the home inspection process both on-site and off. This chapter explains how to conduct the inspection including how to deal with your client (usually the buyer) and the property owner (the seller). The chapter also covers how to write home inspection reports.

LEARNING OBJECTIVES

1. Explain methods of gaining home inspection experience.
2. List the tools of the trade.
3. Describe communication strategies to use with clients (buyers) and owners (sellers) of the subject property.
4. Explain how to conduct the home inspection using the pre-inspection agreement and home inspection reports.

KEY TERMS

Checklist report

Disclaimer

Narrative report

Narrative report with checklist or rating   system

Pre-inspection agreement

Rating system report

Statute of limitations

GAINING EXPERIENCE

Perhaps you have never performed a home inspection and feel unsure of your abilities. You have prepared to a point—you are reading this text-book, quite possibly as part of a home inspection course. Other courses and further study are helpful, but eventually, you must perform. The best way to gain hands-on experience is to practice performing several home inspections before you receive compensation. Ask at least 10 or 15 friends or relatives if you can inspect their properties for free. You should choose different types of residential properties and also consider inspecting properties built during various time periods.

For example, find a home built before 1950; one to three homes built between 1950 and 1970; and then, if possible, every five years thereafter—up until the present date. Also investigate new construction. Several repeat visits to any number of homes under construction can give you a clear picture of the construction process. In addition, careful observation of and conversation with construction crews can update you on the latest building methods.

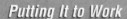
Putting It to Work

As you inspect your practice properties, take notes as you progress through the properties. These notes may serve as future reference to help you look for various problems in similar properties you inspect. Pay attention to property components that have changed dramatically over the years. Consider the advances in the electrical and plumbing areas, energy conservation measures, environmental considerations, and certain building materials.

You Should Know

Even though you do not receive compensation for your practice properties, have your professional (E&O) liability insurance in place. Whether or not you are compensated, you must be protected should liability issues arise.

Learning from Others

Many prospective home inspectors are or have been a professional in one of the home construction, repair, or renovation fields. Whether this is true or not, you can gain valuable knowledge from other technicians and professionals. Electricians, plumbers, carpenters, and heating and cooling technicians, to name a few, are excellent sources of information. If you are acquainted with individuals who do such work, ask to accompany them to some of their jobs. If you do not know any such people, hire them to inspect various components of your home, such as the HVAC, plumbing, and electrical systems, and ask questions.

TOOLS OF THE TRADE

As in any profession, certain tools and equipment are necessary. Whether you work for yourself or others, you have to buy your own tools. Begin now to assemble your tools and equipment. This gives you time to price the more expensive items, such as a ladder, or order what you can't find locally. Also talk to other home inspectors. They can share information about the products and brand names that work best for them. As you progress through your career, you can fine-tune your tools and equipment, adding or subtracting as necessary.

You should not over-purchase tools in the beginning. A great many tools are not needed on a regular basis to perform a home inspection. Remember, you will not be disassembling or repairing items during a home inspection. If you do take an item apart, you are liable for any problems that may arise later. If you cannot observe the condition of an item by a simple probing, let it go.

Putting It to Work

On-Site Equipment

The following is a list of basic tools, supplies, and equipment:

■ *Measuring tapes.* Purchase a 10-15 foot tape. Some inspectors carry a folding ruler.

■ *Binoculars.* A quality pair is indispensable for the roof investigation if you can't walk on the roof.

■ *Camera and photographic equipment.* Photos may be a part of your inspection report. Use them to illustrate items that are difficult to describe in writing. Photos also serve as a reference when you write your report. There are many photo choices on the market today—everything from the standard 35mm to the film-loaded disposable to the Polaroid to the digital camera. The primary consideration is to purchase equipment that you feel comfortable with and that gives a clear and accurate image.

Get in the habit of photographing both the exterior and interior of the property, particularly places where defects, code violations, and other problems appear. Pictures are often better than words, and photos with a few words of explanation provide a concise mode of communicating your observations. Photos kept on file, whether used in the report or not, help protect the home inspector should a dispute arise.

Putting It to Work

■ *Protective clothing.* Encounters with dirt, dust, splinters, and mold, as well as cuts and bruises, are likely during any inspection. Commercial weight slacks or coveralls will serve you well. Buy several pairs of quality work gloves that protect your hands but still allow you to do what is necessary. Thin plastic or latex gloves (the kind medical professionals use) are excellent for close work. Knee pads are useful in crawl spaces and other low-lying areas. You might carry a hard hat to use if you are inspecting a property that is in bad shape or under construction. Property owners often ask inspectors to take off their shoes before entering a home. Because it is difficult to climb up a ladder without shoes, carry disposable shoe coverings. Home inspectors should arrive at the inspection site looking like professionals. The coveralls, knee pads, and other protective clothing can be slipped on over your clothes.

■ *Dust mask or face respirator.*

■ *Electrical circuit tester or voltage meter.* This is used to test whether the circuits have juice running through them. Combination instruments are available too.

■ *Hand pick or awl.*

■ *High-powered flashlights.* In addition to a large flashlight, purchase one small enough to investigate small holes or openings. Be sure to carry spare batteries and extra flashlight bulbs to the job site.

■ *Ladder.* The ladder is one of the most expensive purchases. Purchase one that is long enough, at least 20 feet, to allow access to the tallest roof in the area. A smaller folding stepladder is also necessary. Both the large and small ladders should be ones that fold down to a smaller size, particularly important because the small ladder may be carried into the house. Besides the roof, ladders are used to investigate other exterior segments such as coverings, windows, soffits, and so on. Some inspectors prefer the folding telescopic ladders, but be aware that they are heavy. Others prefer the lighter aluminum ladders. Your ladder should be OSHA (Occupational Safety and Health Administration) approved.

■ *Gas leak detector.* Although the gas meter may not indicate the exact type of gas that is leaking, this is easily deduced from the component where the leak originates. Some common gas leak problems found in the home include a carbon monoxide leak from the furnace, which is hazardous, or a benign methane gas leak from a plumbing pipe. Propane is another common gas found leaking in or around the home.

■ *Level.* Some levels have digital readouts instead of the traditional bubble. When purchasing a level, consider that the shorter the level, the less accurate it is.

■ *Market area maps.* Maps and directions are available through the Internet (e.g., Mapquest.com).

■ *Moisture meter.* This meter can detect moisture inside the walls to a particular depth.

■ *Screwdrivers.* Both Phillips and flathead—one large and small of each should suffice. The larger screwdriver is used to investigate wood rot. The smaller screwdriver is useful for removing switch plate covers or sample paint chips for a lead analysis.

■ *Mirror.* A flame-resistant stainless steel mirror attached to a telescopic handle or an adjustable glass inspection mirror with handle are available. The handles allow a mirror to be placed into hard to reach locations. The mirror reveals items that you may have difficulty seeing otherwise. For example, a mirror is used to check the heat exchanger in a hot air furnace. These mirrors are available with small handles also.

■ *Thermometer.* A thermometer is used to measure the recovery rate of the hot water tank. The *recovery rate* is how long it takes the heater to heat water and maintain a certain temperature.

■ *Toolbox or carrying case and tool belt.* Most of the tools taken into the home fit on your tool belt. The belt is essential because it leaves your hands free to work. Other tools can be left in your vehicle to use as needed. See Figure 4.1 for illustrations of some of these tools.

FIGURE 4.1

Tools of the trade.

a. circuit analyzer
 * Less expensive
   models are available

b. gas tracer

c. thermometer

d. two-prong circuit
   tester

e. telescopic mirror

f. ground fault circuit
   interrupter tester

g. telescopic ladder

h. tool pouch

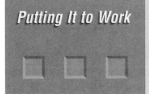

Putting It to Work

A typical tool belt or pouch should contain the following essentials: flashlight, pick or awl, two screwdrivers, ruler or measuring tape, thermometer, gas leak meter, voltage meter, and hand mirror. Other items can be taken from the truck as needed and put away as they are used so they are not forgotten.

■ *Writing and business supplies.* Pens, pencils, graph paper for sketching the house and site layout, business cards, firm pamphlets and promotions, and a clipboard with a home inspection checklist or other report are necessary. If the clients are present at the inspection, bring the pre-inspection agreement if it has not yet been signed. A simple briefcase for the paperwork keeps you organized.

Although the preceding list seems rather formidable, think about the tasks you have to do and the tools that will assist you before making a purchase. Also consider that a roomy station wagon, truck, or van will serve you well over the years and allow you to organize your tools and supplies so that they are easily accessible.

Office Equipment

The home inspection office, whether home based or in a company setting, serves a variety of functions: completing the home inspection report, tracking invoices, making and receiving phone calls, checking library references, marketing the business, updating files, and preparing or reviewing business correspondence. Therefore, basic office equipment is needed. Investigate the types of equipment that serve more than one function. For example, some multifunction machines include a fax, scanner, copier, printer, and telephone. Basic office equipment includes the following:

■ *Computer and software.* Software is available to help complete the pre-inspection agreement and various types of home inspection reports. A generic report form can be printed, brought to the site, and completed as you go through the inspection. Another option is to use a laptop computer on-site and complete the report directly on the computer. After returning to the office, any necessary revisions are made and the report is printed. Software to track accounts receivable, income, and expenses is available.

Putting It to Work

If you are not computer literate, now is the time to become so. Computers and software are very user friendly. Before purchasing expensive home inspection software programs, try a demo program. Generally, demos are free. Most home inspection organizations and software manufacturers offer excellent software at a reasonable price. Technology is here, so use it! (See Appendix C for a list of organizations and their corresponding Web sites.)

■ *Printer.*

■ *Telephone equipment.* The system chosen should include an answering machine and a beeper or cell phone. A toll-free number is useful if you plan to do work at distances greater than 50 miles from your office. Clients who are moving from another town also need to access you from some distance.

■ *Fax machine and a separate fax number.* Software is available that sends and receives faxes directly on the computer if the file is on the computer.

■ *Business forms.* Typical forms include the pre-inspection agreement, client information form, invoices, receipts, and inspection reports.

■ *Office furniture.* Generally, a filing cabinet, desk and chair, lighting, and a few chairs for visitors are sufficient to furnish an office.

HOME INSPECTION PROCEDURE

Home inspectors must develop an orderly method of proceeding from the initial client contact to the final inspection report. For example, companies or individual inspectors may collect inspection fees at different times. Some inspectors require full or partial payment prior to the inspection; others accept payment after the inspection is completed. The following sections offer a sample method. Through personal preference and experience, inspectors can modify the process.

Client Information Form

You may be contacted by the buyer–client or receive a referral from a lender, a real estate agent, or another inspection company. Regardless of who makes the initial contact, certain basic information is required. Figure 4.2 is a sample information form from a home inspection company. Initial basic information should include:

■ Date of the referral or contact.
■ Client's name, billing address, phone number, and e-mail address, if available.
■ Property owner's name, billing address, phone number, and e-mail address, if available.
■ Address of the subject property including the town or city and county.
■ Brief description of the property.

During the initial contact, learn as much as you can about the property. What type of house is it? What is the age and approximate condition of the property? What is the approximate size of the property? These items help to determine what tools to bring to the site and what to charge.	*Putting It to Work* 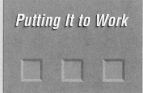

■ Purpose of the inspection. Is it a full or partial inspection, or new construction? Are extra services required such as water quality, lead-based paint, or radon testing?
■ Approximate square footage of the property. This information is important because it defines the scope of the inspection and forms the basis for the fee charged.
■ An indication whether other areas of the property require inspection (e.g., swimming pool, septic system, well).
■ Whether the subject property is inhabited or vacant.
■ Whether the utilities are turned on or not. If not, who will arrange to have them turned on for the inspection?

FIGURE 4.2	*An information form.*

INSPECTION ORDER

Are you the
- ☐ Agent   ☐ Attorney
- ☐ Purchaser   ☐ Lender
- ☐ Seller

Will you be present at the inspection?
- ☐ Yes   ☐ No

Will the agent be present at the inspection?
- ☐ Yes   ☐ No   ☐ Don't Know

Please provide the following client information:

Name

Title

Street Address

City

State/Province

Zip/Postal Code

Country

Work Phone

Home Phone

FAX

E-mail

Please provide the following agent information (if applicable):

Name

Organization

Street Address

City

State/Province

Zip/Postal Code

Country

Work Phone

Home Phone

FAX

E-mail

What inspections would you like performed on the property:
- ☐ Full Residential (Buyer)
- ☐ Full Residential (Seller)

- ☐ HUD 203k Work Write Up or feasibility study
- ☐ Construction Progress Reports
- ☐ Water Test
- ☐ Septic Certification
- ☐ Pre-Listing Inspection
- ☐ Radon
- ☐ Expert Testimony or Documentation
- ☐ Partial Home Inspection
- ☐ Bio-Aerosol (Mold) Testing
- ☐ Asbestos Testing (Evaluation)

What Type of Home:
- ☐ Single-family   ☐ Commercial
- ☐ Multi-family   ☐ Other
- ☐ Condominium

How many square feet is the house?

Age of house

Is there a basement or crawl space?
- ☐ Yes   ☐ No

Does the property have a septic system or well water supply?
- ☐ Yes   ☐ No

Is the house presently occupied?
- ☐ Yes   ☐ No

If no, will the utilities be on?
- ☐ Yes   ☐ No

Please provide the following inspection site information:

Street Address

City

State/Province

Zip/Postal Code

Country

Directions to inspection location (optional)

Special instructions

Source: Closer Look Inspections™, http://www.closerlookinspection.com

If the property owner has moved and no one has authority to turn on the utilities at the time of the inspection, the property can be inspected anyway. The home inspector returns after the clients have moved in and inspects those systems omitted. The section of the inspection report addressing these components is then completed and sent to the clients. To address any problems uncovered during the subsequent inspection, a certain sum of money is placed in escrow (to cover repair or replacement costs) at the closing pending completion of the inspection report.

- Any concerns or questions that the clients have about the property.
- How the client will be billed. Some inspectors bill by the job; others prefer to bill by the hour, particularly if they are unsure of the scope of the inspection.
- Required completion date for the inspection.
- When payment is due.
- Method of payment.

You Should Know

The completion date of the inspection is extremely important because a real estate closing is usually the reason for the inspection. Generally, all contracts of sale are subject to an inspection of the property, so a late inspection report can cause costly delays. Moreover, the decision to purchase the property may rest solely on the inspection results. Be sure that you allow plenty of time to perform the inspection by the desired date.

You Should Know

Many home inspection offices accept various credit cards. Although the credit card companies charge the vendor a small percentage of the sale, many people prefer to pay using a card. Credit cards are reliable because they are accepted or rejected when payment is made. Home inspectors should consider accepting this method of payment.

Once the preliminary information is obtained, the home inspector may be able to set a fee. If not, the inspector can require an initial down payment with the remaining balance (determined after viewing the property and not to exceed a certain amount) due immediately prior to or after the inspection. Many inspection firms have a set price list for the various services offered. Figure 4.3 is a home inspection appointment form that includes a price list.

Pre-Inspection Agreement

During the initial contact, explain that a pre-inspection agreement must be signed prior to the inspection. This agreement can be sent to the client once the appointment is made or it can be signed at the time of the inspection if the client is there. The **pre-inspection agreement** *is a contract that protects both the home inspector and the client. It explains, in general terms, the scope of the inspection (what is included and what is not), the cost, and the procedures to address any dispute that may arise.*

FIGURE 4.3	*A home inspection appointment form with price list.*

INSPECTION ORDER

Client: Ms. Lucy Baynes

Address: 7 Lafleur Street
            New Orleans, Louisiana 70119

Telephone (home): 383-1939   (work):

Referral: NYNEX

Real Estate/Agent:

Inspection Address: 14 Jardin Street
                     New Orleans, Louisiana 70119

Inspection Date/Time: Jan. 8, 2007 (Mon.)   Time: 9:00 a.m.

Services Required:	Fees		
Home Inspection:	$ 250.00		
Termite:	$ 40.00	☒ yes	☐ no
Radon:	$ 45.00	☒ yes	☐ no
Water Purity:	$ 45.00	☐ yes	☒ no
Water Flow:	$ 30.00	☐ yes	☒ no
Dye Test:	$ 50.00	☐ yes	☒ no
Lead Test: (per swab)	$ 10.00	☐ yes	☒ no
Nitrate:	$ 30.00	☐ yes	☒ no
Nitrite:	$ 30.00	☐ yes	☒ no

Weather Condition:

Outside Temperature:

Present at Inspection:

Direction:

Comments:

Source: Anthony D'Agostino, Atlantic Inspection Service, Latham, New York.

Under no circumstances should a home inspection be performed if both parties do not sign a pre-inspection agreement. Give a signed copy to the client.

	You Should Know
If you become a member of a home inspection organization, the state or local chapter can furnish you with a pre-inspection agreement. Agreement forms are included in home inspection software available through these organizations. An attorney can prepare this agreement too. You should not prepare the agreement yourself because contracts must contain certain elements in order to be valid and legally binding.	☐ ☐ ☐

Scheduling the Inspection

Once the client has agreed to have the inspection performed, a date for the inspection is set. After you and the client have selected a choice of available dates, the client, either directly or through a real estate agent, contacts the property owner to determine which date is best. If the property owner has already moved, the real estate agent generally has the key to the property and will let you in.

Inspection Day

A home inspection goes smoothly if you communicate effectively with the buyer–client and the property owner (seller). Although you are working for the buyer, the property owner can furnish you with valuable information about the property. This background information may pinpoint certain problem areas.

Your buyer–clients. Generally, the buyers are present during the inspection and they have questions and concerns about the property. Buyers also like to see how you conduct the inspection—what is inspected and how thoroughly. It is an excellent means for buyers to acquaint themselves with the home.

	You Should Know
Some home inspectors insist that the client be present during the inspection. The inspector can point out where the various systems and components of the property are located and show the client where there are deficiencies. This is helpful because many buyers do not fully understand the nature of a problem from reading the home inspection report. The client's presence allows the inspector to explain his findings in person.	☐ ☐ ☐

	Putting It to Work
Home inspectors should not comment on whether the buyer should proceed with the purchase based on the inspection. A home inspection only reports information regarding the subject property and explains the findings. The decision to purchase is up to the buyers. If a client asks how much the inspector feels the home is worth, the inspector should reply that a real estate agent or appraiser is best suited to answer that question.	☐ ☐ ☐

The property owner. As mentioned in Chapter 1, the property owners may have completed a property condition disclosure form if they have employed a real estate agent. Ask the agent or the owner for a copy of the form prior to the inspection. If you have an opportunity to speak with the owner, the following questions are helpful:

- Are there any current problems with the property?
- Does the property have a septic system or well?
- What is the age of each appliance, the furnace, the hot water heater, the roof, and other house systems?
- Have any recent renovations or repairs been made to the property?
- Is the basement damp or prone to flooding?
- Has there been a recent termite inspection?
- How long has the owner lived on the property?

Although the property owner can be helpful, the inspector must rely on his or her own expertise and not be influenced by the opinions of the owner, a real estate agent, or others.

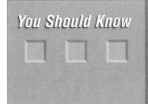

You Should Know   Property owners are a source of information and business. Give the property owner your business card. If the owners are selling, perhaps they are buying in the same area—this may mean a new client for you. Moreover, if the owner is present, he can assist you in a variety of ways: locating the gas and water meters, the distribution panel, the sewer line, and so forth.

EXAMINING THE PROPERTY

Each following chapter of this textbook discusses the specifics of the components that must be inspected. Generally, you must have a method of proceeding through the structure in an orderly and logical manner—from the exterior to the interior.

First, take a look at the site and determine how the home is situated on the site using your compass. Look for drainage problems. Next, look at the property around the house—the walkways, landscaping, and stairways. Then, look at the exterior of the home itself—the framing, facade, foundation wall, doors, windows, patios, decks, and so forth. Check the well and septic system if that is part of the inspection. Examine the roof by either walking it or viewing it with a ladder and binoculars. Next, check the garage. Many homes are built on a slab and some of the items generally found in the basement may be in the garage.

After a thorough inspection of the exterior, go inside the house. Make sure the utilities are turned on. In each room, start with the ceiling and work down to the walls, doors, and windows. Allow plenty of time for the kitchen and bathrooms because these rooms contain many items to be inspected. Next, check the attic and observe the insulation and ventilation. Finally, go into the basement. Many of the house systems, such as electrical, plumbing, and heating, can be checked in the basement. This is also where water and drainage problems appear. If you are testing air quality, such as for the presence of radon, put your equipment in place. Following a home inspection checklist ensures that the property is completely inspected.

Opinions vary as to how long an inspection should take. As you gain experience, you can better estimate the time required for different property sizes and types. The initial client information sheet helps to estimate the scope of the inspection. Proceed slowly and methodically, checking off each item and making comments on your checklist when necessary. An inspection cannot be completed in an hour no matter what the property type. Three hours is generally a minimum time period for a typical 3–4 bedroom single-family home. More time may be required depending on the size and scope of the inspection and the number of extra services requested. Think about the quality of your work rather than the time it takes you. That is your best guide.

You Should Know
Inspection
Timeframe

THE HOME INSPECTION REPORT

The home inspection report generally takes one of four forms: the checklist report with comments, often generated from computer software; the rating system report with comments; the purely narrative or written report; and the narrative report with either a checklist or rating system. The client may want to decide on the form used. Lenders may require a written narrative report. Some home inspection organizations recommend using either the narrative form or the narrative form with a checklist or rating system for a full and complete analysis of the property's condition. Whatever form is chosen, home inspectors must be sure that the findings included are easily understood by the client.

Checklist Report

Many home inspectors bring a preprinted or computer-generated blank checklist report form to the site and complete the report during and after the inspection. A **checklist report** *is a systemized itemization of the various components of a property that is organized into sections that allow the inspector to check off inspected property components and comment on any specific problems.*

With experience, the home inspector can generate a customized checklist. The checklist is modified to include items that are specific to the inspector's clientele and is organized so that it works well for the individual inspector.

Putting It to Work

The home inspection checklist serves many purposes and should be used during the inspection whether or not it is the final report form. First, the checklist provides the home inspector with an organized method of inspecting the property. It is also a reminder of what to inspect and guides the inspector through a thorough investigation. In addition, the checklist serves as a record of the scope of the inspection should a narrative report be generated from the checklist. In this case, inspectors should keep the inspection checklist on file along with all other property information.

The checklist format is also helpful to the client. If the client is present at the inspection, the checklist demonstrates to the buyer that the inspector is methodically examining the property. The checklist gives the buyer feedback about what the inspector is doing and on completion is an easily identifiable report of what the inspector has done. Figure 4.4 is an example of a home inspection checklist report.

FIGURE 4.4	*A home inspection checklist report.*

STRUCTURE

Type of Building:
- ☐ Single Family
- ☐ Two Story & Over
- ☐ Row House/Town House
- ☐ Split Level
- ☐ Duplex
- ☐ Condo

Type of Structure:
- ☐ Wood Frame
- ☐ Masonry
- ☐ Other

Roof Style:
- ☐ Gable
- ☐ Hip
- ☐ Shed
- ☐ Gambrel
- ☐ Mansard
- ☐ Other

Definition of Terms:

Satisfactory: The item inspected is performing its intended function as of the date of inspection.

Not Applicable: The item does not exist on the interior or exterior of the property being inspected.

Not Present (NP): There were no indications or signs at the time of the inspection.

Adequate: Performance within the standards of practice.

Low: Noncompliance with the standards of practice.

GROUNDS

Grading: General Grading, Slope & Drainage
- ☐ Satisfactory
- ☐ Not Applicable

Trees & Shrubbery:
- ☐ Satisfactory
- ☐ Not Applicable

Window Wells:
- ☐ Satisfactory
- ☐ Not Applicable

Sidewalk or Walkway:
- ☐ Concrete
- ☐ Brick
- ☐ Other
- ☐ Patio Blocks
- ☐ Flagstone

- ☐ Satisfactory
- ☐ Not Applicable

Driveway:
- ☐ Concrete
- ☐ Asphalt
- ☐ Gravel
- ☐ Other

- ☐ Satisfactory
- ☐ Not Applicable

Patio or Terrace:
- ☐ Concrete
- ☐ Brick
- ☐ Other
- ☐ Patio Blocks
- ☐ Flagstone

- ☐ Satisfactory
- ☐ Not Applicable

Steps to Building:
STEPS:
- ☐ Wood
- ☐ Concrete
- ☐ Brick
- ☐ Block
- ☐ Other

- ☐ Satisfactory
- ☐ Not Applicable

RAILING:
- ☐ Wood
- ☐ Wrought Iron
- ☐ Steel Pipe
- ☐ Other

- ☐ Satisfactory
- ☐ Not Applicable

Retaining Wall:
- ☐ Brick
- ☐ Block
- ☐ Timber
- ☐ Flagstone
- ☐ Stone
- ☐ Other

- ☐ Satisfactory
- ☐ NP

- ☐ Mortar Joints
- ☐ Dry Joints
- ☐ Weep Holes

- ☐ Satisfactory
- ☐ NP

EXTERIOR

Wood Deck:

PLATFORM:
- ☐ Satisfactory
- ☐ Not Applicable

Decay signs:
- ☐ NP
- ☐ Extensive

RAILING:
- ☐ Satisfactory
- ☐ Not Applicable

Decay signs:
- ☐ NP
- ☐ Extensive

STEPS:
- ☐ Satisfactory
- ☐ Not Applicable

Decay signs:
- ☐ NP
- ☐ Extensive

Porch:

FLOOR:
- ☐ Wood
- ☐ Concrete
- ☐ Other

- ☐ Satisfactory
- ☐ Not Applicable

RAILING OR POSTS:
- ☐ Wood
- ☐ Wrought Iron
- ☐ Other

- ☐ Satisfactory
- ☐ Not Applicable

CEILING:
- ☐ Wood
- ☐ Open Structure
- ☐ Vinyl Siding Vented

- ☐ Satisfactory
- ☐ Not Applicable

| A home inspection checklist report, continued. | **FIGURE 4.4** |

Exterior Wall Covering:

Material: _____

Condition: Decay signs:
☐ Satisfactory   ☐ NP
                      ☐ Extensive

Fascia:
☐ Wood   ☐ Aluminum
☐ Vinyl   ☐ Open Eaves

Condition: Decay signs:
☐ Satisfactory   ☐ NP
☐ Not Applicable   ☐ Extensive

Soffit:
☐ Wood   ☐ Vinyl
☐ Aluminum
☐ Vented   ☐ Not Vented

Condition: Decay signs:
☐ Satisfactory   ☐ NP
☐ Not Applicable   ☐ Extensive

Storm Doors & Windows:
☐ Satisfactory   ☐ Not Applicable

Doors & Trim:

DOORS:
☐ Satisfactory

TRIM:
☐ Jamb   ☐ Threshold
☐ Alum. Clad   ☐ Head

Condition: Decay signs:
☐ Satisfactory   ☐ NP
                      ☐ Extensive

Windows & Trim:

WINDOWS:
☐ Satisfactory

TRIM:
☐ Head   ☐ Jamb
☐ Sill   ☐ Alum. Clad

Condition: Decay signs:
☐ Satisfactory   ☐ NP
                      ☐ Extensive

STYLE:
☐ Double Hung   ☐ Awning   ☐ Slider
☐ Casement   ☐ Hopper   ☐ Fixed

MATERIAL:
☐ Wood   ☐ Metal   ☐ Vinyl
☐ Alum. Clad   ☐ Vinyl Clad

GLASS:
☐ Double Pane - Insulated
☐ Single Pane - Noninsulated

Gutters & Downspouts:
☐ Vinyl   ☐ Aluminum
☐ Seamless   ☐ Galvanized

☐ Satisfactory   ☐ Not Applicable
☐ See Narrative Report

☐ Splash Block   ☐ Drain Boot

☐ Satisfactory   ☐ Not Applicable

Exterior Electrical:
☐ Ceiling/Wall Lights
☐ Satisfactory   ☐ Not Applicable

☐ Wall Lights with Electric Eye
☐ Satisfactory   ☐ Not Applicable

☐ Lamp Post
☐ Satisfactory   ☐ Not Applicable

☐ Lamp Post with Electric Eye
☐ Satisfactory   ☐ Not Applicable

☐ Walkway Lights
☐ Satisfactory   ☐ Not Applicable

☐ Receptacles
☐ Satisfactory   ☐ Not Applicable

☐ G.F.C.I.
☐ Satisfactory   ☐ Not Applicable

Hose Bibs:
☐ Frost Free   ☐ Standard Faucet
(close interior valve in winter)
☐ Satisfactory   ☐ Not Applicable

Water Pressure: P.S.I.
☐ Adequate   ☐ Low

Water Flow: G.P.M.
☐ Adequate   ☐ Low

(continued)

FIGURE 4.4   *A home inspection checklist report, continued.*

GARAGE
☐ Attached   ☐ Detached

WALLS: Material: ☐ Drywall
☐ Covered   ☐ Open Structure

☐ Satisfactory

CEILING: Material: ☐ Drywall
☐ Covered   ☐ Open Structure

☐ Satisfactory

ACCESS:
☐ Scuttle   ☐ Disappearing Stairs

☐ Satisfactory   ☐ No Access

STRUCTURE:
☐ Rafters   Size: _____
☐ Trusses

☐ Satisfactory

ELECTRIC:
☐ Light Switch   ☐ Light Switch–3-Way
☐ Satisfactory   ☐ Not Applicable

☐ Receptacle
☐ Satisfactory   ☐ Not Applicable

☐ G.F.C.I.
☐ Satisfactory   ☐ Not Applicable

Overhead Doors:
OPERATION:
☐ Manual   ☐ Remote control
☐ Satisfactory   ☐ Not Applicable

SAFETY STOP/REVERSE:
☐ Auto   ☐ Electric Eye
☐ Satisfactory   ☐ Not Applicable

DOORS:
☐ Satisfactory   ☐ See Narrative Report

TRIM:
☐ Alum. Clad   ☐ Head   ☐ Jamb
☐ Satisfactory   ☐ See Narrative Report

ROOFING
Roof Covering:
Material: _____
☐ Satisfactory   ☐ See Narrative Report

How Observed:
☐ From ground level with the aid of binoculars.
☐ Access on the roof from a ladder.

Roof Accessories:
☐ Ridge Vent
☐ Satisfactory   ☐ Not Applicable

☐ Roof Vent
☐ Satisfactory   ☐ Not Applicable

☐ Sky Lights
☐ Satisfactory   ☐ Not Applicable

Plumbing Vent:
☐ Flashing with Adhesive
☐ Flashing with Rubber Boot
☐ Satisfactory   ☐ Not Applicable

Flashing:
☐ Galvanized   ☐ Copper   ☐ Aluminum
☐ Satisfactory   ☐ Not Applicable

Chimney:
☐ Brick with Clay Flue   ☐ Metal Liner
☐ Block with Clay Flue   ☐ Chimney Cap
☐ Satisfactory   ☐ Not Applicable
☐ See Narrative Report

☐ **Clean Before Use**

ATTIC
Access:
☐ No access   ☐ Stairs   ☐ Scuttle
☐ Disappearing Stairs
☐ Satisfactory

Ceiling Joists:
Size: _____
Bottom Chord of Truss: _____
☐ Satisfactory

Supporting Structure:
Roof Rafters: _____   Trusses: _____
☐ Collar Ties   ☐ Satisfactory

Roof Sheathing:
☐ Wafer Board   ☐ Plywood   ☐ Plank
☐ Satisfactory

☐ "H" Clips
☐ Satisfactory   ☐ Not Applicable

(continued)

A home inspection checklist report, continued.	FIGURE 4.4

Insulation: Installed In:

☐ Ceiling Joists ☐ Roof Rafters

☐ Satisfactory ☐ Not Applicable

Type:

☐ Vapor Barrier ☐ No Vapor Barrier

Average Thickness:

"R" Value:

Ventilation:

☐ Ridge Vent ☐ Roof Vents ☐ Window

☐ Gable Vents ☐ Soffit Vents ☐ Attic Fan

☐ House Fan

☐ Satisfactory ☐ Not Applicable

☐ Soffit Baffles

☐ Satisfactory ☐ NP

Moisture:

☐ None Noted ☐ Some Stains

☐ Extensive

INTERIOR

Floor Covering:

☐ Satisfactory

Walls:

☐ Satisfactory

Ceiling:

☐ Satisfactory

Stair to Upper Level:

☐ Tread/Riser ☐ Satisfactory

☐ Balustrade ☐ Satisfactory

☐ Wall Railing ☐ Satisfactory

Electrical:

☐ Light or Dimmer Switches

☐ Satisfactory ☐ See Narrative Report

☐ Receptacles

☐ Satisfactory ☐ See Narrative Report

☐ Fan Light

☐ Satisfactory

Heating or Cooling Distribution:

Type: ☐ Satisfactory

Smoke Detector:

☐ Direct Wire ☐ Battery Operated

☐ Satisfactory ☐ See Narrative Report

Windows:

☐ Operable ☐ See Narrative Report

☐ Non Operable

Doors:

☐ Satisfactory ☐ See Narrative Report

Fireplace:

☐ Zero Clearance Metal

☐ Firebrick & Hearth

☐ Wood Stove & Flue

☐ Satisfactory ☐ Not applicable

☐ See Narrative Report

☐ **Clean Before Use**

Damper

☐ Operated ☐ Satisfactory

BATHROOM NO. 1

Location:

Floor Covering:

☐ Satisfactory

Walls and ceiling:

☐ Satisfactory

Tub or Shower Stall:

☐ Free-Standing Tub ☐ Built-In Tub

☐ Fiberglass Enclosure ☐ Whirlpool

☐ Built-In Shower

Base type:

☐ Satisfactory ☐ See Narrative Report

Tub or Shower Door: Safety Glass

☐ Sliding ☐ Yes

☐ Swing ☐ Unknown

☐ Satisfactory ☐ NP

Ventilation:

☐ Window ☐ Satisfactory

☐ Fan ☐ Satisfactory

☐ Fan with Light ☐ Satisfactory

☐ Fan Vented to Exterior ☐ Yes ☐ No

Electrical:

☐ Fan Switch ☐ Satisfactory

☐ Receptacle ☐ Satisfactory

☐ Switch ☐ Satisfactory

☐ G.F.C.I. ☐ Satisfactory

☐ Light ☐ Satisfactory

(continued)

| **FIGURE 4.4** | *A home inspection checklist report, continued.* |

Plumbing:

WATER FLOW:

- [ ] Sink   [ ] Satisfactory
- [ ] Toilet   [ ] Satisfactory
- [ ] Tub or Shower   [ ] Satisfactory

WATER DRAINAGE:

- [ ] Sink   [ ] Satisfactory
- [ ] Toilet   [ ] Satisfactory
- [ ] Tub or Shower   [ ] Satisfactory

Water Temperature: Degrees

Heating & Cooling Distribution:

- [ ] Satisfactory

BATHROOM NO. 2

Location: _____

Floor Covering:

- [ ] Satisfactory

Walls and ceiling:

- [ ] Satisfactory

Tub or Shower Stall:

- [ ] Free-Standing Tub   [ ] Built-In Tub
- [ ] Fiberglass Enclosure   [ ] Whirlpool
- [ ] Built-In Shower

Base type:

- [ ] Satisfactory   [ ] See Narrative Report

Tub or Shower Door: Safety Glass

- [ ] Sliding   [ ] Yes
- [ ] Swing   [ ] Unknown

- [ ] Satisfactory   [ ] NP

Ventilation:

- [ ] Window   [ ] Satisfactory
- [ ] Fan   [ ] Satisfactory
- [ ] Fan with light   [ ] Satisfactory
- [ ] Fan vented to exterior   [ ] Yes [ ] No

Electrical:

- [ ] Fan Switch   [ ] Satisfactory
- [ ] Receptacle   [ ] Satisfactory
- [ ] Switch   [ ] Satisfactory
- [ ] G.F.C.I.   [ ] Satisfactory
- [ ] Light   [ ] Satisfactory

(continued)

Plumbing:

WATER FLOW:

- [ ] Sink   [ ] Satisfactory
- [ ] Toilet   [ ] Satisfactory
- [ ] Tub or Shower   [ ] Satisfactory

WATER DRAINAGE:

- [ ] Sink   [ ] Satisfactory
- [ ] Toilet   [ ] Satisfactory
- [ ] Tub or Shower   [ ] Satisfactory

Water Temperature: Degrees

Heating & Cooling Distribution:

- [ ] Satisfactory

KITCHEN & APPLIANCES

| **Floor Covering:** | **Ceiling:** |
| [ ] Satisfactory | [ ] Satisfactory |

| **Walls:** | **Counter Top:** |
| [ ] Satisfactory | [ ] Satisfactory |

Cabinets:

- [ ] Satisfactory

Electrical:

- [ ] Ceiling Light(s)   [ ] Satisfactory
- [ ] Recess Light(s)   [ ] Satisfactory
- [ ] Switch(s)   [ ] Satisfactory
- [ ] 3-Way Switch   [ ] Satisfactory
- [ ] Receptacles   [ ] Satisfactory
- [ ] G.F.C.I. Over Counter [ ] Satisfactory

- [ ] Fan/Light
- [ ] Satisfactory   [ ] Not Applicable

Plumbing:

SINK:

- [ ] Double Bowl   [ ] Single Bowl
- [ ] Satisfactory

- [ ] Spray Hose
- [ ] Satisfactory   [ ] Not Applicable

- [ ] Water Flow
- [ ] Satisfactory   [ ] No signs of leaks

- [ ] Water Drainage
- [ ] Satisfactory   [ ] No signs of leaks

Ventilation:

- [ ] Exhaust Fan   [ ] Ductless
- [ ] Satisfactory   [ ] Not Applicable

- [ ] Vented to Exterior
- [ ] Satisfactory   [ ] Not Applicable

A home inspection checklist report, continued.   **FIGURE 4.4**

Disposal:
- ☐ Drain Connection   ☐ Satisfactory
- ☐ Electrical Connection
- ☐ Satisfactory   ☐ Not Applicable

Dishwasher:
- ☐ Drain Hose Connection   ☐ Satisfactory
- ☐ Water Connection   ☐ Satisfactory
- ☐ Electrical Connection   ☐ Satisfactory

Range:
- ☐ Gas Connection   ☐ Not App.
- ☐ Electrical Connection   ☐ Satisfactory
- ☐ Burners or Elements   ☐ Satisfactory

Clothes Washer:
- ☐ Drain Hose Connection   ☐ Satisfactory
- ☐ Water Connection   ☐ Satisfactory
- ☐ Electrical Receptacle   ☐ Satisfactory

Clothes Dryer:
- ☐ Gas Connection   ☐ Not App.
- ☐ Electrical Connection   ☐ Satisfactory
- ☐ Vented to the Exterior   ☐ See N. R.

BASEMENT

Stairs:
- ☐ Treads   ☐ Satisfactory
- ☐ Wall Railing   ☐ Satisfactory

Foundation:
- ☐ Block   ☐ Flagstone
- ☐ Poured Concrete
- ☐ Satisfactory   ☐ See Narrative Report
- ☐ Extensive Storage or Finished Area—
- ☐ Visibility Limited

Floor Framing:
- ☐ Open   ☐ Visibility Limited
- ☐ Closed   ☐ See Narrative Report
- Floor Joists: ☐ Satisfactory
- Sub-Flooring: ☐ Satisfactory
- ☐ Plywood   ☐ Plank

Main Bearing Beam:
- ☐ Wood   ☐ Steel   ☐ Satisfactory

Columns:
- ☐ Wood   ☐ Steel   ☐ Satisfactory

Basement Floor:
- ☐ Concrete   ☐ Satisfactory

Basement Floor Covering:
- ☐ Satisfactory   ☐ Not Applicable

Floor Drain:
- ☐ Satisfactory   ☐ Not Applicable

Sump Pit:
- ☐ Sump Pan   ☐ Open Pit
- ☐ Satisfactory   ☐ Not Applicable
- ☐ Sump Pump
- ☐ Satisfactory   ☐ Not Applicable

Dampness:
- ☐ None Noted   ☐ Some Signs
- ☐ Extensive

Water Service:
- ☐ Copper   ☐ Lead   ☐ Satisfactory
- ☐ Galvanized   ☐ Plastic
- Main Shut Off Valve   ☐ Satisfactory
- Main Water Service Pipe Size
- ☐ _____   ☐ Satisfactory

Water Pipes:
- ☐ Copper   ☐ Lead   ☐ Satisfactory
- ☐ Galvanized   ☐ Plastic
- ☐ Pipe Supports   ☐ Satisfactory

Sewage Pipes:
- ☐ Copper   ☐ Lead   ☐ Satisfactory
- ☐ Galvanized   ☐ Plastic
- ☐ Cast Iron
- ☐ Pipe Supports   ☐ Satisfactory

Hot Water Heater: Age: +/- Years Old
- ☐ Gas   ☐ Electric
- ☐ Pressure Relief Valve and   ☐ Satisfactory
  Extension
- ☐ Gas Pipe   ☐ Satisfactory
- ☐ Smoke Pipe & Draft Hood   ☐ Satisfactory
- ☐ Integral w/ Boiler   ☐ Drain Annually

Capacity Gal. _____

Serial No. _____

Heating System:
- ☐ Forced Hot Air   ☐ Forced Hot Water
  Furnace   Boiler
- ☐ Heat Pump   ☐ Gravity Hot Water
  Boiler
- ☐ Satisfactory   ☐ See Narrative Report

Serial No. _____

(continued)

FIGURE 4.4	A home inspection checklist report, continued.

Heat Exchanger:
- ☐ Satisfactory ☐ See Narrative Report

Thermostat:
- ☐ Satisfactory ☐ See Narrative Report

Safety Switch:
- ☐ Satisfactory ☐ Not Applicable

Fuel:
- ☐ Gas ☐ Oil ☐ Electric

Gas Pipe:
- ☐ Satisfactory ☐ Not Applicable

Flue Pipe:
- ☐ Direct Vent (PVC Pipe) ☐ Satisfactory
- ☐ Smoke Pipe & Draft Hood ☐ Corrosion
- ☐ Barometric Draft Damper ☐ Some Signs
- ☐ Auto-Damper ☐ NP

Filter:
- ☐ Electronic ☐ Disposable
- ☐ Satisfactory ☐ See Narrative Report

Humidifier:
- ☐ See Narrative Report

Heating System:
- ☐ Temperature Gauge ☐ Satisfactory
- ☐ Water Pressure Gauge ☐ Satisfactory
- ☐ Pressure Relief Valve ☐ Satisfactory
  and Extension
- ☐ Circulator Pump ☐ Satisfactory

Oil Tank:
- ☐ Interior ☐ Exterior
- ☐ Satisfactory ☐ Needs Service

Cooling System: Energy Source:
- ☐ Split System ☐ Electric
- ☐ Heat Pump ☐ Gas

- ☐ Exterior Compressor ☐ Satisfactory
- ☐ Evaporator Coil ☐ Satisfactory

Compressor Serial No. _____

ELECTRICAL

Service Line Cable:
- ☐ Overhead ☐ Underground

Service Entry Cable:
- ☐ Aluminum ☐ Unknown
- ☐ Satisfactory ☐ Not Visible

Service Entry Cable:

Size: _____ Type: _____

Voltage: _____

Main Panel Box:
- ☐ Satisfactory   Service Rating: ___ Amps
- CIRCUITS:
- ☐ Fuses ☐ Circuit Breakers

Main Panel Box:
Ground Fault Circuit Interrupter:
- ☐ Living Room ☐ Rear Porch ☐ Garage
- ☐ Satisfactory ☐ Not Applicable

CONDUCTORS: (WIRING)
- ☐ Copper ☐ Aluminum ☐ Other

Service Ground:
- ☐ Copper ☐ Aluminum

How Grounded:
- ☐ Ground Rod ☐ Water Pipe Connection
- ☐ Satisfactory

CRAWL SPACE

Entry Way:
- ☐ Readily Accessible
- ☐ Not Readily Accessible
- ☐ Wall Opening ☐ Access Panel
- ☐ 3' or Higher ☐ Less than 3' High

Method of Observation:
- ☐ Wall Opening ☐ Access Panel

Clearance Below Floor Joists or Girders:
- ☐ Greater than 18" ☐ Less than 18"

Moisture:
- ☐ None Noted ☐ Some Signs ☐ Extensive

Ground Covering:
- ☐ Plastic Shtg. ☐ Felt Paper ☐ Concrete
- ☐ Satisfactory ☐ NP ☐ See N. R.

Insulation: ☐ Wall ☐ Floor
☐ Satisfactory ☐ NP

Ventilation: ☐ Satisfactory ☐ NP

Duct Work: ☐ Insulated ☐ Not Ins.
☐ Satisfactory ☐ NP

Pipes: ☐ Insulated ☐ Not Ins.
☐ Satisfactory ☐ NP

(continued)

Source: Anthony D'Agostino, Atlantic Inspection Service, Latham, New York.

Although the checklist offers many advantages, it does not necessarily cover everything that must be said about the property.

Rating System Report

A **rating system report** *uses a numerical evaluation on a scale, for example 1–5, to define the condition of each property component.* Each number may be assigned an evaluation: 1-excellent, 2-good, 3-fair, 4-poor, and 5-unacceptable. This system, like the checklist report, includes space for comments to describe the component's condition or whether it needs repair or presents a safety hazard.

Narrative Report

A **narrative report,** *written in paragraph form, reflects the inspector's observation and opinion of the condition of a subject property.* The report may include photographs, a sketch of the property, and lab reports, if applicable. Many inspectors use the checklist format at the time of the inspection and generate a full narrative report using the checklist (see Figure 4.5 for an example of a narrative report).

Narrative Report with Checklist or Rating System

For a more complete report and additional verification of the inspection findings, many home inspectors affix the checklist or rating system report from the actual home inspection to a narrative report. This **narrative report with checklist or rating system** is useful should any litigation arise because it documents the scope of the inspection and offers a more detailed picture of what was accomplished.

Many houses that you inspect will not be perfect. Because your clients are with you, they might feel somewhat disappointed as you point out problems with various components. Try not to focus only on the problems. Look for and point out property components that are unique, in good shape, or constructed well. Include comments in your report about components that are assets to the structure in addition to the items that are simply satisfactory or deficient.

Putting It to Work

Home Inspection Report Addendum

A typical home inspection report may contain some or all of the following: photographs, a sketch of the property, lab results, and a disclaimer. While on-site, use graph paper to sketch a rough draft of the property's layout. A neater version is prepared later. This sketch clearly indicates the locations of problems such as foundation cracks or drainage issues.

Laboratory test results. A home inspector may be requested to gather samples for environmental testing of items such as lead-based paint, radon, or water quality. If the results are forwarded back to the home inspector before the report is delivered, the results are affixed to the report. When turning in the samples to the lab, instruct the lab to send the results to yourself and the client. If requested, the testing facility will call the home inspector with the results. (Environmental issues are discussed in Chapter 10.)

FIGURE 4.5	*A narrative home inspection report.*

(Note: This narrative was prepared to further explain a checklist report.)

GROUNDS

Driveway
The asphalt driveway pitches toward the garage. Rain water may seep into the garage due to the grade pitching toward the garage.

Steps to Building
Railings should be installed on all steps with three or more risers. This is for safety when ascending and descending the stairs.

EXTERIOR

Porch
Because there was an enclosure around the porch we were unable to inspect the underside of this porch. We suggest that all wood be scraped and painted. Painting of exterior wood is the only protection wood has against the elements and it should be maintained periodically.

Fascia
On the east side of the building there is a portion of aluminum fascia that has fallen off the building. It should be refastened as soon as possible.

Windows and Trim
All wood should be scraped and painted. See comments on porch.

Gutters and Downspouts
The gutters and downspouts should have all the debris removed from them in order for the water to flow properly and not create ice dams in the winter. There are no downspouts on the gutters on the east side of the building. Splashblocks or drain boots should be installed on all downspouts. This will prevent soil erosion and keep water from penetrating the foundation wall.

Hose Bibs
The hose bibs and water lines were frozen.

GARAGE
The shed roof structure is not constructed according to industry standards and appears to be unsafe. We suggest that you contact a professional engineer or the local code enforcement office to evaluate the roof system.

Overhead Doors
There was no power to the automatic door opener and therefore it could not be tested. The overhead doors are starting to deteriorate.

ROOFING

Roof Covering
The roof covering is starting to curl and buckle due to the shingles having reached their age limit. The shingles and accessories will have to be replaced in the near future.
   The flat roof on the garage was covered with ice and we were unable to determine its condition.

Chimney
The metal chimney flue appears to be in satisfactory condition at this time. Before the wood stove is used the flue should be cleaned. This

(continued)

should be done at least once every year to prevent creosote buildup. Creosote build up is the number one cause of chimney fires.

Access   The only access to the attic was an open area above the parlor.

Supporting Structure   The roof rafters over the kitchen area are bearing on a low stud wall in the attic area, and there is no bearing beam in the kitchen ceiling to carry this low stud wall or roof rafters. This is not according to industry standards, and we suggest that you contact a professional engineer or the local code enforcement office to further evaluate the roof system.

Moisture   Due to the building not being heated there is a large amount of frost build up on the roof structure. This moisture may effect the integrity of the roof system and interior finishes.

INTERIOR

Electrical   A representative number of installed lighting fixtures, wall switches and receptacles located throughout the building and garage were inspected and tested and found to be in satisfactory condition unless noted otherwise.

There are some two-prong receptacles in the building that are not grounded. If a tool or appliance is plugged into that receptacle and develops a hot to ground fault, that person can get shocked and possibly electrocuted. This is caused by the old service in the building. A GFCI can be installed and will protect these receptacles. We suggest that a licensed electrician be contacted to further evaluate the proper repair that can be made for receptacles that are not grounded.

Smoke Detector   There are no smoke detectors in the building. Smoke detectors warn you in time to escape from a fire.

Windows   A representative number of windows located throughout the building were operated and found to be functional.

Doors   A representative number of interior doors located throughout the building were operated and found to be functional.

BASEMENT

Stairs   The basement stairs are unsafe and need to be replaced.

Plumbing System   All plumbing lines are frozen due to no heat in the building.

Heating System   The boiler was not operating due to the boiler and heating lines being frozen.

There are indications of a white fungus in the basement that might be a health hazard and should be further evaluated by an environmental laboratory.

(continued)

FIGURE 4.5	A narrative home inspection report, continued.

Home inspectors may include an estimate for repairs in the home inspection report.

A T L A N T I C

INSPECTION SERVICE   COMMERCIAL & RESIDENTIAL

12 BELAIRE DRIVE   LATHAM, N.Y. 12110

(518) 555-1963

February 14, 2007

Eugene Lagrand
162 Front Street
Chicago, Illinois 60610

Re: 192 Lakeview Drive
     Chicago, Illinois 60610

Dear Mr. Lagrand:

The following is our estimate for the repair of the following deficiencies as stated in our building analysis report. This estimate should not be construed as actual cost but only as a guide for these repairs. We suggest that you contact a contractor who specializes in this type of work for actual cost.

Item	Estimate
Garage Roof System	$2200.00
Bearing Beam at Kitchen	$1500.00

If you have any questions, do not hesitate to call at your earliest convenience.

Very truly yours,

Anthony D'Agostino

Anthony D'Agostino

Source: Anthony D'Agostino, Atlantic Inspection Service, Latham, New York.

You Should Know

Home inspectors, unless licensed professional engineers, are not design or structural experts and should not give an opinion about the property's design or structural deficiencies.

Disclaimer. An extremely important addendum to any type of inspection report form is the disclaimer. This section of the report is similar in language and purpose to the pre-inspection agreement. The **disclaimer** *documents the scope of the inspection (what is included and what is not) and specifically indicates which items*

are omitted from the report, including opinions about the structure and design, build-
ing code compliance, and environmental problems (see Figure 4.6).

> A properly written disclaimer is valuable protection for the home inspector. A disclaimer can require that a client pay the cost of any unsuccessful litigation. A disclaimer should be prepared by an attorney familiar with the work of the home inspector.
>
> **You Should Know**

Disclaimer. **FIGURE 4.6**

A T L A N T I C | 12 BELAIRE DRIVE   LATHAM, N.Y. 12110
INSPECTION SERVICE   COMMERCIAL & RESIDENTIAL | (518) 783-1963

SCOPE OF INSPECTION:

This is a limited visual inspection of apparent conditions in readily and easily accessible areas that existed at the time of inspection. Only areas specifically mentioned in this report have been inspected and those areas not mentioned are not part of this inspection. No warranties or guaranties are given or implied for any latent concealed defects. There is no destructive probing or dismantling of any components. Additionally, any repairs after the inspection may reveal defects that are not accessible at the time of inspection. Any and all visual problems observed should be verified with the appropriate contractor, electrician, plumber, or skilled professional for code compliance and cost estimates. ATLANTIC INSPECTION SERVICE is not liable for any defects or deficiencies which could not be reasonably discovered during a limited visual inspection.

ENVIRONMENTAL CONDITIONS:

Unless otherwise indicated, the inspection and report do not address and are not intended to address the possible presence of or danger from any potentially harmful substances and environmental hazards including but not limited to radon gas, lead paint, asbestos, urea formaldehyde, toxic or flammable chemicals, and water and airborne hazards.

CODES:

No check is made for building/housing code conformance. Such codes are normally guides applicable during construction to be executed by duly authorized personnel to interpret and site as per their judgment. There is often wide variance in jurisdictions, changes over time, and judgmental differences. ATLANTIC INSPECTION SERVICE is not an authorized local code official unless otherwise specified.

Source: Anthony D'Agostino, Atlantic Inspection Service, Latham, New York.

TABLE 4.1	Advantages and disadvantages of various home inspection reports.	
TYPE OF REPORT	**ADVANTAGES**	**DISADVANTAGES**
Checklist with comments	▪ can be completed in one step ▪ keeps inspector organized ▪ easy for clients to understand	▪ not enough explanation ▪ does not fully describe property positives
Rating system with comments	▪ can be completed in one step ▪ keeps inspector organized ▪ easy for clients to understand	▪ is subjective and clients may not agree with designated ratings ▪ does not fully describe the problems ▪ does not fully describe property positives
Narrative	▪ more fully describes the inspector's findings ▪ offers a better explanation of problem areas	▪ more work than other forms ▪ requires that inspectors state their findings accurately
Narrative with checklist or rating system	▪ combines the short and long form report giving the most possible information	▪ more work than other types of reports ▪ requires that inspectors state their findings accurately

The Final Inspection Report

Although with the use of the checklist and a Polaroid camera, the home inspection report can be completed by the end of the inspection, it should not be delivered at this point. The inspector should discuss the findings with the client on completion of the inspection, but the written documents must be taken to the office to be finalized and copied. Table 4.1 sets forth the advantages and disadvantages of each type of inspection report.

Putting It to Work

The report should not be overly technical. Keep the language simple so that the client can understand what is in the report.

The report is the inspector's final work product and is not delivered until the inspector has been paid in full for his services. The client should make any final payment before or soon after the inspection is completed.

If time is a factor, the report can be e-mailed or faxed to the client and a hard copy mailed subsequently. Retain a copy of the report along with copies of all items attached to the report. This includes any narrative, checklist, or rating system report used, photos, a sketch of the property, and copies of any lab reports.

Generally, the home inspection report is a confidential document for the client. If, for example, the client is the buyer, the report is given only to the buyer. It is then up to the client to disseminate the report to others. If the client requests, the home inspector may deliver copies of the report to others.

Liabilities of Report Writing

Purchasing real estate is one of the biggest financial decisions many people make. As you complete the inspection report, keep in mind the importance of what you are doing and its effect on your client and third parties who look to the report to assist with the purchase decision. An accurate, honest, and thorough inspection of the property will help protect you should problems arise later. You must give your clients a full and concise picture of the property they are buying. The attached information, such as photos, sketches, lab reports, and any notes you have made (such as conversations with the property owner), serve to support your conclusions. Save copies of the report together with any attached material because they are useful should a dispute about your findings arise at a later date.

> The **statute of limitations** varies from state to state and by the type of claim asserted. *It sets the time frame for commencing a lawsuit and begins to run on the date the claim arose or the date on which the client knew or reasonably should have known of the claim.* Home inspectors must maintain files at least the number of years set forth in the statutes in case a lawsuit is instituted. States that license, certify, or register home inspectors may also have regulations that address the time frame for retaining files.
>
> *You Should Know*

The Home Inspection Report as a Marketing Tool

The content of the home inspection report is the most important part of it, but its presentation also sends a message that you are professional, organized, and prepared. Many home inspectors have a folder professionally printed that contains a business card and information about the company's services, the inspector's experience, and the inspection process. This information may be on separate brochures or letters or printed on the folder itself. This folder is given to clients seeking a home inspector or is used to send the final report. Marketing yourself along with report writing should always be a consideration. The folder is easily shared by your clients with other prospects.

IMPORTANT POINTS

1. The best way to gain hands-on experience is to practice performing several home inspections before you receive compensation.
2. It is a good idea to begin now to assemble tools and equipment. Home inspectors must purchase basic tools for on-site inspections as well as office equipment.
3. Home inspectors may be contacted by the buyer–client or receive a referral from a lender, a real estate agent, or another inspection company. Regardless

of who makes the initial contact, certain basic information is recorded on a client information form.

4. The pre-inspection agreement is a contract that protects both the home inspector and the client. It explains, in general terms, the scope of the inspection, the cost, and the procedures to address any dispute that may arise. A home inspection should not be performed until both parties sign the agreement.

5. Complete a home inspection appointment form once an appointment date is set and mail, e-mail, or fax a copy to the client.

6. Buyer–clients generally accompany the inspector through the inspection process. This is an opportunity for buyers to learn more about the property and observe the inspector. Sellers are a source of information and future business.

7. Home inspectors must have a method of proceeding through the structure in an orderly and logical manner—from the exterior to the interior.

8. An inspection cannot be completed in an hour no matter what the property type. Three hours is generally a minimum time period and additional time may be required depending on the property type, extra services, and the number of deficiencies uncovered.

9. The home inspection report generally takes one of four forms: the checklist report with comments, often generated from computer software; the rating system report with comments; the purely narrative or written report; and the narrative report with either a checklist or rating system.

10. A checklist report form is a systemized itemization of the various components of a property that is organized into sections that allow the inspector to check off inspected property components and comment on any specific problems.

11. The home inspection checklist serves many purposes and should be used during the inspection whether or not it is the final report form.

12. A rating system report uses a numerical evaluation on a scale, for example 1–5, to define the condition of the property component. This system includes space for comments to describe the component's condition.

13. A narrative report, written in paragraph form, reflects the inspector's observation and opinion of the condition of a subject property. For a more complete report, the narrative is combined with a checklist or rating system report.

14. Home inspectors, unless licensed professional engineers, are not design or structural experts and should not give an opinion about the property's design or structural deficiencies.

15. Typical report attachments include photographs, a sketch of the property, lab results, and a disclaimer.

16. An extremely important addendum to any type of inspection report is the disclaimer. The disclaimer documents the scope of the inspection and specifically indicates which items are omitted from the report, including opinions about the structure and design, building code compliance, and environmental problems.

17. Although with the use of the checklist and a Polaroid camera, the home inspection report can be completed by the end of the inspection, it should

not be delivered at this point. The inspector should discuss the findings with the client, but the written documents must be taken to the office to be finalized and copied.

18. Keep a copy of the report along with copies of all items attached to the report. The time period for maintaining records is determined by any applicable state licensure, certification, or registration regulations and statute of limitation guidelines.

19. Many home inspectors have a folder professionally printed that contains pertinent information about the inspection and the home inspector. The completed report can be inserted in the folder.

CHAPTER REVIEW

Field Study Assignment 1

List the people you know who work as professionals in the residential home industry. Ask if you can observe them as they work.

Field Study Assignment 2

Find a new construction site and visit periodically to observe the various stages of construction.

Field Study Assignment 3

Purchase tools and equipment. Visit home centers, such as Home Depot, as well as smaller hardware stores. Visit Web sites that carry tools and equipment. Investigate tool catalogs. Your local hardware store or home center can provide you with a list of catalog companies.

Field Study Assignment 4

Decide where to obtain the home inspection forms discussed in this chapter. Contact home inspection organizations and have them send their catalogs. These catalogs describe the forms in detail. Have any agreements you plan to use reviewed by an attorney. Contracts must comply with any applicable laws.

1. Which of the following is TRUE?
   A. You should obtain errors and omissions insurance before performing a home inspection, whether compensated or not.
   B. Most inspection companies furnish the inspector with tools and equipment.
   C. Home inspectors learn everything they need to know in the classroom.
   D. A ladder is an optional piece of equipment for the home inspector.

2. Which of the following is NOT generally needed to perform a home inspection?
   A. screwdriver
   B. awl
   C. camera
   D. saw

3. Photographs of the subject property:
   A. are never necessary
   B. should only be taken to point out a code violation
   C. assist with explaining certain property defects
   D. should only be taken if specifically requested by the client

4. Which of the following is NOT essential to the small home inspection office?
   A. copier or scanner
   B. computer
   C. fax
   D. secretary

5. The inspection completion date is important because:
   A. it is when the home inspector will be paid
   B. the real estate closing date may depend on it
   C. home inspections must be performed within one week of the signing of a contract of sale
   D. parties to the purchase must be given a date for the home inspection prior to signing the contract of sale

6. Initial information regarding the subject property should NOT include which of the following?
   A. age of the property
   B. racial makeup of the neighborhood
   C. purpose of the inspection
   D. name of the property owners

7. Which of the following must be signed by the client and home inspector prior to performing an inspection?
   A. offer to purchase
   B. property condition disclosure form
   C. pre-inspection agreement
   D. client information form

8. A pre-inspection agreement benefits which of the following?
   A. property owner
   B. client only
   C. home inspector only
   D. both the client and the home inspector

9. Who should prepare the pre-inspection agreement form?
   A. lender
   B. client
   C. attorney
   D. home inspection organization

10. When dealing with the property owner, home inspectors should do which of the following?
    A. Ask that the property owner not be present during the inspection.
    B. Ask the property owner questions about the history and condition of the property.
    C. Use the seller disclosure form as the only basis for the inspection.
    D. Give the property owner a copy of the inspection report.

11. Generally, most home inspections begin with an examination of the:
    A. site
    B. attic
    C. basement
    D. garage

12. Which of the following is a typical time period for the completion of a home inspection?
    A. one-half hour
    B. one hour
    C. two hours
    D. three or more hours

13. Which of the following is NOT a form of home inspection report?
    A. checklist
    B. disclaimer
    C. narrative
    D. rating system

14. A lender that requires a written report receives which of the following report forms?
    A. checklist
    B. rating system
    C. narrative
    D. none of the above

15. Which of the following statements about the checklist report is FALSE?
    A. It guides the inspector through the inspection process.
    B. It provides the basis for a narrative report.
    C. It demonstrates the scope of the inspection to the client.
    D. It provides a detailed written analysis of each property component.

16. Which of the following is NOT included in the inspection report?
    A. sketch of the property layout
    B. photographs
    C. list of all code violations
    D. disclaimer

17. Which of the following is TRUE regarding any environmental testing done on the property?
    A. Home inspectors may not do environmental testing.
    B. Home inspectors may gather samples for laboratory analysis.
    C. Environmental inspections are included in all home inspections.
    D. Home inspectors may not charge extra for any environmental analysis.

18. The Disagreeables refused to pay for their home inspection because their inspector did not comment on certain design defects later discovered about the property. Which of the following is TRUE?
    A. Only licensed professional engineers can comment on design defects.
    B. This was an omission on the part of the home inspector and the clients are right.
    C. The home inspector need only comment on the property's design if specifically indicated in the pre-inspection agreement.
    D. Because comments on design defects are an extra service requiring an extra fee, the Disagreeables must pay for the inspection.

19. The disclaimer attached to the home inspection report protects which of the following?
    A. home inspector
    B. client
    C. property owner
    D. lender

20. Which of the following home inspection report forms should have disclaimers attached?
    A. narrative
    B. checklist
    C. rating system
    D. all of the above

21. The home inspection report should be delivered to the client:
    A. immediately on completion of the inspection
    B. after the report has been finalized by the home inspector
    C. after the property owner has reviewed it
    D. on the date of the closing

22. At the inspection site, the home inspector may do which of the following?
    A. Discuss the inspection findings with the client.
    B. Comment on the property's structural defects and how they might be corrected.
    C. Suggest that the client not buy the property under any circumstances.
    D. Refuse to allow the property owner to accompany the inspector through the inspection.

23. One of the most important tasks that home inspectors must do after the inspection is:
    A. make a copy of the inspection report for their files
    B. call the property owners to let them know about problems with their property
    C. call the town building department with a list of code violations found in the subject property
    D. file a copy of the report with the county clerk's office

24. The Impossibles, the client, sue Jeremy, the home inspector, because a minor code violation was found subsequent to the inspection and had not been reported by Jeremy. Which of the following is TRUE?
    A. Home inspectors are not required to uncover code violations.
    B. Home inspectors are required to uncover code violations.
    C. The Impossibles have no claim against Jeremy because they signed a pre-inspection agreement.
    D. As long as home inspectors attach a disclaimer to the inspection report, they cannot be sued.

25. Mattie recently opened a home inspection business and needs a form for her home inspection reports. She might begin by:
    A. contacting the town building department
    B. visiting a Web site or calling various home inspection organizations for catalogs
    C. asking an attorney to prepare a home inspection report form for her
    D. consulting a real estate agency

ANSWER KEY

1. A	8. D	15. D	22. A
2. D	9. C	16. C	23. A
3. C	10. B	17. B	24. A
4. D	11. A	18. A	25. B
5. B	12. D	19. A	
6. B	13. B	20. D	
7. C	14. C	21. B	

CHAPTER 5

INSPECTING THE SITE

One of the most important considerations when inspecting residential property is the site inspection. This chapter discusses those items that an inspector must examine on the site and the problems that might be encountered.

In an earlier chapter's Field Study Assignment, you selected a practice property (or properties) to inspect. This property will be used to complete the Field Study exercises in this and subsequent chapters.

LEARNING OBJECTIVES

1. List the items included, according to industry standards, in a typical site inspection.
2. Define drainage and explain how proper site grading eliminates drainage problems.
3. Describe what a water table is and its significance.
4. Describe the problems that can occur with landscaping, walkways, driveways, other paved and masonry areas, steps and stoops, patios, porches, attached decks, and balconies.

KEY TERMS

Appurtenance

Baluster

Drainage

Grading

Groundwater

Headroom

Hydrostatic pressure

Percolation rate

Retaining wall

Riser

Slope

Slope gradient

Soil permeability

Stringer

Surface runoff

Topography

Tread

Water erosion

Water table

Weepholes

INDUSTRY STANDARDS

This chapter and the ones that follow discuss the components of the property that must be inspected. Because there currently are no federal uniform guidelines governing home inspections, home inspection organizations have developed standards of practice for the industry. Appendices A and B contain the standards of practice used by two home inspection organizations. The standards set forth the home inspector's tasks by listing those property components that should be inspected and those that should not. As individual states continue to license, certify, and register home inspectors, the states may develop their own standards of practice. For now, many home inspectors find it useful to join a home inspection organization and follow the guidelines provided by that organization's standards of practice.

This textbook provides an overview of the generally accepted components that should be observed, described, or inspected. Sections of the American Society of Home Inspectors® (ASHI) standards are located at the beginning of each chapter to give you an idea of what is expected in each part of a typical residential inspection. For example, Figure 5.1 sets forth the ASHI Standards of Practice for the exterior inspection and includes the site items discussed in this chapter. Some of the components listed in Figure 5.1 are discussed in Chapter 6. The full text of the standards appears in Appendix A.

Putting It to Work

As you inspect a property, your client may ask you about the condition of a swimming pool. Although a pool inspection is not a required part of a home inspection, perhaps you feel qualified to give an opinion as to its condition. You may do this and charge an extra fee for this service. Another option, as with any item that is not part of the standard inspection, is to refer your client to a professional.

You Should Know

If you practice home inspection in a state that requires licensure, certification, or registration, find out if regulations exist as to the standards of practice or standards of care. These regulations are promulgated by the regulatory agency that administers the licensure, registration, or certification.

SITE TOPOGRAPHY

When a property is developed, an initial consideration is the topography of the land—its physical features and contours. **Topography** *includes types of soil; the location of water such as wetlands, springs, or floodplains; forest areas; and the location of rocks, trees, and other vegetation.* These features have an impact on how and where dwellings, utilities, and pipelines are located. If the property is a subdivision, these features determine how the completed subdivision will look. A property's value is primarily determined by its authorized use, its location, and the physical nature of the land.

A major characteristic of land is its *immobility.* The location of the subject property is unchangeable. The home inspection is concerned with the physical nature of the property and any problems that become evident during the examination.

FIGURE 5.1

4. EXTERIOR

4.1 The inspector shall:

A. inspect:

1. siding, flashing and trim.

2. all exterior doors.

3. attached or adjacent decks, balconies, stoops, steps, porches, and their associated railings.

4. eaves, soffits, and fascias where accessible from the ground level.

5. vegetation, grading, surface drainage, and retaining walls that are likely to adversely affect the building.

6. adjacent or entryway walkways, patios, and driveways.

B. describe:

1. siding.

4.2 The inspector is NOT required to inspect:

A. screening, shutters, awnings, and similar seasonal accessories.

B. fences.

C. geological, geotechnical and/or soil conditions.

D. recreational facilities.

E. outbuildings other than garages or carports.

F. seawalls, break-walls, and docks.

G. erosion control and earth stabilization measures.

Applicable ASHI Standards of Practice.

Permission to reprint and reference granted by the American Society of Home Inspectors, Inc. (ASHI) www.ASHI.org

An **appurtenance** *is a right, privilege, or improvement belonging to, and passing with, the land.* Property owners may sell or lease an appurtenance. Examples of appurtenances include mineral, air, and water rights; easements; and the right to a profit from the land by a nonowner. It is possible for an individual to have the right, for instance, to take gravel from land owned by another. Appurtenances, if known to the home inspector, should be noted on the home inspection report.

You Should Know

DRAINAGE AND GRADING

Surface drainage is one of the first considerations when preparing a site for construction. **Drainage** *is the land's ability to draw off surface water.* This is accomplished either naturally or artificially through pipes and other conduits such as drainage tiles (discussed later.) **Grading**, *the arrangement and preparation of the soil for construction,* can place drainage areas where appropriate for water runoff. Proper grading ensures that surface water is directed away from

FIGURE 5.2   *Water penetration of foundation wall.*

The photograph shows evidence of water penetration through a block foundation wall. In this case, the site was not graded and sloped away from the foundation wall. In addition, there were no footing drain tiles.

Source: Anthony D'Agostino, Atlantic Inspection Service, Latham, New York.

the foundation. Water that is not directed away from the foundation will eventually penetrate the foundation wall and cause moisture problems including mold and mildew, heaving, cracking, and perhaps a total collapse of the foundation wall. Figure 5.2 illustrates a foundation damaged due to water penetration. A site composed of slightly rolling hills and valleys provides more natural drainage than does a flat or very steep site.

Proper drainage around the structure prevents wet basements, frost heaving problems, and the buildup of hydrostatic pressure on basement floors, banks, and retaining walls. **Hydrostatic pressure** *is the push of water against a surface.* Appropriate drainage also helps to prevent flood and water erosion and to improve the general attractiveness of the site. **Water erosion** *is the removal of soil material by flowing water. A part of the process is the detachment of soil material by the impact of raindrops. The soil material is suspended in runoff water and carried away.* Sites that are located at the base of an incline are prone to water erosion (see Figure 5.3). In addition, water erosion is often visible in areas where the runoff from gutters tends to wash away the soil.

Putting It to Work

The examination of the site can be a formidable task especially if a property is located on a large lot. Breaking the examination into the categories described later establishes an orderly inspection procedure.

Putting It to Work

Use your pick or awl to check for areas of wood rot or decay. Take care when probing various items so as to not deface or damage the areas.

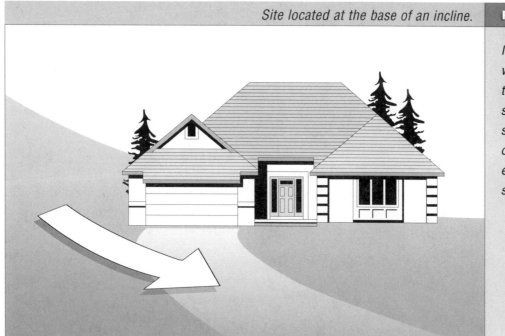

Site located at the base of an incline.

FIGURE 5.3

In this illustration, water running down the incline washes the soil particles down the slope. This eventually causes full or partial erosion of the entire slope.

The inspector's first task is to walk the perimeter of the building site and structure to verify that the site is graded away from the foundation.

Putting It to Work

Another type of erosion in various parts of the country is *wind erosion.* Wind erosion occurs in regions of low rainfall and can be widespread especially in periods of drought. Unlike water erosion, wind erosion generally is not related to slope gradient. Removing or reducing site vegetation increases the potential for wind erosion.

You Should Know

Despite a properly functioning drainage system, poor site planning often results in a less than adequate system. Drainage problems are one of the main sources of trouble that a home inspector may encounter. A surface drainage system should be designed to handle the maximum rate of surface runoff from rain or snowmelt. **Surface runoff** *refers to the loss of water from an area by its flow over the land's surface.* While inspecting drainage problems on a site, the slope, vegetation, and soil type must be considered.

Water draining from a roof that is not properly directed away from the foundation wall by downspouts is as problematic as rainwater and snowmelt directly on the ground. Roof water pools and saturates the ground, with a possibility of penetrating the foundation wall. Check gutters for leaks caused by holes or cracks and also to make sure that they are free of leaves, dirt, water, and other material.

You Should Know

Slope

A **slope** *is land surface that is graded on an angle.* **Slope gradient** *is the inclination of the soil surface from the horizontal.* Slopes are divided into distinct classes from level to very steep. A steep slope, for example, has a gradient of 20–40 percent from the horizontal. A fairly level slope has a gradient of 0–3 percent. Table 5.1 defines the various slope classes. Property that is sloped or graded away from the foundation has fewer drainage problems than one that is not. Slope length also has considerable influence over runoff and potential water erosion.

Ideally, a property should sit up on a site and the land should be graded on all sides. This is not often the case. If a structure is level with the street or sits in the middle of a land parcel that is sloped toward the structure, drainage problems will most likely occur. Water pools around the foundation, and possibly in front of the doorways. If the slope is too steep, water erosion also occurs.

Putting It to Work 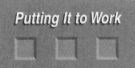	If the basement examination reveals wet spots and the source cannot be found, it may be that the structure is built over old creeks, springs, or other underground drainage areas that are not visible.

TABLE 5.1	SIMPLE SLOPES	COMPLEX SLOPES	LOWER %	UPPER %
Definitions of slope classes.	Nearly level	Nearly level	0	3
	Gently sloping	Undulating	1	8
	Strongly sloping	Rolling	4	16
	Moderately steep	Hilly	10	30
	Steep	Steep	20	60
	Very steep	Very steep	>45	

If the detail of mapping requires slope classes that are more detailed, some of the classes can be divided as follows:

Nearly level:	Level, nearly level
Gently sloping:	Very gently sloping, gently sloping
Strongly sloping:	Sloping, strongly sloping, moderately sloping
Undulating:	Gently undulating, undulating
Rolling:	Rolling, strongly rolling

In a highly detailed survey, for example, slope classes of 0 to 1 percent and 1 to 3 percent would be named "level" and "nearly level."

Source: Soil Survey Staff, Natural Resource Conservation Service, *Soil Survey Manual,* United States Department of Agriculture, Handbook No. 18 (Washington, DC: U. S. Government Printing Office, October 1993).

Soil Quality and Grading of Land

Different soil textures are found throughout the country and soils generally are a combination of various types. Essentially, soil textures include varying mixtures of sand, silt, loam, and clay. Sands are coarse, medium, fine, or very fine. The soil's texture determines the permeability and percolation rate of water. **Soil permeability** *is the ability of the soil to absorb water.* The **percolation rate** *is the speed at which standing water is absorbed by the soil.* Soils such as those composed largely of clay are less permeable than, for example, a fine sandy soil. It follows then that the percolation rate of the sandy soil is much greater than that of the clay soil.

With a septic system, the absorption field is generally composed of soils with rapid percolation rates blended with other less permeable soils to slow down the infiltration rate. Drainage tiles are often used in conjunction with an absorption field to boost the amount of water absorbed.

Putting It to Work

Rain and snowmelt that does not appear as surface runoff infiltrates the soil. The rate of infiltration depends, however, not only on soil type, but moisture content, surface slope, frost in the soil, and rainfall characteristics. Once the water has infiltrated the soil, it encounters varying degrees of flow resistance depending on the type of soil it must go through. Coarse gravels allow water to flow rapidly and in large quantities; tight clays greatly restrict the flow and absorption of water.

Soil that is predominantly composed of either clay or sand is problematic. Clay soil shrinks when losing water and expands when absorbing water. During an expansive period, the clay soil can actually lift areas under the foundation above grade; when the clay dries out, the soil shrinks, causing the foundation to drop more than normal. This motion can cause the foundation wall and floor slab to crack and heave. A predominantly sandy soil, on the other hand, becomes extremely heavy during a wet period, causing dangerous hydrostatic pressure against the foundation wall. In worst case scenarios, the foundation wall can cave in. Figures 5.4 and 5.5 illustrate foundation walls on the verge of collapse due to hydrostatic pressure.

You Should Know

GROUNDWATER AND THE WATER TABLE

Groundwater *is water beneath the surface of the earth that can be collected with wells, tunnels, or drainage galleries or that flows naturally to the earth's surface via seeps or springs.* The **water table** *is the uppermost boundary of the groundwater.*

Some of the water that infiltrates soil is held by soil particles, but most of it eventually reaches the water table below where the soil is saturated. Generally, the water table follows the natural contours of the land, and its depth from the surface varies with the soil type and amount of rainfall. During wet periods, the water table is close to the surface; during extended dry periods, it is many feet beneath. Wetlands are areas of land where the water table is either at or near the

FIGURE 5.4   *Example of hydrostatic pressure.*

The foundation wall is bowing, causing horizontal and vertical cracks. This wall is on the verge of collapse.

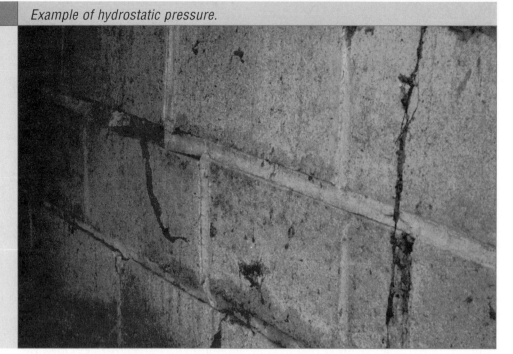

Source: Anthony D'Agostino, Atlantic Inspection Service, Latham, New York.

surface most of the time. The main problem with a high water table is that it causes hydrostatic pressure on the floor slab. This hydrostatic pressure, in turn, causes the floor slab to buckle or heave upward. Should the water table drop with a corresponding decrease in pressure, the floor can sink. This pressure causes cracking and heaving of both the floor slab and the foundation wall. Footing drain tiles are regularly used to counteract problems associated with a high water table.

FIGURE 5.5   *Foundation wall on the verge of collapse.*

Source: Anthony D'Agostino, Atlantic Inspection Service, Latham, New York.

Footing Drain Tile

Footing drain tile is used around concrete or masonry foundations that enclose habitable or usable space below grade (see Figure 5.6). *Drain tile* is perforated hollow pipe used to disperse liquid into the ground. These pipes, placed around the perimeter of a footing, are recommended for any site where the water table can be expected to extend beyond the top of the footing. The pipes are laid on a bed of gravel or stone with a slight grade toward a sump pump inlet in the basement. They are covered with more gravel and encased with filter paper so that solids cannot block the perforations and impede the water flow.

Drainage tiles are generally four inches in diameter. They are composed of various materials including clay, porous concrete, perforated corrugated steel, or bell and spigot concrete. The use of perforated, corrugated plastic drainage is increasing. A significant problem with the drain tile itself is that it becomes ineffective if blocked by soil washing into it. Blockage frequently occurs as a result of poor construction practices (e.g., laying broken or poorly aligned pipe or allowing silt or clay deposits to wash into the pipe before backfilling takes place).

Another type of site drainage is the French drain, typically semicircular concrete furrows that are filled with gravel or stone. The drain helps to direct the surface water away from the foundation wall. It is found either on the surface of the site or slightly below grade.

Putting It to Work

Drain tiles are found in most new construction. With homes built before 1960, if water is a problem, there might not be any drain tiles around the perimeter of the footing.

You Should Know

Footing drain tile. **FIGURE 5.6**

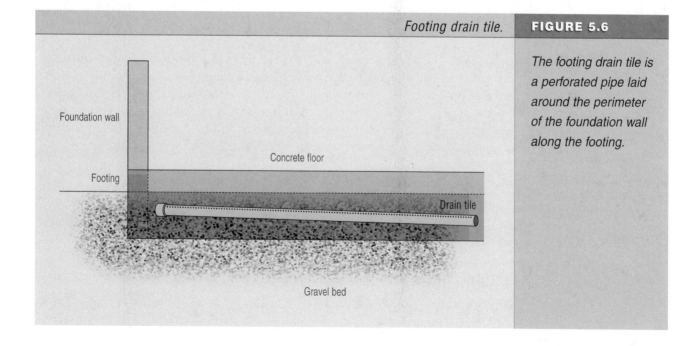

Foundation wall

Concrete floor

Footing

Drain tile

Gravel bed

The footing drain tile is a perforated pipe laid around the perimeter of the foundation wall along the footing.

Floodplains are low, flat, periodically flooded lands adjacent to rivers, lakes, and oceans that are subject to *geomorphic* (land shaping) and *hydrolic* (water flow) processes. For land use planning purposes, the regulatory floodplain is usually viewed as all lands within reach of a 100-year flood. A 100-year flood is defined as a flood event that has a one percent chance of occurring in any given year. The Federal Emergency Management Agency (FEMA) produces floodplain maps and defines areas bounded by the 100-year floodplain. One of the purposes of this mapping is the implementation of the National Flood Insurance program. Home inspectors should know whether the property they are inspecting is in or near a floodplain because special building codes may apply. In addition, affected home owners must have flood insurance. Local building and health departments are sources of information.

Inspecting for drainage problems. Inspectors should check to see if a property has a sump pump situated in a pit in the basement; if so, drainage is probably an issue. The *sump pump* removes surface and groundwater that penetrates through the ground to the footing.

Look for ruts or gullies on the ground or large bare spots where grass or other vegetation refuses to grow. This may indicate a greater and swifter flow than the soil and ground cover can absorb. The installation of a drainage conduit provides a solution.

LANDSCAPING

Landscaping serves more purposes than simply aesthetic appeal. Landscaping conceals unsightly areas, serves as a noise barrier, defines certain spaces, prevents soil erosion, and removes pollutants from the area. Surveys have shown that older trees around a house improve salability and greatly increase a home's value.

Trees

In many cases, natural vegetation, such as mature trees, may be on the site before excavation. The developer may wish to keep them in place. It is recommended that the house initially be situated at least 20 feet from any existing vegetation, especially mature trees that are to be preserved, so as not to disturb the root system. Over a period of time, however, certain areas of the property become overgrown with trees. This causes a variety of problems including too much shade. The lack of sunlight allows the structure's exterior covering to mildew and rot.

In most cases, it is safe to plant trees within 5 to 10 feet of the structure as long as the branches are cut back periodically.

Shrubs and Flower Beds

Shrubs and flower beds should be graded away from the foundation wall. Shrubs should be trimmed away from the foundation wall and transplanted regularly to avoid overcrowding. Crowded shrub beds promote insect infestation, mildew, and fungus.

Inspecting trees, shrubs, and flower beds. Look for tree branches that are growing toward the structure and blocking windows and overhanging the roof. These branches, including dead ones, should be trimmed away. The biggest problem with overgrown tree branches is that leaves, twigs, and other matter clog gutters and attract insects toward the house, causing pest infestation. Tree branches can also be hazardous if a storm breaks and then blows them toward vulnerable areas of the structure such as windows, glass patio doors, above-ground cables attached to the structure, or swimming pools where plastic liners are vulnerable to damage.

Proper landscaping around the perimeter of a property can help avoid drainage problems, so an examination of the beds will reveal whether there might be problems. Look for flower and shrub beds where standing water has pooled. If this is the case, check the gutter downspouts and make sure the water is being discharged away from the foundation rather than into a plant bed or next to the foundation wall. In some cases where water pools around plant beds, window wells are used to prevent water from seeping through the basement windows. These wells are also used to keep rodents, leaves, and other debris from entering the house through the windows. The bottoms of these wells should contain absorbent material such as gravel. If the floor of the window well is filled with water, it may indicate a drainage problem. Often, window wells have a plastic covering to prevent the entry of water and debris.

RETAINING WALLS

Retaining walls are used extensively in residential landscaping. **Retaining walls** *are structures made from a variety of materials, such as brick, stone, slate, poured concrete, concrete block, and pressure-treated wood, that are used to hold back areas of earth.* The most common cause of a retaining wall's failure is inadequate drainage. Retaining walls without adequate drainage are subject to substantial hydrostatic pressure, sufficient to cause collapse if they are not designed to withstand such pressure. It is important that the wall is backfilled with suitable porous material. This material may be crushed stone, pea stone, or gravel. The retaining wall should have either drainage tiles with adequate filters to drain water from the base or weepholes. **Weepholes** *are small perforations in retaining wall material that allow water drainage.* Brick, concrete, and concrete block walls should have weepholes. Sometimes weepholes are not as satisfactory as drainage tiles because they tend to become blocked with fine soil. Retaining walls built with wood materials do not require weepholes because the water flows out between the wood slats.

Brick retaining walls contain mortar to hold the bricks in place. A solid brick or concrete wall may be as high as five or six feet. Lower walls, generally not higher than two or three feet, such as those made of fieldstone or slate, are often constructed without mortar or other adhesive substances. Poured concrete retaining walls contain embedded steel reinforcements and must have the footing below the frost line to prevent heaving.

Inspecting retaining walls. Besides drainage issues, retaining walls can pose a number of other problems. Improperly anchored wood retaining walls can eventually heave or sag, causing complete collapse. Concrete walls develop cracks that are problematic if not repaired to prevent further stress and greater damage. Vertical cracks that appear open toward the top of the wall and narrow or hairline toward the bottom may indicate a problem with settlement. Horizontal cracks may indicate too much pressure originating from the back of the wall. Inspectors may notice a few shrinkage cracks caused by the shrinkage of the mortar or other binding material. These cracks are harmless because they do not penetrate the depth of the wall. The inspector should note whether the wall is standing vertically or is sloped slightly toward the embankment. A wall that is heaving or bowed forward indicates pressure problems from earth, water, or both that can eventually cause the wall's total collapse.

WALKWAYS, DRIVEWAYS, AND OTHER PAVED AND MASONRY AREAS

Asphalt or concrete is most often used for driveways and walkways. Brick, gravel, and packed soil are other materials encountered on a routine inspection. Forces that cause deterioration include temperature changes, moisture, superimposed loads, and the movement of underlying soil. Weather conditions, tree roots, and erosion cause underlying soil movement. In addition, many home owners residing in colder climates use salt to de-ice their walkways and driveways. Salt often causes pitting and cracking to the surface of asphalt and concrete.

Inspecting driveways and walkways. Poured concrete walkways and driveways may crack, crumble, or heave over time. Asphalt, too, may develop cracks, ruts, or holes. Walkways and driveways left in disrepair are safety hazards. Safety hazards should be noted on the home inspection report.

Inspectors should look for wheel depressions in asphalt driveways. These depressions may indicate the poor compaction of the driveway bed. Numerous soft spots in the asphalt may indicate drainage problems.

You Should Know   Generally, building code requirements call for a walkway from the front door of the house to the street or driveway. The minimum property standards promulgated by HUD require walkways to all dwellings within a development and walkways that lead to various other facilities within the development.

FIGURE 5.7

Components of a stairway.

Source: Basics for Builders: Framing and Rough Carpentry, by Scot Simpson. Kingston, MA: The R.S. Means Company, Inc.

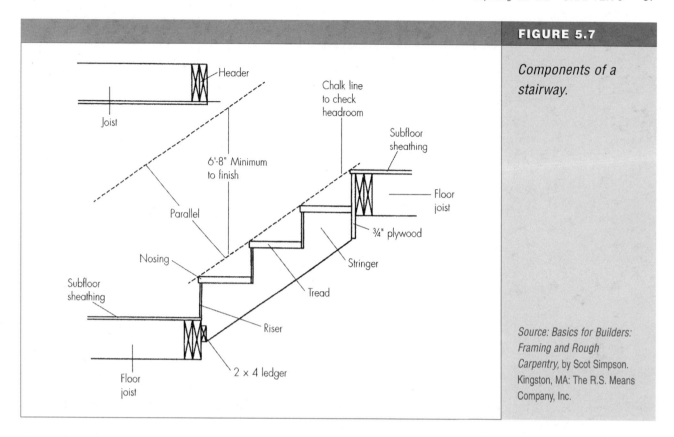

STEPS AND STOOPS

Stairways and single steps are located at various places on the site. There may be a single stairway in the middle of a walkway leading toward the house or there may be a three- or four-step stairway leading to the house entry. A stair is composed of three main parts: the tread, the riser, and the stringer (see Figure 5.7). The **riser** *is the vertical area of the step that supports the tread.* The **tread** *is the horizontal surface of the stair;* and the **stringer** *or carriage supports the stairway. The space between the stair and the overhang* (or the ceiling inside the structure) *is called the* **headroom.** Local building codes designate headroom space. *Poles or posts that run from the stair handrail vertically to the tread are known as* **balusters.** The spacing of the baluster must meet code requirements; the poles are to be spaced four inches apart so that children cannot poke their heads through the posts and become stuck. The platform at the end of the stairway is called the *stoop.* The stoop must have adequate space to turn around or stand. The minimum dimensions of the stoop are generally designated in local building codes.

Inspecting the stairway. Outdoor stairways are composed of a variety of materials including brick, poured concrete, pressure-treated lumber, or a combination of these materials. The stairway must generally have a concrete footing and foundation because without it the steps will sink, heave, or tilt to one side. The handrail may be constructed of wood, wrought iron, or steel or designed as a wall with concrete or brick. Building codes define rail requirements for both indoor and outdoor stairways. Generally, any platform above grade must have a rail. Stair rails should be inspected for stability and the condition of the rail itself, including corrosion on metal railings and rot and decay on wood railings.

PATIOS, PORCHES, ATTACHED DECKS, AND BALCONIES

atios, porches, decks, and balconies are simple or elaborate depending on the general architecture of the structure and the property owner's wishes.

Patios

Patios generally abut the property and are accessed from the house through a simple doorway, most commonly sliding glass doors or French doors. Patio material consists of poured concrete, brick, slate, or stones laid in a concrete base.

Inspecting the patio. As with walkways and driveways, patios may pose a safety hazard if they are cracked or have ruts, holes, or pieces broken off the edges. The patio slab should meet the surrounding vegetation without being a hazard when walking from the patio to the lawn area. The patio slab should be sloped away from the structure so that water can drain away. If wood or metal rails, fences, or sidewalls surround the patio, these too should be inspected in a fashion similar to the stair rails.

Putting It to Work

Findings of conditions that constitute safety hazards, whether defined as such by code requirements or not, should always be noted on the inspection report. These safety hazards should be reported and explained to the client so that they can be eliminated before the client takes possession of the property. The home inspector should refer the client to those professionals who can remedy the particular safety hazard.

Porches

Porches are enjoying a resurgence in popularity and are found in many new constructions as well as older homes. A porch is an extended part of the house structure and is composed of a roof, support columns, floor, and crawl space. Due to code requirements, virtually all porches have railings. Porches are composed of a variety of materials including wood, concrete, concrete block, or brick. If the porch floor is concrete, there is a footing and foundation to support it. Wooden porches are supported by piers driven into the ground and a floor joist system supports the porch floor. (See Chapter 6 for a discussion of floor joist systems.) If the porch floor is wood, it might have latticework enclosing the crawl space.

Inspecting the porch. If possible, examine the crawl space to evaluate the condition of the floor joist and bearing beams by checking for wood rot and decay. Porch railings may be wood, wrought iron, or walled in by brick or concrete. The porch materials are examined in a fashion similar to other exterior structures. Look for surface cracks if the material is wood or concrete, loose mortar if the material is brick or concrete block, and rot and deterioration of wood or brick posts or columns. Figure 5.8 illustrates a porch bearing beam decayed by water penetration. Figure 5.9 illustrates a porch on the verge of collapse because there is no foundation or footing to support it. Like the stairway, porch railings and balusters must meet code requirements. Balusters not placed according to code pose a safety hazard.

FIGURE 5.8

A porch bearing beam decayed by water penetration.

Source: Anthony D'Agostino, Atlantic Inspection Service, Latham, New York.

FIGURE 5.9

A porch on the verge of collapse.

Source: Anthony D'Agostino, Atlantic Inspection Service, Latham, New York.

Decks

Decks have many different shapes, sizes, and elevations and are generally constructed from pressure-treated lumber. This lumber requires a waterproof stain, paint, or seal to protect the wood. Figure 5.10 illustrates the components of a basic deck. Like the porch, a deck generally has its own concrete footing. On top of the footing is a post anchor, that is, a metal framing connector, to hold the post

FIGURE 5.10   *Components of a deck.*

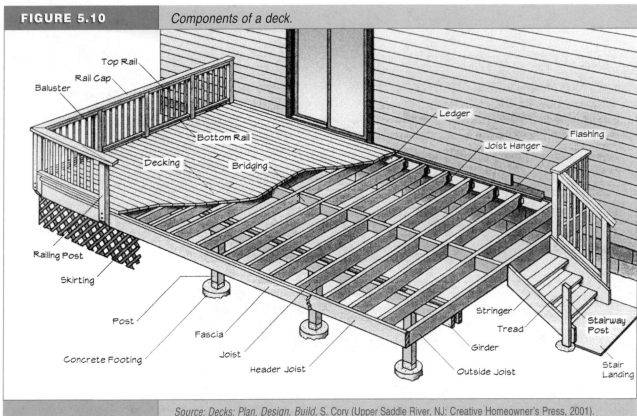

Source: Decks: Plan, Design, Build, S. Cory (Upper Saddle River, NJ: Creative Homeowner's Press, 2001).

in place. The posts support either the deck or railing. A girder is positioned horizontally across the posts and carries the load of the floor joists. Beams rest on the post or alongside the post. The joists support the decking. Bolted to the house frame is a ledger that connects the deck to the structure. Decking boards are nailed or screwed to the joists or attached by decking clips. Decks may or may not have rails and balusters and, like a porch, may have latticework or skirting to keep animals and other objects from getting under it. The deck may have a stairway attached to it.

Inspecting the deck. Decking boards should be spaced wide enough to allow water to seep through so that it does not pool on the deck and rot the wood. Decks must meet code requirements as to rails, balusters, stairways, and supports. Like the porch, moisture can be a problem on the underside of the deck, especially one that is constructed very close to the ground. If possible, check for signs of wood rot, fungus, and other moisture problems under the deck. Tall decks that reach to the second story of the property should be checked for stability. The posts should be securely fastened to the footing and not show signs of wood rot or other decay. Exercise caution when stepping onto a deck that appears to be a safety hazard.

Balconies

Balconies are extensions from the house structure and are supported as such. They are often additionally supported by piers running from the ground up under the balcony floor. All balconies must have rails and balusters that meet code requirements.

Inspecting the balcony. Check for water that has penetrated from the intersection of the balcony and structure wall. This water penetration can cause moisture problems inside the structure. Balconies may also become unstable over time and, as with the roof, home inspectors must exercise extreme caution before stepping onto a balcony.

IMPORTANT POINTS

1. Because there currently are no federal uniform guidelines governing home inspections, home inspection organizations have developed standards of practice for the industry. Many home inspectors find it useful to join a home inspection organization and follow the guidelines provided by that organization's standards of practice.

2. A typical site inspection, according to industry standards, includes the inspection of the following: drainage and grading; landscaping, trees, shrubs, and other vegetation; retaining walls; walkways, driveways, and other paved and masonry areas; steps and stoops; patios, porches, decks, and balconies; and any railings.

3. The home inspection is most concerned with the physical nature of the property and any problems that become evident during the examination.

4. An appurtenance is a right, privilege, or improvement belonging to, and passing with, the land. Property owners may sell or lease an appurtenance.

5. Drainage is the land's ability to draw off surface water.

6. Proper grading ensures that surface water is directed away from the foundation.

7. Proper drainage around the structure prevents wet basements, frost heaving problems, and the buildup of hydrostatic pressure on basement floors, banks, and retaining walls.

8. Water erosion is the removal of soil material by flowing water. Another type of erosion in various parts of the country is wind erosion, which occurs in regions of low rainfall and can be widespread especially in periods of drought.

9. Property that is sloped or graded away from the foundation has fewer drainage problems than one that is not. Slope length also has considerable influence over runoff and potential water erosion.

10. Soil textures include varying mixtures of sand, silt, loam, and clay. The soil's texture determines the permeability and percolation rate of water.

11. Groundwater is water beneath the surface of the earth that can be collected with wells, tunnels, or drainage galleries or that flows naturally to the earth's surface via seeps or springs. The water table is the uppermost boundary of the groundwater.

12. Footing drain tiles, placed around the perimeter of a footing, are recommended for any site where the water table can be expected to extend beyond the top of the footing.

13. Proper landscaping around the perimeter of a property can help avoid drainage problems, so an examination of the beds will reveal whether there might be problems.

14. The most common cause of a retaining wall's failure is inadequate drainage.

15. Forces that cause walkway and driveway deterioration include temperature changes, moisture, superimposed loads, and the movement of underlying soil.

16. A stair is composed of three main parts: the tread, the riser, and the stringer. The space between the stair and the overhang is called the headroom. Local building codes designate the headroom space. Poles or posts that run from the stair handrail vertically to the tread are known as balusters. The spacing of the balusters must meet code requirements; the poles are to be spaced four inches apart.

17. As with walkways and driveways, patios may pose a safety hazard if they are cracked or have ruts, holes, or pieces broken off the edges.

18. A deck may be on an extension of the house footing or the deck may have been added later and is not supported as a part of the house structure.

19. The balcony support originates from the house structure. It may also be additionally supported by posts or beams running from the ground up under the balcony floor.

CHAPTER REVIEW

Field Study Assignment 1

Using your practice property and a copy of the inspection checklist from Figure 4.4, inspect the site. Note any problems you encounter for further exploration and discussion.

Field Study Assignment 2

Research the water table levels in the area where you will inspect properties to learn how it impacts building standards, codes, and specifications. This information can be obtained from local building or health departments, developers, contractors, and other home inspectors.

Field Study Assignment 3

Visit a new construction site and observe what factors were taken into consideration when locating the structure on the site. Pay attention to the slope and grading of the site. If possible, look for the placement of footing drain tile around the perimeter of the footing.

1. Standards of practice for home inspection can be found primarily through:
   A. federal guidelines
   B. state guidelines
   C. home inspection organizations
   D. individual inspection companies

2. JayCee, a home inspector, was asked to inspect the automatic garage door opener. She did not fully understand the mechanism. What should she do?
   A. Inspect it as best as she can.
   B. Advise her clients to seek the services of a qualified professional.
   C. Tell her clients that state law does not allow her to touch mechanical parts.
   D. Agree to disengage the mechanism and bring it to a qualified professional for them.

3. Which of the following is NOT included in a typical site inspection?
   A. playground equipment
   B. porches
   C. decks
   D. patios

4. Which of the following IS included in a typical site inspection?
   A. retaining walls
   B. swimming pools
   C. awnings
   D. docks

5. Topography refers to:
   A. physical features of land
   B. hydrostatic pressure
   C. demography
   D. appurtenances

6. To ensure that surface water is directed away from the foundation, the site must be properly:
   A. drained
   B. backfilled
   C. pressurized
   D. graded

7. Which of the following is NOT prevented by proper drainage?
   A. water erosion
   B. wind erosion
   C. wet basements
   D. foundation heaving problems

8. The primary source of problems encountered during a site inspection is:
   A. drainage issues
   B. landscaping issues
   C. cracked driveways
   D. collapsed retaining walls

9. A nearly level slope has a gradient of:
   A. 1–3 percent
   B. 4–6 percent
   C. 7–9 percent
   D. 9–11 percent

10. If a slope is too steep, which of the following is most likely to occur?
    A. wind erosion
    B. pooling of water in front of the structure's doorways
    C. water erosion
    D. a wet basement

11. Which of the following is NOT a type of soil texture?
    A. sand
    B. silt
    C. loam
    D. gravel

12. Soil permeability refers to:
    A. the ability of the soil to absorb water
    B. the speed at which standing water is absorbed by the soil
    C. soil density
    D. soil texture

13. The water table is:
    A. a measurement of hydrostatic pressure
    B. the uppermost boundary of the groundwater
    C. the slope of a river or stream
    D. a table of liquid weights and measures

14. To counteract problems associated with a high water table, which of the following are used?
    A. drain tiles
    B. a layer of coarse gravel
    C. filter paper
    D. tiebacks

15. Drain tile is most commonly placed around the:
    A. perimeter of the site
    B. perimeter of the footing
    C. basement window wells
    D. foundation wall

16. The biggest problem associated with tree branches growing into the structure is:
    A. unsightliness
    B. too much shade
    C. pest infestation
    D. damage to windows

17. The most common retaining wall failure is caused by:
    A. the use of pressure-treated wood
    B. pest infestation
    C. cracked mortar
    D. inadequate drainage

18. A dry retaining wall is one that is constructed:
    A. indoors
    B. without mortar or other adhesive
    C. using fieldstone only
    D. with wood

19. Brick retaining walls generally contain which of the following to alleviate drainage problems?
    A. peepholes
    B. weepholes
    C. cracks in the mortar
    D. filter paper

20. Walkways should be inspected for:
    A. curb appeal
    B. location
    C. composition
    D. safety hazards

21. Which of the following is NOT a section of a stairway?
    A. anchor
    B. riser
    C. tread
    D. stringer

22. Generally, building codes require that stair balusters are placed:
    A. one inch apart
    B. two inches apart
    C. three inches apart
    D. four inches apart

23. The main problem associated with the edge of a patio that does not properly meet the surrounding vegetation is that it:
    A. looks unsightly
    B. causes weeds to grow between the patio and the lawn
    C. causes a trip hazard
    D. deteriorates the patio edge

24. The crawl space under a porch should be examined for which of the following?
    A. square footage
    B. damage to floor joists
    C. soil composition
    D. accessibility

25. Which of the following is FALSE?
    A. Water can penetrate from the balcony platform and cause moisture problems inside the structure.
    B. Balconies should be inspected for stability.
    C. Inspectors must step onto balconies under all conditions.
    D. Balconies must have rails around the platform.

ANSWER KEY

1. C	8. A	15. B	22. D
2. B	9. A	16. C	23. C
3. A	10. C	17. D	24. B
4. A	11. D	18. B	25. C
5. A	12. A	19. B	
6. D	13. B	20. D	
7. B	14. A	21. A	

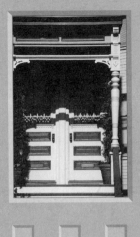

CHAPTER 6

INSPECTING THE EXTERIOR

H ome inspectors must have basic knowledge of the construction of the property's structural components. Only then can an intelligent inspection of the property be done. This chapter focuses on an analysis and inspection of the exterior components. As you read, refer to Figure 6.1 in order to visualize the residential structure.

LEARNING OBJECTIVES

1. List the items that are included in the inspection of the property's exterior.

2. Describe the structural components' interconnections.

3. Briefly summarize the primary problem areas to examine during the exterior inspection.

KEY TERMS

Balloon framing	Fixed-pane windows	Lally columns	Roof truss system
Bearing wall	Flashing	Light	Sash
Casing	Floating slab	Monolithic slab	Sheathing
Control joints	Floor joist	Muntins	Sill plate
Cornice	Floor truss	Pitch	Slab-on-grade
Counterflashing	Footing	Platform framing	construction
Creosote	Foundation wall	Plumb	Soffit
Cricket	Frieze board	Post-and-beam	Sole plate
Double top plate	Girder	framing	Spalling
Eave	Glazing	Rafters	Stile
Fascia	Header	Rails	Stud
Felt paper	House wrap	Rebars	Threshold
		Ridge beam	Wood rot

FIGURE 6.1   *The basic parts (structure) of a house.*

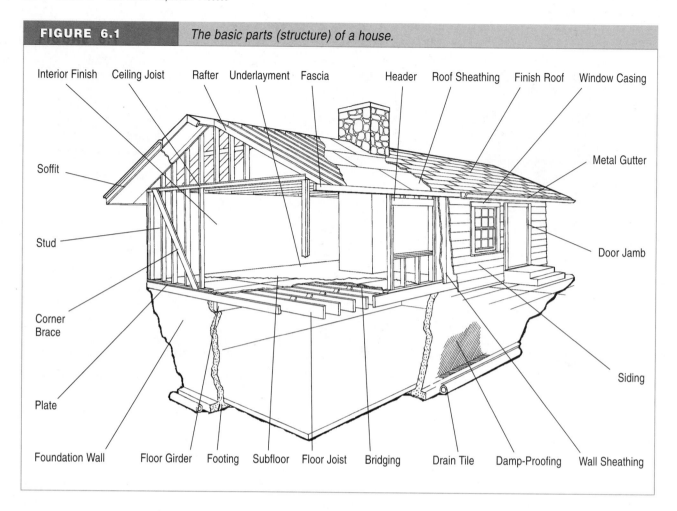

Interior Finish Ceiling Joist   Rafter   Underlayment Fascia   Header   Roof Sheathing   Finish Roof   Window Casing

Soffit   Metal Gutter

Stud   Door Jamb

Corner
Brace

Plate   Siding

Foundation Wall   Floor Girder   Footing   Subfloor   Floor Joist   Bridging   Drain Tile   Damp-Proofing   Wall Sheathing

SCOPE OF THE EXTERIOR INSPECTION

F igure 6.2 sets forth the ASHI Standards of Practice for the inspection of the structure, the exterior, and the roof system. The site components of the exterior were discussed in Chapter 5. (See Appendix A for the complete ASHI Standards.)

FOUNDATION AND FOOTINGS

H ouses are generally built on a foundation that forms a basement, crawl space, or slab (discussed later; see Figure 6.3). The most important foundation building block is the footing. The **footing** *is the concrete base below the frost line that supports the foundation of the structure.* To construct the footings, the building lines are laid out with batter boards, temporary wood members on posts that form an L-shape outside the foundation's corners. The width of the footing is at least twice the width of the foundation wall that is erected on it. In many cases, the footing depth is equal to the foundation wall thickness. Local building codes, however, generally determine footing measurements. Soil type is also a consideration. In light soils, the footing is wider to spread the weight of the load; in heavier clay soils, it is narrower. In wet and coastal areas, homes are constructed on posts or piers.

FIGURE 6.2

3. STRUCTURAL SYSTEM

3.1 The inspector shall:

   A. inspect:

   1. the structural components including foundation and framing.

   2. by probing a representative number of structural components where deterioration is suspected or where clear indications of possible deterioration exist. Probing is NOT required when probing would damage any finished surface or where no deterioration is visible or presumed to exist.

   B. describe:

   1. the foundation and report the methods used to inspect the under-floor crawl space and attics.

   2. the foundation.

   3. the floor structure.

   4. the wall structure.

   5. the ceiling structure.

   6. the roof structure.

3.2 The inspector is NOT required to:

   A. provide any engineering or architectural service or analysis.

   B. offer an opinion as to the adequacy of any structural system or component.

4. EXTERIOR

4.1 The inspector shall:

   A. inspect:

   1. siding, flashing and trim.

   2. all exterior doors.

   3. attached or adjacent decks, balconies, stoops, steps, porches, and their associated railings.

   4. eaves, soffits, and fascias where accessible from the ground level.

   5. vegetation, grading, surface drainage, and retaining walls on the property when any of these are likely to adversely affect the building.

   6. adjacent or entryway walkways, patios, and driveways.

   B. describe:

   1. siding.

4.2 The inspector is NOT required to inspect:

   A. screening, shutters, awnings, and similar seasonal accessories.

   B. fences.

   C. geological, geotechnical and/or hydrological soil conditions.

   D. recreational facilities.

   E. outbuildings other than garages and carports.

   F. seawalls, break-walls, and docks.

   G. erosion control and earth stabilization measures.

(continued)

FIGURE 6.2	
Applicable ASHI Standards of Practice, continued.	**5. ROOF SYSTEM**
	5.1 The inspector shall:
	A. inspect:
	1. roofing materials.
	2. roof drainage systems.
	3. flashing.
	4. skylights, chimneys, and roof penetrations.
	B. describe:
	1. roofing materials.
	2. methods used to inspect the roofing.
Permission to reprint and reference granted by the American Society of Home Inspectors, Inc. (ASHI) www.ASHI.org	5.2 The inspector is NOT required to inspect:
	A. antennae.
	B. interiors of flues or chimneys which are not readily accessible.
	C. other installed accessories.

The purpose of the footing is to support the foundation wall and, consequently, the entire weight load of the structure. The footings must provide an adequate base for the structure to prevent settling of the house. Figure 6.4 illustrates a typical residential footing and foundation.

Foundation Walls

Foundation walls *generally are composed of poured concrete, masonry (concrete) block, or brick. The height of the foundation wall determines whether the structure has a full basement or a crawl space.* In masonry block foundation walls, the block forms the back half of the wall and is sometimes covered with a brick veneer on the front. Vertical masonry piers are built inside these foundation walls to provide additional support for the house.

FIGURE 6.3	*Types of foundations.*

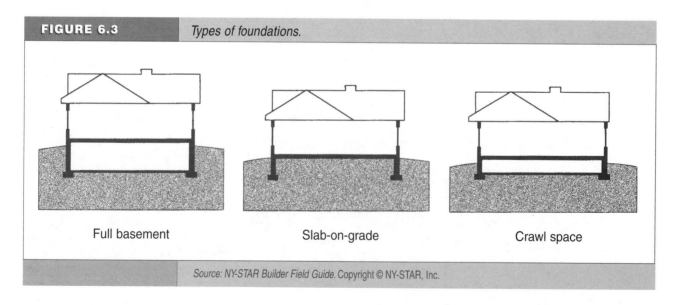

Full basement   Slab-on-grade   Crawl space

Source: NY-STAR Builder Field Guide. Copyright © NY-STAR, Inc.

The permanent wood foundation, or PWF, is a new type of foundation that possesses drainage features that help prevent moisture problems. A PWF is composed of load-bearing lumber-framed walls sheathed with plywood. The lumber and plywood are pressure treated with preservatives to prevent decay from moisture and insects. PWFs are generally allowed by all building codes. The construction design and granular footing keep ground moisture away from the basement walls. During construction, the plywood joints are sealed with butyl caulking. The walls are covered with a vapor barrier prior to being backfilled, partially with P-rock, to facilitate drainage and eliminate leaks due to hydrostatic pressure caused by soil expansion around the basement. PWF is crack and cold weather resistant. In a PWF system, the wall studding is already in place, eliminating the need to construct a separate wall inside the foundation for insulation. PWF systems use conventional framing techniques similar to those used to frame the main floor exterior walls. Walls may be framed to any height depending on whether there is a basement or crawl space.

Currently a new type of concrete application is the use of preformed or precast Styrofoam blocks for building foundations. The blocks are stacked and tied together, then filled with concrete to form sturdy foundations that have high R-values. Although foam blocks have been available for several years, they are only recently being used in residential homes. This foundation type is used in areas with extreme weather and in the construction of properties near beaches.

Footing and foundation.   **FIGURE 6.4**

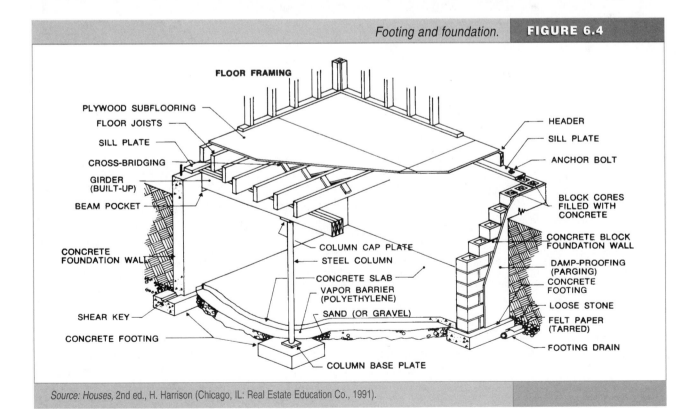

Source: *Houses,* 2nd ed., H. Harrison (Chicago, IL: Real Estate Education Co., 1991).

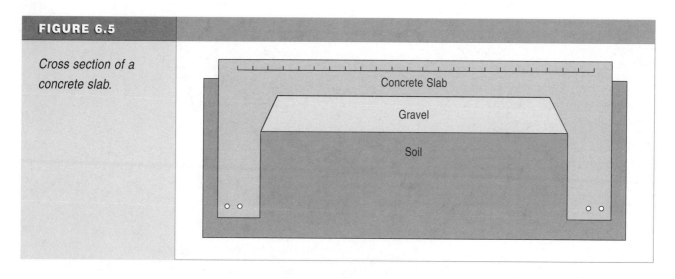

FIGURE 6.5

Cross section of a concrete slab.

Concrete Slab

Gravel

Soil

Slab-on-Grade Construction

On level terrain, **slab-on-grade construction** is possible. *The foundation is a concrete slab instead of a foundation wall. The concrete slab is poured directly on the ground, eliminating the crawl space or basement.* The slab provides the floor of the dwelling and the support for the exterior and interior walls. **Floating slabs** *are constructed by pouring the footing first and then pouring the slab. If the footing and slab are poured at the same time, it is called a* **monolithic slab.** The concrete slab method is less expensive than the foundation wall system or basement but is not practical in all building situations. Although slab construction works well in warmer climates, it may be problematic in areas where the ground freezes in winter. This freezing can shift the slab and cause the floor to be very cold. However, many houses in colder climates are built with a slab foundation without any problem.

Around the slab, the concrete forms a beam that is two feet deep. The rest of the slab is four or six inches thick. Figure 6.5 shows a cross section of a floating slab. A six-inch layer of gravel lies under the slab and a four-millimeter plastic vapor barrier lies between the slab and the gravel. In addition, depending on local conditions, building codes require that these areas be treated with termiticide. Embedded in the concrete is six-by-six-inch wire mesh and steel reinforcing bars (rebars).

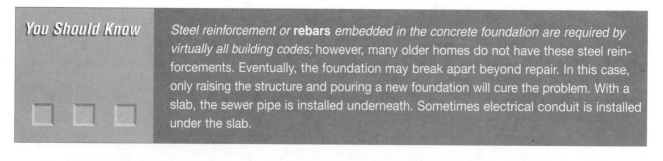

You Should Know

Steel reinforcement or **rebars** *embedded in the concrete foundation are required by virtually all building codes;* however, many older homes do not have these steel reinforcements. Eventually, the foundation may break apart beyond repair. In this case, only raising the structure and pouring a new foundation will cure the problem. With a slab, the sewer pipe is installed underneath. Sometimes electrical conduit is installed under the slab.

Inspecting the Foundation and Footings

The foundation inspection includes examining for cracks, bulges, or undue settlement. Solid materials may expand or contract due to temperature variations. Cracks must be evaluated to determine whether they are cosmetic or in need of repair. A type of foundation crack is the shrinkage crack, which occurs as the foundation cures and may require monitoring. Concrete block also shrinks during curing and may expand when exposed to moisture and temperature variations.

Cracks that are V-shaped, wider at the top and narrower toward the bottom of the foundation wall, generally indicate a problem that requires correction. V-shaped cracks usually worsen over time and may require excavation below the existing foundation to build a supporting foundation. These cracks are caused by the uneven settlement of the footing. To avoid this problem, prior to pouring the footing, the ground underneath the footing must be compacted.

A wall crack that continues into the foundation floor may involve the footing and could be a settlement crack of structural significance. Often foundation cracks occur if the footings are not deep enough or wide enough to support the structure's load. Hydrostatic pressure or soil conditions, such as heavy sand or clay that expands and contracts (see Chapter 5), are reasons why a foundation wall can settle too much, lean, or bulge. A foundation that is damaged in this respect may have to be replaced. Leaning or bulging foundations are usually observed visually or with the assistance of a level designed for that purpose.

Brick foundations may expand over time due to moisture and temperature conditions. Brick walls above grade may expand and contract enough to cause major damage if control joints are not used during construction. **Control joints** *are vertical spaces in the brick wall joints that allow for the expansion and contraction of the brick and mortar.* Figure 6.6 depicts a collapsed brick foundation.

Horizontal cracks in the foundation are due to a number of factors:

- frost in cold climates
- backfill damage
- wet soils causing a heavy load against the foundation
- hillsides causing a heavy load against the foundation

A collapsed brick foundation wall.   **FIGURE 6.6**

The peeling paint could be lead based because the property in this photograph is 50 years old.

Source: Anthony D'Agostino, Atlantic Inspection Service, Latham, New York.

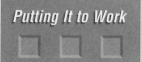
Putting It to Work

To gauge whether there has been foundation movement, look for evidence of previous repairs to the foundation walls. If so, recurrent movement is a problem. The inspector should also examine for old versus new cracks and active versus static cracks.

STRUCTURE FRAMING

F raming refers to the wooden skeleton of the home. Refer to Figure 6.7, which depicts framing from the bottom plate to roof. Wood framing members are pieces of lumber with a nominal two-inch thickness. For example, a 2" × 4" is a piece of lumber two inches thick by four inches wide. These *framing members, known as* **studs**, *are commonly 2 × 4s, 2 × 8s, 2 × 10s, or 2 × 12s and are used vertically for wall construction.* These wood framing members are also used as joists for floor and ceiling framing. Usually, 2 × 6s or 2 × 8s are used as rafters in the roof framing system.

FIGURE 6.7

Framing from bottom plate to roof.

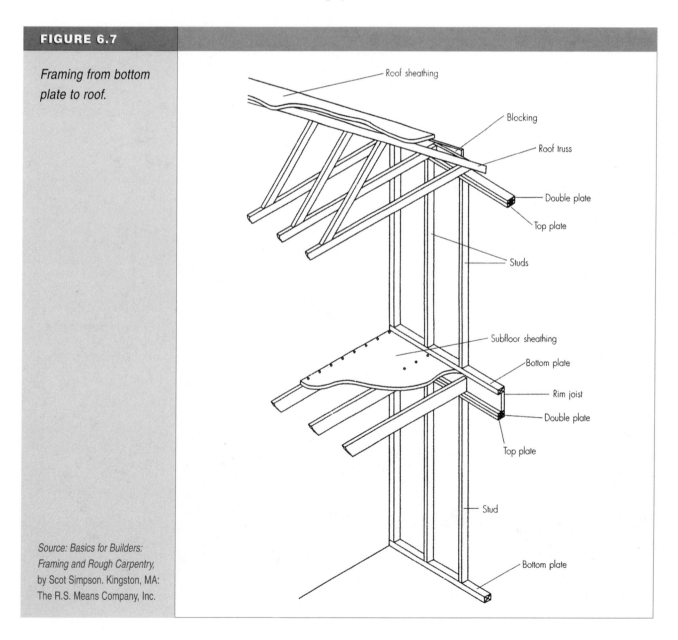

Source: Basics for Builders: Framing and Rough Carpentry, by Scot Simpson. Kingston, MA: The R.S. Means Company, Inc.

Timber is sized in "nominal," as opposed to "actual," dimensions. A nominal dimension rounds off the actual dimension to the next highest whole number. For example, a piece of timber that actually measures 1.5" × 3.5" is rounded off to the nominal 2" × 4".

Flooring

The top of the foundation wall is finished off with a course of solid masonry. On top of this rests the foundation sill plate. The sill plate is usually made from a pressure-treated 2" × 6" or 2" × 8" piece of lumber. If pressure-treated lumber is not used for the sill, then metal flashing must be placed between the foundation wall and the wooden member. The wooden sill is fastened to the foundation wall by anchor bolts. The **sill plate** *is the first wooden member of the house and is used as the nailing surface for the floor system.*

The box sill, or banding, rests on the sill plate and is the same size wooden member as the floor joists (2" × 8", 2" × 10", or 2" × 12"). The banding runs around the top of the foundation wall, attached to the sill plate.

The **floor joists** *span the distance between the foundation walls and the girder and provide support for the subfloor. The main carrying beam, or* **girder**, *is either a steel beam or several wooden members fastened together (usually 2 × 10s, 2 × 12s, or larger) that spans the distance from one side of the foundation to the other.* The joists rest on the girder for support.

Various types of columns are used to *support the main carrying beam of the structure; for example,* **lally columns**, *round steel columns filled with concrete that vary in diameter and rest on a base plate, which is the column footing pad.* They are placed in the basement or crawl space and their height is adjusted accordingly. The spacing of the lally columns is determined by the main carrying beam's size and material. In older structures, wood columns may be found. Check for signs of wood rot in these older columns.

Typical framing places wooden members at 16 inches on center. The phrase "16 inches on center" means that the center of one 2" × 4" stud is 16 inches away from the center of the next. Depending on the area to be spanned, the joists are doubled or even tripled to support the load. Some modern construction methods use wooden floor trusses in place of single floor joists. A **floor truss** *is a support member constructed in a factory by nailing a number of smaller members (2 × 4s or 2 × 6s) together in a number of triangular patterns to provide maximum strength.* Either 1/2-inch or 5/8-inch plywood or OSB (oriented strand board) subflooring rests directly on top of the joists.

Once the floor joists are in place, a plywood subfloor is nailed to the joists. Different grades of plywood can be used and the grade is determined by the material that will rest on top of it. When laying the subfloor, adhesive applied to the joist creates an effective bond and cuts down on squeaky floors. A gap of 1/8-inch between the ends and edges is recommended because the plywood and floor joists both expand and contract.

The expansion and contraction of wood is a common occurrence because wood has the ability to absorb moisture from the air. It expands when it absorbs moisture and shrinks when it loses moisture. The moisture content of wood affects its size, dimension, stability, decay resistance, glue bonding, and ability to accept paint.

FIGURE 6.8   *A cracked floor joist.*

A wood knot that should over time cause the floor joist to crack.

Source: Anthony D'Agostino, Atlantic Inspection Service, Latham, New York.

Inspecting the Floor

Floor framing problems can be observed in the basement. During construction, holes are drilled through floor joists for pipes or electrical wiring. If improperly drilled, these holes compromise the integrity of floor joists. In addition, knots in the floor joist wood can shrink over time, causing them to crack (see Figure 6.8). Should one of the floor joists weaken, the joist can twist out of place, causing a weakness in that area of the floor. Moreover, floors that squeak are generally caused by plywood sheathing that is not correctly nailed and glued to the floor joists. Another possibility is that the sheathing is not properly butted together, causing an up and down movement of the floor.

A sagging floor may be caused by a sagging main bearing beam. The sagging bearing beam can be caused by support columns spaced too far apart to support the load that the beam must carry. If possible, inspectors should check that there are double floor joists under wall partitions whether a bearing wall or not. If not, the weight of the wall causes the floor sheathing to sag.

Walls

The floor system usually serves as a stage or platform for the wall system. Wall framing forms the structure's exterior and interior walls. The walls are usually built using 2" × 4" studs, 16 inches on center. The **bearing walls** *support the ceiling or the roof and include the outside wall frame.* They are erected first. Nonbearing walls or partitions are walls that enclose interior space but do not support the structure. See Figure 6.9 for a cross section of a bearing wall.

You Should Know

In older homes, diagonal pieces of lumber are used at the corners for further reinforcement. This was before plywood, a much stronger material than previously used, was available.

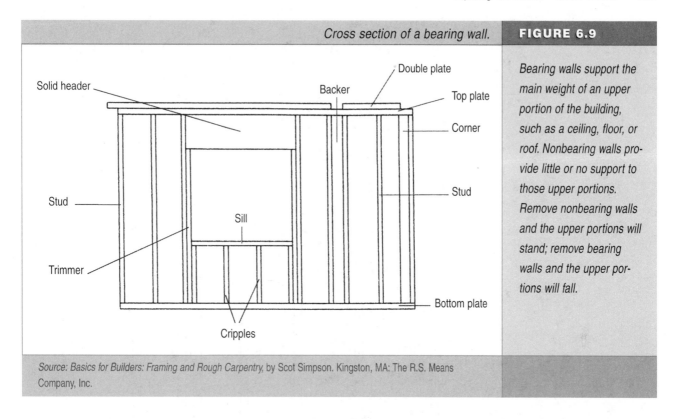

Source: Basics for Builders: Framing and Rough Carpentry, by Scot Simpson. Kingston, MA: The R.S. Means Company, Inc.

Cross section of a bearing wall. **FIGURE 6.9**

Bearing walls support the main weight of an upper portion of the building, such as a ceiling, floor, or roof. Nonbearing walls provide little or no support to those upper portions. Remove nonbearing walls and the upper portions will stand; remove bearing walls and the upper portions will fall.

A horizontal base plate, also called a **sole plate**, *serves as the foundation for the wall system. A* **double top plate** (Figure 6.10), *is used to tie the walls together and provide additional support for the ceiling and roof system.* The double top plate is made up of two or more structural timbers that are bolted together with a metal plate sandwiched between for additional strength.

Openings in the wall for doors or windows must be reinforced to pick up the missing support of the vertical load. This process is done with 2 × 8s, 2 × 10s, or 2 × 12s, known as headers, or lintels, erected over the top of the opening. Headers form a solid wood bridge over the opening and extend to the bottom of the top plate. Sandwiched in between the header's studs is a 1/2-inch thick piece of plywood. The **headers** *are actually beams that support the ceiling and the roof*

FIGURE 6.10

A wall double top plate.

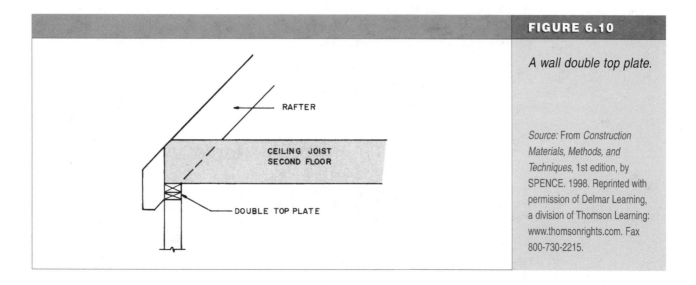

Source: From *Construction Materials, Methods, and Techniques,* 1st edition, by SPENCE. 1998. Reprinted with permission of Delmar Learning, a division of Thomson Learning: www.thomsonrights.com. Fax 800-730-2215.

FIGURE 6.11

Placement of the header within the frame.

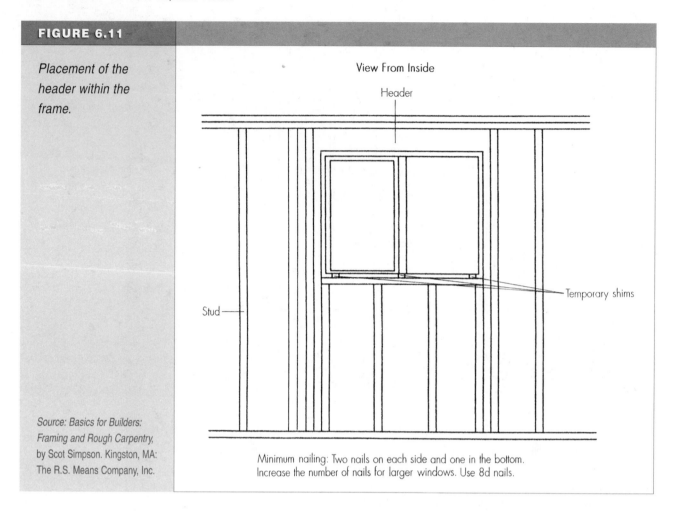

View From Inside

Header

Temporary shims

Stud

Minimum nailing: Two nails on each side and one in the bottom. Increase the number of nails for larger windows. Use 8d nails.

Source: Basics for Builders: Framing and Rough Carpentry, by Scot Simpson. Kingston, MA: The R.S. Means Company, Inc.

over the door and window openings. When a header spans more than five feet, double-length studs are constructed on either side of the header. Figure 6.11 illustrates the placement of the header within the frame.

The construction of the exterior walls follows a similar pattern. In the corners, the top plate on one wall overlaps the top plate of the next and the walls are nailed together to bind the corner. Then, the interior walls fit into the top plates of the exterior walls.

Inspecting the Wall Framing

Wall framing errors left uncorrected during the construction process convert to hard-to-fix problems later. If the walls are not plumb or the rooms are not square, for example, not only do the building load paths shift but the dimensions change too. A **plumb** wall refers to *a position or measurement that is truly and exactly vertical, 90 degrees from a level surface.* Sheet goods applied to the wall's interior or exterior may have unsightly, hard-to-hide joints and corners and may require time-consuming trimming and other repairs.

It is not a simple matter for the home inspector to check the integrity of the wall framing. Wall framing is generally covered by exterior framing. It may be visible, however, in some areas of the structure such as the basement and the garage. Evidence gleaned from other structural components can provide clues as to the wall framing's integrity. If bulges are observed on the walls, for instance, there could be a problem with the studs. Water may have penetrated the stud, most probably during construction, and caused the stud to warp. Under no circumstances should the inspector dismantle the wallboard to further examine a suspected problem with the studs.

Framing Types

The type of framing described in the preceding section is known as **platform framing** because *the structure's framing rests on a subfloor platform.* Platform framing is the most common type of framing used in residential construction.

An alternative to platform framing is **balloon framing.** This method *uses a single system of wall studs that run from the foundation through the first and second floors to the ceiling support.* This method is rarely used in residential construction.

A third type of framing is **post-and-beam framing.** These *members are much larger than ordinary studs and may be 4 or 6 inches square. The larger posts are placed several feet apart instead of 16 or 24 inches on center.* Like balloon framing, this type of framing is seldom used in residential construction. Figure 6.12 illustrates framing types.

Frame types. **FIGURE 6.12**

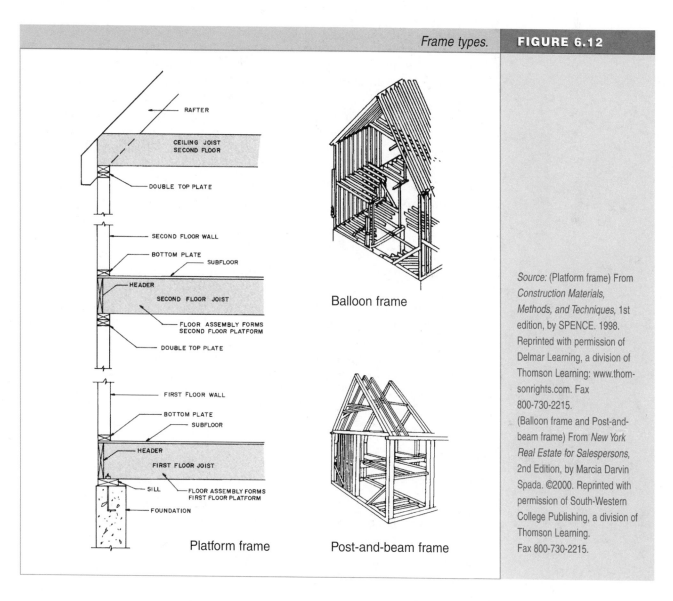

Balloon frame

Platform frame

Post-and-beam frame

Source: (Platform frame) From *Construction Materials, Methods, and Techniques,* 1st edition, by SPENCE. 1998. Reprinted with permission of Delmar Learning, a division of Thomson Learning: www.thomsonrights.com. Fax 800-730-2215.
(Balloon frame and Post-and-beam frame) From *New York Real Estate for Salespersons,* 2nd Edition, by Marcia Darvin Spada. ©2000. Reprinted with permission of South-Western College Publishing, a division of Thomson Learning. Fax 800-730-2215.

FIGURE 6.13

Types of windows.

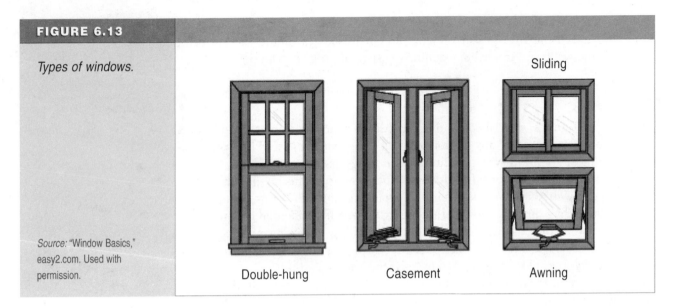

Sliding

Double-hung   Casement   Awning

Source: "Window Basics," easy2.com. Used with permission.

WINDOWS

The exterior of the window is surrounded by trim composed of wood, vinyl, or aluminum. Building paper around the window and flashing along the window's top and bottom serve as weatherproofing.

Most windows fall into four basic types: double-hung, casement, sliding, and awning. What differs from one window type to another is how the sash moves to open the window. Another window type seen more commonly on porches or in older homes is the jalousie window. Hopper windows are commonly used for basements. In some cases, the sash may be stationary such as with **fixed-pane windows** *that do not open or close* including the picture window and variations of the bay window. Figure 6.13 illustrates and describes window types.

The element common to all of the window types is the sash. A **sash** *is the frame that surrounds and secures the glass.* The sash can be made of wood, metal, or plastic. The sashes are built from four frame components: *top and bottom pieces are called* **rails** and *the sides are called* **stiles**. In many cases, a window sash is divided into smaller windows. The *dividers are called* **muntins**. Some windows have fake muntins that simply snap in. *The material that surrounds the window on the inside is known as the* **casing**. Figure 6.14 shows the components of a window.

The material inside the pane is known as **glazing**. Generally, a window is glazed with *glass that may be one or more layers, known as a* **light**. Glass windows may have a single layer or two or more layers. These layers form an airtight seal. Should the seal break, through normal wear and tear or because the window is cracked or broken, moisture can enter between the layers, forming condensation.

Inspecting the Windows

The following items are checked during the window inspection:

- The operability of the windows. (Double-hung windows should be checked to see if the top and bottom sashes are operable.)
- Sash cords and sash weights in older windows. Often the cords are frayed and broken, rendering the window inoperable. Newer windows are spring operated, eliminating the cords and weights.

FIGURE 6.14

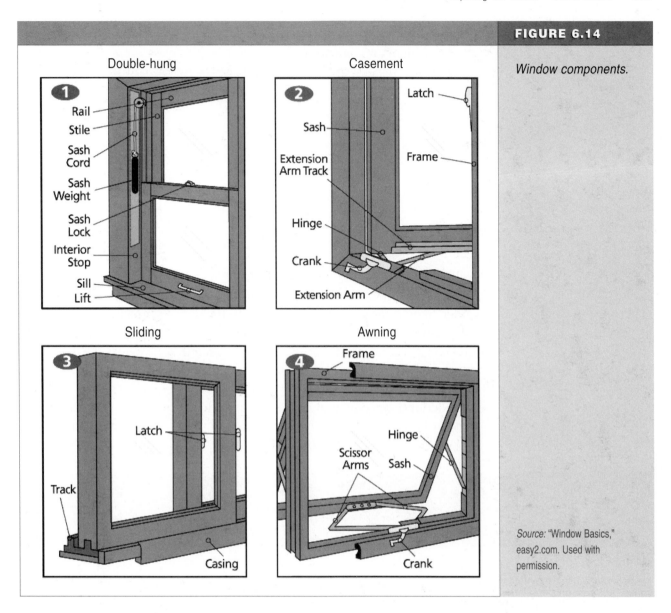

Window components.

Source: "Window Basics," easy2.com. Used with permission.

- Wood rot around window casings. **Wood rot** *is caused by a type of fungus that destroys wood. It is as damaging as termite or other insect infestation.* Instead of flashing, a wood molding may be installed along the top of the window to catch the water. This molding is subject to wood rot, which allows water to penetrate through to the exterior wall.

- The presence and condition of caulking should be noted where the window trim meets the siding and between all trim joints. Observe any peeling or chipped paint.

- The window's framing and sash should be free of peeling and cracking paint. Check for wood rot.

- Broken glazing material should be noted, as should multiple light windows with a broken seal. These windows should be replaced. All windows should have tempered safety glass.

- The basement windows should be caulked around the perimeter to prevent water penetration. Note any breakage, missing caulking, and water seepage.

DOORS

Exterior doors are constructed of wood, metal, glass, or a combination of these materials. According to building codes, in new construction, the door from the garage into the house must be fire resistant. Figure 6.15 depicts a door's components.

Inspecting the Doors

Check the condition of the door's **threshold**—*the area on the ground in front of the door that keeps rain and snow from entering the structure.* The threshold is susceptible to normal wear and tear and wood rot. Inspectors should open and close all exterior doors. Examine the following:

- condition of caulking and paint
- whether or not the hinges are properly affixed
- whether the door shuts firmly and tightly and that the locks are in working order. Should the door not shut properly, the door itself may be warped or the headers above the door are sagging due to water penetration.
- sliding glass doors should be opened and closed to see whether the door stays in its tracks. A malfunctioning sliding door may indicate that the door frame is warped or that the components that slide the door are broken or missing.
- all exterior doors containing glass must use tempered safety glass that shatters into small pieces, not dangerous large chunks. Newer doors with glass have engraved safety insignias in the corner.

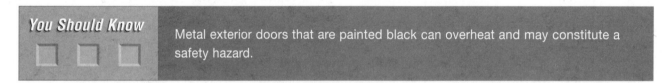

You Should Know

Metal exterior doors that are painted black can overheat and may constitute a safety hazard.

FIGURE 6.15

Components of a door.

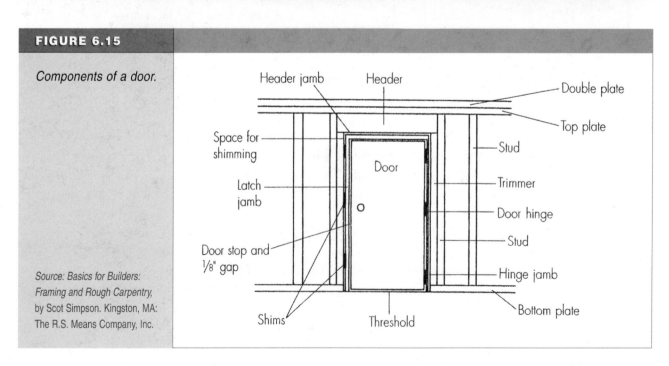

Source: Basics for Builders: Framing and Rough Carpentry, by Scot Simpson. Kingston, MA: The R.S. Means Company, Inc.

TRIM

Trim is found throughout the exterior of the structure: around doors, windows, corners, and the bottom of the siding. Other decoration to the siding may include shutters, window boxes, and mailboxes. Trim protects the edges of the siding and prevents water, insects, and debris from penetrating between the siding and the sheathing.

Inspecting the Trim

Inspect trim made of wood for wood rot, peeling paint, missing caulking between seams and joints, warping, and splitting. Use an awl or screwdriver to prod and poke the wood slightly to assess damage. If a section of trim looks rotted or warped, check behind the trim to assess any damage to the siding.

> **You Should Know**
>
> Vinyl or aluminum trim is much less problematic than wood trim. The main item to inspect with these materials is whether pieces of trim are missing or loose.

CEILING AND ROOF FRAMING

The ceiling joists rest on the top plate of the wall. These joists are placed directly over the vertical studs for maximum bearing strength. The joists span the structure between the outer walls. In traditional framing, these joists are usually 2 × 8s, and the inner walls help bear the load of the roof. With the contemporary use of **roof truss systems**, *the truss carries the load-bearing function to the outer walls.* Because a roof truss is made up of a number of smaller members (usually 2 × 4s), the attic space is almost completely lost. Trusses are tied to the walls with small metal plates. Figure 6.16 shows the roof truss system.

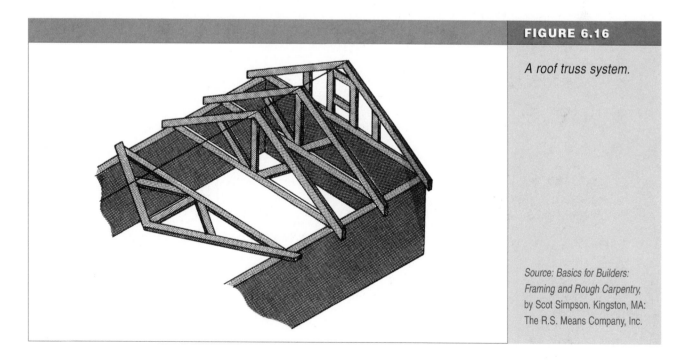

FIGURE 6.16

A roof truss system.

Source: Basics for Builders: Framing and Rough Carpentry, by Scot Simpson. Kingston, MA: The R.S. Means Company, Inc.

> ### You Should Know
> ### Roof Truss
> ### System
>
> A roof truss system has many advantages. It is very strong and because it is built from only 2 × 4 lengths of lumber, it is generally less expensive than a traditionally built roof. Truss systems also allow the builder more freedom to build a custom-shaped roof at a lower cost. Moreover, a truss can span a large distance. It transmits the load of the roof to the exterior walls. Because the interior walls are not load bearing, they can be easily moved later.

> ### Putting It to Work
>
> The roof truss system, once installed, should not be altered. An alteration to any of the joists compromises the integrity of the design and the load-bearing capacity of the trusses.

The **ridge beam** *is the highest part of the framing and forms the apex, or top line, of the roof.* **Rafters** *are the long wooden members that are fastened to the ends of the ceiling joists and form the gables of the roof.* Rafters are usually 2 × 6s or 2 × 8s. The rafters are fastened to the ridge at the peak of the gable. Figure 6.17 explains roof framing terms. Because most homes today are built with trusses, the ridge beam is eliminated.

Characteristics to look for when identifying the roof style include roof shape, or type, which includes the pitch. The **pitch** *is the slope of the roof.* Construction technique, style, and customized forms are other identifying factors. The roof is one of the most easily identifiable systems of a house and often serves as a general description of the entire structure. In contemporary residential construction, two varieties of roof styles are common: the traditional gable roof and the hip roof. Figure 6.18 is an illustration of these two types and other common roof types.

The roof should extend at least six inches beyond the exterior of the structure. Common construction practices use a 12-inch overhang on the front and

FIGURE 6.17

Roof framing terms.

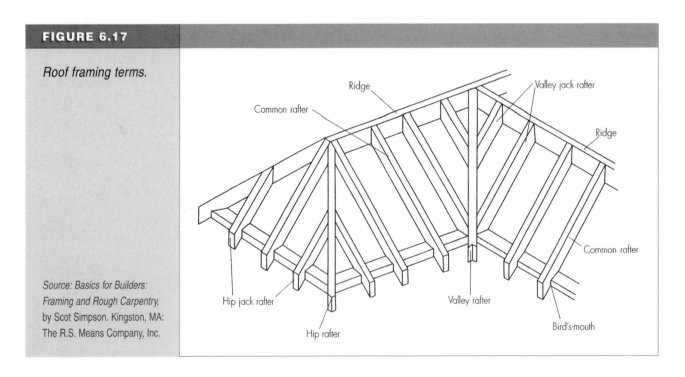

Source: *Basics for Builders: Framing and Rough Carpentry,* by Scot Simpson. Kingston, MA: The R.S. Means Company, Inc.

FIGURE 6.18

Common roof types.

Source: From *New York Real Estate for Salespersons,* 2nd Edition, by Marcia Darvin Spada. ©2000. Reprinted with permission of South-Western College Publishing, a division of Thomson Learning. Fax 800-730-2215.

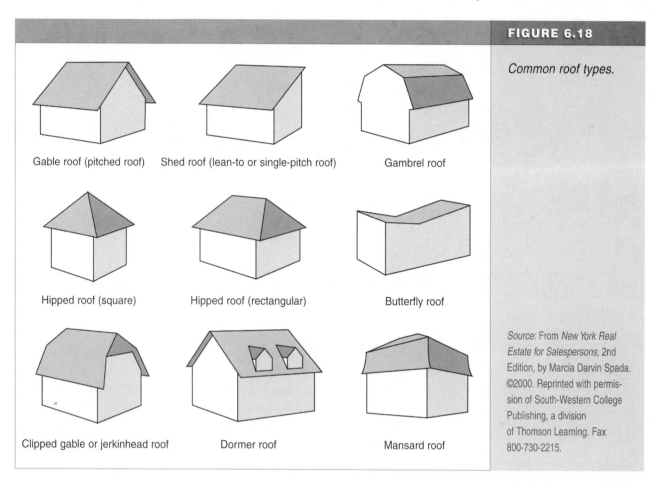

Gable roof (pitched roof)   Shed roof (lean-to or single-pitch roof)   Gambrel roof

Hipped roof (square)   Hipped roof (rectangular)   Butterfly roof

Clipped gable or jerkinhead roof   Dormer roof   Mansard roof

rear, with a 6-inch overhang on the side. These overhangs, which are part of a sloped roof, are known as the eaves. An **eave** *is the lowest part of the roof that projects beyond the walls of the structure. The eave trim is known as the* **cornice**. The larger the overhang, the more protection from sun and rain for the exterior walls, windows, and doors.

Flashing

The proper construction of roof junctions is vital to ensure weather tightness. Metal valleys and flashing are used to help the shingles or shakes (discussed later) keep the structure sound and dry. Most roof leaks occur where water is channeled off the roof or where the roof abuts a vertical wall or chimney. To prevent leaking, flashing strips are installed near the edge of the eave, near other corners of the roof, around the base of the chimney and other structural members that protrude through the roof, and at all intersecting angles. **Flashing** *is a metallic material that is used in certain areas of the roof and walls to prevent water from seeping into the structure.* Metal flashing should be no less than 26-gauge galvanized steel or its equivalent and should be painted on both sides with metal or bituminous paint. Figure 6.19 illustrates flashing details for typical roof projections and Figure 6.20 depicts typical chimney flashing.

Step flashing extends under the shingles or shakes and up the vertical surface. It is covered by *a second layer of flashing called* **counterflashing**. Figure 6.21 shows roof valley flashing details.

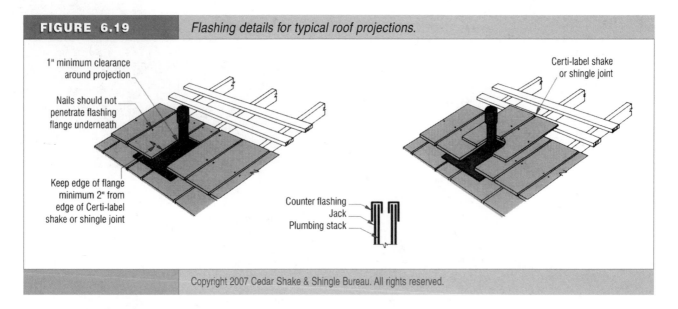

FIGURE 6.19   *Flashing details for typical roof projections.*

1" minimum clearance around projection

Nails should not penetrate flashing flange underneath

Keep edge of flange minimum 2" from edge of Certi-label shake or shingle joint

Certi-label shake or shingle joint

Counter flashing
Jack
Plumbing stack

Soffit, Fascia, and Frieze Board

The overhang or eave is made up of three components: the soffit, the fascia, and the frieze board. The **soffit** *is the area under the roof extension.* It is made of wood, aluminum, or vinyl, depending on the type of siding. The soffit is perforated or has vents so that air can flow through the ridge vents to ventilate the attic.

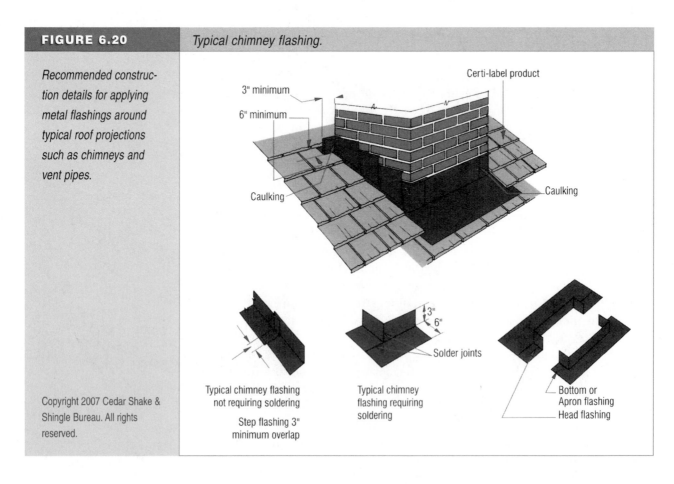

FIGURE 6.20   *Typical chimney flashing.*

Recommended construction details for applying metal flashings around typical roof projections such as chimneys and vent pipes.

Certi-label product

3" minimum

6" minimum

Caulking

Caulking

Typical chimney flashing not requiring soldering

Step flashing 3" minimum overlap

Typical chimney flashing requiring soldering

3"
6"
Solder joints

Bottom or Apron flashing
Head flashing

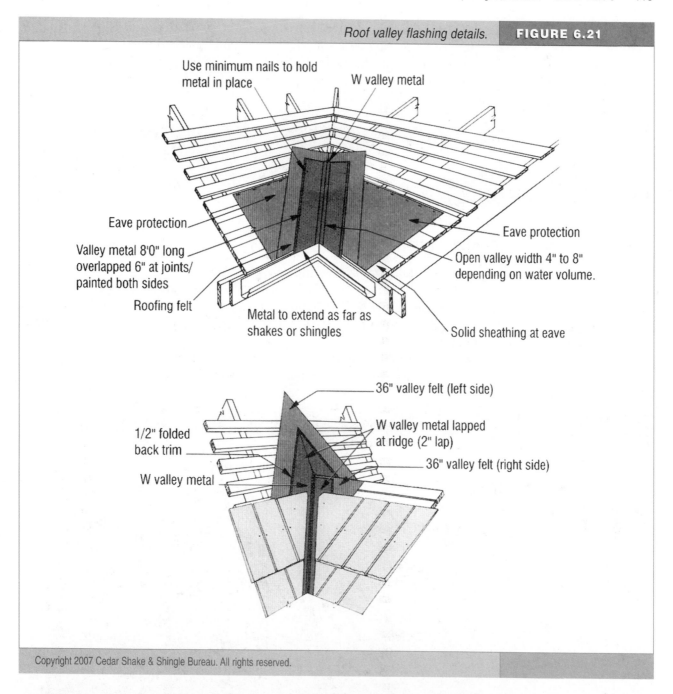

Roof valley flashing details. **FIGURE 6.21**

Use minimum nails to hold metal in place

W valley metal

Eave protection

Valley metal 8'0" long overlapped 6" at joints/ painted both sides

Roofing felt

Metal to extend as far as shakes or shingles

Eave protection

Open valley width 4" to 8" depending on water volume.

Solid sheathing at eave

36" valley felt (left side)

1/2" folded back trim

W valley metal lapped at ridge (2" lap)

W valley metal

36" valley felt (right side)

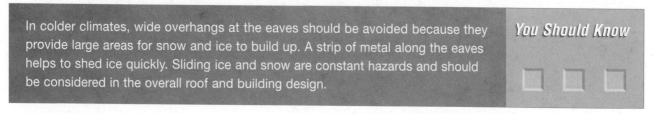

In colder climates, wide overhangs at the eaves should be avoided because they provide large areas for snow and ice to build up. A strip of metal along the eaves helps to shed ice quickly. Sliding ice and snow are constant hazards and should be considered in the overall roof and building design.

You Should Know

The area of material facing the outer edge of the soffit is called the **fascia**. The fascia boards are perpendicular to the soffit. Fascia wood may be capped with a sheet of painted aluminum that is bent into shape on the site. The fascia is typically a 1 × 6 or a 1 × 8. If guttering is installed on the roof, it is fastened to the fascia. The third component of the overhang is the frieze board. This is a wooden member (usually a 2 × 4, 2 × 6, or 2 × 8) that is fastened directly under the soffit, against the top of the wall. The purpose of the frieze board is both decorative and functional. The **frieze board** *prevents wind and moisture from penetrating the junction of the soffit and sheathing.*

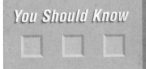

You Should Know   Intersecting roof surfaces at hips and ridges (see Figure 6.22) should be capped to ensure a weather-tight joint. Hip and ridge units, made on-site or at the factory, may be used, but must have alternate overlaps and concealed nailing.

Roofing Materials

A properly installed roof covering can last 20 or more years depending on the type. The roof decking is covered with a variety of materials. Roofing materials must be strong enough to withstand the assault of intense weather conditions. The sun's heat elevates rooftop temperatures 50 to 75 degrees Fahrenheit above ambient temperature. Ultraviolet radiation accelerates the aging of the asphalt shingle layers and other roof material. Moisture, pollution, snow loads, ice, tree limbs, and seismic shock also stress roofing materials. Thermal shocks to the roof in the form

FIGURE 6.22   *Intersecting roof surfaces at hips and ridges.*

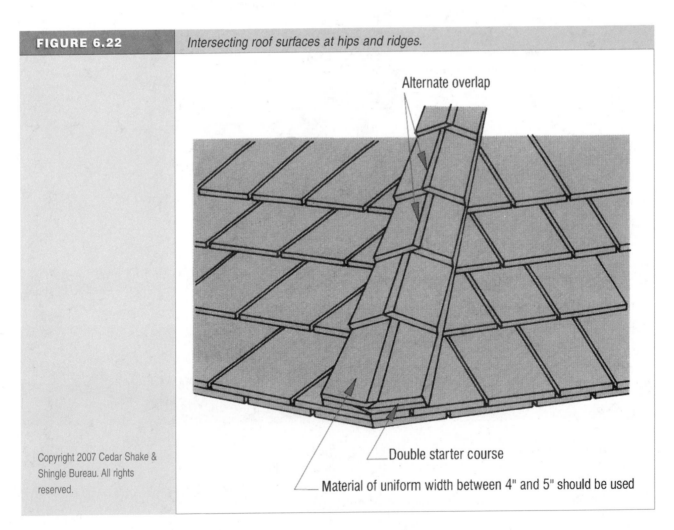

of intense heat and then extreme cold cause the roof deck to expand and contract, placing tremendous stress on roof coverings. Improper attic ventilation is also a contributing factor to roof deterioration and is discussed in Chapter 7.

Shingles

Once the structural skeleton of the roof system is in place, it is covered with either plywood or particleboard decking. On top of this, roofing felt paper (tar paper) is applied to aid weatherproofing. Commonly used weights for residential housing are the 15 and 30 underlayments. Thirty-weight felt was commonly used with older organic asphalt shingles. Today, lighter and thinner fiberglass composite shingles are generally combined with 15-weight felt.

Fiberglass composite and asphalt shingles are the most common roof coverings. There are two basic types of asphalt shingles. Each consists of a core material that is coated with asphalt and then covered with granules. The core, or base material, may be either fiberglass mat or organic felt. Shingles made of each type of base material possess certain characteristics that recommend them for particular applications.

The purpose of the shingle is to provide the waterproofing integrity for the roof. Asphalt is made from a petroleum derivative and contains oils that provide ductility and pliability. Over time, these oils rise to the surface of the shingle, where they are washed away by rainwater. The intense heat of the roof combined with the shedding of the oil oxidizes or hardens the asphalt over time. Asphalt shingles are coated with colored ceramic-coated mineral granules to protect the asphalt from the sun's ultraviolet rays.

Shingles are available in three types (see Figure 6.23). The three-tab shingle is the industry standard and derives its name because there are three "tabs" on each shingle. The shingles are typically 3 feet long, are installed with a 5 1/2-inch exposure, and weigh approximately 240 pounds per 100 square feet. Three-tab shingles are available in a wide range of colors and should last 25 to 30 years.

The applique shingle is a three-tab shingle with a second layer of asphalt and granules applied. This unreinforced applique is a decorative enhancement that serves no function other than to create a look of dimensionality. Laminated shingles differ from the applique variety in that two or more reinforced shingles are bonded together using a special laminating asphalt. The laminated shingle has a

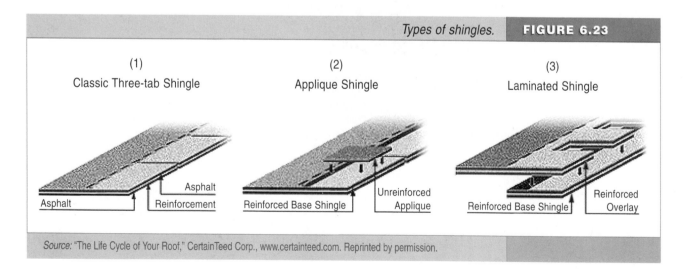

Types of shingles. **FIGURE 6.23**

(1)
Classic Three-tab Shingle

(2)
Applique Shingle

(3)
Laminated Shingle

Asphalt

Asphalt
Reinforcement

Reinforced Base Shingle

Unreinforced
Applique

Reinforced Base Shingle

Reinforced
Overlay

Source: "The Life Cycle of Your Roof," CertainTeed Corp., www.certainteed.com. Reprinted by permission.

more textured appearance and provides added protection. Also referred to as an architectural or dimensional asphalt shingle, they are typically 3 feet long, are installed with a 5 1/2-inch exposure, and weigh approximately 250–365 pounds per 100 square feet. Available in a wide range of colors and with manufacturer warranties of up to 40 years, laminate shingles are currently the most popular for residential roofing.

Wood Shingles and Shakes

Although shingles are made from a variety of materials, shakes are made from wood. Most wood shingles and shakes are made from cedar. The material is durable, wind resistant, and has good thermal and acoustical properties. Cedar shakes and shingles used in the southeastern United States with a climate index of 65 degrees or greater should be pressure treated. Fungicidal chemicals may also be added to inhibit moss, fungus, and mildew. Cedar shakes and shingles can last 30 years or more. Cedar shingles are thinner than shakes and produce a crisp uniform appearance. Cedar shingles are also used as siding.

You Should Know  Shingles and shakes are applied over spaced sheathing or roof plank (see Figure 6.24). Wood shingles are applied over 1 × 4 board. Spaced sheathing is usually 1 × 4 or 1 × 6 softwood board. Solid sheathing is acceptable and may be required in seismic regions and under treated shakes and shingles. Figure 6.25 illustrates the different dimensions of cedar shakes.

FIGURE 6.24   *Wood shingles applied over 1" × 4" boards.*

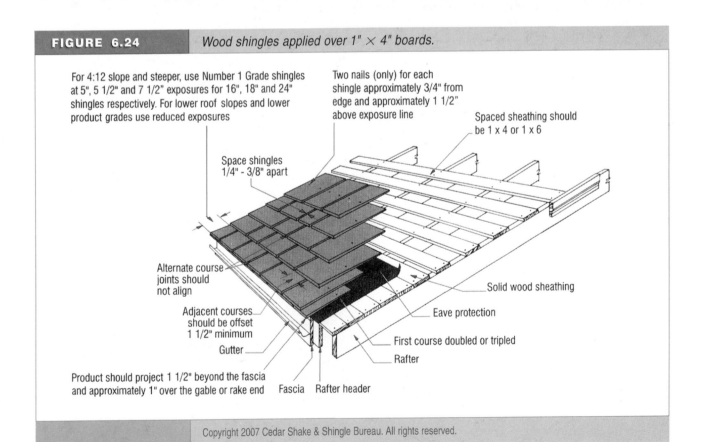

For 4:12 slope and steeper, use Number 1 Grade shingles at 5", 5 1/2" and 7 1/2" exposures for 16", 18" and 24" shingles respectively. For lower roof slopes and lower product grades use reduced exposures

Two nails (only) for each shingle approximately 3/4" from edge and approximately 1 1/2" above exposure line

Spaced sheathing should be 1 x 4 or 1 x 6

Space shingles 1/4" - 3/8" apart

Alternate course joints should not align

Adjacent courses should be offset 1 1/2" minimum

Gutter

Product should project 1 1/2" beyond the fascia and approximately 1" over the gable or rake end

Fascia

Rafter header

Solid wood sheathing

Eave protection

First course doubled or tripled

Rafter

Different dimensions of cedar shakes. **FIGURE 6.25**

Hand–Split and Re–Sawn Shakes

Recommended Use–For walls and roofs 4:12 pitch and steeper where a high quality appearance and performance are desired.

Description–Lengths 18-inch, thickness 1/2" (medium) and 3/4" (heavy) minimums; length 24-inch, thickness 3/8", 1/2" (medium) and 3/4" (heavy) minimums. Width 4" minimum and 14" maximum. Clear heartwood; 20% maximum flat grain.

Roof Exposure– 18-inch shakes- 7 1/2" maximum; 24-inch medium and heavy shakes- 10" maximum; 24-inch (3/8") shakes-7 1/2" maximum (5" per UBC).

Wall Exposure–Single course: 8 1/2" for 18-inch shake; 11 1/2 " for 24- inch shake. Double course: 14" for 18-inch shake; 18" for 24-inch shake.

Taper Sawn Cedar Shakes

Description–Lengths 18-inch, 24-inch; width 4" minimum, 14" maximum; thickness 5/8" nominal (5/8", 3/4", 7/8", yet uniform in each bundle or pallet).

Roof Exposure–10" for 24-inch shake; 7 1/2" for 18-inch shake.

Wall Exposure–Single course: 11 1/2" for 24-inch shake; 8 1/2" for 18-inch shake.
Double course: 18" for 24-inch shake: 14" for 18-inch shake.

Recommended Use–For walls or roofs on 4:12 pitch and steeper where a high quality, durable and uniform appearance is desired.

Starter-finish Course–Length 15-inch. For use on the underlying starter course at eave lines and for the final course at ridges where trimming would otherwise be necessary and full-length are not needed.

Slate

Slate is a natural stone, impermeable to water and resistant to freeze–thaw cycles. Slate roofs can last more than 75 years. Pieces of slate are available in various lengths, colors, and widths; its thickness generally ranges from 3/16-inch to 1 1/2-inches. Slate roofs can be installed with uniform or graduated lengths and thicknesses for variation. Figure 6.26 illustrates a slate roof.

Tile

Clay tile styles, Spanish, French, and flat, are found in a variety of colors and can last in excess of 75 years. Concrete tile is very similar to clay tile in style; however, concrete tile weighs less and is less expensive. Concrete tiles can last up to 50

FIGURE 6.26

A slate roof.

Source: Anthony D'Agostino, Atlantic Inspection Service, Latham, New York.

years. Certain concrete tiles hold up well in cold weather climates, while others are better suited for areas of the country without a freeze–thaw cycle.

Flat Roofs

A number of materials are used to protect the flat roof including bitumen, copper, and galvanized steel.

Bitumen roofing. Often, flat roofs are covered with roll roofing. The roofing material is manufactured and packed in a roll and nailed to the roof deck. Sometimes rolled roof is used as an underlayment. Bitumen material, such as asphalt or coal tar, is modified with either a granular coating to protect it from foot traffic or an aluminum coating to protect against the harsh sun. The advantage of modified bitumen is that it is relatively easy to repair and maintain.

Copper. Copper is used as a flat roofing material and as roofing for bay windows, dormers, and cupola tops. Shingles, flashing, and chimney caps are also made from copper.

Galvanized steel. More affordable than copper, galvanized steel is widely used for flashing and chimney caps. It is also used for standing- and flat-seam roofs. The use of prefinished galvanized steel eliminates the need for paint and ensures that the sheet metal roof does not rust. Often seen in commercial applications, standing-seam galvanized steel roofing is becoming popular once again in the residential market.

Inspecting the Roof

Damage to the roof is detected by examining the exterior surface and the attic. The attic inspection is discussed more fully in Chapter 7. Storm damage, damage from tree branches falling onto the roof, and aging all contribute to roof deterioration. Inspectors should look for the following:

FIGURE 6.27

Asphalt shingles curled around the edges.

This illustration depicts shingles that have deteriorated and curled due to normal wear and tear.

Source: Anthony D'Agostino, Atlantic Inspection Service, Latham, New York.

- loose or missing shingles
- stains on the interior of attic walls and ceilings
- shingles curled around the edges (see Figure 6.27)
- shingles that are blistered, cracked, stained, or buckled (see Figures 6.28 and 6.29)
- gutters filled with granules from the shingles (small amounts are normal; large amounts could mean that the shingles are near the end of their useful

FIGURE 6.28

Problems seen as shingles age.

Blisters:
During the course of natural weathering, small bubble-like raised areas known as blisters may appear on the surface of the shingles. The blisters may be small and pea-sized or as large as a quarter. The blisters may open, exposing the asphalt, or closed. Blisters frequently result when minimum ventilation requirements are not met.

Blisters

Staining:
Over a period of time, shingles may develop dark brown or black streaks that are sometimes mistaken for soot, dirt, moss or tree droppings. In actuality, this discoloration may be caused by algae growth. Although most roofing systems are susceptible to algae discoloration, it is not readily visible on white or light-colored shingles.

Staining

Surface Cracking:
Another manifestation of the normal aging process may be the development of surface cracks. For example, as the flexibilizing oils of the asphalt are depleted due to heat, the shingle becomes more brittle, to the point where surface cracking may appear. The stresses created by thermal shock and the movement of the roof deck also increase the likelihood of surface cracking.

Applique Surface Cracking

Curling:
As the asphalt hardens over time, the granules that were once securely embedded begin to break away. Also, as this hardening advances, the asphalt layers begin to shrink. As the asphalt layer shrinks, it is being countered by the shingle reinforcement, which resists shrinking. The top and bottom coatings shrink and the reinforcement remains stable. As a result, the edges of the shingle may begin to curl over time.

Curling

Source: "The Life Cycle of Your Roof," CertainTeed Corp., www.certainteed.com. Reprinted with permission.

FIGURE 6.29   *Damaged wood shingles.*

Wood shingles are warped and are detaching from the roof. Deck moss and other material is growing through them.

Source: Anthony D'Agostino, Atlantic Inspection Service, Latham, New York.

life). Granule loss exposes the asphalt underneath to ultraviolet rays that can compromise the material.

■ worn or missing roof flashings. If the flashing around the chimney is on the downslope of the roof, it should have a cricket to prevent snow and ice buildup. The **cricket** *is composed of metal flashing and keeps snow and water from building up against the chimney* (see Figure 6.30).

■ roof deck bowing, expansion, movement, and waviness

■ buckling of the shingles as a result of deck movement

■ stressing, splitting, and rotting of wood shakes and shingles

FIGURE 6.30

A roof cricket.

Source: Anthony D'Agostino, Atlantic Inspection Service, Latham, New York.

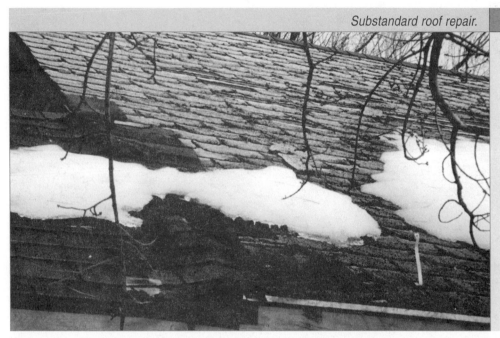

Substandard roof repair.

FIGURE 6.31

In this illustration, the home owner built an addition to the structure and overlapped the sections of the roof. Because of this, water is penetrating through the shingles to the inside wall of the structure.

Source: Anthony D'Agostino, Atlantic Inspection Service, Latham, New York.

- proper penetration of and adequate flashing around all vents that penetrate the roof
- clogged roof drains on flat roofs
- missing or cracked pieces of slate
- missing or cracked pieces of tile
- substandard roof repair (see Figure 6.31).

The condition of the roof can also be observed from the attic. Check the following items:

- framing rafters and roof decking for warping, buckling, bowing, cracking, water stains, and wood rot (see Figure 6.32)
- leakage around the chimney that penetrates through to the roof decking
- other water stains such as around vent pipes
- damage to the integrity of the roof truss system

When possible, find out from the property owner when the roof and roofing material was installed. Put this date in your home inspection report and cite the source of the information.

Putting It to Work

ROOF PROJECTION COMPONENTS

Chimneys

The chimney works with the stove or fireplace in a circular pattern. The chimney should extend at least 3 feet above the highest point where it passes through the roof and at least 2 feet higher than any portion of the building within 10 feet. If the roof is flat, the chimney should be at least 3 feet above the roof.

FIGURE 6.32   *Problems with a roof rafter.*

The crack over the doorway indicates a problem with the roof system. In this case, an old roof that covered a porch was incorrectly attached to newer roof decking. The roof rafters are missing where the old roof meets the new, causing movement of the rafter system. This subsequently compromised the roof decking.

Source: Anthony D'Agostino, Atlantic Inspection Service, Latham, New York.

Heat in the chimney causes a draft that pulls in combustion air and makes the fire burn hotter. When there is heat and fuel in the air, oxygen is needed to complete the reaction. This in turn delivers more heat to the chimney and creates more draft. An insulated chimney creates more draft with less heat because the insulation keeps the exhaust hot until it is expelled outside. In the winter, a well-designed and properly installed chimney makes some draft and flows some air upward even when no fire is burning.

In cold weather regions, chimneys should be located at the ridge or gable ends of the roof away from possible snow pressure. Chimneys and other wood-burning appliances are a serious fire hazard if not properly installed and maintained.

Masonry Chimneys

A masonry chimney should rest on its own foundation below the frost line. When chimney fires occur in masonry chimneys—whether the flues are an older, unlined, type or are tile lined to meet current safety codes—the high temperatures at which they burn (around 2,000 degrees Fahrenheit) can "melt" mortar, crack tiles, cause liners to collapse, and damage the outer masonry material. When tiles crack and mortar is displaced, a pathway is created for flames to reach the structure's combustible wood frame. Heat can conduct through a perfectly sound chimney to ignite nearby combustibles.

Prefabricated, Factory-Built, Metal Chimneys

Factory-built metal chimneys that are designed to vent wood-burning stoves or prefabricated metal fireplaces must pass special tests established by Underwriters Laboratories (UL®). Under chimney fire conditions, damage to these systems still may occur, usually in the form of buckled or warped seams and joints on the inner liner. When prefabricated, factory-built metal chimneys are damaged by a chimney fire, they must be replaced. When possible, look for signs of a chimney fire. Some of the signs include:

- "puffy" creosote with rainbow-colored streaks that has expanded beyond the creosote's normal form. **Creosote** *is a black tar-like substance that builds up inside the chimney through normal use.*
- warped damper, metal smoke chamber, connector pipe, or factory-built metal chimney
- cracked or collapsed flue tiles, or tiles with large chunks missing
- discolored and distorted rain cap
- creosote flakes and pieces found on the roof or ground
- roofing material damaged from hot creosote
- cracks in exterior masonry
- evidence of smoke escaping through masonry mortar joints or tile liners

Proper chimney installation includes the following:

- the chimney is a good distance away from wood framing
- metal flues have a one-inch clearance all the way around
- metal chimneys are triple wall
- thermal insulation is not be too close to the chimney
- the stovepipe or chimney is placed through the ceiling or wall so as not to cause ignition of the wood framing

Structural damage to metal prefabricated chimneys is caused by the inner liners corroding, rusting, buckling, or collapsing, or by the seam separating. The damage results from a fire that is too hot, especially in high-efficiency stoves and fireplace inserts, or from a creosote fire. Wood framing can be exposed to excessive temperatures or toxic gases can leak to the interior of the home.

Structural damage in masonry chimneys is evidenced by cracks in and separation of the tile inner liner and the surrounding bricks or blocks. This is caused by the ignition of creosote that has built up inside the chimney. Many older chimneys do not have a tile liner. If the chimney does not have a liner, the addition of a properly installed liner is advisable.

Other items to look at during a chimney inspection are:

- whether the chimney is cracked
- whether the metal rain cap in securely in place
- whether a metal spark arrester is installed on top of the chimney to keep sparks from setting the house on fire
- whether the chimney is securely fastened to the roof

Skylights

Skylights have enjoyed great popularity over the last 20 years and are commonly found in residential structures. Skylights provide only light or both light and ventilation. They are either domed or flat and are made of glass or plastic in aluminum frames.

Inspecting the Skylights

The primary problem with skylights is water leakage around the perimeter. Evidence of leakage is most easily observed on the interior of the structure in the form of wet or stained spots. Another component to check is the skylight frame—it should be free of rust or corrosion. The skylight frame is best observed from the roof when possible.

Vent Stacks

Vent stacks typically originate from the bathroom or kitchen of the house and allow gases to escape from the structure through the roof. Plumbing vent stacks also allow air into the system so that the water drains properly (more fully discussed in Chapter 8).

Inspecting the Vent Stacks

Older houses may have vent stacks or pipes that are located on the perimeter of the structure and go up past the roofline. This may cause a problem because the pipe is subject to frost damage that can block the gases from escaping. Pipes that end at or near a window are also problematic because gases can escape back into the structure. Roof vent stacks should be flashed like other roof penetrations. Asphalt cement is often used to seal joints. Figure 6.33 illustrates a problem with a vent pipe.

You Should Know   Plastic vent pipe extended through the roof may be dislodged by sliding snow.

| **FIGURE 6.33** | *Problem with a vent pipe's installation.* |

This illustrates a vent pipe for a bathroom exhaust fan. It is incorrectly installed through the roof vent and then directed upward to the roof.

Source: Anthony D'Agostino, Atlantic Inspection Service, Latham, New York.

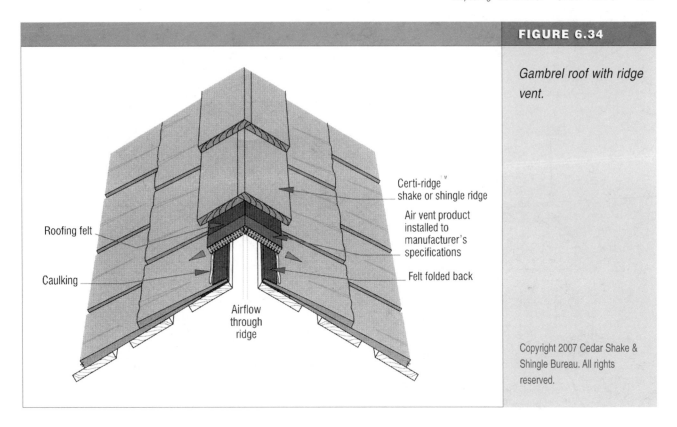

Copyright 2007 Cedar Shake & Shingle Bureau. All rights reserved.

FIGURE 6.34

Gambrel roof with ridge vent.

Roof Vents

Roof vents allow ventilation to the attic. All roof vents should be caulked at the joints.

Inspecting the Roof Vents

Evidence of leakage is observed on the roof deck or the attic's roof.

The ridge vent runs along the peak of any roof. In older homes, a triangular gable-end vent is typical. Ridge vents offer better circulation and prevent small animals from accessing the attic. Figure 6.34 illustrates a gambrel roof with ridge vent.

You Should Know

EXTERIOR COVERING

Once all framing members are in place, including the roof rafters, *a plywood covering called* **sheathing** *is placed over the exterior.* Oriented strand board (OSB board), also known as wafer board, is also used as sheathing. *Insulation materials,* either **house wrap** or **felt paper,** *are nailed over the sheathing.* A final covering is placed over the insulation, typically brick or siding. Siding can be wood, vinyl, or a metal, such as aluminum. Often a combination of materials, such as fieldstone, brick, or siding, is used. Some communities or subdivisions have regulations governing which exterior materials are used and home inspectors working with new construction should be aware of their existence. On the structure's interior walls, a drywall (Sheetrock) wallboard or plasterboard is used.

FIGURE 6.35   *A structure covered with vinyl siding.*

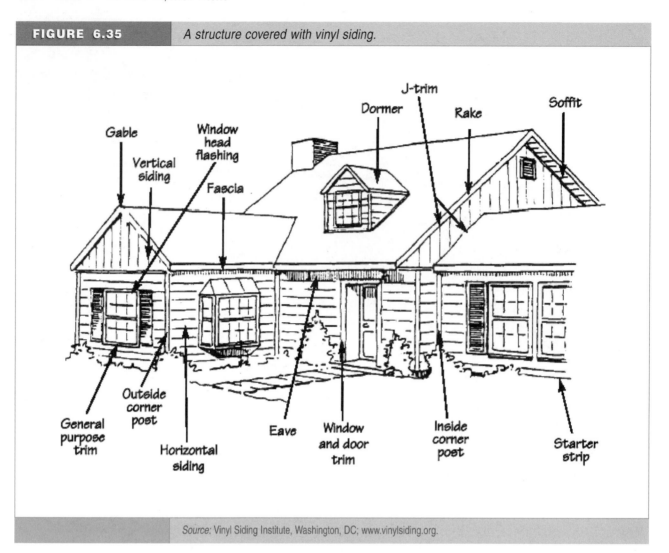

Source: Vinyl Siding Institute, Washington, DC; www.vinylsiding.org.

Aluminum and Vinyl Siding

Many houses use standard aluminum or vinyl siding. Figure 6.35 illustrates a structure covered with vinyl siding. Both of these products do not require much maintenance. The major problem with both types is that strips may become loose and detach from the exterior wall. Loose or missing siding allows water to work its way through the exterior wall to the interior frame.

Vinyl siding is made from thin, flexible sheets of plastic about two millimeters thick; it is precolored and bent into shape during manufacturing. The sheets are 12 feet long and about a foot high. Installation begins at the wall's bottom and the sheets interlock as they go up the wall. Vinyl siding can expand and contract 1/2-inch or more over a 12 1/2-foot length due to changes in temperature.

Vinyl and aluminum siding are installed with a number of accessory pieces (see Figure 6.36) to prevent water penetration. Before the siding can be hung, a number of accessories must be installed, including starter strips, corner posts, window flashing, trim, and J-channels over the rooflines. J-channels are used around windows and doors to receive the siding. Allowance should be made for expansion and contraction by leaving a 1/4-inch gap between the siding and all

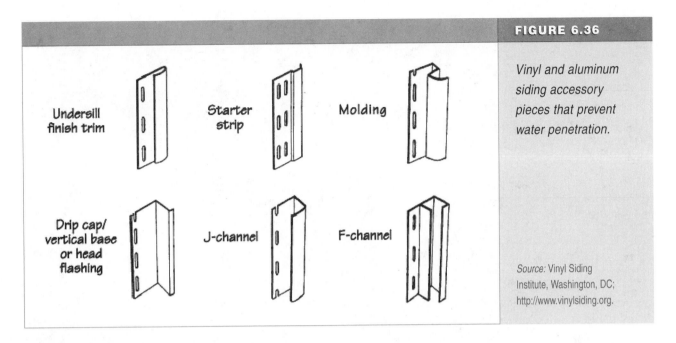

FIGURE 6.36

Vinyl and aluminum siding accessory pieces that prevent water penetration.

Source: Vinyl Siding Institute, Washington, DC; http://www.vinylsiding.org.

corner posts and channels (increase to 3/8-inch when installing in temperatures below 40 degrees Fahrenheit). Figure 6.37 illustrates siding components.

Inspecting Aluminum and Vinyl Siding

Carefully check the siding to be sure that all pieces are firmly secured and that none are missing.

Vinyl J-channels should not be in contact with roofing shingles because the shingles may transfer enough heat to the J-channels to cause their distortion.

You Should Know

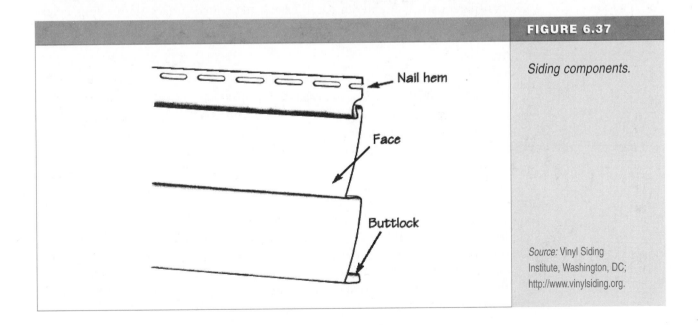

FIGURE 6.37

Siding components.

Source: Vinyl Siding Institute, Washington, DC; http://www.vinylsiding.org.

FIGURE 6.38   *Wood siding deteriorated by wood rot.*

This wood siding, composed of 4' x 8' sheets with vertical grooves, has succumbed to irreparable wood rot.

Source: Anthony D'Agostino, Atlantic Inspection Service, Latham, New York.

Wood Siding

As with aluminum and vinyl siding, wood can also become detached from the structure's exterior wall.

Inspecting Wood Siding

Because popping nails may indicate the expansion or contraction of the siding, inspectors should observe that the siding pieces are firmly secured. Wood has a tendency to warp or split over time. This condition allows water to penetrate the wood and the sheathing, causing wood rot. Figure 6.38 illustrates wood siding deteriorated by wood rot.

The only protection for exterior wood siding is a clear weatherproof varnish, transparent stain, or exterior paint. Check all painted surfaces for peeling, cracking, and bare spots.

Putting It to Work

Inspect the paint finish on a wood surface for peeling or bubbling. Should this be an issue, the problem could be that moisture is seeping from the interior through to the exterior wall because the vapor barrier that insulates the structure is not functioning properly or was never installed.

Brick

Brick veneer is attached directly to the sheathing with accordion-shaped metal brick ties. Behind the brick, there is a one-inch space for water to channel behind the brick and down through weepholes that are spaced evenly along the bottom course of the veneer. Weepholes are created by leaving out some mortar between the bricks. Flashing is affixed to the wall under the brick so that water does not penetrate the foundation wall.

Inspecting Brick Veneer

The main problem with brick veneer is that it can become loose and detach from the sheathing. Inspectors should examine for signs of **spalling** (i.e., *the crumbling of brick*) and for loose or cracked bricks. Another sign of trouble is mortar that is either cracked or crumbling. Always check for the presence of weepholes.

Stucco

Stucco is a cement plaster that is applied directly to concrete or masonry surfaces. When used in conjunction with wood-frame construction, it is applied over a metal lath in several coats. The first scratch coat is cement, the second is a bonding coat, and the third is a finish coat that either must be painted or contains pigment.

Inspecting Stucco

The main problem with stucco is that it tends to crack due to the expansion of the plywood sheathing underneath it. Check stucco for cracks because any size crack to stucco allows moisture to penetrate.

Exterior Insulating Finish System

Exterior insulating finish system (EIFS) is similar to stucco in appearance and is used as an exterior wall covering in many parts of the country. The use of EIFS has caused problems because water can seep into the wall cavities and become trapped there. Unlike brick or stucco, EIFS does *not* have an internal water barrier and the water has no way of draining out. This water seepage causes the wood-framing members to rot and decay. Mold, fungus, and mildew form inside the walls. In addition, the moisture causes unsightly streaking, and rust and calcium buildup. Eventually, the covering can pull away from the house frame.

EIFS allows water to penetrate through any exterior joint including windows and flashing. Some solutions include retrofitting certain sections of the wall and installing a drain pan under each windowsill to transport any water leaking through the window. In some cases, replacement of the material is needed.

Inspecting EIFS

Inspectors who examine EIFS use a special wall moisture meter to detect areas that contain moisture. However, in certain areas, inspectors must be certified to examine EIFS. Unless inspectors are very knowledgeable about EIFS, they may be subject to liability problems for inspecting this material.

IMPORTANT POINTS

1. Items included in an exterior inspection are the foundation and footings, including the crawl space; floor construction and wall framing, if visible; exterior wall covering, including flashing, siding, veneers, trim, paint, and caulking; exterior windows and doors and the corresponding framing and trim; the roof system, including the roof covering, drainage system,

flashing, skylights, and other roof penetrations; eaves, soffits, and fascias, if accessible from the ground; and chimneys, flues, dampers, and associated components.

2. Houses are generally built on a foundation that forms a basement, crawl space, or slab. The most important foundation building block is the footing. The footing is the concrete base below the frost line that supports the foundation of the structure. A slab-on-grade foundation is a concrete slab poured directly on the ground that eliminates the crawl space or basement.

3. The foundation inspection includes examining for cracks, bulges, or undue settlement.

4. Framing refers to the wooden skeleton of the structure. Wood framing members are wooden pieces of lumber with a nominal two-inch thickness.

5. Some floor framing problems may be observed in the basement. Floors that squeak are generally caused by plywood sheathing that is not correctly nailed and glued to the floor joists. Another possibility is that the sheathing is not properly butted together, causing an up and down movement of the floor. A sagging floor may be caused by a sagging main bearing beam.

6. Openings in the wall for doors or windows must be reinforced to pick up the missing support of the vertical load. This process is done with 2 x 8s, 2 x 10s, or 2 x 12s, known as headers, or lintels, erected over the top of the opening.

7. Wall framing errors left uncorrected during the construction process convert to hard-to-fix problems later. Wall framing is generally covered by exterior framing although it may be visible in some areas of the structure, such as the basement and the garage. Evidence gleaned from other structural components can provide clues as to the wall framing's integrity.

8. Platform framing is the most common type of framing used in residential construction. With this type of framing, the structure rests on a subfloor platform. Other less common types of framing are balloon framing and post-and-beam framing.

9. Wood rot is caused by a type of fungus that destroys wood. It is as damaging as termite or other insect infestation.

10. The following items are checked during the window inspection: the operability of the windows, sash cords, and sash weights; the window casings for wood rot, missing caulking, and peeling or chipped paint; and all windows for broken glazing material.

11. Exterior doors may be made from a combination of materials including glass. All exterior doors containing glass must use tempered safety glass that shatters into small pieces instead of hazardous large chunks.

12. A roof truss system has many advantages. It is strong, generally less expensive than a traditionally built roof, and allows the builder more freedom to build a custom-shaped roof at a lower cost.

13. The roof is one of the most easily identifiable systems of a house. In contemporary residential construction, two varieties of roof styles are common: the traditional gable roof and the hip roof.

14. Metal valleys and flashing are used to help the shingles or shakes keep the structure sound and dry. Most roof leaks occur where water is channeled off the roof or where the roof abuts a vertical wall or chimney.

15. Fiberglass composite and asphalt shingles are the most often used roof covering. Asphalt is the main substance in roofing shingles.

16. Other roof coverings include wood shakes and shingles, rolled roofing, slate, tile, and metal including copper and galvanized steel.

17. During the roof inspection, look for the following: stains on the interior of the attic walls and ceilings; shingles that are loose, missing, curled, blistered, cracked, stained, or buckled; gutters filled with granules from the shingles; worn or missing roof flashings; bowing, expansion, movement, or waviness of the roof deck; stressing, splitting, and rotting of wood shakes and shingles; proper penetration of and adequate flashing around all roof penetrations; clogged roof drains on flat roofs; missing or cracked pieces of slate; and substandard roof repair.

18. Structural damage in masonry chimneys is evidenced by cracks in and the separation of the tile inner liner and the surrounding brick or block structure. Structural damage to metal prefabricated chimneys is caused by the inner liners corroding, rusting, buckling, or collapsing, or by the seam separating.

19. Roof penetrations, such as chimneys, skylights, vent stacks, and roof vents, are examined for proper flashing and water leaks.

20. A final covering is placed over the sheathing and felt paper, generally brick or siding. Siding can be aluminum, wood, or vinyl. Other exterior covering materials include fieldstone, brick, and stucco.

CHAPTER REVIEW

Field Study Assignment 1

Using your practice property and a copy of the inspection checklist from Figure 4.4, inspect the exterior. Note any problems you encounter for further exploration and discussion.

Field Study Assignment 2

Identify and name the type of roof and roof covering material on your subject property. Identify the siding material used on your subject property.

 **REVIEW QUESTIONS** *Choose the letter that best answers the question.*

1. Which of the following is NOT included in a standard home inspection?
   A. screens, awnings, and shutters
   B. wall framing, if visible
   C. chimney
   D. roof drainage system

2. Which of the following determines whether the structure has a basement or crawl space? The height of the:
   A. footing
   B. foundation wall
   C. girder
   D. sill plate

3. One of the main reasons why a foundation wall may lean or bulge is:
   A. a warm climate
   B. hydrostatic pressure
   C. insufficient insulation
   D. pest infestation

4. Which of the following is used as the nailing surface for the floor system?
   A. double top plate
   B. soffit
   C. lintel
   D. sill plate

5. If a floor sags over a wall partition, the problem may be:
   A. not enough support from the floor joists
   B. sheathing that is not glued or nailed to the floor joists
   C. sheathing that is not properly butted together
   D. support columns that are too close together

6. Beams that support the ceiling and the roof over the door and window openings are known as:
   A. double top plates
   B. bearing beams
   C. headers
   D. girders

7. Bulges observed on the interior walls of the structure may indicate a problem with the:
   A. studs
   B. foundation
   C. main bearing beam
   D. sill plate

8. Which of the following is NOT a window component?
   A. stiles
   B. stringer
   C. rails
   D. muntin

9. A roof truss system carries the load of the roof to the:
   A. interior walls
   B. ridge beam
   C. main carrying beam
   D. exterior walls

10. A metallic material that is used in certain joints and junctures of the roof and walls to prevent water from seeping into the structure is known as:
    A. flashing
    B. control joints
    C. fascia
    D. tie backs

11. Which of the following is NOT a component of the eave?
    A. soffit
    B. threshold
    C. fascia
    D. frieze board

12. The purpose of the ceramic-coated granules on asphalt shingles is:
    A. to protect the shingles from water penetration
    B. to protect the shingles from ultraviolet rays
    C. for decoration only
    D. to inhibit mold

13. Shakes are made of:
    A. asphalt
    B. concrete
    C. wood
    D. copper

14. Which of the following is NOT a material used for a roof covering?
    A. copper
    B. slate
    C. cedar
    D. brick

15. Randy, a home inspector hired by the buyers, observed that the asphalt shingles used as a roof covering were curled around the edges. The property owners were very upset and claimed that the roof was only five years old. How should Randy best respond to the situation?
    A. Note his observations in the home inspection report and advise his clients of his findings.
    B. Advise the property owners to sue the installer of the shingles.
    C. Advise his clients not to purchase the property unless the roof is repaired first.
    D. Advise the property owners to take the property off the market until the roof is repaired.

16. Leakage around a brick chimney through to the roof decking is generally an indicator that:
    A. there has been a chimney fire
    B. the flashing surrounding the chimney is either missing or compromised
    C. the roof decking is improperly nailed to the rafters
    D. the mortar is either cracked or disintegrated

17. The danger of cracked tiles and mortar displacement in a chimney is that this condition creates:
    A. more creosote
    B. a greater draft
    C. a pathway for flames to reach the combustible wood frame of the structure
    D. a hotter fire

18. The main problem to look for when inspecting skylights is:
    A. corrosion to the frame
    B. leakage
    C. placement on the roof
    D. whether or not the size and shape meet code requirements

19. The main problem with vent pipes that extend over a window is that:
    A. gases can escape back into the structure
    B. they are unsightly
    C. they never function properly
    D. the condensation from the window causes them to corrode

20. Roof vents allow ventilation to pass through to the:
    A. underlayment
    B. attic
    C. chimney
    D. ridge beam

21. The main problem with vinyl siding is that:
    A. it rusts
    B. it tends to warp
    C. it may become loose or detach from the structure
    D. it is subject to fungus growth

22. The primary protection for exterior wood siding is:
    A. some form of paint
    B. termiticide
    C. formaldehyde
    D. fungicide

23. Andy was inspecting a property in a subdivision where he knew that all of the properties were restricted to the use of wood or brick for the exterior covering. The back wall of the subject property was covered with aluminum siding. How should Andy handle this?
    A. He should report this to the home owner's association.
    B. He should notify the town building department.
    C. He should advise his clients about the violation and include it in his home inspection report.
    D. He should say and do nothing.

24. Spalling refers to:
    A. weepholes
    B. cracks in asphalt
    C. material that is crumbling
    D. material compromised by wood rot

25. The main problem with stucco is that it:
    A. can only be used in colder climates
    B. tends to crack
    C. has a life expectancy of only five years
    D. requires painting every year

ANSWER KEY

1. A	8. B	15. A	22. A
2. B	9. D	16. B	23. C
3. B	10. A	17. C	24. C
4. D	11. B	18. B	25. B
5. A	12. B	19. A	
6. C	13. C	20. B	
7. A	14. D	21. C	

INSPECTING THE INTERIOR

A detailed and careful inspection of the interior is an important part of the home inspection process. It is often the most complex because of the diversity of components found inside even the most seemingly simple structure.

LEARNING OBJECTIVES

1. List the items that are included in the interior inspection of the subject property.

2. Describe the general procedure for performing the interior inspection.

3. Explain the significance of insulation and identify its locations within the structure.

4. Describe the importance of a vapor barrier.

5. Briefly summarize the main problems to look for during the interior inspection.

KEY TERMS

Ash dump door

Ash pit

Ash pit cleanout door

Building envelope

Catalytic combustor

Damper

Efflorescence

Extension springs

Flue

Flue collar

Grout

Gypsum board

Internal reversing mechanism

Lift handle

Metal lath

Non-catalytic stove

Photoelectric eye

Resilient floor covering

R-value

Section joint

Subfloor

Throat damper

Torsion springs

Trim

Vapor barrier

Wythe

SCOPE OF THE INTERIOR INSPECTION

igure 7.1 sets forth the ASHI Standards of Practice for the inspection of a structure's interior, insulation and ventilation, and fireplaces and solid fuel–burning (SFB) appliances.

BASIC INSPECTION PROCEDURE

he interior inspection should proceed in an orderly fashion using the home inspection checklist. The inspection encompasses many of the same components in each room. Examine the walls, ceilings, floors, windows, doors, stairways, and counters and cabinets in the kitchen and bathroom (additional kitchen and bathroom inspection items are discussed in Chapter 8). The fireplace or other SFB appliances, the attic, basement, and garage are also included if these are part of the house. Some inspectors like to start at the top floor and work down. Others prefer to begin with the front entrance and any stairways that might be present.

Enter the living room, dining room, and kitchen and systematically examine each of these rooms. Examine the closets using the same criteria as the rest of the rooms. Check the counters and cabinets in the kitchen. Next, inspect the bedrooms and bathrooms and any other interior rooms. Check the operation and function of all doors and windows. Codes generally require that each room have at least one window, including a room in the attic. The window's purpose is not only to provide light and air, but also to facilitate escape and allow air into the room in case of fire. Examine the windowsills to see if there is wood rot, cracks in the wood, peeling paint, or other defects. Apply the same principles of inspection to all hallways and corridors. Use your circuit tester to check the wall receptacles (see Chapter 9). Examine the heat distribution components (see Chapter 8). Unless the property is in an extremely warm locale, each room should have a heat source. Complete the interior inspection with a thorough examination of the garage, attic, and basement.

You Should Know
Stairway
Components

The interior stairway components are much the same as the exterior stairway discussed in Chapter 6. There may be differences in building code requirements, however. When you inspect the interior stairway, make sure it has a tightly secured railing. Check that the treads are securely fastened to the risers, that they are of equal width, and not broken or warped. Examine the risers to see if they are of equal height. Codes specify the sizes of treads and risers. With the balusters, make sure that they are no more than four inches apart (as discussed in Chapter 6).

Putting It to Work

You need at least a flashlight and a telescopic mirror to assist you with the interior inspection. If you wear a tool belt, other items as needed are readily available.

FIGURE 7.1

Applicable ASHI Standards of Practice.

10. INTERIOR

10.1 The inspector shall inspect:

    A. walls, ceilings, and floors.

    B. steps, stairways, and railings.

    C. countertops and a representative number of installed cabinets.

    D. garage doors and garage door operators.

10.2 The inspector is NOT required to inspect:

    A. paint, wallpaper, and other finish treatments.

    B. carpeting.

    C. window treatments.

    D. central vacuum systems.

    E. household appliances.

    F. recreational facilities.

11. INSULATION AND VENTILATION

11.1 The inspector shall:

    A. inspect:

        1. insulation and vapor retarders in unfinished spaces.

        2. ventilation of attics and foundation areas.

        3. mechanical ventilation systems.

    B. describe:

        1. insulation and vapor retarders in unfinished spaces.

        2. absence of insulation in unfinished spaces at conditioned surfaces.

11.2 The inspector is NOT required to disturb insulation.

12. FIREPLACES AND SOLID FUEL BURNING APPLIANCES

12.1 The inspector shall:

    A. inspect:

        1. system components.

        2. chimneys and vents.

    B. describe:

        1. fireplaces and solid fuel burning appliances.

        2. chimneys.

(continued)

FIGURE 7.1

*Applicable ASHI
Standards of Practice,
continued.*

12.2 The inspector is NOT required to:

    A. inspect:

        1. interiors of flues or chimneys.

        2. firescreens and doors.

        3. seals and gaskets.

        4. automatic fuel feed devices.

        5. mantles and fireplace surrounds.

        6. combustion make-up air devices.

        7. heat distribution assists (gravity controlled and fan assisted).

    B. ignite or extinguish fires.

    C. determine draft characteristics.

    D. move fireplace inserts or stoves or firebox contents.

You Should Know

Sometimes, an inspector must return to an already inspected area to further investigate an issue that arises in another part of the property. Although all of this work does not appear on the home inspection report, inspectors must follow through on their observations. They should not, however, assume the role of a professional electrician or plumber in explaining or answering client concerns. Always recommend that clients contact the appropriate professional should they have concerns regarding any of the inspector's findings.

DOORS AND LOCKING MECHANISMS

The basic components of doors and windows are discussed in Chapter 6. Exterior doors are heavier and usually solid. Most interior doors are made of hollow-core wood, but some may be solid. Figure 7.2 diagrams an interior door and Figure 7.3 illustrates the common door types found in a residential property. Begin your door inspection with the front door. Does it shut firmly and lock easily? Not all doors and windows have locks. Exterior doors must lock from both the inside and outside. Interior doors, if they have locks at all, lock only from the inside of the room. Open and shut all doors to test for operability. The door between the garage and the structure must be fireproof and must automatically swing shut to prevent gas fumes and other noxious vapors from entering the house.

Inspecting Doors and Locking Mechanisms

The following are completed during the inspection:

- Check that the door hinges and hinge screws are in place. Interior doors generally have two hinges; exterior doors have three because they are heavier.
- Make sure the header above the door is not sagged or bowed (see Chapter 6).
- Verify that sliding or bifold doors move easily in their tracks and do not come loose. If the sliding door is also an exterior door, check the locking mechanism.

Diagram of an interior door.   **FIGURE 7.2**

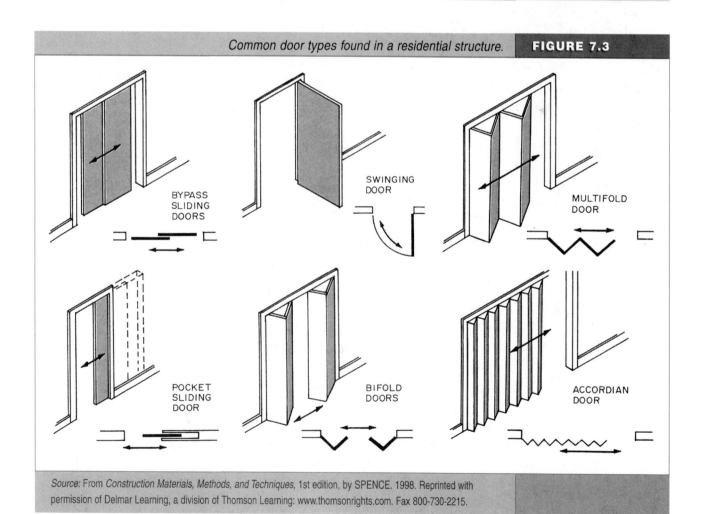

Interior door openings are trimmed on both sides with a casing after the finish wall material is installed.

Source: From *Construction Materials, Methods, and Techniques,* 1st edition, by SPENCE. 1998. Reprinted with permission of Delmar Learning, a division of Thomson Learning: www.thomsonrights.com. Fax 800-730-2215.

Common door types found in a residential structure.   **FIGURE 7.3**

Source: From *Construction Materials, Methods, and Techniques,* 1st edition, by SPENCE. 1998. Reprinted with permission of Delmar Learning, a division of Thomson Learning: www.thomsonrights.com. Fax 800-730-2215.

- Observe that each door has a working doorknob so that an individual is not trapped in a room if the door is shut.
- Verify that the door is level with the ceiling above it and the floor below it.
- Check the operability of the door. Is it easy to open and close or does it stick or make a great deal of noise?
- What is the condition of the door? Is it scratched, warped, or have pieces missing? Does it securely fit the door jamb or is it cut too short at the top or bottom so that it does not fit into the space properly? Often, older door casings are not square because of the structure's settlement.
- Examine the locks to ascertain operability.

WALLS, CEILINGS, AND FLOORS

The inspection of the walls, ceilings, and floors comprises a large segment of the interior inspection. Interior walls are either load bearing or non-load bearing. Figure 7.4 illustrates the framing of a non–load-bearing wall. Hidden inside the wall and ceiling cavities are the electrical wires and plumbing pipes that comprise the structure's mechanical systems.

Walls

Walls are composed of a variety of materials such as gypsum board, plaster, solid wood, plywood, and fiberboard. Different rooms in the interior may include one or more of these materials. Many walls and ceilings are composed of gypsum board, also known as drywall, wallboard, or the brand name Sheetrock. **Gypsum board** *is a type of wall panel composed of an inner core of noncombustible gypsum*

| FIGURE 7.4 | Non–loading-bearing wall. |

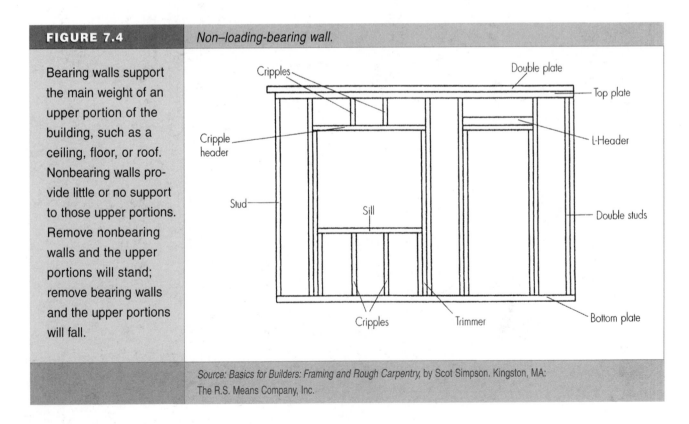

Bearing walls support the main weight of an upper portion of the building, such as a ceiling, floor, or roof. Nonbearing walls provide little or no support to those upper portions. Remove nonbearing walls and the upper portions will stand; remove bearing walls and the upper portions will fall.

Source: Basics for Builders: Framing and Rough Carpentry, by Scot Simpson. Kingston, MA: The R.S. Means Company, Inc.

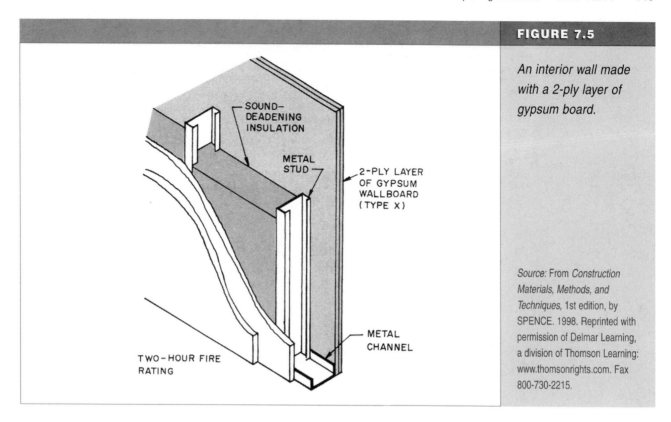

FIGURE 7.5

An interior wall made with a 2-ply layer of gypsum board.

Source: From *Construction Materials, Methods, and Techniques,* 1st edition, by SPENCE. 1998. Reprinted with permission of Delmar Learning, a division of Thomson Learning: www.thomsonrights.com. Fax 800-730-2215.

and paper surfacing on the front, back, and edges. It is manufactured according to American Society of Testing and Materials (ASTM) standards. Figure 7.5 illustrates an interior wall made with a 2-ply layer of gypsum board. Gypsum is a rock-forming mineral that is used in plaster, wallboard, some cements, fertilizers, and paint. It is also known as plaster of paris.

Prior to the mid-1950s, most ceilings and walls were formed from plaster-coated metal or wooden laths (discussed later). Although gypsum board is currently used to form the walls, certain areas still require a plaster application (e.g., archways, rounded walls, and other unique shapes) if one-quarter-inch gypsum wallboard will not work. Many forms of gypsum board are fire resistant. Code requirements designate those interior walls, if any, that must have fire resistant properties. Gypsum board is fastened to wood studs and ceiling joists with special nails and screws. The joints between the boards are covered with tape and a joint compound (see Figure 7.6).

Plaster

Generally, plaster walls are found in homes that are 50 or more years old; however, plaster is still used today in certain applications. It is applied over a metal lath in three coats. In older homes, the plaster walls were constructed using a wooden lath; in recent years, a metal lath is used. **Metal laths** *are available in a variety of styles and generally resemble a meshlike or honeycomb pattern. The lath supports the plaster that hardens around it* (see Figure 7.7). The first coat of plaster is the scratch coat—the plaster is forced into the spaces of the lath. The second coat, called the brown coat, is applied over the scratch coat. After the second coat hardens, the finish coat is applied. At this point, the surface may be smoothed or textured.

FIGURE 7.6

Gypsum board covered with tape and joint compound.

Source: From *Construction Materials, Methods, and Techniques,* 1st edition, by SPENCE. 1998. Reprinted with permission of Delmar Learning, a division of Thomson Learning: www.thomsonrights. com. Fax 800-730-2215.

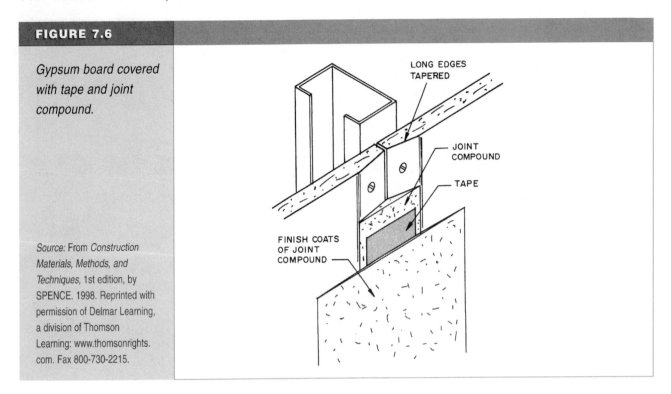

Paneling

Some walls have a layer of wood paneling glued, screwed, or nailed to it. Paneling is made from either hardboard or solid wood. Hardboard is wood that is ground down into fibers and then compressed to form a solid sheet. The wood is then imprinted with a grain that is similar to different varieties of wood. Paneling is also constructed from plywood and finished with a wood grain. Solid wood paneling is made from either hardwood or softwood and finished in a variety of patterns and colors. The paneling is generally available in 4' × 8' sheets. The paneling may be nailed or screwed directly to the studs. In other cases, the paneling is nailed, screwed, or glued to the gypsum board underneath. Inspectors can often

FIGURE 7.7   *Metal lath.*

(A) Metal lath is tied to metal studs with 18-gauge wire. (B) A three-coat plaster wall finish over metal lath.

Source: From *Construction Materials, Methods, and Techniques,* 1st edition, by SPENCE. 1998. Reprinted with permission of Delmar Learning, a division of Thomson Learning: www.thomsonrights.com. Fax 800-730-2215.

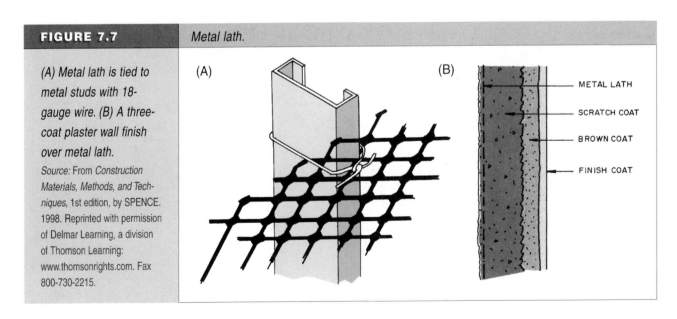

determine whether there is gypsum board underneath by tapping on the paneling and listening for a hollow sound that indicates the absence of gypsum board.

Ceilings

Ceilings hide the floor above it or the roof decking and are composed of a number of materials including wood and exposed beams, gypsum panels, plaster, metal, or any number of fibrous panels. Ceilings may be flat, curved, or constructed with a variety of sloping surfaces that provide unique design details to the structure. A cathedral ceiling that follows the contours of the roof rafter is an example of a sloping ceiling shape. Most ceilings today are constructed with the same gypsum board that makes up the walls. In older homes, plaster ceilings are common. Other variations also exist.

Exposed Ceiling

In some cases, the floor above the ceiling or the roof decking is exposed and used as the ceiling. Post-and-beam construction or log homes are examples of an exposed ceiling structure. In this case, the wood must be finished with varnish. Some ceilings are decorated with a combination of plaster or gypsum board and exposed beams.

Suspended Ceiling

A suspended ceiling is often found in the basement, but may be in other parts of the house. Suspended ceilings allow electrical and plumbing components to be hidden under the ceiling panels. Suspended ceiling panels are hung from the floor above by wires that hold a metal grid (see Figure 7.8). The ceiling panels are

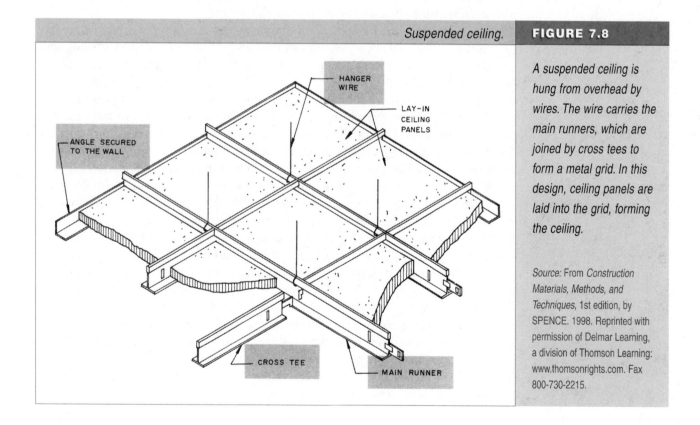

Suspended ceiling. **FIGURE 7.8**

A suspended ceiling is hung from overhead by wires. The wire carries the main runners, which are joined by cross tees to form a metal grid. In this design, ceiling panels are laid into the grid, forming the ceiling.

Source: From *Construction Materials, Methods, and Techniques*, 1st edition, by SPENCE. 1998. Reprinted with permission of Delmar Learning, a division of Thomson Learning: www.thomsonrights.com. Fax 800-730-2215.

placed within the grid. Some suspended ceiling materials are fire resistant and may have acoustical properties. Ceiling panels are available in aluminum, fiberglass-reinforced polymer gypsum, and gypsum panels faced with vinyl, fabrics, and other substances.

Ceiling Tiles

Ceiling tiles can be attached directly to a preexisting ceiling finish with adhesive, staples, screws, or nails. They can be installed over gypsum board, plaster, wood, wood strips, and other materials. Ceiling tiles are made from polymer plastic, fiberglass, mineral fibers, tin, or other metals. They are generally found in squares of 12 to 24 inches. Many of them, such as the plastic variety, can be painted with an oil-based paint. Decorative strips often cover the joints between tiles. Ceiling tiles may be fire resistant and have acoustical properties.

Inspecting the Walls and Ceilings

If the walls and ceilings are constructed with gypsum board, the workmanship is checked first. Are shrinkage cracks due to the normal expansion and contraction of the framing or are they due to poor workmanship? Poor workmanship is evidenced by joints that are not properly seamed or walls that are not plumb. Small cracks commonly appear in the corners of the room and around the headers above doors and windows. Generally, they are harmless and a result of the structure's normal movement. A slight bulge may appear in the drywall here and there. This may be caused by popping nails or screws that are moving out from the studs. This happens due to the normal expansion and contraction of the wood framing. Nail popping only becomes a problem when the nails back out through the tape and joint compound and become visible. A number of popping nails may also indicate inadequacies in the structure's framing.

Another issue to investigate is water damage. Check to see if the walls are free of stains and dry; water can loosen the tape and joint compound. A wall or ceiling may sag if it has been damp or wet or if the drywall is too thin. Drywall should be no less than three-eighths-inch thick. If there are water stains on an outside wall (one that is on the inside of the exterior wall) or adjacent ceiling, the inspector should determine the source. It could be coming from a leak in the roof or a window. Check the roof or windows, even if previously examined, to determine the cause. Ceiling stains that appear on the first floor interior ceiling are possibly from water spilled on the second floor or a plumbing leak. If there are bulges in a wall, the cause may be a twisted stud, but that is nearly impossible to confirm.

Plaster walls and ceilings may reveal slightly different problems. When areas of plaster become wet and then dry, certain areas may turn to a powder-like state. Examine dry plaster walls for signs of powder even if the wall is dry when it is inspected. Aging plaster walls can be problematic. Over time, plaster cracks, blisters, and breaks apart, particularly if neglected. Plaster is affected by changes in temperature. If a property is empty and is left cold for a length of time, plaster can deteriorate. Like drywall, plaster will crack due to natural shrinkage over time or from the structure's movement. Hairline cracks, one-eighth inch or less, are not harmful. A hollow sound behind a plaster wall in an older home (before the use of metal laths) may indicate that the plaster is no longer adhering to the wood lath behind the wall. Because plaster dries out over time and loses its moisture, if moisture is present, there may be a problem.

In walls constructed of either drywall or plaster, larger cracks (those wider than one-quarter to one-half inch) may indicate an underlying structural problem (e.g., the nonbearing walls are not properly supported and are pushing down on the wall material or the floor joists below the wall or ceiling joists above it may be compromised and are not supporting the wall at the top or the bottom). In addition, if the ceiling joists are causing the ceiling to sag, this not only stresses the plaster or drywall, but the adjacent walls. If an inspector observes problems with the foundation wall, such as evidence of too much movement due to foundation settlement, this can affect the walls, ceilings, and floors.

Wood paneling may have a small space between the joints due to its normal expansion and contraction, but the space should be no more than one-quarter inch. If there is a moisture problem behind the wall, paneling can warp, bow, or come lose from the wall. If a piece is missing, examine the wall for water stains or moisture.

When examining a suspended ceiling, find out why it was constructed. Was it constructed to cover up a problem with the ceiling above it? Remove a ceiling panel and check for water stains, bulges, or other defects. Determine whether the metal grid that supports the ceiling panels is securely fastened to the ceiling above it.

Ceiling tiles should undergo the same scrutiny. If any of the tiles are loose or missing, check the ceiling for water stains and to determine whether it is damp or soft. Missing ceiling tiles often suggest that the entire ceiling may be compromised and that all of the ceiling tiles are in danger of dislodging. Look at the joints between the tiles. Are there places where the trim, decorative pieces, or filler is missing?

Floors

Under most finished flooring is a subfloor. The **subfloor** *is a plywood surface nailed to the floor joists that serves as the surface for the floor finish.* Plywood subfloor is generally five-eighths-inch thick. Dimension lumber, a type of wood plank ranging from two to six inches thick and five to twelve inches wide that serves the same purpose as plywood, is found in older homes. Waferboard, a type of pressed wood, is also used as subfloor material. Floor finishes are not often addressed by building codes because they do not pose a safety hazard. Building codes may, however, address the ingress and egress from rooms; window, light, and air requirements; and the size of the passageways leading to and from rooms. Carpeting, which is not generally part of the home inspection, must meet fire safety standards promulgated by the National Fire Protection Association and other standards set forth by the U.S. Department of Commerce.

Floor Materials

Floors are covered with a variety of materials including resilient flooring such as vinyl, asphalt, and rubber. **Resilient floor covering** *is a manufactured interior floor covering in either sheet or tile form that returns to its original form after being bent, compressed, or stretched.* Other flooring materials include wood and clay tile.

Resilient flooring. Vinyl flooring, composed of a polyvinyl chloride material, is available in both sheets and tiles in a variety of thicknesses. Vinyl sheets are available in 6-, 9-, and 12-foot-wide rolls up to 50 feet long. Vinyl tiles are available in

9-, 12-, 18-, and 36-inch squares and some rectangular shapes. Vinyl sheets and tiles are glued to the floor with factory-recommended adhesives.

Asphalt resilient flooring is available in 9- or 12-inch square tiles in different grades and is very durable and fire resistant. Asphalt tiles are bonded to wood or concrete floors using factory recommended adhesives.

Rubber flooring is a form of resilient flooring available in tiles and sheets. The most common tile sizes are 12- and 36-inch squares. Sheets range from 36 to 50 inches wide. Rubber flooring is comfortable for walking and has a type of gridded surface that aids traction.

An older resilient floor covering, linoleum, is found in many properties. It is manufactured in sheets and is made of cork and oil on a cloth backing.

Wood. Wood floors are composed of either hard- or softwoods. Floors in new construction may have a factory-applied finish. Older floors may have been sanded and finished on site with either a clear or opaque varnish or paint. Wood floors are composed of either narrow strips of wood in a variety of thicknesses or wider planks. Newer wood-look floors are available as a hardwood veneer with a vinyl top layer that simulates the look of wood. Wood floor materials are affixed to the floor using a combination of adhesives and nails.

Clay tile. Clay floor tile is another flooring material used in many homes because of its durability. Tiles are classified as either quarry tile, paver tile, or ceramic tile. Quarry tile does not have a glaze and the surface is sometimes roughened to make the tile slip resistant. Paver tiles are either glazed or unglazed and are weather resistant. These tiles are primarily used in commercial applications. Ceramic tile is either glazed or unglazed and is used for flooring, countertops, and exterior applications. Ceramic tiles made for the floor may have textured surfaces to avoid slippage. Portland cement mortar or other combinations of mortar that include Portland cement, sand, resins, and water are used to affix clay tiles to the underlayment. **Grout,** *a mixture of Portland cement, lime, and sand, is mixed with water to fill and seal the spaces between the tiles.*

Inspecting the Floor

First check the floor to make sure it is level with no raised bumps or sags. Sometimes inspectors roll a ball or marble across a floor to determine whether the floor is level, but a carpenter's level will do the trick. If the subfloor is set on a concrete slab, it's possible that floor problems are caused by the settling of the slab. If the slab settles too much, the interior walls also sink, causing the floor to improperly meet the slab and interior walls. In some properties, the floor may sag or appear uneven. Sagging floors occur because the floor joists cannot support the load on the floor's surface. Similarly, an uneven surface may be caused by one or more floor joists that are either broken or twisted.

Resilient flooring is subject to tears and may come loose from the subfloor. Look for missing or loose tiles. This loosening is seen as a bump or ripple in the floor surface. If water compromises the subfloor underneath, this can cause the tiles or sheets to become loose or heave. Examine the joints between the sheets and tiles to make sure that the materials are bonded to the subfloor and that there are no gaps between the squares or sheet seams.

Hardwood floors should be smooth and level. If expansion and contraction has taken place, it is evidenced by ripples in the floor surface. Like other wood components, wood floors are subject to wood rot. If the floor has been damaged by water, it may appear swelled or buckled. If there are raised bulges, it may mean that the floorboards are loose because they are not nailed down properly. Because floorboards are laid together tightly, the boards do not have space to expand and will buckle upward should there be moisture under them. If the floor squeaks, it is possible that the subfloor is not properly nailed or glued to the floor joists.

Clay tile should be subjected to the same scrutiny. Look for cracked, chipped, loose, or missing tiles. Check that the tiles are firmly adhered to the floor and that there is no missing grout around the tiles.

Damage to the floor surface may be a trip hazard and is noted on the home inspection report.	**You Should Know** ☐ ☐ ☐

While you are examining the floors, walls, and ceilings, the trim will no doubt catch your eye. **Trim** *is made of either metal or wood and is used to finish windows, doorways, and the areas where the floor meets the wall and the wall meets the ceiling. It is also used in cabinetry, built-in shelving, and other areas.* When examining the trim, determine that it is not warped or bowed and that the corner joints are properly mitered. Nail holes should be covered with wood fill, sanded, and finished with a coat of paint or varnish.	**Putting It to Work** **Trim** ☐ ☐ ☐

INSULATION AND VAPOR BARRIERS

Most of the subject property's insulating material is not visible. An unfinished attic, if insulated, is one area where insulation is visible. Other areas include unfinished spaces such as a crawl space, basement, garage, or dormer. Home inspectors should check the insulation's type, quality, and effectiveness where visible. The primary purpose of insulation is to resist the flow of heat from one area to another. It provides the double benefit of preventing heat loss in the winter and protecting against heat overload in the summer.

Building or energy codes mandate minimum R-values for insulation in various parts of a residential structure and designate the areas where insulation must be installed. The required performance of the insulation depends on the type of heating system. Insulation is rated according to an R-value. Because the **R-value** *means the degree of resistance to heat transfer through the walls (heat is kept in or out), the larger the R-value, the greater the degree of insulation.* Most brand-name insulation products are marked with their particular R-value.

Although some newer houses have insulation that meets optimal standards, most older homes are under-insulated unless they've been retrofitted.

Although home inspectors examine the insulation, they should not analyze or report on the R-value in the inspection report. Any client concerns regarding the performance of the insulation are directed to a heating or structural specialist.	**Putting It to Work** ☐ ☐ ☐

Insulation Types and Locations

Insulation is available in a variety of forms and falls into five categories: flexible, loose fill, rigid or wallboard, reflective, and sprayed. Flexible insulation is available in two types: blanket (or quilt) and batt. Figure 7.9 illustrates where insulation is placed in the structure.

| FIGURE 7.9 | *Insulation placement.* |

Insulation is placed wherever the interior walls, ceilings, or floors are exposed to exterior temperatures.

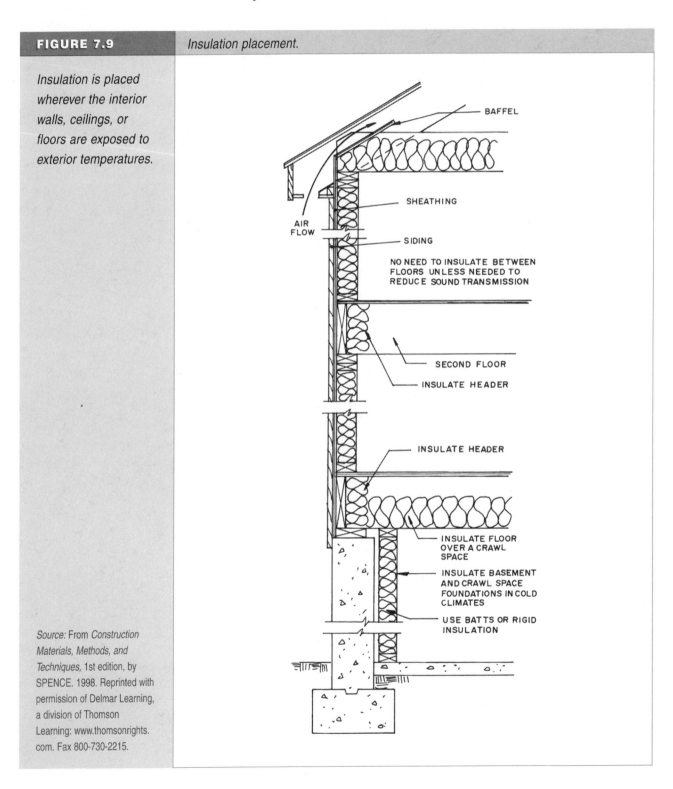

Source: From *Construction Materials, Methods, and Techniques,* 1st edition, by SPENCE. 1998. Reprinted with permission of Delmar Learning, a division of Thomson Learning: www.thomsonrights.com. Fax 800-730-2215.

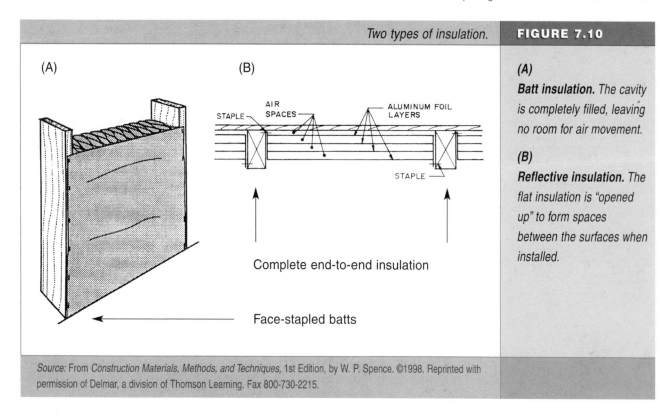

■ *Blanket insulation* ranges from one to three inches thick and comes in 15.5-inch wide rolls of fiberglass or other fibrous material. The insulation is stapled or nailed between the studs, under the rafters, or over the ceiling. It is designed to fit in the space between the joists and studs. Blanket insulation is enclosed with a paper cover. One side may be treated as a vapor barrier to help keep moisture out of the wall cavities. The cover sheet is often surfaced with aluminum foil or other reflective insulation that helps to keep the heat out.

■ *Batt insulation* is made of a fibrous material, such as fiberglass, and ranges from two to six inches thick. Figure 7.10(A) shows batt insulation installed between studs.

■ *Loose-fill insulation* is composed of lightweight materials such as perlite, vermiculite, wood paper, or cotton fibers. It can be poured or blown in to fill the spaces between studs on a horizontal surface or in hard-to-reach areas. It is often used on attic floors.

■ *Rigid insulation* is a fibrous material in the form of lightweight wallboard that combines strength with heat and acoustical insulating properties. These boards are used in roof and wall sheathing and concrete slab flooring.

■ *Reflective accordion insulation,* shown in Figure 7.10(B), receives its value not from the thickness but from its reflective surface. It must be exposed to an air space to be effective and can be installed up to four layers thick that are opened up to provide the air space.

■ *Unfazed rolls* (without paper covering) and loose blown-in insulation can be added on top of existing attic insulation to improve the home's energy efficiency.

■ *Spray-on insulation* is a hot, viscous mixture that is sprayed into the inside of the sheathing and solidifies.

Vapor Barriers

Codes may require that all building envelope materials that absorb moisture be protected by a vapor barrier on the insulation applied to the warm (inside) wall of exterior walls. Water vapor is generated from the activities inside the structure, such as cooking and bathing, as well as moisture conditions generated from the exterior. As warm air rises in the structure, so does the moisture. The **vapor barrier** *is composed of sheets of moisture-resistant material, such as polyethylene film, kraft paper, or aluminum foil, that is bonded to insulation. The vapor barrier prevents warm interior air from mixing with cold exterior air and forming condensation within the wall.* Should condensation occur, the structure, in effect, "sweats" and this causes the wood framing members to rot and, in turn, damage other components.

Kraft paper is coated with wax or asphalt and is used on the inside of the insulation. Aluminum foil has heat-reflective properties in addition to its use as a vapor barrier. Polyethylene film is nailed to the studs on the side facing inside the structure and is placed under the subfloor and on the ceiling. It may also be used to cover the ground in a crawl space. Other vapor barriers include various types of latex and oil-based paints. A properly installed vapor barrier keeps moisture from entering the structure's living space and becoming trapped in the attic or penetrating the insulation. Most new homes are built with vapor barriers installed. Figure 7.11 illustrates the difference between insulation with and without a vapor barrier. Some homes built 15 or 20 years ago do not have vapor barriers.

ATTIC

 thorough inspection of the attic can reveal a number of problems, including compromised insulation, ventilation, wiring, and roofing materials.

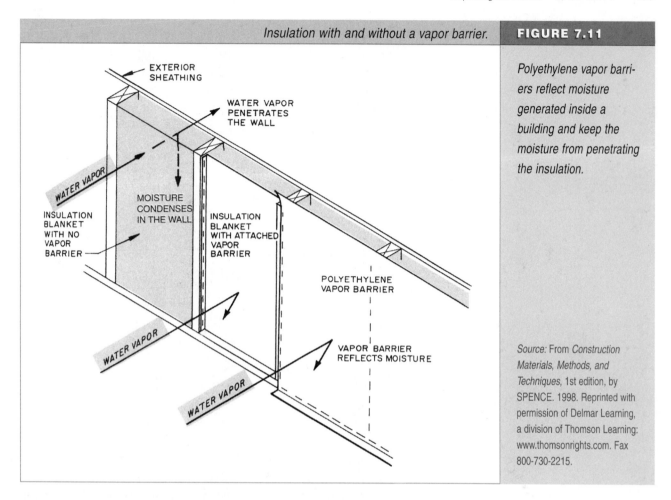

Insulation with and without a vapor barrier.   **FIGURE 7.11**

Polyethylene vapor barriers reflect moisture generated inside a building and keep the moisture from penetrating the insulation.

Source: From *Construction Materials, Methods, and Techniques,* 1st edition, by SPENCE. 1998. Reprinted with permission of Delmar Learning, a division of Thomson Learning: www.thomsonrights.com. Fax 800-730-2215.

Opening and Accessibility

The attic inspection may be hindered by accessibility problems. In some homes, the attic may be completely inaccessible. Attics can be accessed by a pull-down stairway sometimes located in the garage, or a scuttle, an opening in the ceiling (such as in a closet), that requires a ladder to reach. The latter type of opening may render the attic inaccessible to the home inspector. Once in the attic, the inspector may find that he cannot stand up or easily move about the space. Some attics have flooring, others do not. If an attic inspection does not take place, the reasons are noted on the home inspection report.

Insulation

In the winter, attic insulation forces the warm air to stay in the structure's living area and prevents it from entering the attic. In the summer, insulation keeps the attic heat from combining with the cooler air inside the structure. Attic insulation keeps the house cooler even though air-conditioned and makes air conditioners more efficient.

Wiring

Electrical wiring hidden from sight in the attic may pose a safety hazard. Home inspectors should proceed with caution especially if the electrical power is not turned off. One of the problems commonly found in the attic is electrical wiring

Source: From *Construction Materials, Methods, and Techniques,* 1st edition, by SPENCE. 1998. Reprinted with permission of Delmar Learning, a division of Thomson Learning: www.thomsonrights.com. Fax 800-730-2215.

FIGURE 7.12

Insulation around a recessed light.

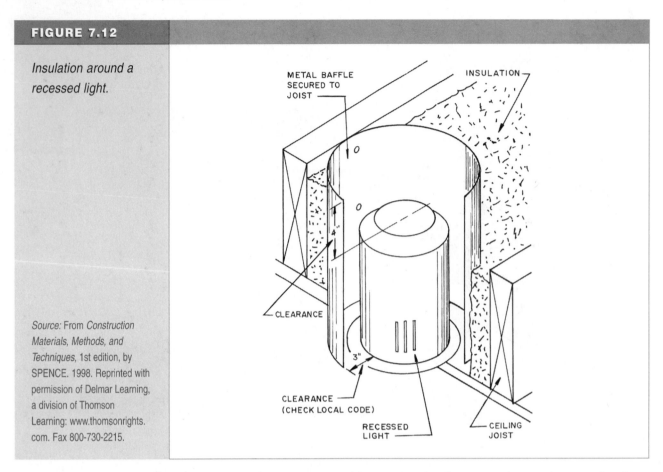

hidden under the insulation. Older wiring that has worn down poses a safety hazard. In addition, recessed light fixtures on the attic ceiling may be covered with insulation or insulation may have fallen on them. Code requirements generally designate that insulation be kept three to four inches away from recessed light fixtures. Incandescent lights may generate enough heat to cause a fire. Fire-resistant material is used to create a baffle around the light. It extends at least four inches above the insulation and is fastened to a ceiling joist (see Figure 7.12).

Ventilation

All ventilation systems have a central exhaust fan and several ducts to remove stale air from various places in the house. This fan is usually installed in the basement or attic, keeping fan noise away from the living space. How fresh air is introduced to replace exhausted air depends on the type of heating or air-cooling system in the home. All systems have a central exhaust fan that pulls stale air out of the kitchen, bathrooms, and other locations where pollutant concentrations are usually highest. Figure 7.13 shows different types of ventilation systems.

Much of the time, attics in older homes are not properly vented. A major source of roof damage originates in the attic. Inadequate insulation and the absence of a vapor barrier and ventilation compromise the roof system, causing extensive moisture damage. Therefore, proper ventilation of the attic space is essential. Ventilation permits air to circulate through the attic. In the winter, it prevents warm, moist air from being trapped in the attic where condensation can cause damage. Ventilation keeps the roof deck cooler, lessening the possibility of ice dams (discussed later). In the summer, ventilation prevents damaging heat

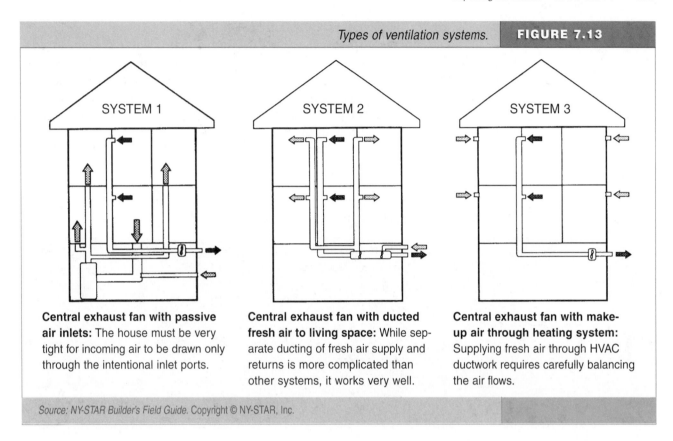

FIGURE 7.13

Types of ventilation systems.

SYSTEM 1

SYSTEM 2

SYSTEM 3

Central exhaust fan with passive air inlets: The house must be very tight for incoming air to be drawn only through the intentional inlet ports.

Central exhaust fan with ducted fresh air to living space: While separate ducting of fresh air supply and returns is more complicated than other systems, it works very well.

Central exhaust fan with make-up air through heating system: Supplying fresh air through HVAC ductwork requires carefully balancing the air flows.

Source: NY-STAR Builder's Field Guide. Copyright © NY-STAR, Inc.

and humidity from being trapped in the attic. Preventing this heat buildup not only cools the attic, but also the entire structure.

If the attic isn't properly ventilated, moisture is trapped, causing the deterioration of the insulation and the wood framing. In addition, inadequate attic ventilation can damage the roof system. The movement of air prevents or inhibits moisture condensation on the undersurface of the shingles or shakes or on the roof decks.

Two kinds of air movement help ventilate the roof. First, warm, moist air rises naturally in the attic and is exhausted out through the ridge vent. Second, wind passing over the ridge vent draws air and moisture out of the attic. Vents should be located in the soffits and the gable ends or, preferably, at the ridge lines. The gable is that part of the wall immediately under the end of a pitched roof cut into a triangular shape by the sloping sides of the roof. Gable vents may be the least effective type of vent because air circulates only near the gables and does not cover the entire roof. Ridge vents are installed along the peak of the roof. There are several other types and locations of roof vents. Soffit ventilation plugs should be screened and louvered to deter insects. Attic fans supply additional air movement.

Another problem caused by a lack of ventilation in the attic is that the attic insulation loses its R-value as it takes on moisture.

You Should Know

Inspecting the Attic

Should condensation occur in an improperly insulated or ventilated attic, mildew and wood rot compromises the wood rafters and eventually the roof deck. In some cases, the plaster or wallboard on the ceilings can crack and paint can peel or blister. The home inspector must first determine that the attic contains insulation that is placed firmly between the ceiling joists or roof rafters. If this is the case, the inspector must verify that there is an air space between the insulation and the sheathing. If there is no air space, moisture condensation can decay the sheathing or roof rafters. In addition, the insulation should not be pushed up against the eaves because it blocks the airflow through the soffit into the attic space. To ensure that a space exists between the rafters and the insulation, *baffles* made of a polystyrene material are placed in the space between the insulation and the sheathing.

Determine whether there is adequate flow of air both across the attic space and from the attic floor through to the roof. The roof rafters are examined for warping, bowing, and signs of wood rot.

<table>
<tr><td>You Should Know
Ice Dams</td><td>Ice dams occur when heat from the attic melts snow on the roof and the water flows down the roof and refreezes at the eaves. The water freezes because the gutters and eaves (overhangs) are not heated. As the ice builds up, melting and refreezing water backs up under the shingles and seeps into the structure through seams in the roof sheathing, gaps around plumbing stacks, and nail holes. This ice buildup settles in the gutters and under roof shingles, causing roof damage. As the ice dams melt, water leaks into the house, damaging the walls and ceilings. Proper attic insulation and ventilation, as well as a waterproof shingle underlayment applied to the roof deck, can prevent ice dams from forming.</td></tr>
</table>

GARAGE

Garages are either attached or detached. Many garages are several steps down from the entrance to the property. The attached garage floor should be 4 to 12 inches lower than the floor of the main part of the house; however, this is not always the case. This requirement is necessary because of the gas fumes and other vapors from the car exhaust that emanate from the garage. Because gas particles are heavier than air, they sink. A lower garage keeps these noxious fumes out of the main part of the house.

Many garages are not completely finished and some or all of the garage may have exposed construction. If the construction is visible, examine the vertical studs, ceiling joists, and roof rafters. If covered with drywall or other material, inspect the walls and ceiling to see if they are cracked, water stained, or show signs of decay. Garage walls adjacent to living areas should be insulated. If there are living quarters above the garage, the ceiling should be insulated. Some type of wall finish should cover the garage framing members that are adjacent to the living space because uncovered framing is a fire hazard. If a furnace is located in the garage, it should be enclosed and have a source of ventilation. Gasoline or oil leaking from a vehicle can be accidentally ignited by a furnace flame. In cold regions, plumbing pipes located in the garage should be insulated to prevent freezing. If there is access to an attic from the garage, check the opening. Determine whether the hatch cover and the pull-down stairs are operable. Is there adequate lighting to move up the stairway and into the attic?

Some garages contain drainage pits to catch water and snowmelt. Is the floor pitched toward the drain? The garage floor should be built up slightly above the driveway to prevent water from entering. The garage floor, walls, and ceiling are checked, in a manner similar to other interior walls, for water leakage, cracks, and undue movement. Garages should have light switches at all doors. Many mechanical overhead garage door openers have a timed lighting system that turns the garage ceiling light on when the door opens and automatically switches it off sometime later.

Detached Garage

A detached garage may be quite close to the house and connected to it by a small breezeway, a shared roof, or other covering to assist with access during inclement weather. The exterior of the attached garage is examined using all of the criteria applied to the exterior of the rest of the house (see Chapter 6). It is possible that the detached garage has been allowed to deteriorate and may be in worse condition than the main house. Carefully examine the floor slab for cracks, breakage, and heaved areas. Some detached garages do have dirt floors. This condition is unacceptable because it promotes pest infestation, moisture problems, and corresponding wood rot to the framing members. The electrical system is checked in both attached and detached garages. Exterior wiring is used in detached garages. Hanging wires, open junction boxes, extension cords used to operate garage door openers or space heaters, and other makeshift wiring is unacceptable and a fire hazard.

Doors and Door Operators

The garage door is probably the largest moving object in the structure and is generally constructed of wood or galvanized steel. Doors in newer homes may have a coat of corrosion protection on top of the galvanized steel and a baked-on enamel paint finish that is almost maintenance free. A vinyl weather seal may encircle the perimeter of the door.

The garage door is composed of several components. *The area between garage door sections is known as a* **section joint**. Cables are used to lift the garage door and are attached to two corner brackets affixed to the lower left and right corners of the door. Garage doors are balanced either by torsion springs or extension springs. **Extension springs** *are generally mounted just above the horizontal track, perpendicular to the closed garage door. They provide lifting power by stretching (extending).* If an extension spring breaks, broken spring parts cause injury by flying around the garage. However, a safety cable, installed inside each extension spring, can contain the spring and prevent injury. Many garage doors do not have a safety cable. **Torsion springs** *are usually mounted above the closed door, parallel and horizontal to the top section of the door. They provide lifting power for the door by winding and unwinding while the door is being opened or closed.* The torsion spring is under high tension. A **lift handle** *is affixed to the door (or a pull rope is attached to the bottom bracket in the lower corner) and is used with a door that is opened and closed manually.* If an automatic opener is attached to the door, the lift handle or pull rope should be removed because it can snag people or loose clothing while the door is being opened.

Door Opener

Garage door openers are electric motorized devices that open and close garage doors. *Most openers include an* **internal reversing mechanism** *that causes the door to reverse when it hits an obstruction.* However, a garage door opener with an inadequate or poorly maintained reversing mechanism is a safety hazard. The sensitivity of the internal reversing mechanism can fall out of adjustment so that the door does not reverse when it hits an obstruction.

Two additional measures are available to ensure the safety of garage door openers. One is the photoelectric eye. **Photoelectric eyes** *are sensors mounted five to six inches off the floor on both sides of a garage door.* These sensors operate with a garage door opener and send an invisible beam across the door opening. If that beam is broken while a motorized door is closing, the garage door opener causes the door to reverse direction to the fully open position.

Another alternative is a sensing edge that is attached to the bottom edge of a garage door. When this sensor contacts an obstruction during the door's closing, the opener causes the door to reverse direction to the fully open position.

A federal law requires that, beginning in 1993, all residential garage door openers sold in the United States include additional protection against entrapment, such as photoelectric eyes or a sensing edge. The law also requires that if the sensors become inoperative, the opener will not function. Garage door openers are usually operated by a wall-mounted push button, a hand-held remote control, or a keyless entry pad that requires the entry of a numerical code. Inspectors should ensure that the door operates properly.

Inspecting the Door and the Door-Opening Mechanism

Garage doors may be out of balance. This is usually indicated when the door feels heavy while pushing it up to open or the door does not stay open by itself. Most doors should stay open, without manual assistance, when about three or four feet above the floor.

Another safety hazard in a garage door is the space between the section joints. It is easy to get fingers caught in the joints and then squeezed as the garage door begins to move. Newer overhead doors are equipped with finger-protected section joints that prevent this problem. Check the tracks on the door to see if they are secure. Open and close the door by hand to observe operability.

If the garage door is operated mechanically, inspectors should determine that the reverse mechanism is operational. This can be done by placing an object, such as a block of wood, in the path of the overhead door while the door is open. If the door does not reverse when it hits the obstruction, the mechanism is not functioning properly and is noted as a safety hazard on the inspection report. The garage door opener should be plugged into a receptacle above the door; there should not be a lead wire running from the ceiling to a receptacle on a side wall.

BASEMENT

Problems with the foundation wall and floor slab are primarily discussed in Chapter 6. This section provides additional information. One of the main problems found in the basement is water penetration through the foundation wall that causes the basement to be permanently damp. An unfinished basement wall may show white stains. This staining is called efflorescence. **Efflorescence** *is caused by the masonry mineral salts that combine with the water as it penetrates through the floor or wall.* Water often seeps into the basement where the floor meets the wall (see Figure 7.14). Although a basement may be finished, it is usually not totally finished. Even in a finished basement, there are areas where you will be able to inspect the structural components.

FIGURE 7.14

Water penetration through the foundation and floor that caused efflorescence.

Source: Anthony D'Agostino, Atlantic Inspection Service, Latham, New York.

Some basements have a trap connected to the sewer line. The trap is located in a pit in the floor or on a wall, connected to the outgoing sewer pipe. If the pit is wet or there is water below the wall trap, this may indicate a leak or crack in the pipe. The pit should be dry and show no signs of leakage. The trap must be capped at all times to prevent gases and sewage from backing up into the basement.

Check all areas of the basement for water stains and rust. Examine metal objects stored in the basement for signs of rust. If the basement is paneled, water penetration shows up as water stains on the paneling or wood rot. Drywall finishes are susceptible to mold and mildew that may be visible as black, gray, or greenish spots in the wall. If the floor is carpeted and water has penetrated through the slab, the carpet may show signs of mold. Water damage to resilient floor tiles is evidenced by raised or buckled tiles and efflorescence between the tile joints. It is important to differentiate between water damage from the floor slab or foundation wall and water damage coming from above the basement. A spill or overflowing sink or shower is a one-time event, whereas defects in the foundation wall or floor are chronic issues.

Many furnaces and hot water heaters are located somewhere in the basement. This area should be free from exposed wood of any kind, including wall studs, sheathing, ceiling joists, or wood paneling. Areas in close proximity should be covered with fire-resistant drywall. Ensure that there is adequate ventilation around the furnace. If the furnace is not in an enclosed room, this is sufficient. A furnace room, however, must have openings for outside air. Many furnace rooms have louver doors that provide this ventilation. Ensure that the ventilation to a furnace room is not blocked. Examine basement stairs using the same criteria as other interior stairways.

Crawl Spaces

In older homes, crawl spaces may be inaccessible or are damp because there is a dirt floor. Vapor barriers can be installed in crawl spaces to reduce moisture.

There should be a source of ventilation such as a window or windows spaced around the foundation. If the property has both a basement and crawl space, then the ventilation is provided from the basement. If the crawl space is located underneath a section of the interior structure, check the floor joists and subfloor for any leaks, wood rot, mold, or twisted joists.

You Should Know

Home inspectors should exercise extreme caution when entering a crawl space. Watch for broken glass, hanging wires, rodents, and other animals.

FIREPLACES AND SOLID FUEL BURNING APPLIANCES

ireplaces and other solid fuel burning (SFB) appliances must comply with code requirements. Earthquake regions have codes with special requirements. See Chapter 6 for a discussion of chimneys.

Types of Fireplaces and SFB Appliances

A standard brick fireplace generally has a 36-inch opening, is about 28 inches high, and 16 to 20 inches deep. The inner walls angle inward and the back wall slopes forward, but sometimes the walls are vertical. Figure 7.15 illustrates a cross

FIGURE 7.15

A cross section of a fireplace.

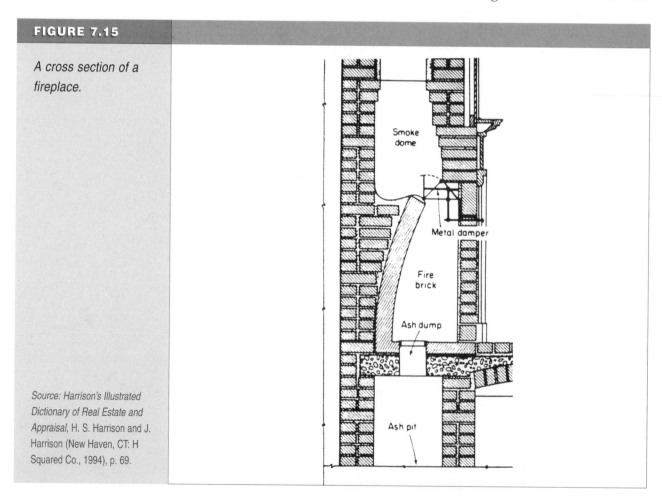

Source: Harrison's Illustrated Dictionary of Real Estate and Appraisal, H. S. Harrison and J. Harrison (New Haven, CT: H Squared Co., 1994), p. 69.

section of a fireplace. Factory-built fireplaces, constructed from steel, cast iron, firebrick, and other manufactured materials, are installed on-site and are equipped with factory-built chimneys. Gas fueled fireplaces may be connected to the gas heating system and can be constructed inside a masonry fireplace.

Types of Stoves

■ Franklin and other non-airtight cast-iron stoves look like a fireplace except that they freestand on a hearth and are connected to a chimney with a stovepipe. They have loose-fitting doors, are not airtight, and operate with the doors either open or closed. Other types of non-airtight stoves include barrel stoves (an oil barrel with a load door, legs, and a flue collar), small camp stoves, and turn-of-the-century potbelly stoves.

■ Airtight stoves achieve a long burn time by allowing very low rates of air-flow into the stove, causing a slow, smoky fire. There is a greater risk of creosote buildup and an increased chimney fire potential.

■ A radiant stove uses fire to heat the stove. The stove then heats the home by emitting infrared radiation.

■ Circulating stoves transfer heat to air moving across the hot surface. The air heats up and rises. The rising air draws more air after it, causing the air to circulate. A circulating stove has panels spaced out from the firebox and allows air to circulate between the firebox and the panels.

EPA-certified stoves. Newer EPA-certified stoves with stricter emission standards allow primary air to enter the stove through a long, thin slit across the top of the firebox. This creates a better mixture of oxygen with the fuel load for a more efficient primary combustion. Instead of letting the combustible gasses emitted by the fuel load escape up the flue, the gasses are burned through a catalytic combustor or a non-catalytic secondary combustion air system. A **catalytic combustor** *is a ceramic round, square, or rectangular insert with numerous small channels, or tubes, running through it. Applied to the ceramic surface is a layer of a catalytic chemical, generally platinum or palladium.* When sufficient temperatures are reached, this chemical coating reacts with smoke passing through the channels, reducing the smoke's ignition temperature and burning the smoke. As smoke passes through the combustor and is burned, it creates heat instead of pollution. The chemical coating is not burned or consumed in the process.

Non-catalytic stoves (called non-catstoves) *maximize combustion efficiency by providing a secondary combustion air system.* Smoke and gasses emitted by the fuel load are burned by the injection of secondary air into the stove. These stoves have a set of perforated stainless steel tubes (or a perforated baffle, or some similar device) across the top of the firebox. These tubes introduce air across the top that mixes with the combustible gasses rising from the fuel load, maximizing the combustion of the gases.

Wood-Burning Stove and Other Manufactured SFB or Gas-Burning Appliance Requirements

As with chimneys, metal fireplaces should be approved by Underwriters Laboratories (UL®). Freestanding fireplaces should be at least three feet from unprotected walls, drapes, or other flammable materials. Wall protection should be installed if the fireplace is closer than three feet. A brick pad or insulated fireproof material is placed on the floor beneath the appliance. Pipes connecting freestanding stoves and fireplaces to a chimney are at least 24-gauge steel that is UL® listed and installed in accordance with the listing. No pipe should be longer than 10 feet nor more than 75 percent of the vertical height of the chimney, whichever is less.

Both the fireplace and chimney should be supported properly. Wall-hung chimneys and fireplaces may place too much weight on walls and partitions, causing the floors to settle and masonry flues to crack. A modified fireplace (a firebox inserted into an existing fireplace) should have a steel liner at least one-quarter-inch thick to decrease the likelihood of rusting.

Fireplace and SFB Appliance Components

Flue

All fireplaces and SFB devices contain a **flue**, *which is the enclosed passageway in a chimney through which smoke and other gases move upward* (see Figure 7.16). The flue must be an adequate size: equal to at least one-tenth of the area of the fireplace opening for a chimney more than 15 feet tall or at least one-eighth of the area of the fireplace opening for a chimney less than 15 feet. Each fireplace must have its own flue, but more than one flue may be located in the same chimney. If a furnace and a fireplace connect to the same chimney, for example, there must be at least two vertical passageways up through the inside of the chimney. Separate flues are required because if there are breaks in the linings, smoke can cross over to one of the adjacent flues and leak into the home through a chimney-connected appliance in another room. Each flue must be constructed with *a solid brick partition* called a **wythe** (see Figure 7.17).

Damper

The **damper** *is a plate or valve that closes the fireplace flue when the fireplace is not in use, preventing heat loss.* It must be fully opened before lighting the fire. A **throat damper** *is a damper located in the throat of the fireplace, just above the fire-*

FIGURE 7.16

Diagram of a flue.

Source: Harrison's Illustrated Dictionary of Real Estate and Appraisal, H. S. Harrison and J. Harrison (New Haven, CT: H Squared Co., 1994), p. 70.

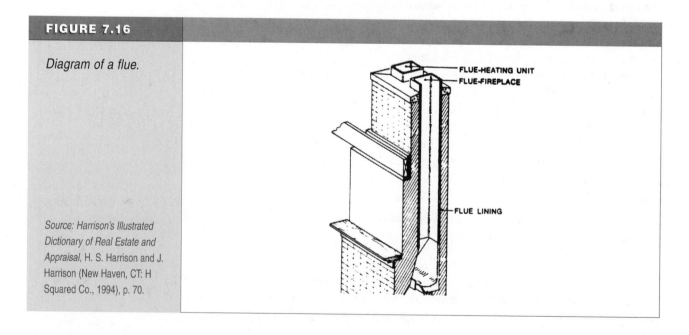

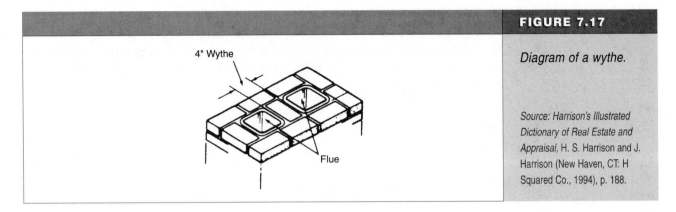

FIGURE 7.17

Diagram of a wythe.

Source: Harrison's Illustrated Dictionary of Real Estate and Appraisal, H. S. Harrison and J. Harrison (New Haven, CT: H Squared Co., 1994), p. 188.

box. This is the most common type of damper and is operated by either a handle inside the firebox or a knob above the fireplace opening that is connected to a rotating metal shaft attached to the damper. A top-sealing damper is located at the top of the chimney and is operated by a cable extending down the flue to a handle in the firebox.

Older wood-burning stoves may have a pipe damper, a round valve in the stovepipe, that is closed or opened to reduce or increase the flow of gasses through the stove. Newer catalytic stoves have a bypass damper in the form of a metal plate that allows smoke and gasses to bypass the catalytic unit. After the stove is heated to the temperature required for the catalytic unit to operate, the bypass damper is closed, forcing the smoke through the catalytic combustor. Many non-catstoves are designed without any damper.

Cleanout Door

At the base of the flue is a metal cleanout door. Standard fireplaces do not have this door because soot and debris are removed at the fireplace opening. If inspectors observe a door in the basement that is centered below the fireplace, it is probably an ash pit door (discussed later).

Hearth

The outer hearth is the area beyond the fireplace and should extend at least 16 inches into the room and 8 to 12 inches on either side of the fireplace opening. The hearth is composed of noncombustible, heat-resistant materials, such as brick, stone, tile, or concrete, and is at least four inches thick. The inner hearth is the floor of the fireplace itself.

> **You Should Know**
>
> Freestanding stoves sit on a hearth and are connected to a round hole in the chimney by a stovepipe.
>
> ☐ ☐ ☐

Firebox, Ash Dump Door, Ash Pit, and Ash Pit Cleanout Door

Some fireboxes are lined with masonry firebricks or a refractory cement; others are lined with steel or cast-iron panels. The **ash dump door** *is the metal door located in the inner hearth of some fireplaces and leads to an ash pit. The* **ash pit** *is a* *cavity underneath the firebox that is used as a receptacle for ashes and is accessible through a cleanout door. The* **ash pit cleanout door** *is a metal door located at the base of the chimney that leads to the ash pit.* Every stove includes some type of lever, dial, or handle that is used to adjust the amount of air entering the firebox and regulate heat output.

Baffle

In wood-burning stoves, the baffle is a device that slows or changes the direction of the gasses in the stove. Most baffles are steel, cast-iron, or refractory brick plates installed at the top of the firebox. Smoke and gasses must move around the baffle before exiting. This increases the amount of time the gasses remain in the stove, allowing for total combustion.

Inspecting Fireplaces and Manufactured Wood-Burning Appliances

■ Examine, when possible, for cracks, blockages, and leaks in the flue lining, bricks, and mortar.

■ Look for creosote buildup.

■ In masonry fireplaces, check the brickwork for wear and breakage.

■ Check the damper—it should freely open and close. Corrosion and debris are the most common causes of stuck dampers. Examine the smoke chamber above the damper. Sometimes the damper is too low, forcing smoke to spill back into the room. A misplaced damper can be removed and replaced or smoke guards that lower the top of the fireplace opening can be installed. Check that the damper is not warped, rotten, broken, or corroded. A stuck damper blade may be caused by a buildup of sand, soot, and debris behind the damper. The chimney may need cleaning.

Putting It to Work	When checking the damper, watch for debris coming down from the flue.

■ Check for excessive black smoke stains above or on the sides of the fireplace opening. Smoke stains around the fireplace opening are an indication of the improper use of the fireplace or a smoking problem. Sometimes smoke stains are caused by leaky gaskets around the frame of a fireplace door or a partial or complete blockage of the flue. Animal nests, leaves, debris, or the internal collapse of chimney brickwork can cause blockages. The remedy is a chimney cap with a screen mesh installed on the chimney.

■ Examine for water leaking into the fireplace. The chimney cap should prevent water from running down the flue. Cracks or holes in the crown of the chimney or in other areas may allow leakage. It is also possible that pooling water is soaking through the structure.

■ Examine for efflorescence, or white stains, on the fireplace walls. Efflorescence is an early indicator of water damage, often seen inside the fireplace due to water pooling above the damper and soaking through.

■ Observe that there is adequate clearance around the fireplace or wood-burning device.

■ While inspecting wood-burning stoves, check the condition of the stovepipe leading to the chimney. If it is rusty or soft or has holes in it, it must be replaced. If there is soot, creosote, or signs of leakage on the outside of the stove or stovepipe, this may be the result of installation defects or a problem with stove operation. Check the inside and the outside of the stove for cracks, bulges, warping, rust, or other signs of damage or wear.

■ Examine the **flue collar**, the opening on the top, rear, or side of a wood-burning stove to which the stovepipe is connected.

Note the type of fireplace on the inspection report. Is it wood- or gas-burning, masonry or metal, freestanding or built into the structure?

Putting It to Work

IMPORTANT POINTS

1. The interior inspection includes the examination and observation of all interior rooms; accessible doors and locking mechanisms; walls, ceilings, floors, steps, stairways, and railings; the garage, garage doors, and garage door openers; the attic including opening(s), accessibility, framing, sheathing, insulation, ventilation, and exposed wiring; flues, dampers, and associated components; fireplaces and other SFB appliances; and mechanical ventilation systems.

2. Once a problem is noted in one part of the structure, the inspector may have to examine another section of the structure to determine the cause.

3. Exterior doors must lock from both the inside and outside. Interior doors, if they have locks at all, lock only from the inside of the room. Open and shut all doors to test for operability.

4. Interior walls are either load bearing or non-load bearing.

5. Many walls and ceilings are composed of gypsum board, also known as drywall or wallboard.

6. Before gypsum board, most ceilings and walls were formed from plaster-coated metal or wooden laths.

7. Plaster walls are generally found in homes that are 50 or more years old.

8. If the walls and ceilings are constructed from gypsum board, the workmanship is checked first.

9. The main question to answer during the examination of a suspended ceiling is whether it was constructed to cover up a problem with the ceiling above it.

10. Examine the joints between the resilient floor sheets and tiles to make sure that the materials are bonded to the subfloor and that there are no gaps between the squares or sheet seams.

11. When examining the trim, determine that it is not warped or bowed and that the corner joints are properly mitered.

12. Generally, all areas exposed to exterior temperatures require insulation. Home inspectors should check the insulation's type, quality, and effectiveness where visible.

13. Codes may require that all building envelope materials that absorb moisture be protected by a vapor barrier on the insulation applied to the warm (inside) wall of exterior walls.

14. The attic inspection may be hindered by accessibility problems. In some homes, the attic may be completely inaccessible. Electrical wiring hidden from sight in the attic may pose a safety hazard.

15. All ventilation systems have a central exhaust fan and several ducts to remove stale air from various places in the house.

16. A major source of roof damage originates in the attic. Inadequate insulation and the absence of a vapor barrier and ventilation compromise the roof system, causing extensive moisture damage.

17. The attached garage floor should be 4 to 12 inches lower than the floor of the habitable space, but many garage floors are not.

18. If the garage door is operated mechanically, inspectors must check to see if the reverse mechanism is operational.

19. One of the main problems found in the basement is water penetration through the foundation wall that causes the basement to be permanently damp.

20. Freestanding fireplaces should be at least three feet from unprotected walls, drapes, or other flammable materials.

21. Wall-hung chimneys and fireplaces may place too much weight on walls and partitions, causing the floors to settle and masonry flues to crack.

CHAPTER REVIEW

Field Study Assignment 1

Using your practice property and a copy of the inspection checklist from Figure 4.4, inspect the interior of your subject property. Omit the inspection of the kitchen, bathroom, plumbing, and electrical because this is discussed in future chapters. Note any problems you encounter for further exploration and discussion.

Field Study Assignment 2

Find and identify the type of insulation used in your subject property. Examine the insulation to see whether it is bonded to a vapor barrier. If so, what kind of material is used?

1. Which of the following is included in an interior inspection?
   A. garage door opener
   B. electromagnetic fields
   C. indoor air quality
   D. central vacuum system

2. One of the tasks of the home inspector is to:
   A. advise the clients as to whether they should buy the property
   B. find all code violations
   C. reinspect an area that may yield information regarding a problem in another part of the structure
   D. show prospects their credentials

3. A major difference between exterior and interior doors is that:
   A. interior doors rarely have locks
   B. interior doors have more hinges than exterior doors
   C. interior doors are heavier than exterior doors
   D. interior doors are generally hollow

4. Metal laths are used in the application of which of the following:
   A. ceiling tiles
   B. plaster
   C. gypsum board
   D. suspended ceilings

5. One of the main problems to look for when inspecting ceiling tiles and suspended ceilings is:
   A. hidden damage in the ceiling underneath
   B. electrical code violations
   C. out-of-date design
   D. little or no insulation around the tile material

6. A random and slight bulge in the drywall could be an indicator of:
   A. mold or mildew
   B. a popping nail
   C. the detachment of the glue that holds the drywall seams together
   D. the drywall turning to a powdery substance

7. Cracks found on a plaster wall may indicate an underlying structural problem if they are:
   A. one-sixteenth-inch wide
   B. one-eighth-inch wide
   C. one-half-inch wide
   D. none of the above

8. An example of resilient flooring is which of the following:
   A. clay tile
   B. wood plank
   C. carpeting
   D. rubber

9. One of the main causes of a sagging floor is:
   A. warped floorboards
   B. inability of the floor joists to support the load on the floor's surface
   C. cracked or chipped ceramic tile
   D. walls that are not plumb

10. Insulation is required:
    A. inside all interior walls
    B. underneath all floor joists
    C. in all areas where the structure is exposed to exterior temperatures
    D. in all ceiling joists

11. Insulation is rated according to:
    A. a BTU
    B. an ohm
    C. an R-value
    D. a heat retention index

12. A vapor barrier should be applied to the:
    A. inside wall of exterior walls
    B. attic floor only
    C. inside wall of interior walls
    D. plumbing pipes only

13. Which of the following is NOT an issue in the attic inspection?
    A. accessibility
    B. drainage
    C. ventilation
    D. hidden wiring

14. Moisture condensation in the attic most directly effects which of the following roof components?
    A. roof rafters
    B. fascia
    C. soffit
    D. ridge vent

15. Proper ventilation and insulation most directly prevent which of the following weather conditions from forming:
    A. water buildup in the gutter
    B. ice dams
    C. water leakage into the structure
    D. wind damage

16. An attached garage is constructed lower than the rest of the structure because:
    A. it is aesthetically more pleasing
    B. it keeps dust and debris from entering the house
    C. all codes require that a stairway from the garage lead up into the house
    D. it prevents gas fumes and other vapors from entering the house

17. The garage door is balanced by the:
    A. torsion spring
    B. lift handle
    C. photoelectric eye
    D. sensing edge

18. The internal reversing mechanism on the garage door opener is important because it:
    A. keeps the garage door locked
    B. causes the door to open back up if it hits an obstruction
    C. prevents peoples' fingers from catching in the section joints
    D. resets the opener mechanism if the garage door is opened manually

19. Efflorescence is caused by:
    A. mold
    B. mineral salts
    C. wood rot
    D. fluorescent paint

20. Where might water most likely leak through the basement wall?
    A. from the ceiling
    B. from the trap
    C. where the floor slab and foundation wall meet
    D. none of the above

21. The most important problem to diagnose when evidence of water is found in the basement is:
    A. whether efflorescence has occurred
    B. the location of the crawl space
    C. the source of the problem
    D. the location of the furnace room

22. How many feet from draperies, unprotected walls, and other flammable materials must free-standing fireplaces be placed?
    A. one foot
    B. three feet
    C. five feet
    D. seven feet

23. A solid brick partition in a chimney that has more than one flue is known as a:
    A. wythe
    B. cast-in-place liner
    C. flue collar
    D. bypass damper

24. Excessive black smoke stains above or on the sides of the fireplace opening may indicate:
    A. a fire that was too hot
    B. a hearth that is too small
    C. the absence of a baffle
    D. partial or complete blockage of the flue

ANSWER KEY

1. A	7. C	13. B	19. B
2. C	8. D	14. A	20. C
3. D	9. B	15. B	21. C
4. B	10. C	16. D	22. B
5. A	11. C	17. A	23. A
6. B	12. A	18. B	24. D

CHAPTER 8

INSPECTING THE PLUMBING, HEATING, AND AIR-CONDITIONING SYSTEMS

The inspection of residential plumbing, heating, and cooling systems varies from property to property. There is a vast difference in the equipment and materials used in older versus newer systems. This chapter covers the most common systems you will examine and observe.

LEARNING OBJECTIVES

1. List the items that are included in the inspection of the plumbing, heating, and cooling systems.
2. Describe the general procedure for the vent and pipe system inspection.
3. Describe the general procedure for inspecting the heating and cooling systems.
4. Explain how to examine the plumbing fixtures.

KEY TERMS

Aquifer

Backflow preventer

Boiler

BTU

Cesspool

Cleanout

Compressor

Condenser

Convector

Evaporator

Float valve

Forced warm air system

Freon

Gate valve

Globe valve

Heat exchanger

Hydronic system

Main soil stack

Main vent stack

Nonpotable water

Plenum

Plumbing fixture

Potable water

Pressure regulator valve (PRV)

Refrigerant

Septic system

Soil or waste stack

Steam system

Temperature pressure relief valve

Thermocouple

Thermostat

Trap

Valve

Vent system

Water hammer arrestor

SCOPE OF THE INSPECTION

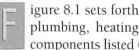igure 8.1 sets forth the ASHI Standards of Practice for the inspection of the plumbing, heating, and air-conditioning systems. Note that some of the components listed (e.g., chimneys and flues) are discussed in other chapters.

PLUMBING SYSTEM

The plumbing in a house consists of two systems: the water supply system used for drinking, cooking, and washing and the drainage system for wastewater. These systems must be separated from each other to prevent contamination. Local building codes are very specific as to the structure of the plumbing system and the materials used.

Inspecting the Plumbing System

The most time-efficient way to inspect the plumbing system is to perform it as you inspect the property room by room. The plumbing system is integral to the functionality of the property and its components appear throughout the house. When you inspect the basement, for example, this is the time to examine the furnace, hot water heater, drainage, and other pipes. If this equipment is located in the garage or other location, then it is inspected at that time. All plumbing fixtures are inspected in the rooms where they appear. In the average house, this is the kitchen and bathroom.

Water Supply Systems

Most suburban and municipal areas have access to public water supply systems. These systems, generally regulated by local health departments, are the recommended source of water supply. A public water supply source can be a municipality such as a city, village, or town. The water supply system in the house delivers potable water to all of the fixtures. **Potable water** *is water that is safe for drinking.* **Nonpotable water** *is wastewater or recycled water used in plumbing fixtures and is not safe for consumption.* Water is brought under pressure from a municipal water main into the house piping system. The service pipe that brings the water into the house is generally three-quarter-inch in diameter, but larger pipes can be found in older homes. All water fixtures should have separate cutoffs so that a repair can be made without shutting down the entire system.

You Should Know

Although lead pipes are still used for a variety of applications, this pipe material should never transport drinking water. Lead can easily leach into the water supply and is a health hazard, especially to children. In older homes, it is important to recognize whether a property is still using lead pipes for the main water supply. Inspectors can use a simple magnet, such as from a refrigerator, to test the composition of the pipes. If the magnet adheres to the pipe, it is composed of galvanized steel; if not, it is most likely composed of lead. Lead pipe is also recognized by a bulb-shaped joint. In most applications, galvanized steel pipe is used to carry drinking water through the service supply line. Chapter 10 more fully discusses the dangers of lead in paint and drinking water.

FIGURE 8.1

Applicable ASHI Standards of Practice.

6. PLUMBING SYSTEM

6.1 The inspector shall:

A. inspect:

1. interior water supply and distribution systems including all fixtures and faucets.
2. drain, waste, and vent systems including all fixtures.
3. water heating equipment and hot water supply system.
4. vent systems, flues, and chimneys.
5. fuel storage and fuel distribution systems.
6. drainage sumps, sump pumps, and related piping.

B. describe:

1. water supply, drain, waste, and vent piping materials.
2. water heating equipment including energy source(s).
3. location of main water and main fuel shut-off valves.

6.2 The inspector is NOT required to:

A. inspect:

1. clothes washing machine connections.
2. interiors of flues or chimneys which are not readily accessible.
3. wells, well pumps, or water storage related equipment.
4. water conditioning systems.
5. solar water heating systems.
6. fire and lawn sprinkler systems.
7. private waste disposal systems.

B. determine:

1. whether water supply and waste disposal systems are public or private.
2. water supply quantity or quality.

C. operate automatic safety controls or manual stop valves.

8. HEATING SYSTEM

8.1 The inspector shall:

A. open readily openable access panels

B. inspect:

1. installed heating equipment.
2. vent systems, flues, and chimneys.

B. describe:

1. energy source(s).
2. heating systems.

(continued)

FIGURE 8.1

Applicable ASHI Standards of Practice, continued.

8.2 The inspector is NOT required to:
  A. inspect:
     1. interiors of flues or chimneys that are not readily accessible.
     2. heat exchangers.
     3. humidifiers or dehumidifiers.
     4. electronic air filters.
     5. solar space heating systems.
  B. determine heat supply adequacy or distribution balance.

9. AIR CONDITIONING SYSTEMS

9.1 The inspector shall:
  A. open readily openable access panels.
  B. inspect:
     1. central and through-wall equipment.
     2. distribution systems.
  C. describe:
     1. energy source(s).
     2. cooling systems.

9.2 The inspector is NOT required to:
  A. inspect electronic air filters.
  B. determine cooling supply adequacy or distribution balance.
  C. inspect window air conditioning units.

Permission to reprint and reference granted by the American Society of Home Inspectors, Inc. (ASHI) www.ASHI.org

---

Putting It to Work

If a property is serviced by municipal water, a water meter (Figure 8.2) is generally found along the outside foundation wall, in the basement, or elsewhere in the interior. Households that rely on well water generally have a storage tank that is located in the basement.

Inspecting the Public Water Supply Entrance

The inspector must do the following:

- Check the location of the main service line and the condition of the pipe. Galvanized steel pipes are coated with zinc and as the zinc corrodes, the pipes may rust. Look for leaking or rusted pipe.
- Check to see whether the main service pipe is made of lead.
- Find the location of the water meter.
- Determine whether there is a pressure-reducing valve near the water meter. This is used when the municipal water pressure is too great for the house's piping system.
- Find the main shut-off valve and examine its condition.

Well Water

Groundwater is a significant water source for millions of people. Homes in rural areas may depend on individual and community well-water supplies. Therefore,

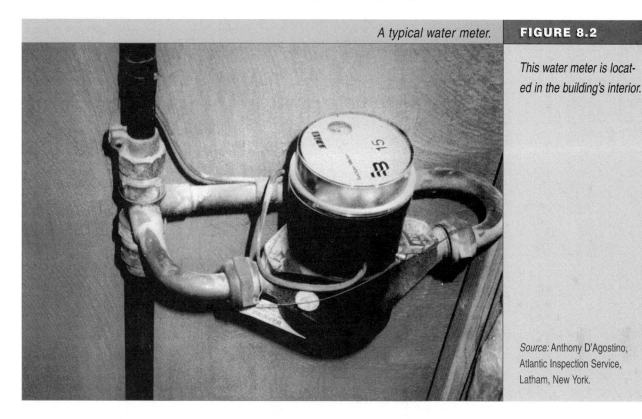

A typical water meter. **FIGURE 8.2**

This water meter is located in the building's interior.

Source: Anthony D'Agostino, Atlantic Inspection Service, Latham, New York.

home inspectors encounter wells at many of the properties they inspect. Home inspection standards generally do not require a water quality examination or an analysis of the well's function (see Chapter 10 for a complete discussion). However, a well inspection can be performed if the clients want the well inspected and the inspector is competent to do so. If problems are suspected or uncovered during the inspection, the inspector should recommend that a professional make any further evaluations and repairs.

Departments of health often furnish guidelines for the proper location, construction, and protection of well water. If guidelines are not followed or an area becomes heavily populated, the sanitary quality of the well water can be jeopardized. There are several types of wells: drilled, dug, and spring. Studies have shown that drilled wells are the better type. Dug wells can be excavated by hand or by mechanical equipment. A spring is classified as rock or earth, depending on the source. Figure 8.3 illustrates a cross section of a drilled well.

Typical code specifications governing well construction include:

- Wells are built at a depth of more than 20 feet below the ground surface.
- The well should be situated in an accessible location not subject to flooding. The location must be a sufficient distance from potential sources of pollution on the owner's property or any adjoining properties.
- Wastewater systems must be separated from buildings, property lines, wells, and waterways according to specified minimum distances.

Table 8.1 identifies the minimum separation distances from the well to the components of a wastewater system required by one municipality. Figure 8.4 illustrates a home's layout pattern as it relates to the well water and wastewater disposal systems.

FIGURE 8.3

A cross section of a drilled well.

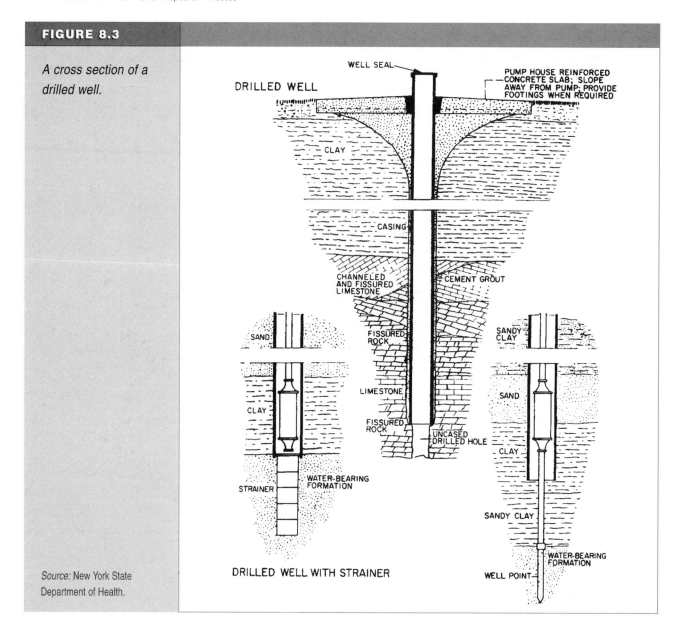

DRILLED WELL

WELL SEAL

PUMP HOUSE REINFORCED CONCRETE SLAB; SLOPE AWAY FROM PUMP; PROVIDE FOOTINGS WHEN REQUIRED

CLAY

CASING

CHANNELED AND FISSURED LIMESTONE

CEMENT GROUT

FISSURED ROCK

LIMESTONE

FISSURED ROCK

UNCASED DRILLED HOLE

SAND

CLAY

STRAINER

WATER-BEARING FORMATION

DRILLED WELL WITH STRAINER

SANDY CLAY

SAND

CLAY

SANDY CLAY

WATER-BEARING FORMATION

WELL POINT

Source: New York State Department of Health.

Well Components

Well water is water pumped up from the ground below the water table. Underground water flows along streams or aquifers. **Aquifers** *are below ground-level rock beds over which water flows.* Well water is derived from the aquifer and the water above it. A private water supply system is composed of the well, a pump, the storage tank, and the connecting pipe between the well and the storage tank.

Types of well pumps. The well pump types commonly found in residential wells include the piston pump, the jet or ejector pump, and the submersible pump.

SYSTEM COMPONENTS	TO WELL OR SUCTION LINE	TO STREAM, LAKE, WATERCOURSE, OR WETLAND	TO DWELLING	TO PROPERTY LINE
House sewer (watertight joints)	25' if cast iron pipe, 50' otherwise	25'	10'	10'
Septic tank	50'	50'	10'	10'
Effluent line to distribution box	50'	50'	10'	10'
Distribution box	100'	100'	20'	10'
Absorption field	100'	100'	20'	10'
Seepage pit	150'	100'	20'	10'
Dry well (roof and footing)	50'	25'	20'	10'
Raised or mound system	100'	100'	20'	10'
Evapotranspiration- absorption system	100'	50'	20'	10'
Composter	50'	50'	20'	10'

Separation distances from wastewater system components. TABLE 8.1

Source: New York State Department of Health.

1. A *piston pump* is available in two types: one for shallow wells and one for deep wells. A piston pump uses the up-and-down motion of a piston to displace water in a cylinder.

As a piston is driven in one direction, water fills the chamber behind it. The water is forced into the system when the piston reverses direction. Water flow in and out of the chamber is controlled by valves. Shallow piston pumps are used in wells up to 22 feet deep. With deep piston pumps, the pump cylinder is attached to the bottom of a drop pipe. As the piston moves up and down, it pumps water up through the pipe. For shallow wells, the motor and piston are on the ground. Deep piston pumps have the motor on the ground and the piston assembly in the well. Piston pumps are primarily found in older wells.

2. A *jet (ejector) pump* (Figure 8.5) delivers water under pressure by the centrifugal pump through the nozzle of the ejector. The centrifugal pump then picks up the water flow, sending part of the water through the discharge pipe and the rest back to the ejector. If the well is shallow, the pump is on the ground surface and the jet and centrifugal pump are adjacent to each other. Water can be lifted from a depth of 22 feet. For deep wells, the centrifugal pump is still on the ground, but the jet assembly is submerged in the well casing. Water can be lifted with this pump from a depth of 85 feet.

3. A *submersible pump* (Figure 8.6) is a type of centrifugal pump that has several impellers mounted together on a vertical shaft. The impellers and motor are

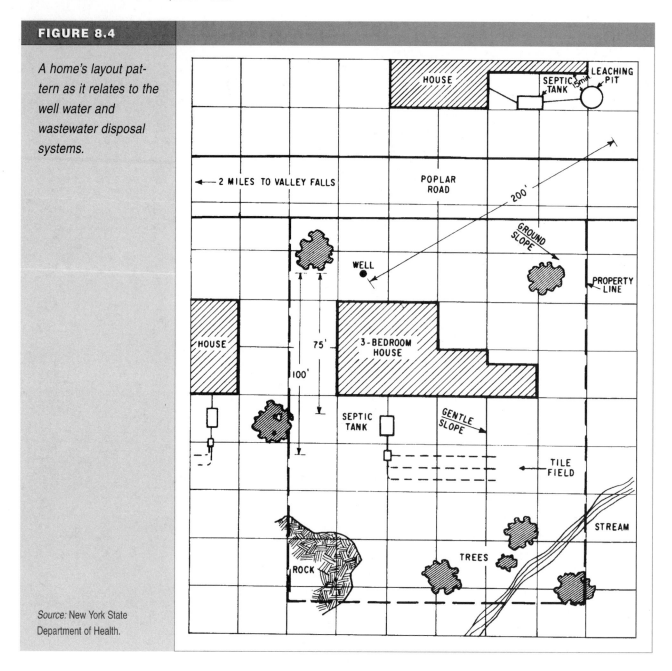

FIGURE 8.4

A home's layout pattern as it relates to the well water and wastewater disposal systems.

Source: New York State Department of Health.

in a housing that is positioned below the water level. A submersible pump can lift water from a depth of 1,000 feet. The pump capacity and pressure depend on the diameter, speed, and number of impellers.

Well-water storage tanks. The purpose of a well-water storage tank is to prevent the well from pumping every time the household uses water. Types of well-water storage include the following:

■ *Pressure tank.* As the pressure tank fills with water, the air inside the tank is compressed. As more water is added, the pressure inside the tank increases because the air takes up less volume. As the water is used, the compressed air pushes the water out of the tank under pressure. As the water level drops in the tank, the volume that the air occupies grows and the pressure it exerts decreases.

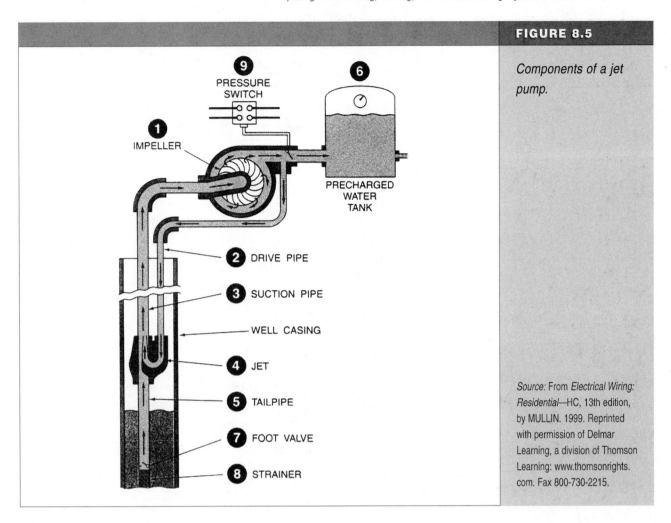

FIGURE 8.5

Components of a jet pump.

Source: From *Electrical Wiring: Residential*—HC, 13th edition, by MULLIN. 1999. Reprinted with permission of Delmar Learning, a division of Thomson Learning: www.thomsonrights. com. Fax 800-730-2215.

■ *Elastic pressure cells.* These cells have a capacity of about three gallons. A cell is composed of a metal cylinder with an elastic liner on the inside. As the pump delivers water under pressure to the cell, the elastic liner is compressed as the cylinder is filled. Then, when a faucet is turned on, the water is forced out of the cell by the pressure provided by the expanding liner.

■ *Gravity tank.* This is a large tank located above the level of the structure. It differs from other storage tanks because the pressure in a gravity tank is not derived from the amount of water in the tank; rather, it is derived from the elevation above the water outlets.

■ *Reservoirs.* Water may also be stored in reservoirs built at pump level that supply little or no pressure to the system. Made of poured concrete or steel, they serve as storage holding tanks and are generally used when a continuous but small supply is needed. With this sort of arrangement, a second pump is required to pump water, under pressure, from the intermediate storage to the faucet.

Inspecting the Well Components

Inspectors must not disassemble or remove any well equipment. Nor are they responsible for making a determination as to the water quality (see Chapter 10). Much of a well inspection consists of identifying that there is a well and

FIGURE 8.6

A submersible pump.

Source: From *Electrical Wiring: Residential—HC*, 13th edition, by MULLIN. 1999. Reprinted with permission of Delmar Learning, a division of Thomson Learning: www. thomsonrights.com. Fax 800-730-2215.

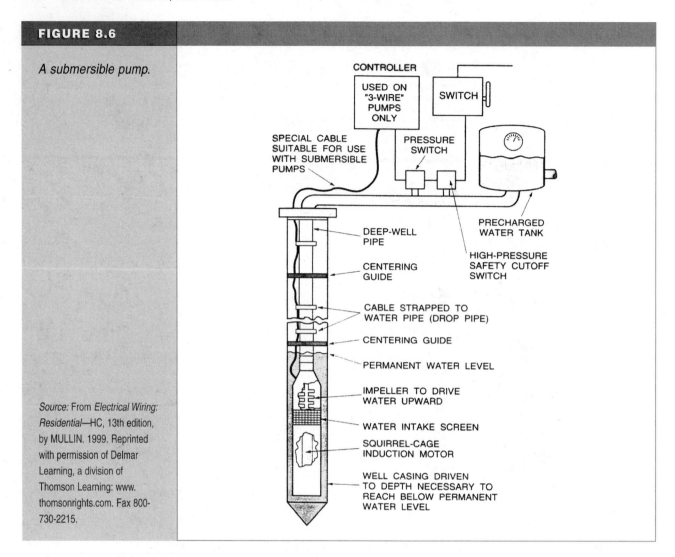

CONTROLLER
USED ON "3-WIRE" PUMPS ONLY

SWITCH

SPECIAL CABLE SUITABLE FOR USE WITH SUBMERSIBLE PUMPS

PRESSURE SWITCH

PRECHARGED WATER TANK

DEEP-WELL PIPE

CENTERING GUIDE

HIGH-PRESSURE SAFETY CUTOFF SWITCH

CABLE STRAPPED TO WATER PIPE (DROP PIPE)

CENTERING GUIDE

PERMANENT WATER LEVEL

IMPELLER TO DRIVE WATER UPWARD

WATER INTAKE SCREEN

SQUIRREL-CAGE INDUCTION MOTOR

WELL CASING DRIVEN TO DEPTH NECESSARY TO REACH BELOW PERMANENT WATER LEVEL

determining the well's location and the location of its components, the type of well, and the pump's operability.

In order to determine whether the pump is working, the inspector has to run the water. Once the pressure tank is empty enough, the pump should kick in. At the same time, the inspector observes the pressure gauge to ascertain whether the reading indicates that the holding tank's pressure is dropping. After a time, the pressure tank should fill and the pump automatically turns off. If the pump does not turn on to fill the tank or does not turn off after the tank is filled, it may be malfunctioning. To repair the pump, it must be pulled from the well. Inspectors should advise their clients that a plumber, an electrician, or an individual who specializes in well repair must examine and repair the pump.

Inspectors should also examine, as much as possible, the condition of the storage tank. Check for leaks, rust, and corrosion and examine the functionality of the main shut-off valve between the well pipes and the storage tank.

Sanitary Waste Systems

With houses that are part of a municipal wastewater system, the wastewater drains through the house drainage system into a house sewer that connects to the municipal sewer system or is deposited in a private wastewater system. Within the house, waste and water from the plumbing fixtures move down the fixture drain and through soil or waste pipes, known as soil stacks, that connect to branch soil pipes and, finally, to the main soil or waste stack. **Soil or waste stacks** *are vertical pipes into which waste flows from waste pipes connected to each fixture.* The **main soil stack** *connects to the house drain where the waste leaves the system.* Pipe diameters (discussed later) are sized to promote the rapid flow of the waste material. The system relies on the pull of gravity. Because of this, drainage pipes are generally larger in diameter, typically up to four inches, than water supply pipes. The horizontal slope of the pipe is regulated by plumbing codes. Figure 8.7 illustrates the main components of a typical residential sanitary piping system. Figure 8.8 illustrates typical cast-iron soil pipe fittings. Figure 8.9 shows how a floor joist was improperly cut away to fit a drainage pipe.

Venting Requirements

The **vent system** *consists of pipes that provide a flow of air to and from a drainage system.* These vent pipes allow air to circulate to ensure the rapid and silent flow of waste and stop backpressure. Vent piping permits gases and odors in the drainage piping to circulate up through the system and escape into the air.

Every plumbing fixture is connected to a vent pipe, which is then connected to a roof vent pipe or vent stack. The **main vent stack** *is the top of the main soil stack and connects to all of the home's toilets.* Secondary vents connect to other fixtures such as sink traps. Building codes specify venting requirements.

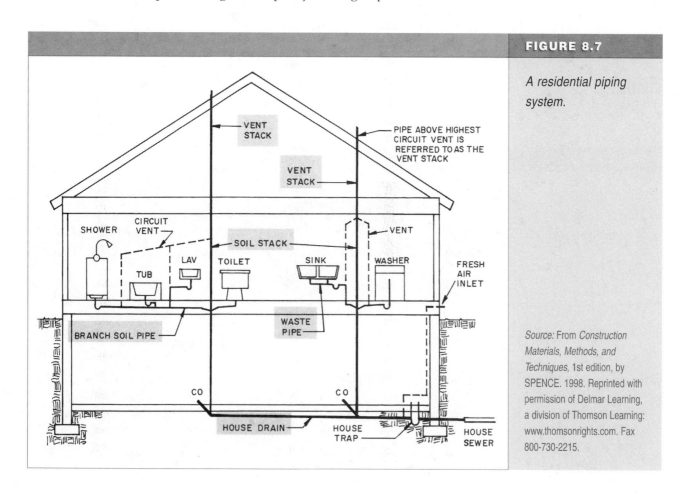

FIGURE 8.7

A residential piping system.

Source: From *Construction Materials, Methods, and Techniques*, 1st edition, by SPENCE. 1998. Reprinted with permission of Delmar Learning, a division of Thomson Learning: www.thomsonrights.com. Fax 800-730-2215.

FIGURE 8.8

Typical cast-iron soil pipe fittings.

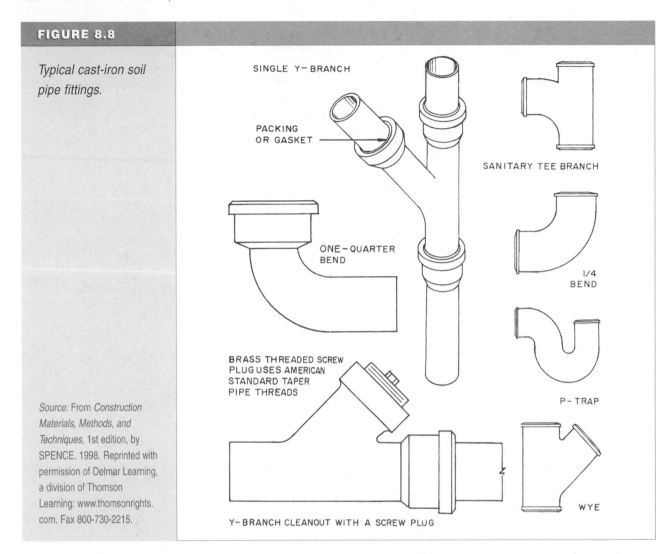

SINGLE Y-BRANCH

PACKING OR GASKET

ONE-QUARTER BEND

BRASS THREADED SCREW PLUG USES AMERICAN STANDARD TAPER PIPE THREADS

Y-BRANCH CLEANOUT WITH A SCREW PLUG

SANITARY TEE BRANCH

1/4 BEND

P-TRAP

WYE

Source: From *Construction Materials, Methods, and Techniques,* 1st edition, by SPENCE. 1998. Reprinted with permission of Delmar Learning, a division of Thomson Learning: www.thomsonrights. com. Fax 800-730-2215.

FIGURE 8.9

A floor joist was improperly cut away to fit a drainage pipe.

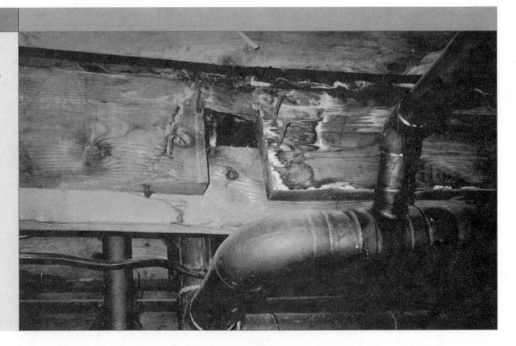

Source: Anthony D'Agostino, Atlantic Inspection Service, Latham, New York.

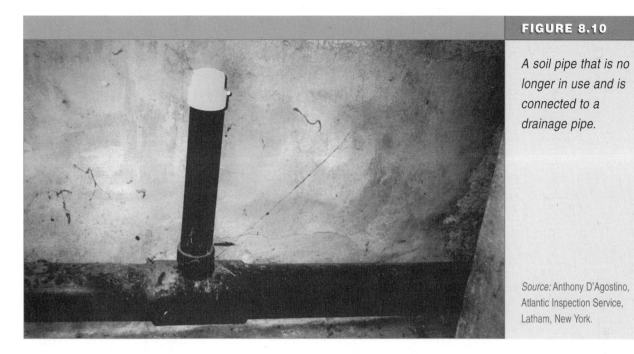

FIGURE 8.10

A soil pipe that is no longer in use and is connected to a drainage pipe.

Source: Anthony D'Agostino, Atlantic Inspection Service, Latham, New York.

The vent pipe keeps the water in a fixture's trap under atmospheric pressure so that it is not siphoned out if another fixture is added. A drain may have a **cleanout**, which is *a pipe fitted with a removable plug.* An auger may be run to dislodge an obstruction in the pipe.

Inspecting the Vent System

The first item to look for when inspecting the vent pipes is whether or not there is a plumbing vent stack venting through the roof. The absence of the vent stack is a violation of plumbing codes. To check for the vent stack's presence or improper venting, run water in a sink and let it drain. If there are gurgling or sucking noises, it is possible that the fixture is not vented to the outside. The inspector should also check every fixture for foul smells. Sewer gasses are unmistakable and another indicator of the absence of or improper venting. Figure 8.10 illustrates a soil pipe, no longer in use, connected to a drainage pipe. Because the soil pipe has no cap, it allows sewer gases to vent into the structure.

On-Site Wastewater Treatment Systems

In most rural and some suburban residential areas, individual wastewater treatment systems are used to dispose of household wastes. *A typical household wastewater treatment system consists of a house sewer, a septic tank, a distribution box, and an absorption field or seepage pit.* This is known as a **septic system.** Figure 8.11 diagrams a typical septic system.

In a household septic system, the house sewer is the pipeline connecting the house to the drain and septic tank. Because untreated waste clogs the absorption field if not properly treated, the septic tank provides this needed treatment. The distribution box evenly distributes the flow from the septic tank to the absorption field or seepage pits. The absorption field is a system of narrow trenches partially filled with a bed of washed gravel into which perforated joint pipe is placed. The discharge from the septic tank is distributed through these pipes into the trenches

---

FIGURE 8.11

A house septic system.

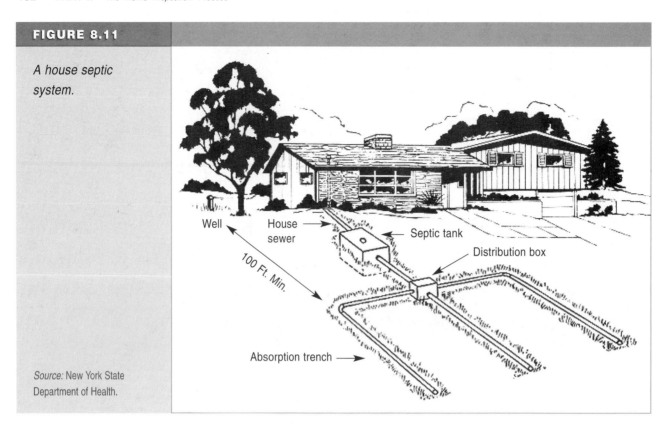

Source: New York State Department of Health.

---

and surrounding soil. The seepage pit is a covered pit with a perforated or open-jointed lining through which the discharge from the septic tank infiltrates the surrounding soil. According to many health department regulations, if soil and site conditions are adequate for absorption trenches, seepage pits cannot be used.

House sewer construction, including materials, must comply with code requirements of minimum separation distances between a wastewater system and wells, streams, lakes, wetlands, the house, and the property line. Refer back to Table 8.1.

Inspecting the Septic System

Because the septic system is underground and the house drain looks the same whether connected to a private or municipal system, the presence of a septic system may not be obvious. An inspection of the septic system is not typically part of a home inspection, but home inspectors who work in rural areas may examine the system for the same reason they examine a private water supply system. When inspecting the system, the inspector should find the location of the absorption field, with the help of the property owner, if possible. One problem the inspector may encounter is that some home owners have a cesspool instead of a fully functioning septic system. A **cesspool** is *simply a pit (sometimes lined with plastic) composed of stones and gravel through which raw sewage collects.* This is a health and safety hazard and a violation of plumbing and building codes.

Septic systems require regular maintenance and should be cleaned every three years to prevent sludge buildup. If the tank is not regularly cleaned, the sludge will leach out into the absorption field and interfere with the absorption trenches. Inspectors should try, if possible, to ascertain the age of the septic tank by asking the property owner.

The absorption field should be examined for any questionable liquids oozing through the ground. There should be no foul smelling odors in the area of a properly functioning septic system.

Seepage and overflow in septic systems can sometimes be observed by using a tracer dye. The inspector flushes the dye into the sanitary waste system and then checks the pipes for leaks and the ground surface for evidence of the tracer.

Putting It to Work

Pipes

Because most pipes are hidden behind walls, ceilings, and floors, they cannot all be accessed for inspection. Exposed pipe is generally found in the basement and in cabinets under plumbing fixtures. Pipes are sometimes protected from freezing with insulation. For example, pipes in a crawl space should be protected with insulation in colder climates. Pipes for water supply and house drainage systems come in a range of types and have advantages and disadvantages (discussed later). Older homes contain different piping materials than those that are common today.

Pipe Fittings

Pipes must be connected using certain types of fittings. Water pipes use butt-welded, socket, and threaded fittings. The bell and spigot connection is used on sewer lines. Coupling is a type of fitting that simply connects one pipe to another. Elbow fittings change the direction of the pipe. Pipe ends are closed by installing a coupling and screwing a plug into it. A cap screws over the end of the pipe. Figure 8.12 illustrates types of pipe and fitting connections.

Valves

In addition to pipe sizing, water pressure can be regulated by other means. A booster pump or other similar system is used to increase water pressure. Valves

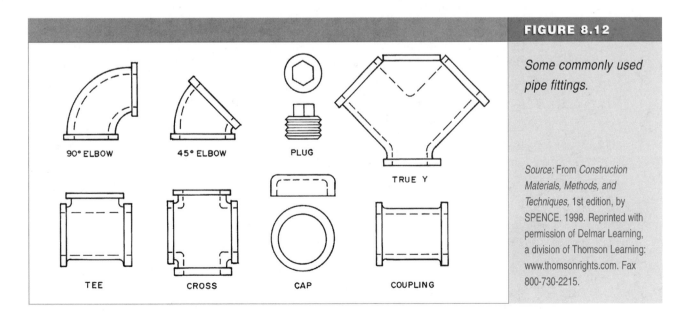

FIGURE 8.12

Some commonly used pipe fittings.

90° ELBOW   45° ELBOW   PLUG   TRUE Y   TEE   CROSS   CAP   COUPLING

Source: From *Construction Materials, Methods, and Techniques*, 1st edition, by SPENCE. 1998. Reprinted with permission of Delmar Learning, a division of Thomson Learning: www.thomsonrights.com. Fax 800-730-2215.

are also used with pipes to control the flow of water. A **valve** *is a device used to regulate the flow of a liquid or gas. It may force the flow in a certain direction.* Valves found in residential construction and equipment include:

- The **gate valve** *is mostly used as the main water shutoff valve to the property.* It is also used to stop the flow of water to fixtures and equipment such as when repairs are made.

- A **globe valve** *is used at points where it is needed infrequently* such as in bathrooms. A globe valve *can adjust or stop the flow of water.*

- A **pressure regulator valve (PRV)** limits the water pressure. *Also called a pressure-reducing valve, it is used to reduce and automatically maintain the pressure of water within predetermined parameters.* This valve may be used to reduce incoming water pressure. This prevents damage to the pipe and equipment.

- A **temperature pressure relief valve** *is used in hot water and steam systems.* This valve *allows hot water and steam to escape if the water temperature and pressure buildup are too high for the equipment.*

- A **float valve** *is used to control water levels in tanks.* As the water level rises, the float rises and shuts off the water when a set capacity has been reached.

- A **water hammer arrestor** contains a hydraulic piston that absorbs the shock waves produced by sudden changes in water flow. This reduces the commonly heard banging in pipes. The **backflow preventer** *keeps water from backing up in the system.*

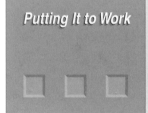

Putting It to Work

Inspectors should locate, but not operate, the main shutoff valve. Check the valve for leaks. Generally, the main shutoff valve is found inside the house. Missing or leaking shutoff valves are noted on the inspection report. The other types of valves mentioned previously are components of various plumbing fixtures and heating and cooling equipment and are discussed again later in the chapter.

Pipe Condensation

Condensation forms on cold water pipes when warm air encounters them. This condensation must be avoided because it causes moisture to form in the wall cavity. This moisture can penetrate the wall or ceiling material. To avoid this problem, cold water pipes should generally be wrapped with insulation. Currently, preformed fiberglass or foam insulation is used and is generally one-half to one inch thick. The insulation is generally taped to the pipe.

To prevent dripping from pipes and plumbing equipment, including hot water heating systems and pipes carrying hot water or refrigerant, insulation is useful. If hot and cold water pipes are parallel, they should be a minimum of six to seven inches apart to reduce a heating and cooling exchange. Figure 8.13 depicts a pipe wrapped with insulation.

Traps

To prevent sewer gases and odors from entering the house, drains are protected by traps. A **trap** *is a curved section of drainpipe that fills with water, providing a seal.* Drains that penetrate a wall generally have a P-trap and those that go through the

Pipe insulation. **FIGURE 8.13**

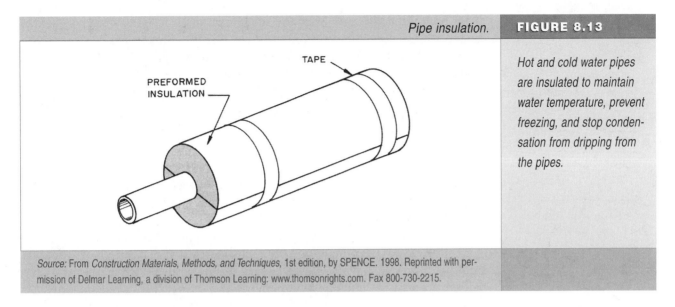

Hot and cold water pipes are insulated to maintain water temperature, prevent freezing, and stop condensation from dripping from the pipes.

Source: From *Construction Materials, Methods, and Techniques,* 1st edition, by SPENCE. 1998. Reprinted with permission of Delmar Learning, a division of Thomson Learning: www.thomsonrights.com. Fax 800-730-2215.

floor have an S-trap. The water held by the trap is replaced each time the fixture is used. Lavatories typically have a P-trap. Bathtubs often use a drum trap. Figure 8.14 illustrates types of traps.

Piping Materials

The most common pipe materials used in plumbing systems include cast-iron, copper, plastic, brass and galvanized steel.

1. *Cast-iron pipe.* This type of pipe is typically used for underground plumbing in the house drainage system because it is strong and durable. It is available in light and heavy weights, and building codes usually specify the required weight for the application. The disadvantage of cast-iron pipe is that it is heavy, time-consuming to install, and eventually can rust on the inside.

2. *Copper pipe.* This type of pipe is used for both water supply and drainage systems. Copper pipe is longer lasting than brass or steel pipe, is corrosion resistant, and is easy to work with. In the water supply system, copper pipe can be

Types of traps. **FIGURE 8.14**

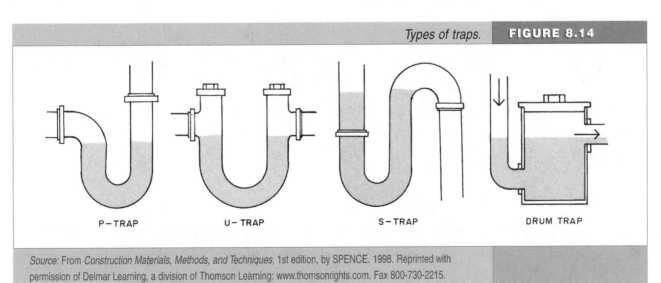

P-TRAP   U-TRAP   S-TRAP   DRUM TRAP

Source: From *Construction Materials, Methods, and Techniques,* 1st edition, by SPENCE. 1998. Reprinted with permission of Delmar Learning, a division of Thomson Learning: www.thomsonrights.com. Fax 800-730-2215.

used for hot- and cold-water lines and for branch pipes to house fixtures such as sinks and washing machines. In the drainage system, copper pipe is used for the main soil stack, soil pipes, and vent pipes. For plumbing applications, copper pipe is available in rigid or flexible form in different thicknesses. Building and plumbing codes generally determine what type should be used for a certain application.

3. *Plastic pipe.* This type of pipe is being used more often in plumbing systems and is approved by building codes for many different applications. When it was first developed, it was used only for the cold-water supply, outdoor sprinkler systems, and swimming pool plumbing. The older plastics were not as resilient or heat resistant as metal pipes. For home plumbing, essentially three types of plastic pipe are used: PVC (polyvinyl chloride), ABS (acrylonitrile butadiene styrene), and SRP (styrene rubber plastic).

Plastic is lightweight, economical, resistant to corrosion, and easy to install. When compared to metal pipe, however, plastic is less resistant to heat, expands and contracts more when heated and cooled, has less crush resistance, withstands less internal pressure, and may require more support because of its flexibility. All three types can be used for sewer systems, and ABS and PVC can be used for wastewater and vent systems. ABS pipe is used in one- and two-family homes for drainage, but some building codes disallow its use in multifamily dwellings or in commercial and industrial applications because it contains a flammable petroleum product. Codes generally disallow plastic pipe for drinking water.

4. *Brass pipe.* Brass pipe is no longer used in many plumbing installations, but inspectors will find it in older homes. Brass is expensive and has been replaced by other materials that do the job just as efficiently. In some homes, brass pipe can still be found in exposed pipes that have sometimes been chrome plated. It is at times still used where there is a hard water problem.

5. *Galvanized steel pipe.* Steel pipe was used extensively until about 1960 for the water supply and less often for the drainage system. In the water supply, steel pipe is still used for hot and cold water and for branch pipes to fixtures. Steel pipe is infrequently used in the drainage system for the main soil stack, soil pipes from fixtures, and vent pipes. Steel is not used for underground plumbing.

Pipe Size for Adequate Pressure

The minimum acceptable pressure in a water distribution system is the lowest pressure that permits safe, efficient, and satisfactory operation. The maximum acceptable pressure is the highest pressure that does not cause damage to the system. Building codes stipulate the minimum pressure for various plumbing fixtures, as well as the maximum allowable pressure.

A pipe that is sized too small will not allow the available water pressure to flow through to the fixture. Sometimes problems occur in older houses where the galvanized steel pipes become clogged, particularly with a buildup of mineral deposits over a long period.

Inspecting the Pipes

Most of the structure's pipe system is hidden behind walls and ceilings. Therefore, the inspector must examine the property to find the areas where pipe is exposed. This includes the basement, garage, attic, and under sinks and other exposed plumbing fixtures.

Examine all accessible pipes for the following:

- *Leakage.* All pipes should have tight-fitting joints. Examine the ceiling above and floor below any pipe, when possible, for water stains.

- *Rust and corrosion.* Pipes have a certain life span and older pipes may have reached theirs. For example, galvanized steel pipe that is coated with zinc may begin to rust internally over time. As the steel rusts, it obstructs and narrows the diameter. This reduces the pipe's ability to supply an adequate water flow. This type of problem is more prevalent in homes 50 or more years old because steel pipe was used more regularly then. Copper, a much longer lasting pipe, was not available back then, nor was plastic. Rust may also be observed by turning on the faucet to see if the water appears discolored. This rust could originate with the pipe or the joints.

- *Pipe sizing for adequate pressure.* One way to ascertain that the property has adequate pressure is to turn on all of the faucets. There should still be a good stream of water coming from each of the faucets. If not, the pipe diameter could be too narrow.

- *Noisy pipes.* Turn on the water, flush the toilets, and listen for any noises in the pipes. Water hammer (discussed earlier) occurs when a pipe is loose and moves when water moves through the pipe. This pipe movement causes a banging noise in the pipes.

- *Insulation.* Check that all domestic water lines are insulated properly and that condensation is not visible. If possible, feel the insulation to see if it is dry.

HEATING SYSTEMS

In most heating systems, a furnace is used to heat the air, which is then discharged either directly or through ducts into the space being heated. A residential heating system is usually one of the following types: hot water, steam, forced warm air, or electric.

1. *Hot water system. Whenever liquids, such as water, are heated or cooled, the process is referred to as a* **hydronic system**. Figure 8.15 illustrates types of hydronic heating systems. A hot water system consists of pipes, a boiler, and room-heating units such as radiators or convectors. The water is heated in the boiler and then propelled through the pipes by one or more circulator pumps to the radiators or convectors, where the heat is transferred to the air in the various rooms. Convectors are the more common heating medium. A **convector** *is a heat-emitting unit in which heat is produced by the movement of air around a metal surface.* Figure 8.16 illustrates types of fin-tube convectors. Older homes have upright convectors that look something like radiators. The more common type is the fin-tube baseboard convectors that usually run along the baseboards of a room. One or more walls may have convectors depending on the room's size and configuration.

You Should Know
Boilers

Boilers *are used to transfer heat from a fuel source to a fluid, such as water, and are constructed from cast iron, steel, or copper. The container is pressurized and transfers heat to the water, producing either hot water or steam.* Boilers are classified as either high-pressure or low-pressure. Residential applications generally are limited to low-pressure boilers that are typically used as heating boilers.

FIGURE 8.15	*Three types of hydronic systems.*

SINGLE-PIPE SYSTEM	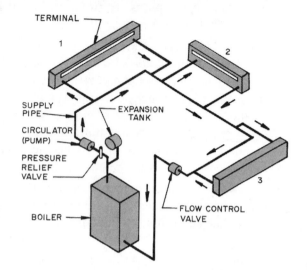	A single-pipe hydronic system carries the water from the boiler through each terminal and back to the boiler.
TWO-PIPE DIRECT RETURN	The two-pipe hydronic direct-return hot water system has a separate return line for the cooled water, which flows in a direction opposite the supply line.	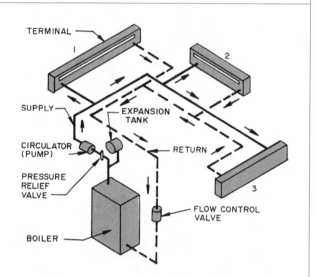
TWO-PIPE REVERSE RETURN	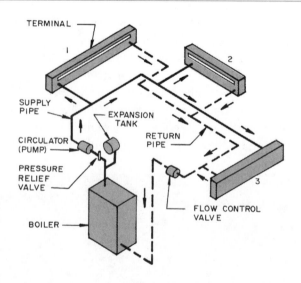	The two-pipe reverse-return hydronic hot water system has the return water flowing in the same direction as the hot supply water providing about the same pipe resistance to water flow for each terminal.

Source: From *Construction Materials, Methods, and Techniques,* 1st edition, by SPENCE. 1998. Reprinted with permission of Delmar Learning, a division of Thomson Learning: www.thomsonrights. com. Fax 800-730-2215.

Types of fin-tube convectors. **FIGURE 8.16**

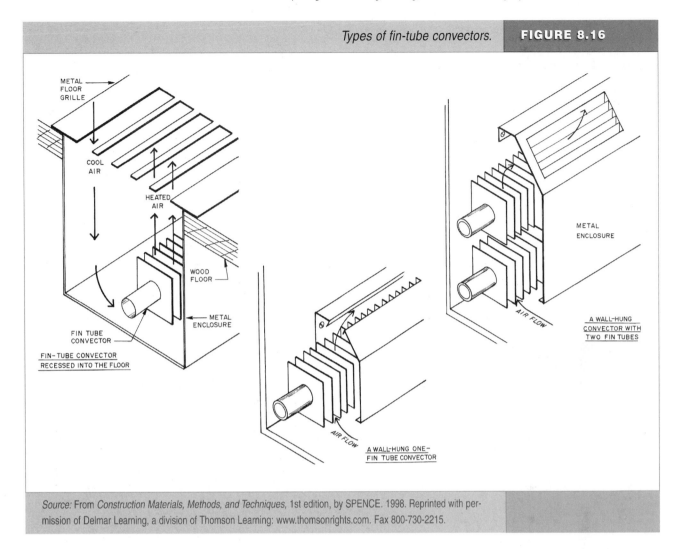

2. *Steam system.* A **steam system** *consists of a boiler, where steam is produced, and a system of pipes that conveys the steam to radiators, convectors, or other types of room-heating elements.* Steam can produce a large amount of heat with a small amount of circulating fluid. The most common types of steam systems are one-pipe systems in which the steam and condensation (evaporation) are carried in one pipe; a two-pipe system in which the steam and condensation are carried in two different pipes; and a vacuum return steam system, which is a low-pressure two-pipe system. This type is generally used on larger buildings because it requires a lower steam pressure and can fill the system with steam rapidly. Figure 8.17 illustrates types of steam heating systems. Steam heat is usually found in older homes.

3. *Forced warm air system.* A **forced warm air system** *consists of a furnace that contains a fan or blower, a heat source such as gas or oil, a heat exchanger, a casing, controls, and a filter.* The heat exchanger transfers the heat into the building through the ductwork via the fan. *The system works by extracting cool air from in and out of doors and passing this cool air through the heat sources. The warmed air then flows through ducts to the various rooms of the house.* The system can also be designed to provide cooling through the same ducts. Depending on the size of the system, forced warm air systems can be adapted for residential, commercial, and industrial applications.

FIGURE 8.17	*Types of steam heating systems.*

SINGLE-PIPE STEAM HEATING SYSTEM	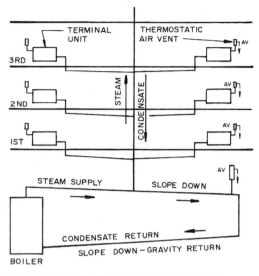	A single-pipe steam heating system uses the same pipe system for the steam supply and condensate return.
TWO-PIPE STEAM HEATING SYSTEM	Two-pipe steam heating systems have separate piping lines for the steam supply and the return condensate. 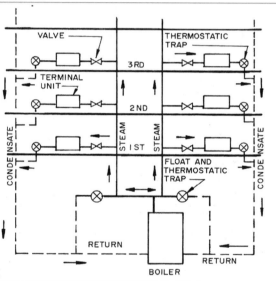	
TWO-PIPE VACUUM RETURN SYSTEM *Source:* From *Construction Materials, Methods, and Techniques,* 1st edition, by SPENCE. 1998. Reprinted with permission of Delmar Learning, a division of Thomson Learning: www.thomsonrights.com. Fax 800-730-2215.	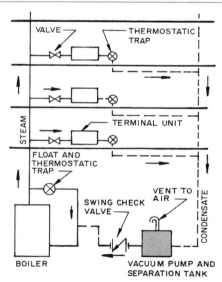	The two-pipe vacuum steam heating system uses a vacuum pump to increase the pressure difference and discharges gas that is not condensable into the atmosphere.

Warm air systems include three types: upflow, downflow, and horizontal. An upflow warm air furnace moves air out of the top of the unit into the duct systems. It is used in the basement when ducts are run under the floor; or on the main floor when the ducts are run in the attic. A downflow warm air furnace moves the air out of the bottom of the unit. This type is used when the ducts are in a concrete slab floor or below the floor in a crawl space. A horizontal warm air furnace is mounted in the attic or hung below the floor joists. Horizontal warm air furnaces that have heating and cooling capabilities can be installed outdoors on a concrete slab. Those that have downflow capabilities can be installed on the roof. Figure 8.18 illustrates the air-flow patterns of these furnace systems.

Upflow, downflow, and horizontal warm air furnaces.   **FIGURE 8.18**

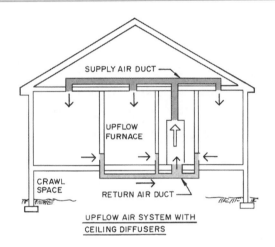

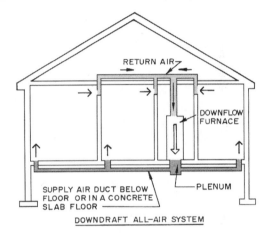

Downflow warm air heating systems are used in a building with a crawl space or concrete floor.

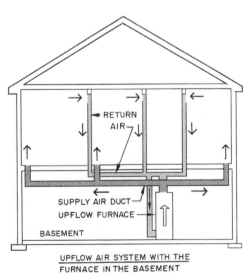

Typical upflow warm air heating systems.

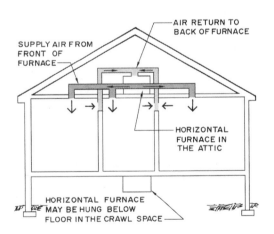

Horizontal warm air furnaces are hung below the floor or in the attic.

Source: From *Construction Materials, Methods, and Techniques,* 1st edition, by SPENCE. 1998. Reprinted with permission of Delmar Learning, a division of Thomson Learning: www.thomsonrights.com. Fax 800-730-2215.

4. *Electric resistance heating systems.* Residential electric heating is usually in the form of baseboard heaters placed directly along the walls of a room. The units consist of three basic elements. There is a resistor, which is the material used to produce heat by passing a current through it. When electricity passes through a wire, the molecules are stirred up and heat is created. The resistor is embedded in insulation and a protective metal sheathing. The unit contains a terminal that connects it to the power supply. This type of installation of electric heat is more economical than other types of heat because it does not require a furnace or duct-work. Other types of electric heating systems include a hot-air electric furnace and radiant panels. The electric furnace works in much the same manner as other furnaces. An electric resistance element is used to supply the warm air and the furnace delivers the warmed air through ductwork to various parts of the structure. Electrical radiant panels are composed of a system of electrical elements embedded in the ceiling, floor, or wall panels of a structure. Heat is transferred evenly to the surrounding objects and people rather than to the air. Radiant heat systems cannot perform the dual function of heating and cooling as do many of the other devices discussed. Figure 8.19 illustrates electric radiant heat imbedded in a ceiling panel, a plaster ceiling, and a concrete floor.

You Should Know

Radiant heating might also use hot water, steam, or electricity. Tubes to carry the heated water or steam may be constructed in the same manner as for electricity.

Heating Fuel and Power

There are three types of heating fuel: electricity, oil, and gas.

1. *Electric heat.* Electrical heating devices have a resistance heating element that heats the circulating air directly or through a metal sheath enclosing the element. Rising utility costs over recent years have made the electric furnace less economical in residential applications because the cost of electricity is generally more expensive than other types of fuel.

2. *Oil-fired heat.* Oil-fired furnaces include a burner and controls and are available in a variety of shapes and styles. Oil-fired furnaces are used to generate warm air or can be combined with an air-cooling system (discussed later). Oil-fired heat, although economical, requires the fuel to be delivered and stored. The oil is pumped from a storage tank outside the house. Code requirements regulate the location of both above- and belowground storage tanks. Figure 8.20 illustrates a typical installation for an oil-fired furnace.

Small aboveground and underground heating oil storage tanks for residential use may be subject to state or local regulation, but most domestic tanks generally are not. The regulation and maintenance of above- and underground storage tanks are discussed further in Chapter 10.

3. *Gas-fired heat.* In a gas-fired furnace, combustion takes place within a metal heat exchanger. The products of the combustion are conveyed through a flue or vent. Gas furnaces can burn either natural gas or liquefied petroleum air gases. Gas-fired heating is a popular form of heating because it is economical, convenient, and the oil delivery is eliminated.

Types of electric radiant heating systems. **FIGURE 8.19**

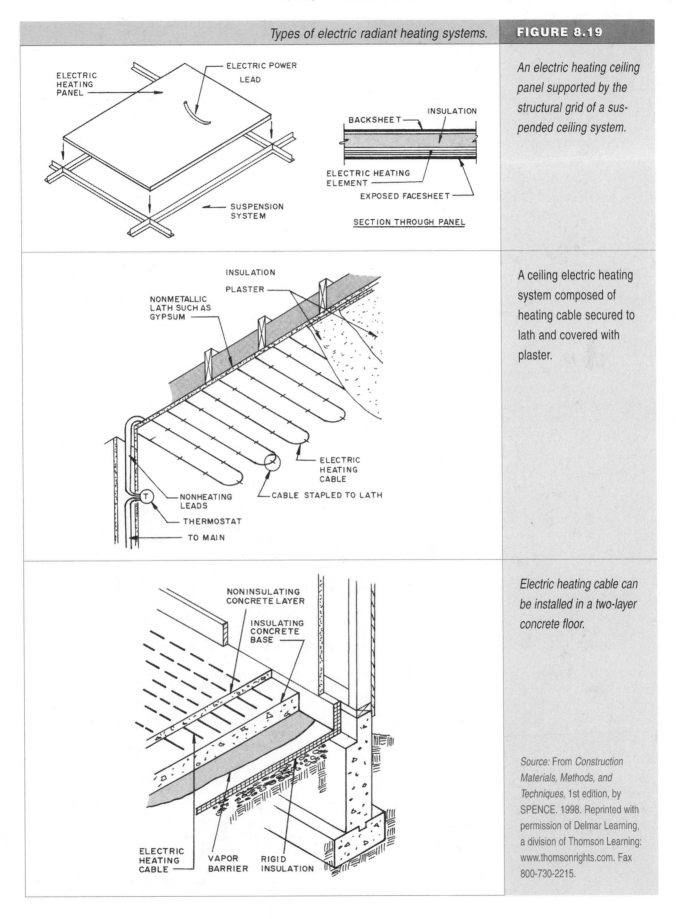

An electric heating ceiling panel supported by the structural grid of a suspended ceiling system.

A ceiling electric heating system composed of heating cable secured to lath and covered with plaster.

Electric heating cable can be installed in a two-layer concrete floor.

Source: From *Construction Materials, Methods, and Techniques,* 1st edition, by SPENCE. 1998. Reprinted with permission of Delmar Learning, a division of Thomson Learning: www.thomsonrights.com. Fax 800-730-2215.

FIGURE 8.20

An oil-fired warm air furnace.

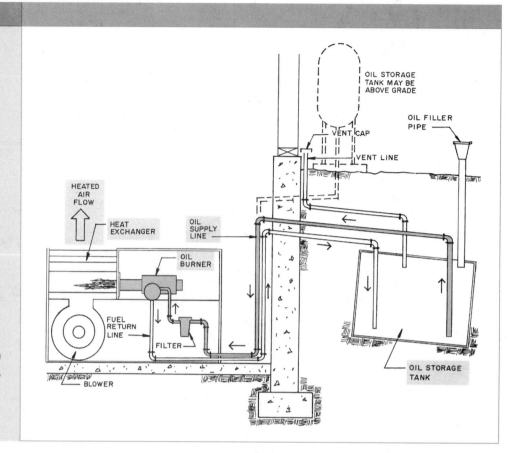

Source: From *Construction Materials, Methods, and Techniques,* 1st edition, by SPENCE. 1998. Reprinted with permission of Delmar Learning, a division of Thomson Learning: www.thomsonrights.com. Fax 800-730-2215.

You Should Know
Thermostats

A **thermostat** *is a control device that automatically responds to temperature changes by opening and closing an electric circuit. This action regulates the temperature of the space in which the thermostat is located. Thermostats work mechanically or electronically.* Some properties are divided into zones with different thermostat settings for each. A typical thermostat has a metal coil that is pressure sensitive and expands or contracts due to heat or cold. This triggers an on-off switch in the thermostat.

You Should Know
Heating System
Efficiency Ratings

Heating system efficiency is now rated by a Department of Energy rate of efficiency requirement. Furnaces are rated by the Annual Fuel Utilization Efficiency (AFUE). AFUE is the percentage of heat delivered by the furnace as compared to the furnace's input rating. The higher the AFUE rating, the lower the cost of fuel. All new furnaces are required to meet at least 78 percent AFUE. For example, if a furnace has a 100,000 BTU input rating and has an 80 percent efficiency rating, this furnace will render 80,000 BTUs to the building. The remaining 20,000 BTUs are not used as heat energy. Older furnaces, 10 or more years old, most probably fall well below AFUE efficiency requirements. Ninety percent of high efficiency heating systems are gas-powered. These systems do not require a chimney but generally utilize a PVC vent pipe.

Inspecting the Furnace

The inspection of the furnace must be modified depending on the type of system found in the subject property. Systems should be inspected using the following guidelines:

■ Check that each room has at least one heating vent, convector, radiator, or other means of heating. The number of heating supply and return grills depends on the size of the ductwork and the heating system. In general, the heat convectors (hydronic system) or supply outlets (warm air system) are placed against exterior walls. These convectors and supply ducts should have adjustable openings. Check that they are working properly and are not bent or misshapen to a point where they are stuck in an open or closed position. The return ducts for the warm air system are located on the interior walls.

■ Attempt to find out the age of the heating system by looking for the date on the unit itself, service stickers left on the equipment, or from the property owner. Furnaces vary as to longevity. If a furnace is properly maintained with regular cleaning, lubrication, and repairs, it can last about 25 years. If the home inspector observes that it has not been regularly maintained, he should recommend that a heating specialist be called in.

■ Examine the furnace itself. Is there evidence of leaking, cracks, rust, or corrosion to the body of the furnace?

■ Check for an abnormal amount of soot in and around the furnace. If so, the vent pipe connected to the furnace that vents into the chimney may need removal and cleaning. A pipe clogged with soot produces a back draft that may cause dangerous carbon monoxide to enter the structure.

■ Check that the heater has a safety switch. This switch is necessary so the furnace can be shut off if there is a malfunction in one or more of the controls. Inspectors should suggest that a safety switch be installed if none is visible.

■ A lack of ventilation in an enclosed furnace room is a safety hazard. A hot water heater or boiler and a hot air furnace in a six-foot by four-foot room with a solid door, for example, does not receive adequate ventilation. Inadequate ventilation can cause a back drafting through the vent pipes that allows dangerous carbon monoxide fumes to enter the structure.

■ If the property has an oil-fired furnace, the inspector should locate the oil storage tank. If the inspector finds that the subject property has an underground tank, this should be mentioned in the inspection report. Because of the location in the ground, underground tanks are impossible to inspect. The main problem with these tanks is leakage into the surrounding soil (see Chapter 10). To protect the environment and for ease of maintenance, the inspector should suggest that the underground tank be removed by a certified specialist and an aboveground tank installed. Figure 8.21 depicts the presence of an underground oil storage tank in the front yard. In this illustration, the pipes projecting from the ground indicate the presence of the tank.

■ Examine aboveground oil storage tanks for leaks, rust, and corrosion.

■ Check the location of the thermostat and make sure that it is registering. Inspectors can use the thermostat to check the operation of the heating system. This operation should not be performed in warm weather, however, in a dual heating–air-conditioning hot air system. It also should not be performed when a

FIGURE 8.21

FIGURE 8.21

An underground storage tank.

Source: Anthony D'Agostino, Atlantic Inspection Service, Latham, New York.

separate air-conditioning unit is on because the excess heat can damage the air conditioner's evaporator coils (discussed later).

■ In gas-fired systems, check the pilot light. The pilot light ignites the gas in the furnace. A standing pilot light is a type of pilot light that burns all of the time. *If the pilot goes out, a device known as a* **thermocouple** *automatically closes the gas valve that controls the flow of gas and stops the flow.* This is a safety device so that if the pilot goes out, gas fumes do not enter the structure.

■ Observe the gas burners inside the heat exchanger. The **heat exchanger** *is the area where combustion or the burning of fuel for heat takes place.* If the flames look too high, then the gas is not burning at the proper rate of combustion. If the flame looks too yellow and rolls out of the furnace, it may be an indication that gas is ejecting from the body of the furnace. This can cause damage to the outside of the heater, as well as to the controls, and constitutes a safety hazard. Other problems with the burners, such as an uneven flame, may indicate clogged burners or an uneven flow of gas to the burner. Any suspected problems with the burners should be reported to the client and a heating specialist recommended.

You Should Know   New furnaces possess electronic ignition systems rather than pilot lights. The gas is ignited by an electric spark. The same systems also appear on gas-fired ovens and cooktops.

■ With gas-fired furnaces, a black solid iron pipe should carry the gas from its source (the metered gas line) to the furnace. Flexible piping is not recommended because it tends to leak over time. Check that the pipe has a shutoff valve. There should also be a drip leg attached to the pipe right before the pipe enters the furnace. The drip leg is a pipe that allows sediment, condensation, and other debris from the gas pipe to flow out before the gas enters the furnace.

FIGURE 8.22

A hot water furnace with three circulating pumps.

Source: Anthony D'Agostino, Atlantic Inspection Service, Latham, New York.

■ With a hot water (hydronic) system, turn the thermostat on and make sure the circulator pumps go on. Figure 8.22 is a picture of a hot water furnace with three circulating pumps. Check to see that the heated water is circulating through the pipes in the system. Observe the temperature pressure gauge that gives a reading as to the water pressure in the system and the temperature of the heated water. When the heater has cycled, turn off the thermostat to make sure the system shuts the circulator pumps down.

■ To check the hot air system, turn on the thermostat and let the system cycle. Eventually, you will hear the blowers turn on. If the system is working satisfactorily, turn the thermostat off and check to see that the blowers also shut down. Also check that the air filter is in place and if so, remove it to make sure that it is clean. Filters should be changed once a month while the furnace is in operation.

Some furnaces may have humidifiers attached to them. The problem with this arrangement is that the humidifier may be leaking. Unless humidifiers are maintained, there is enormous potential for mold spores, allergens, and bacteria to thrive in the stagnant water pool, which is then circulated directly to the air in the home. Individual room humidifiers with distilled water may be better alternatives.

Putting It to Work

AIR-CONDITIONING

With the integration of HVAC (heating, ventilating, and air-conditioning) systems into home construction, cooling the air using central air-conditioning is standard in new construction. Central air-conditioning units are located outside of the air-conditioned space. They can be placed indoors in the basement of the structure, outside on the roof, or adjacent to the structure's outside walls.

Major Components

The mechanical components of an air conditioner are a liquid refrigerant, an evaporator coil, a compressor, and a condenser. A **refrigerant** *is any substance that produces a cooling effect by absorbing heat as it vaporizes (disperses into the air).* The refrigerant must be nontoxic and nonflammable. *The most common refrigerant used in air conditioners is* **freon.** The **evaporator** *takes heat from the air surrounding it and brings it to the refrigerant.* The **compressor** then *creates a flow of refrigerant from one part of the system to the other.* The **condenser** *liquefies the refrigerant gas by cooling it.*

<table>
<tr><td>*You Should Know
Air Conditioners*</td><td>Whether the system is air-cooled or water-cooled depends on the type of condenser used in the system. An air-cooled condenser consists of a fan or a natural draft that blows air across a large-surface coil. This type of condenser is used in smaller units. In a water-cooled condenser, water circulates through tubes or coils inside of a shell. Refrigerant circulates through the space between the tubes or coils. The water-cooled condenser is suited to medium-sized units. Sometimes air-conditioning condensers are a combination of water-cooled and air-cooled and are called evaporative condensers.

    Air conditioners not combined with other types of units are single systems with two parts. The outdoor segment of the air conditioner is composed of the compressor, condenser, and fan. The indoor unit is composed of an evaporator coil, a condensate tray, a refrigerant line, a fan, and an air filter. This system has its own ductwork and may be located in the basement or attic.</td></tr>
</table>

Combination Systems

Because an air-conditioning unit conditions air, a single forced warm air heating system can also include cooling, ventilating, and dehumidifying systems. Cooled air, fresh air from outdoors, and dehumidified air can travel through the same ducts as the heated air. Because the same ductwork is used for all functions, this is one of the most economical installations.

When the air conditioner is combined with a forced warm air furnace, pipes carry the refrigerant from the compressor, located outdoors, to an indoor coil (known as an evaporator) located inside the furnace. The warm air from the room passes over this chilled coil and is cooled. This chilled air then travels back from the furnace through the plenum. The **plenum** *is a large metal conduit box in the form of a duct located inside the heating system where hot air builds up pressure and is then forced out to room heating elements.* The refrigerant circulates through the space between the tubes or coils in the furnace and moves back to the outdoor air-conditioning compressor where the heat it has absorbed is transferred to the atmosphere. The refrigerant then moves back to the interior coils to repeat the process.

Hot water and steam heat furnaces employ a similar system. When oil, gas, or electric warm air is used to heat, a cooling coil unit is placed on the furnace and connected to the outside air conditioner. Figure 8.23 illustrates an outside air-conditioning unit connected to an indoor furnace.

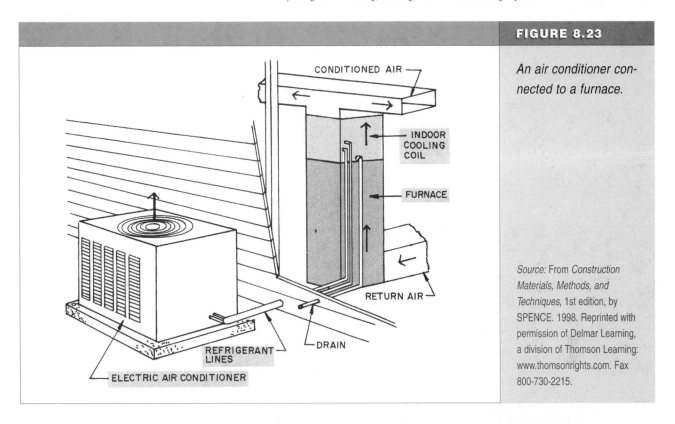

FIGURE 8.23

An air conditioner connected to a furnace.

Source: From *Construction Materials, Methods, and Techniques,* 1st edition, by SPENCE. 1998. Reprinted with permission of Delmar Learning, a division of Thomson Learning: www.thomsonrights.com. Fax 800-730-2215.

Most components of an HVAC system are assigned a BTU rating. **BTU** *stands for British thermal unit and is a measure of heat energy. A BTU is the amount of heat required to raise the temperature of one pound of water by one degree Fahrenheit.* The capacity of an air-conditioning unit is rated in tons of refrigeration, and 12,000 BTUs is equal to a one-ton capacity. Therefore, an air conditioner rated at 12,000 BTUs per hour can melt one ton of ice per day, and it takes 40 BTUs to cool one cubic foot of space.

You Should Know
BTU Ratings

Heat Pumps

Another type of heating and cooling system combination is the heat pump. Air source heat pumps extract heat from the outside, even in moderately cold weather, and transfers the heat into the home. This heat transfer cycle is reversed in the warmer months to extract heat from the interior of a building, transfer it to the outdoors, and produce air-conditioning (cooling).

Heat pumps can be distinguished from one another according to how they draw on the heat source. Air-to-air heat pumps draw on the outside air as a heat source. Ground-source heat pumps (Figure 8.24) draw on the consistent temperature of the ground to bring heating and cooling into the house. Other types of heat pumps include water-to-water and air-to-water.

The most common heat pump is the air-to-air. This pump includes a compressor similar to the ones used in a refrigerator. A refrigerant or gas is circulated in the coils. When the unit is in the heating mode, the coils in the outdoor unit enable the refrigerant to absorb heat from the outdoor air. The refrigerant is moved to the compressor where it is compressed, raising its temperature. It moves

FIGURE 8.24

The inside unit of a ground-source heat pump.

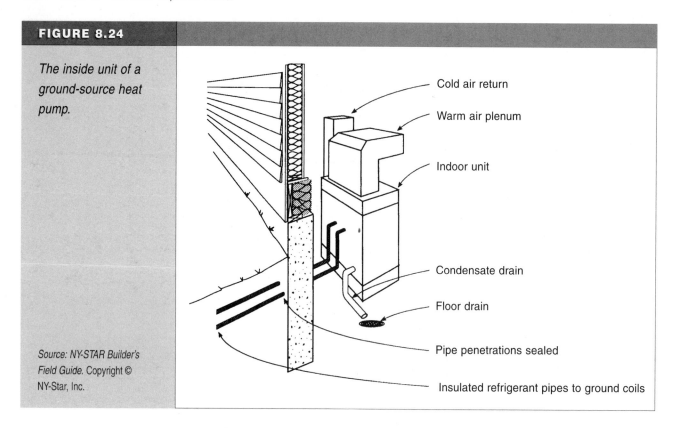

- Cold air return
- Warm air plenum
- Indoor unit
- Condensate drain
- Floor drain
- Pipe penetrations sealed
- Insulated refrigerant pipes to ground coils

Source: NY-STAR Builder's Field Guide. Copyright © NY-Star, Inc.

to indoor coils when indoor air is blown over them by a blower that removes the heat and moves it through ducts into the structure. In the cooling mode, the reverse happens. Heat is absorbed by the inside coils and dispersed to the outside air by the outside coils. Figure 8.25 illustrates the heating cycle of an air-to-air electric heat pump. Air-to-water heat pumps are used to cool air in a room and transfer the heat to water or another liquid to be heated. Therefore, a living space and swimming pool could be heated at the same time.

A disadvantage of both types of heat pump is that they can operate only in moderate climates. When the temperature drops below 34 degrees, the heat pumps are ineffective. The limitation of the air-to-air heat pump system is that the temperature of the air outside is typically the lowest when the need for heat inside is the greatest. The ground-source system is troublesome in winter because the frozen ground around the pump insulates it and prevents it from extracting heat.

Another drawback to the heat pump is that the heat coming out of the vent feels cooler than that generated by a furnace. In climates with cold winters, home owners who use a heat pump often have a backup heating system to maintain a comfortable living environment. The advantage of the heat pump is that the air cooling and heating systems are built into the same unit.

Inspecting the Air-Conditioning

■ Make sure that the unit is on level ground. It should sit on a concrete slab or be raised up on blocks. Check that the unit is not covered by trees, bushes, or other vegetation. It should be clean and not covered with leaves, dirt, and other outdoor debris. The unit must have adequate clearance on all sides and be situated on the shady side of the structure if possible. If you plan to turn the air conditioner on, check that the disconnect switch on the outdoor unit is not activated.

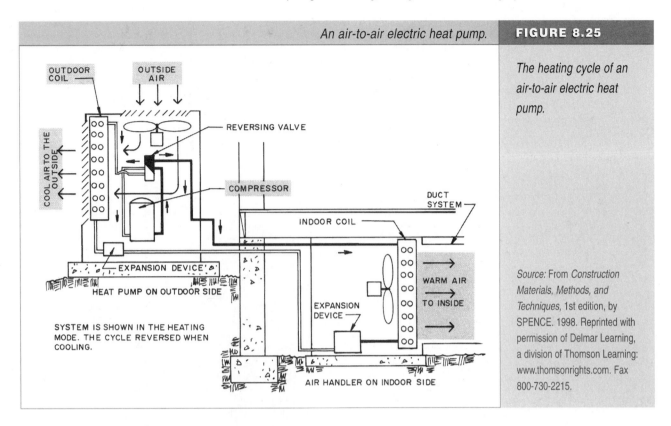

FIGURE 8.25

An air-to-air electric heat pump.

The heating cycle of an air-to-air electric heat pump.

Source: From *Construction Materials, Methods, and Techniques,* 1st edition, by SPENCE. 1998. Reprinted with permission of Delmar Learning, a division of Thomson Learning: www.thomsonrights.com. Fax 800-730-2215.

■ Turn on the thermostat that controls the air conditioner and listen for the fan to go on. It should take about 20 minutes or more, depending on the weather, for the air conditioner to cool the house. Once the unit is operating, check the ducts and make sure cold air is coming out. The air conditioner should not be turned on when the temperature is less than 65 degrees because this can damage the compressor. Listen to the fan and observe any unusual noises.

■ When heat passes over the evaporator and is cooled, condensation occurs. A tray, called an evaporator coil pan or condensate tray, catches the water produced by this evaporation. Check that the condensation from the evaporator coil is not leaking out of the evaporator coil pan. If the inside unit is located in the attic, for example, you can look for stains on the attic ceiling. This very well may be coming from the air-conditioning unit rather than a leak in the roof.

■ Verify that the air filter is installed. Filters should be changed once a month during the air-conditioning season.

■ If possible, check for ice buildup on the evaporator coil. If present, advise your clients to check with an air-conditioning specialist.

■ Enter each room and see that it is cooling evenly. If not, there may be a leak in the ductwork to one of the rooms.

WATER HEATERS

Several types of hot water systems are found in residential construction. Gas and electric water tanks are common, as are systems that are connected to the heat source. Typically, single-family homes require at least a 40- to 50-gallon hot water tank.

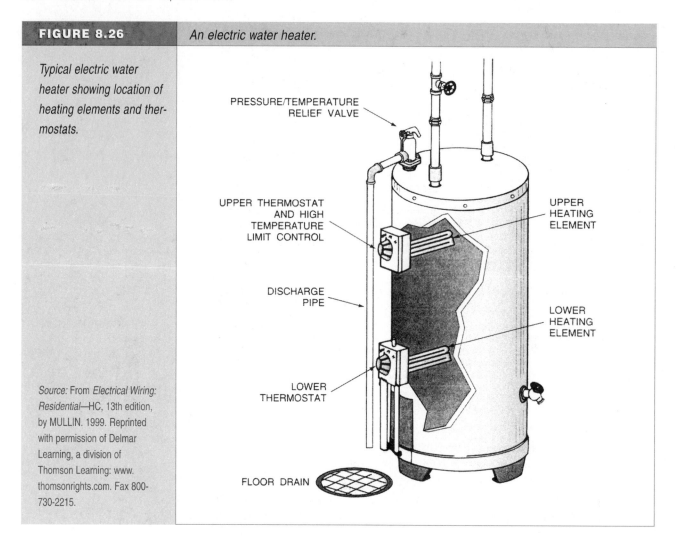

Source: From *Electrical Wiring: Residential*—HC, 13th edition, by MULLIN. 1999. Reprinted with permission of Delmar Learning, a division of Thomson Learning: www.thomsonrights.com. Fax 800-730-2215.

FIGURE 8.26   *An electric water heater.*

Typical electric water heater showing location of heating elements and thermostats.

PRESSURE/TEMPERATURE RELIEF VALVE

UPPER THERMOSTAT AND HIGH TEMPERATURE LIMIT CONTROL

DISCHARGE PIPE

LOWER THERMOSTAT

UPPER HEATING ELEMENT

LOWER HEATING ELEMENT

FLOOR DRAIN

Types of Heaters

1. *Gas water heaters* consist of a vertical storage tank enclosed in an insulated metal tank. The gas is automatically controlled by a thermostat inside the tank so that the incoming cold water turns on the gas. When the water is heated, the thermostat lowers the flame.

2. *Electric water heaters* (Figure 8.26) are also insulated tanks. With this type of tank, two heating elements are immersed inside the tank and heat the water. Electric heaters can be constructed to take 120 or 240 volts of electricity; currents of 240 volts are more efficient and economical.

3. *Summer–winter hookup* is a method of heating water that is sometimes found in residential construction. A copper coil is immersed in the hot water of the house-heating boiler. Pipes connect this coil to a hot water storage tank. Water flows from the pipes that connect the boiler to the storage tank, where it is then stored. In this type of hookup, the tanks are horizontal rather than vertical as with the gas and electric water tanks. In addition, some houses have a hot water system that has no hot water storage tank. Hot water is supplied by immersing a large number of coils directly into the boiler water. This is called a *tankless coil system*.

Inspecting the Water Tank

In general, water tanks do not have a long life. The age limit for most water heaters is approximately 15 years. The following items should be examined and observed during the inspection of hot water heaters:

■ To allow the hot water and steam to escape if the water temperature or pressure buildup is too high for the equipment, hot water heaters must have a temperature pressure relief valve. If the pressure gets too high, the valve automatically discharges water before it reaches the boiler. The valve is located at or near the top of the tank, but must have a pipe extension attached to it that runs down the side of the tank. Occasionally, you will notice that there is no pipe extension on the pressure relief valve. A pipe extension should be added and should extend to six or eight inches above the basement floor. The extension is a safety device that prevents people from being scalded. As a safety measure, the pressure relief valve should be opened every six months to ensure its correct operation. If the valve does not open or close properly, it should be replaced. Water heaters have been known to explode due to a faulty pressure relief valve.

■ Inspectors may suggest that the water in the bottom of the tank be drained annually to reduce sediment buildup. Sediment can be drained through the drain valve at the bottom of the water heater.

■ To ascertain the recovery rate of the water tank, test the hot water temperature with a thermometer. Run the water for approximately five minutes. This is equal to approximately 50 percent of the water in the tank. Retest the water temperature. The temperature should be no more than 10 degrees less than the starting temperature. If not, the rate at which the water tank produces hot water is unsatisfactory.

■ To prevent scalding, water tanks should be set no higher than 120 degrees.

■ Gas- and oil-fired hot water heaters should be located in a well-ventilated area—not an enclosed airless room (as described earlier).

■ Gas, propane, and oil heaters have a flue pipe extending from the heater to the chimney. Inspectors should look for a draft hood that must be placed at the top of the heater so that carbon monoxide fumes do not escape back from the chimney into the structure.

■ Check all gas-fired equipment, including hot water heaters and furnaces, for gas leaks. Also, check that the burner flame is not burning too strong. Flames that are too high because of an improper mixture of gas and air have a tendency to puff out, possibly burning the outside components of the water heater. (This is described more fully in the discussion of furnaces.) Figure 8.27 illustrates how a hot water heater was actually burned on the outside by the flames. Both of these issues are safety hazards and should be reported immediately to the client and property owner and noted as a safety hazard on the inspection report.

KITCHENS AND BATHROOMS

The kitchen and bathroom are approached on two levels. First, there is the basic inspection of the interior room. Second, there is the inspection of the various plumbing fixtures. A **plumbing fixture** *is an appliance requiring a*

FIGURE 8.27

A hot water heater scorched on the exterior by flames that puffed out.

Source: Anthony D'Agostino, Atlantic Inspection Service, Latham, New York.

water supply and drainage system. All plumbing fixtures require clean water to assist in the discharge of the waste materials. Minimum requirements for plumbing fixtures are outlined by plumbing codes. These fixtures must withstand wear and tear caused by water, bacteria, and other waste. Therefore, plumbing fixtures must have a smooth, nonporous surface and be made from stainless steel, copper, brass, enameled cast iron, vitreous china, molded plastic, gel-coated fiberglass, acrylic-faced fiberglass, and sometimes granite, marble, and other natural and synthetic materials.

Putting It to Work

Although the kitchen and bathroom may not be large areas, it is likely that the inspector will spend more time in these rooms than a bedroom of comparable or larger size.

While inspecting the kitchen and bathroom, you should examine the permanently installed cabinets and countertops in each of those rooms. Cabinets are usually composed of wood or wood materials. Wood cabinets are often made from particleboard with a plastic laminated surface. Metal cabinets are typically found in older homes. Kitchen and bathroom cabinets are generally either base cabinets or wall cabinets. Figure 8.28 illustrates the components of wall and base cabinets.

Wall and base cabinet components.	**FIGURE 8.28**

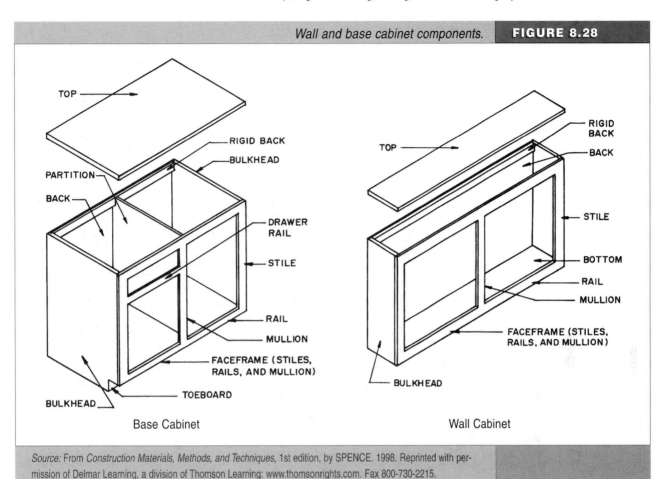

Base Cabinet   Wall Cabinet

Countertops vary in materials. They can be made from plywood or OSB board bonded to a plastic laminate top manufactured from melamine-formaldehyde. Counters are also fashioned from natural stone, such as granite or marble; simulated stone; or ceramic tile bonded to a wood base.

When inspecting the cabinets, check that the base cabinets are securely fastened to the wall and that the counters are securely affixed to the cabinets. To check the functionality of the drawers and cabinets, open and close them. Make sure the drawers roll easily and that the cabinet doors close firmly. Examine the counters for significant dents, holes, and cracks.

While examining the counters and cabinets, the inspector is not looking for aesthetic appearance or the quality of the materials. The main objective is to check that the counters and cabinets are functional and securely affixed to the floor and wall.

Putting It to Work

Although the Americans with Disabilities Act (1992) provides guidelines for the accessibility to various kitchen and bathroom plumbing fixtures, the Act is mandatory only for public places and large apartment buildings. Inspectors may, however, encounter homes designed for the physically challenged.

You Should Know

Plumbing Fixture Types

Plumbing fixtures most commonly inspected in the kitchen and bathroom include sinks, toilets, bathtubs, and showers.

Sinks

Sinks are fashioned from stainless steel, enameled cast iron, glass, marble, and various natural and synthetic stones. In the kitchen, triple-, double-, and single-bowl sinks are found. One of the sink's bowls may have a garbage disposal attached underneath. Sinks can be mounted with the finished rim resting over a countertop, flush with the countertop, or supported from underneath the countertop. Other sinks are molded one-piece units and are one with the countertop material. Any of these sinks may be built into a cabinet that conceals the under part of the bowl and plumbing. Other sink types consist of a one- or two-piece bowl and pedestal with no cabinetry. Some sinks are wall hung.

Bathroom sinks can be made from the same materials as kitchen sinks, but the pedestal-style sink with no cabinet is more commonly found in the bathroom. Most bathroom sinks are fitted with pop-up stoppers controlled by levers and rods that drain the water from the sink.

The kitchen sink is central to much of the kitchen plumbing. Under the sink is flexible tubing for the hot and cold water supply. The water runs through these supply lines directly to the faucet. Each of the supply lines has a shutoff valve. Older homes may not have shutoff valves. The kitchen sink is also connected to a wastewater drainpipe. Figure 8.29 illustrates a kitchen sink drainpipe connected to the wastewater drain line. In this illustration, the home owner attempted to use duct tape to close one end of the drain line. The drain line should be properly capped so that gases and waste material do not escape into the structure.

A trap (discussed earlier) is part of the drainage system and is located under the sink. The hot and cold water supply lines may be connected to a dishwasher, garbage disposal, icemaker, or hot water dispenser. Separate sprayers that are part

FIGURE 8.29

A drain pipe.

Source: Anthony D'Agostino, Atlantic Inspection Service, Latham, New York.

| *Kitchen sink components.* | **FIGURE 8.30** |

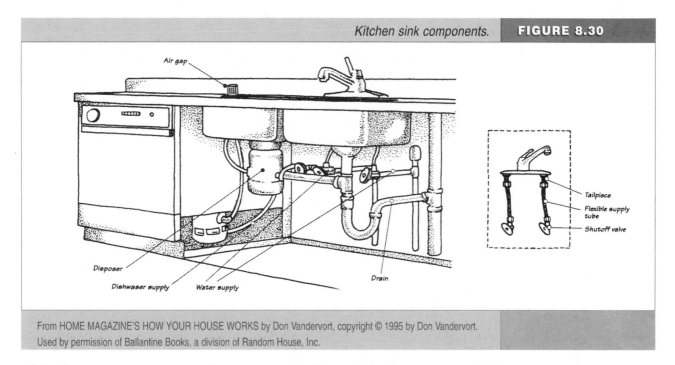

From HOME MAGAZINE'S HOW YOUR HOUSE WORKS by Don Vandervort, copyright © 1995 by Don Vandervort. Used by permission of Ballantine Books, a division of Random House, Inc.

of the faucet units connect to the water supply through the faucet. Figure 8.30 illustrates the components of kitchen sink plumbing.

Inspecting the sinks. The kitchen sink should be tested for water flow and the proper drainage from the sink. Are the hot and cold water supply lines hooked up correctly? Because the dishwasher water source is the same as for the sink, check the pipe connection that leads from the dishwasher to the water supply lines for leakage. Check that the drain and water source are hooked up correctly and that the sink has a P-trap to block any sewer gases from escaping through the pipe. Inspectors may find that some homes have an S-trap under the sink. An S-trap is not as effective as a P-trap because S-traps tend to have the water sucked out of the trap when it drains. This allows sewer gases to escape through the drain into the structure. The dishwasher drain should be connected above the trap for the sink. Figure 8.31 illustrates a dishwasher drainpipe connected to a three-inch drainpipe. Because there is no P-trap, sewer gases can back up into the structure through the dishwasher drainpipe.

All sinks should be securely fastened to the counter or to the wall if the sink is a wall mount.

Home inspectors must check the function and operation of all faucets. Observe whether the faucets shut off fully without leakage. It is a good idea to check the faucet a few minutes after you have turned it off to see if there is a slow leak. You can accomplish this by drying the bowl of the sink after turning off the faucet and then going back to check for moisture. Stains in the sink bowl or around the faucet area are also signs of leakage. Observe whether the hot and cold water are flowing through the proper side of the faucet. Make sure the faucet is securely fastened to the countertop so that water cannot seep under it. Check that the handles of the faucet are not missing or damaged to the point that the faucet is not operational. Faucets should be free of rust and corrosion. Cracked or missing ceramic faucets should be replaced.

Putting It to Work
Faucets

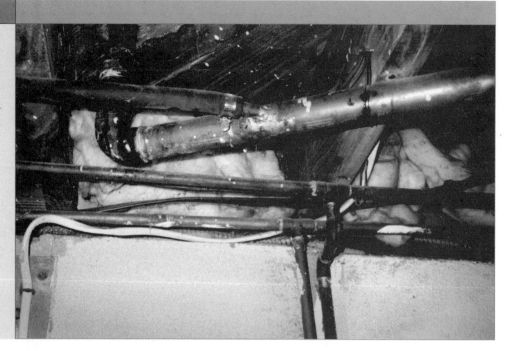

FIGURE 8.31

This dishwasher drainpipe is connected to a three-inch drainpipe. Because there is no P-trap, sewer gases can back up into the structure through the dishwasher drainpipe.

Source: Anthony D'Agostino, Atlantic Inspection Service, Latham, New York.

Toilets

Toilets (water closets) are generally floor mounted in a residential property and use a flush tank. They are constructed from vitreous china or enameled iron. The toilet drains wastewater through a valve system. A water tank is part of the toilet. The tank handle is connected inside the tank to a flush valve that lifts when the handle is depressed. This motion allows the water in the tank to flow into the bowl. These toilets are gravity toilets and rely on a water pressure of about 15 pounds per square inch (psi) to flush. The water pressure from the water flowing into the bowl forces the waste down through the pipe.

As the tank empties out and the handle is released, a float ball drops and activates a ballcock that allows the tank to once again fill with water. The water fills into the tank through a refill valve. Some toilets have ballcocks that operate on water pressure without a float ball. The water reaches the ballcock through a supply tube connected to a valve outside the toilet. Figure 8.32 diagrams the parts of a toilet.

You Should Know

In 1992, the U.S. Department of Energy mandated low-flush toilets as a water conservation measure. Therefore, newer toilets are engineered to use much less water to complete the operation than older ones. The newer toilets use 1.6 gallons per flush, half the amount of water used by older 3.5-gallons-per-flush toilets. Pressure-tank toilets, another more expensive alternative, have a secondary container inside the tank. It uses the water pressure entering the main tank to compress air trapped in the inner tank. Each flush is pressure assisted to push out wastes instead of siphoning them out as with a gravity toilet. This pressure toilet operates with 25 to 35 psi of water pressure.

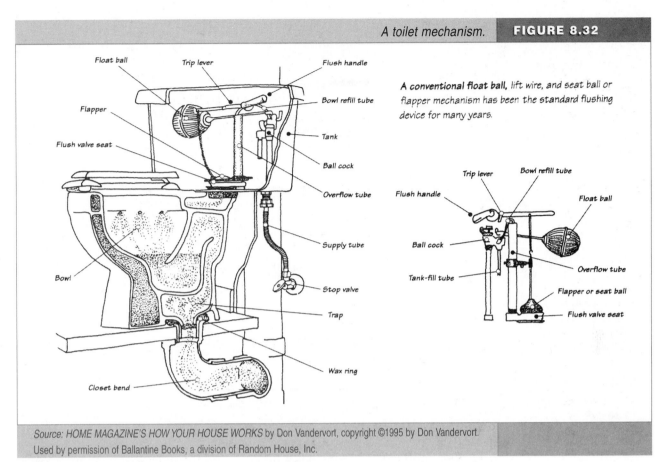

A toilet mechanism.   **FIGURE 8.32**

Float ball
Trip lever
Flush handle
Flapper
Bowl refill tube
Flush valve seat
Tank
Ball cock
Overflow tube
Bowl
Supply tube
Stop valve
Trap
Wax ring
Closet bend

A conventional float ball, lift wire, and seat ball or flapper mechanism has been the standard flushing device for many years.

Trip lever
Bowl refill tube
Flush handle
Float ball
Ball cock
Overflow tube
Tank-fill tube
Flapper or seat ball
Flush valve seat

Source: *HOME MAGAZINE'S HOW YOUR HOUSE WORKS* by Don Vandervort, copyright ©1995 by Don Vandervort. Used by permission of Ballantine Books, a division of Random House, Inc.

Bathtubs and Showers

Bathtubs are available in a variety of shapes and sizes. Some have two sides closed and fit into a corner. Others have one side closed and are fitted between end walls. Whirlpool tubs have pumps that circulate the water. Some bathtubs are made from gel-coated fiberglass and the tub and wall enclosure form a single unit. This smooth surface leaves no cracks to form mold. Showers are made from porcelain, enamel steel, or fiberglass. Both bathtubs and showers installed today must have control valves that limit the water temperature to a maximum of 120 degrees.

Inspecting the bathroom plumbing fixtures. The bathroom plumbing fixtures should be inspected as follows:

■ Check the sink, drain, and trap in the same way as the kitchen sink. Look for cracks in the sink bowl and check that the sink is securely fastened to the wall or the countertop. Figure 8.33 illustrates the plumbing of a typical bathroom sink.

■ Flush the toilet and observe that the water drains properly. Rock the bowl in a gentle back and forth motion to make sure it is tightly secured to floor. Many toilets connect to the floor with a gasket ring. Make sure there is no leakage where the toilet meets the floor and gasket ring. Remove the tank top and look inside. Flush the toilet again and observe that the moving parts are functioning properly. If the toilet is sluggish and the waste is slow to go down, there may be a blockage in either the waste pipe or the toilet trap. Other causes could be a deficient amount of water in the bowl. Because the water pressure is causing the flushing operation, too little water compromises this. Check that the toilet has a

FIGURE 8.33

A typical bathroom sink.

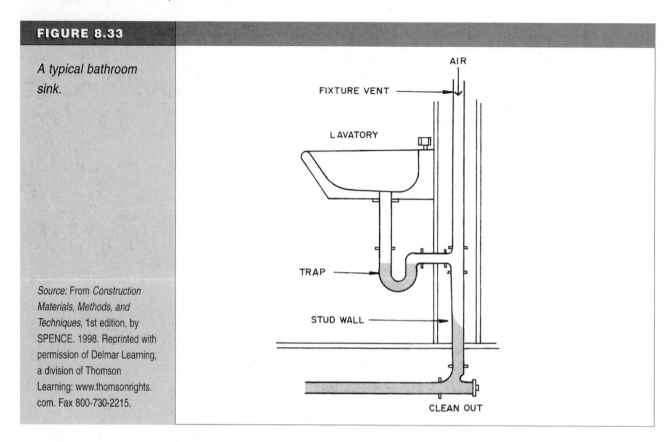

Source: From *Construction Materials, Methods, and Techniques*, 1st edition, by SPENCE. 1998. Reprinted with permission of Delmar Learning, a division of Thomson Learning: www.thomsonrights. com. Fax 800-730-2215.

separate shutoff valve. This avoids a flood should the toilet malfunction. A separate shutoff eliminates the need to shut off the entire water supply system if there is a problem with the toilet.

■ Check the faucets in the shower, tub, and sinks.

■ To check the bathroom for acceptable drainage, fill the tub with about one-half-inch of water. Open the drain and flush the toilet at the same time. If the water dribbles down the drain, it indicates that there is a blockage somewhere in the drain line.

Putting It to Work

If, when checking the tub drainage and flushing the toilet, the toilet wastewater backs up into the tub, then the drain line leading from the tub or the toilet is clogged.

■ If tiles enclose the shower and tub, verify that the seam where the bathtub ends and the tile begins is properly caulked. The same is true for tub enclosures that are lined with fiberglass.

■ Tap the ceramic tiles on the floor, tub, and shower enclosure to see if they are securely fastened to the wall. Also, notice if any of the tiles are bulging away from the wall. Bulging tiles may be an indicator of moisture behind the tiles.

■ Check that the stall shower is not leaking through to the floor below. Find the point under the shower and examine the ceiling for moisture or stains. This is the best way to detect if the shower is leaking. Although home inspectors cannot check the problem directly, the leak may be caused by a rusted metal shower pan inside the floor of the shower. Older showers were constructed with a combination of a ceramic tile floor and a metal shower pan to catch the overflow of water that does not readily go down the drain. Instead, the water may leak through the grout into the pan and sit there, eventually causing the pan to rust. Newer showers are constructed with fiberglass or plastic pans and do not have this problem.

| You may notice that some property owners have put sheet fiberglass over ceramic tile in a shower or tub enclosure. This was installed quite possibly to cover up a decaying tile problem underneath. It can, therefore, indicate that moisture might exist behind the tiles. | *Putting It to Work* |

| Recommend to your clients that they have whirlpool tubs professionally cleaned and inspected. If possible, home inspectors should ask the property owner to fill and turn on a whirlpool tub. The home inspector should not do this. | *Putting It to Work* |

IMPORTANT POINTS

1. In general, the inspection of the plumbing, heating, and air-conditioning includes the water supply and distribution systems; water and fuel shutoff valves; wastewater and drainage systems; accessible pipes used for water supply and drainage; pipe vent systems; hot water heaters; heating equipment; the air-conditioning system; and plumbing fixtures including sinks, tubs, shower, faucets, and toilets. Inspectors may include other items, such as a well or septic system inspection, if their expertise allows, and there is client demand.

2. If a property is serviced by municipal water, a water meter is generally found along the outside foundation wall or in the basement.

3. A private water supply system is composed of the well, a pump, the storage tank, and the connecting pipe between the well and the storage tank.

4. Much of a well inspection (though not required by industry standards of practice) consists of identifying that there is a well and determining the well's location and the location of its components, the type of well, and the pump's operability.

5. With houses that are part of a municipal wastewater system, the wastewater drains through the house drainage system into a house sewer that connects to the municipal sewer system or is deposited in a private septic tank.

6. The first item to look for when inspecting the vent pipes is whether or not there is a plumbing vent stack venting through the roof. The absence of the vent stack is a violation of plumbing codes.

7. To inspect a septic system, the absorption field should be examined. Look for any questionable liquids oozing through the ground. There should be no foul-smelling odors in the area of a properly functioning septic system.

8. Most of a structure's pipe system is hidden behind walls and ceilings. Therefore, the inspector must examine the property to find the areas where pipe is exposed.

9. Examine all accessible pipes for leakage, rust and corrosion, pipe sizing for adequate pressure, and noise in the pipes. Check that all cold water pipes are insulated properly and that condensation is not visible.

10. A residential heating system is usually one of the following types: hot water, steam, forced warm air, and electric. Check that each inhabited room in the structure has at least one heating vent, convector, radiator, or other means of heating.

11. When inspecting the heating system, look for evidence of leaking, cracks, rust, or corrosion to the body of the furnace. Also, check for an abnormal amount of soot in and around the furnace. Verify that the furnace has a safety switch.

12. A lack of ventilation in an enclosed furnace room is a safety hazard.

13. The heating system inspection includes checking the location of the thermostat and making sure that it is registering. In gas-fired systems, check the pilot light and observe the gas burners inside the heat exchanger.

14. The mechanical components of an air conditioner are a liquid refrigerant, an evaporator, a compressor, and a condenser.

15. When an air conditioner is combined with a forced warm air furnace, pipes carry the refrigerant from the compressor, located outdoors, to an indoor coil, known as an evaporator, located inside the furnace.

16. Air source heat pumps extract heat from the outside, even in moderately cold weather, and transfer the heat into the home. This heat transfer cycle is reversed in the warmer months to extract heat from the interior of a building, transfer it to the outdoors, and produce air-conditioning (cooling).

17. To inspect the air-cooling system, first check that the exterior compressor is on level ground. Observe that the fan inside the compressor is working and check that the condensation from the evaporator coil is not leaking out of the evaporator coil pan. Verify that the air filter is installed and, if possible, check for ice buildup on the evaporator coil.

18. To inspect the hot water heater, note whether there is a pipe extension on the pressure relief valve. Also test for the recovery rate of the hot water and make sure that the water tank is set no higher than 120 degrees.

19. All gas-fired equipment, including hot water heaters and furnaces, is checked for gas leaks.

20. When inspecting the cabinets and counters in the kitchen and bathroom, check that the base cabinets are securely fastened to the wall and that the counters are securely affixed to the cabinets. Open and close the drawers and doors to check for operability.

21. The kitchen sink should be tested for water flow and the proper drainage from the sink.

22. Bathroom fixtures that must be inspected include the sink, tub, shower stall, and toilet. Toilets should be flushed to see whether the water drains properly. Check that they are secured to the floor.

23. Bathroom tiles should be examined for moisture behind them.

CHAPTER REVIEW

Field Study Assignment 1

Using your practice property and a copy of the inspection checklist from Figure 4.4, inspect the plumbing, heating, and air-conditioning components of your subject property. Note any problems you encounter for further exploration and discussion.

Field Study Assignment 2

To further reinforce what you have learned in this chapter, identify the following while inspecting the plumbing, heating, and air-conditioning at your practice property:

- the drainage pipes and the water supply pipes
- the pipe material
- the type of heating system
- whether the property uses a municipal or a private water supply
- whether the property has a septic system
- the types of traps in the drainage system
- the type of water tank

REVIEW QUESTIONS *Choose the letter that best answers the question.*

1. One way of telling whether a property is serviced by municipal water is if:
   A. lead pipe is not used in the water supply service pipe
   B. there is a water meter in or outside the home
   C. the property has adequate water pressure
   D. the water is potable

2. If a well is on-site and the home inspector agrees to inspect it, she should do which of the following?
   A. Test for water quality.
   B. Remove the submersible pump and examine it.
   C. Examine the condition of the pressure tank.
   D. Repair any items that are causing immediate problems.

3. It is clear to Sam, a home inspector, on testing the water flow that the well pump is not working. How should he proceed?
   A. Sam should remove the pump from the well for a closer look.
   B. Sam should advise his clients not to purchase the property until the pump is fixed.
   C. Sam should advise his clients of the problem and suggest they hire a well professional to further investigate the problem.
   D. Sam should report the malfunction to the health department.

4. Soil stacks are vertical pipes that are part of the:
   A. drainage system
   B. water supply system
   C. chimney system
   D. heating system

5. The purpose of vent pipes in a drainage system is to:
   A. allow backpressure into the system
   B. stop outside air from entering the system
   C. avoid the use of traps
   D. ensure the rapid flow of waste

6. The examination of the absorption field when inspecting a septic system is important because it:
   A. is the only way to evaluate whether the system is functioning
   B. is the only indicator that a septic system exists on the property
   C. usually violates plumbing codes
   D. may indicate a malfunctioning system if liquids are oozing through to the surface

7. A pressure tank is used in conjunction with a(n):
   A. compressor
   B. well
   C. septic system
   D. air-cooling system

8. The valve used as the main shutoff valve to the property is known as the:
   A. gate valve
   B. globe valve
   C. pressure regulator valve
   D. float valve

9. A type of pipe that is no longer used in plumbing applications is:
   A. copper
   B. cast-iron
   C. brass
   D. galvanized steel

10. The problem with older steel galvanized pipes is that they:
    A. form sediment that becomes toxic over time
    B. rust internally, narrowing the diameter of the pipe
    C. are a violation of plumbing codes
    D. are not functional after 25 years of use

11. A steam heating system is a type of:
    A. hydronic system
    B. forced warm air system
    C. resistance heating system
    D. radiant heating system

12. Which of the following need NOT be observed as part of the heating system inspection?
    A. an abnormal amount of soot in and around the furnace
    B. ventilation in a furnace room
    C. gas burners inside the heat exchanger
    D. underground oil storage tanks

13. A device that automatically closes the gas valve should the pilot light go off is known as the:
    A. globe valve
    B. temperature pressure relief valve
    C. thermocouple
    D. drip leg

14. Which of the following is NOT a component of an air-conditioning system?
    A. condenser
    B. resister
    C. evaporator
    D. compressor

15. The heat source for an air-to-air heat pump is:
    A. the ground temperature
    B. outside air
    C. electric resistors
    D. thermal panels

16. If part of the air-conditioning unit is in the attic and there is moisture on the ceiling below, what air-conditioner component might be causing the moisture?
    A. compressor
    B. condenser
    C. fan
    D. evaporator coil pan

17. When a large number of coils are immersed directly into the boiler water to supply hot water, this is known as:
    A. a summer–winter hookup
    B. a tankless coil system
    C. an evaporative condenser
    D. a recycled condensation

18. A safety device that should be attached to the pressure relief valve on a hot water heater is known as:
    A. an extension pipe
    B. a thermocouple
    C. a heat exchanger
    D. a convector

19. To prevent scalding, water tanks should be set at no more than:
    A. 90 degrees
    B. 98.6 degrees
    C. 110 degrees
    D. 120 degrees

20. One of the most important features to observe in the inspection of counters and cabinets is:
    A. the type of material
    B. the aesthetic appearance
    C. the placement in the room
    D. whether they are securely affixed to the floor and wall

21. The purpose of a trap under the sink is to:
    A. catch dirt and debris before it goes down the drain pipe
    B. to prevent sewer gases from traveling up the pipe into the structure
    C. to provide an opening to gain access to the drain pipe
    D. to provide an alternate drainage route

22. The mechanism that allows a toilet to flush is:
    A. hydraulic pressure
    B. gravity
    C. water pressure
    D. electromagnetic fields

23. Toilets are generally constructed from:
    A. vitreous china
    B. gel-coated fiberglass
    C. molded ceramic tile
    D. copper with enamel covering

24. One of the problems with ceramic tiles on bathroom floors and walls is that they:
    A. pose a safety hazard
    B. need to be replaced every five to seven years
    C. may loosen and cause moisture to form behind them
    D. absorb water

25. An older stall shower is leaking through to the floor. The most likely cause is:
    A. people who shower for more than five minutes
    B. a rusted metal shower pan
    C. rotted floor joists
    D. too much water pressure

ANSWER KEY

1. B	8. A	15. B	22. C
2. C	9. C	16. D	23. A
3. C	10. B	17. B	24. C
4. A	11. A	18. A	25. B
5. D	12. D	19. D	
6. D	13. C	20. D	
7. B	14. B	21. B	

CHAPTER 9

INSPECTING THE ELECTRICAL SYSTEM

T he electrical system inspection requires a basic understanding of electricity and how it delivers power to the outlets in the building. While inspecting the electrical system, inspectors must take care to protect themselves and any clients that are present from electric shock.

LEARNING OBJECTIVES

1. List the items that are included in the electrical system inspection.
2. Define basic electrical system terminology.
3. Describe the general procedure for the electrical system inspection.

KEY TERMS

Amperage

Branch circuit wiring

Bus bars

Circuit

Circuit breaker

Conductor

Electric current

Fuse

Ground fault circuit interrupter (GFCI)

Insulator

Junction box

Neutral bus bar

Ohm

Outlet

Overcurrent protection devices

Raceway

Receptacle

Service drop

Service entrance cable

Service lateral

Service lateral conductor

Switch

Transformer

Voltage

SCOPE OF THE ELECTRICAL INSPECTION

igure 9.1 sets forth the ASHI Standards of Practice for the electrical system inspection.

FIGURE 9.1	
Applicable ASHI Standards of Practice.	**7. ELECTRICAL SYSTEM** 7.1 The inspector shall: 　A. inspect: 　　1. service drop. 　　2. service entrance conductors, cables, and raceways. 　　3. service equipment and main disconnects. 　　4. service grounding. 　　5. interior components of service panels and sub panels. 　　6. conductors. 　　7. overcurrent protection devices. 　　8. a representative number of installed lighting fixtures, switches, and receptacles. 　　9. ground fault circuit interrupters. 　B. describe: 　　1. amperage and voltage rating of the service. 　　2. location of main disconnect(s) and sub panels. 　　3. presence of solid conductor aluminum branch circuit wiring. 　　4. presence or absence of smoke detectors. 　　5. wiring methods 7.2 The inspector is NOT required to: 　A. inspect: 　　1. remote control devices. 　　2. alarm systems and components. 　　3. low voltage wiring, systems, and components. 　　4. ancillary wiring systems and components not a part of the primary electrical power distribution system. 　B. measure amperage, voltage, or impedance.
Permission to reprint and reference granted by the American Society of Home Inspectors, Inc. (ASHI) www.ASHI.org	

Putting It to Work

A search of the Internet will reveal several reputable companies that sell tools specifically for the home inspector. These companies have catalogs that fully describe the type of tool and its uses. A large variety of tools are available in various price ranges to assist with the electrical inspection. Now is the time to investigate the possibilities.

A variety of tools are helpful when performing the inspection of the electrical system. A three-prong branch circuit analyzer device, plugged into the receptacle, tests for proper wiring (discussed later), excess voltage drop (when less than 120 voltage enters the receptacle), ground fault circuit interrupter (GFCI) function, and loose receptacle connections. It also indicates inadequate and high-resistance grounds that are safety hazards. Separate GFCI testers are also available. This device plugs into the receptacle and electrically trips the GFCI outlet to make sure the GFCI is functioning properly. Two-prong testers are available to test two-slot receptacles in older homes. In addition, a pair of binoculars helps inspect the service drop.

Putting It to Work
Electrical
Inspection Tools

The National Electric Code (NEC) is a national standard for electrical installation and service and is written to safeguard people and property from hazards arising from the use of electricity. The code was developed by the National Fire Protection Association so that consumers, local code enforcement agencies, insurance companies, and other organizations have a uniform standard of electrical performance and safety. The code is used for all electrical installations and remodeling projects.

You Should Know
National Electric
Code

Although inspectors are not responsible for code enforcement, a familiarity with the sections of the NEC that pertain to the inspection is helpful. This chapter examines certain NEC requirements. Inspectors may not find current code standards in all properties they inspect because the code changes every three years. Those properties that were built prior to a code regulation are not in violation. Local codes may be more restrictive but must follow the requirements of the national code.

Putting It to Work

INSPECTION PROCEDURE

The inspection of the electrical system proceeds in the same order as the information in this chapter is presented. Begin with the exterior where the service enters the house. If the electric meter and the main panel board or main disconnect are located outdoors, inspect this equipment first. Proceed to the interior and locate the main panel board if not found outside. After an examination of the main disconnect and the interior details of the main panel board, move through the structure. Check the garage and attic for wires, cables, and junction boxes. While performing the inspection, examine the operation of light switches, light fixtures, plugs, ground fault circuit interrupters (GFCIs), light fixtures, and the presence and workability of smoke detectors.

ELECTRICITY

lectric current *is the flow of electrons along a conductor such as a copper wire.* The electrons are produced by a generator or battery that forces electrons to follow the conductor to an appliance such as a lightbulb. The electrons then flow back to the source. There are two types of electric current: direct and alternating. Direct current, or DC, has a constant flow in one direction. Alternating current or AC flows in one direction and then in the opposite direction. Each complete repetition is called a cycle. The number of repetitions per second is called the frequency.

You Should Know
Measurements of Electricity

Power is the rate at which energy is used. The unit of electric power in electric circuits is expressed in watts or kilowatts. One kilowatt is equal to 1,000 watts. One watt-hour of energy represents one watt of power use for one hour. A watt is used to specify the rate at which electrical energy is dissipated. Electrical capacity requirements are determined when a house is built and are normally delineated in watts or kilowatts. Moreover, the amperage required for different electrical uses is calculated in watts or kilowatts. House electrical circuits are installed according to these kilowatt requirements.

You Should Know

Electricity is produced by a generator. Types of generators include hydroelectric, fossil fuel, and nuclear powered. Alternating current is produced by an AC generator, also called an alternator, that may be powered by any of the mentioned sources.

Conductors

Electricity moves along wires called **conductors**. *A good conductor has little resistance to the flow of electricity.* Copper and aluminum are the two most commonly used wiring materials because they are good conductors of electricity. Copper conducts electricity better than aluminum, so if an aluminum wire is used, it must have a larger diameter to carry the same amount of current. *The resistance to the flow of electricity is measured in ohms. An* **ohm** *is a unit of electrical resistance of a conductor.* **Insulators** *are materials that are poor conductors of electricity and are, therefore, placed around wires to prevent electrical shock.* Materials such as glass, ceramic, and plastics are examples of insulators. *Electricity travels in a path called a* **circuit**. Switches (discussed later) can be placed in the circuit's path to interrupt the flow of electricity. Figure 9.2 illustrates the current flow in an electrical circuit.

Voltage and Amperage

Voltage *is the electrical pressure that pushes through wires.* Voltage is very similar to water pressure; it is the push. A voltage service of 120/240 volts is standard; less voltage does not meet the requirements of a residential property. Inspectors can generally verify the voltage by looking at the aboveground cable coming into the structure. If there are three cables that often means that the service is 120/240; if there are only two that means the service is probably 120 volt. Lighting and small appliance loads use 120 volts; 240 volts is generally necessary for heavier residential applications. **Transformers** *are used to change alternating current from one voltage to another, reducing it to a level that can be used in the residence.* The voltage going into the transformer (from the power company) is the primary voltage. This

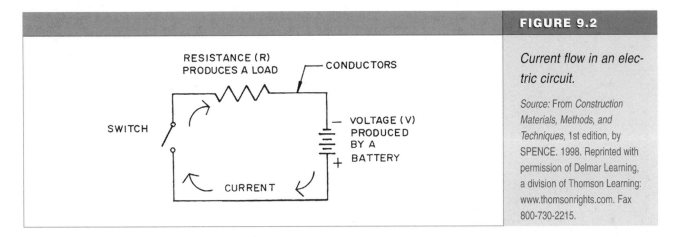

FIGURE 9.2

Current flow in an electric circuit.

Source: From *Construction Materials, Methods, and Techniques,* 1st edition, by SPENCE. 1998. Reprinted with permission of Delmar Learning, a division of Thomson Learning: www.thomsonrights.com. Fax 800-730-2215.

240 voltage can be wired for 120 volts for household usage. The transformer also has a neutral line that is grounded so that there are three lines coming into the house: two live ones and one neutral.

Amperage *is the amount of current or electricity flowing through a wire.* The main panel board is where circuit breakers or fuses are located and is discussed more fully later. Most residential service is 100 amperes, commonly called amps. Home inspectors may, however, inspect new construction that has 150- or 200-amp service. Service with less than 100 amps is generally substandard for the needs of a typical residential house.

It is the job of the inspector to describe the amperage service of the property. It is not always an easy one. There is no direct relation between the service size and the number of fuses or the total rating of all fuses or circuit breakers. The ratings may total more than the service size.

Putting It to Work

INCOMING SERVICE

Electric power is brought to the house through outside cables and is then delivered through a series of conductors to the house wiring system. Two types of service exist: some houses are located in areas that have aboveground cables; others have underground or buried cables. *Aboveground cables that come from the nearest utility pole connecting to the service entrance conductors of the house or building are called a* **service drop.** Transformers are generally located on the utility pole. Figure 9.3 illustrates a service drop.

High voltage underground cable is often installed for new construction. Pad-mounted transformers are placed near the rear lot line or another location in the subdivision. *Electrical service that runs underground is called a* **service lateral.** *The conductors installed between the transformers and the meters are called the* **service lateral conductors** (see Figure 9.4). The utility company's responsibility is to bring electricity to the service drop or lateral of the property. According to requirements set forth in the NEC, the aboveground service conductor or cable must have a minimum clearance of three feet from windows that open, doors, porches, balconies, ladders, stairs, fire escapes, or other similar locations. The cable (drip loop) must be 10 feet above the finished grade at the building. The drip loop is

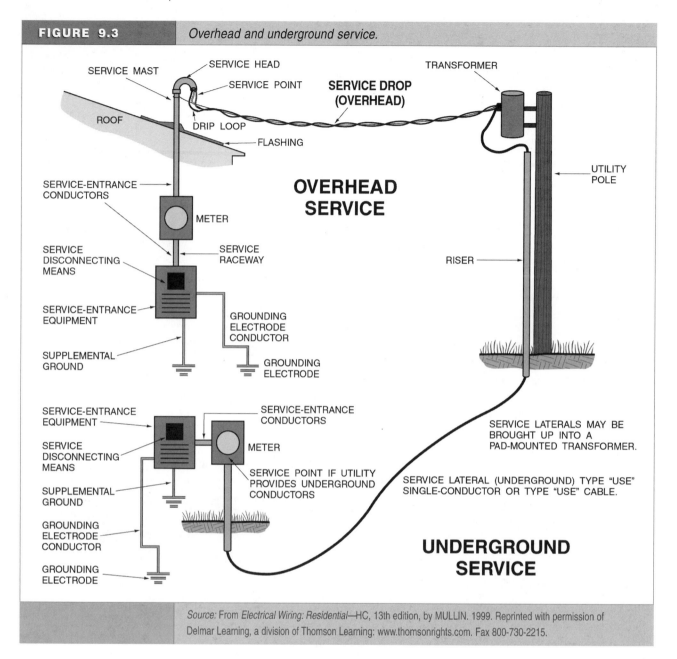

FIGURE 9.3   *Overhead and underground service.*

Source: From *Electrical Wiring: Residential—HC*, 13th edition, by MULLIN. 1999. Reprinted with permission of Delmar Learning, a division of Thomson Learning: www.thomsonrights.com. Fax 800-730-2215.

located at the connection of the service drop and the entry conductor from the building. Figure 9.5 illustrates the clearance requirements for a service drop.

The property owner is responsible for every other aspect of the service beyond that point of entry. For example, property owners are responsible for all inside wiring, blown fuses, and, in most cases, for the electric meters that measure usage. The meter that measures usage is generally on the exterior of the structure. From the service entrance and through the panel board, branch circuit wiring is run to various parts of the house.

Service Entrance Cable

A **service entrance cable** (**SE cable**) *is a single conductor or several conductors, with or without covering, used for aboveground service entrance.* SE cable is generally run

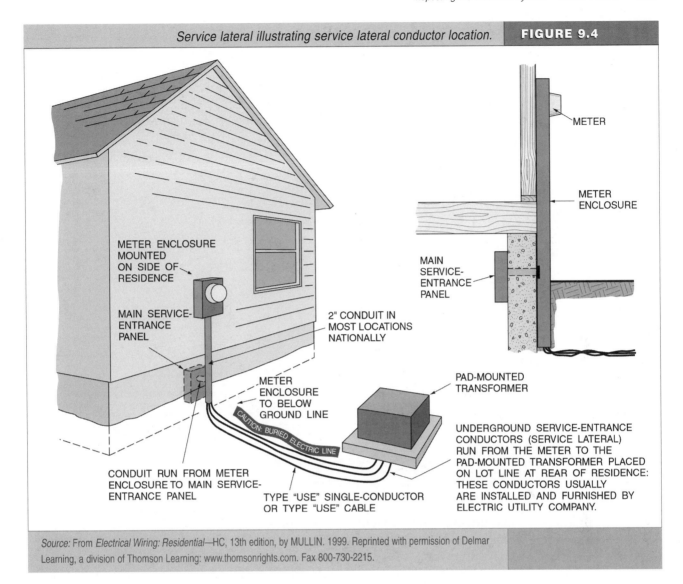

FIGURE 9.4

Service lateral illustrating service lateral conductor location.

METER

METER ENCLOSURE

MAIN SERVICE-ENTRANCE PANEL

METER ENCLOSURE MOUNTED ON SIDE OF RESIDENCE

MAIN SERVICE-ENTRANCE PANEL

2" CONDUIT IN MOST LOCATIONS NATIONALLY

METER ENCLOSURE TO BELOW GROUND LINE

CAUTION: BURIED ELECTRIC LINE

PAD-MOUNTED TRANSFORMER

CONDUIT RUN FROM METER ENCLOSURE TO MAIN SERVICE-ENTRANCE PANEL

TYPE "USE" SINGLE-CONDUCTOR OR TYPE "USE" CABLE

UNDERGROUND SERVICE-ENTRANCE CONDUCTORS (SERVICE LATERAL) RUN FROM THE METER TO THE PAD-MOUNTED TRANSFORMER PLACED ON LOT LINE AT REAR OF RESIDENCE: THESE CONDUCTORS USUALLY ARE INSTALLED AND FURNISHED BY ELECTRIC UTILITY COMPANY.

Source: From *Electrical Wiring: Residential—HC*, 13th edition, by MULLIN. 1999. Reprinted with permission of Delmar Learning, a division of Thomson Learning: www.thomsonrights.com. Fax 800-730-2215.

from the utility company's service point outdoors to the meter base and then to the main panel board. The outer jacket depicted in Figure 9.6 is used when the SE cable is exposed to sunlight. Type SE cable is used as interior wiring to hook up major appliances. For this application, the circuit conductors must be insulated.

A different service cable, Type USE, is for underground use. This type of cable is not permitted inside the structure and must move from the ground and terminate in a meter. To protect the conductors from damage, they are run through a **raceway** *that goes from the bottom of the meter through to a point below the ground level. Raceways are used to support, enclose, and protect electrical wires.* They may also be run from the bottom of the meter pedestal. Figure 9.7 illustrates a supported raceway.

Grounding

Electrical systems must be grounded; that is, they are connected to the earth to limit excess voltage from lighting, line surges, or unintentional contact with higher voltage lines. Grounding stabilizes the voltage, protecting the system. Proper

| FIGURE 9.5 | *Clearance requirements for a service drop.* |

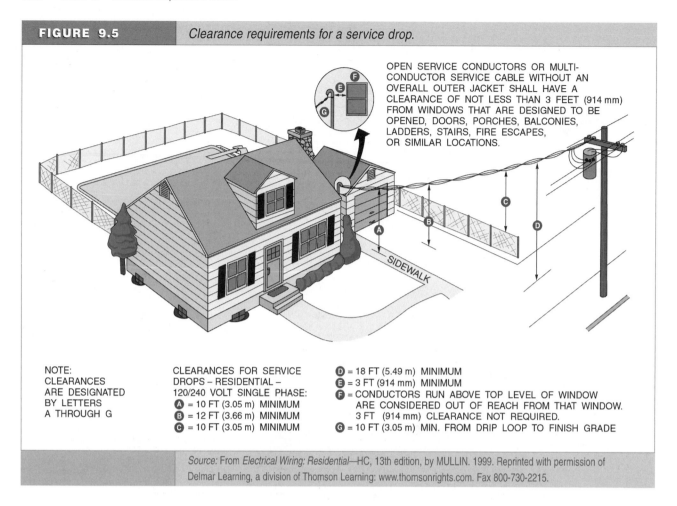

OPEN SERVICE CONDUCTORS OR MULTI-CONDUCTOR SERVICE CABLE WITHOUT AN OVERALL OUTER JACKET SHALL HAVE A CLEARANCE OF NOT LESS THAN 3 FEET (914 mm) FROM WINDOWS THAT ARE DESIGNED TO BE OPENED, DOORS, PORCHES, BALCONIES, LADDERS, STAIRS, FIRE ESCAPES, OR SIMILAR LOCATIONS.

NOTE:
CLEARANCES
ARE DESIGNATED
BY LETTERS
A THROUGH G

CLEARANCES FOR SERVICE DROPS – RESIDENTIAL – 120/240 VOLT SINGLE PHASE:
Ⓐ = 10 FT (3.05 m) MINIMUM
Ⓑ = 12 FT (3.66 m) MINIMUM
Ⓒ = 10 FT (3.05 m) MINIMUM

Ⓓ = 18 FT (5.49 m) MINIMUM
Ⓔ = 3 FT (914 mm) MINIMUM
Ⓕ = CONDUCTORS RUN ABOVE TOP LEVEL OF WINDOW ARE CONSIDERED OUT OF REACH FROM THAT WINDOW. 3 FT (914 mm) CLEARANCE NOT REQUIRED.
Ⓖ = 10 FT (3.05 m) MIN. FROM DRIP LOOP TO FINISH GRADE

Source: From *Electrical Wiring: Residential*—HC, 13th edition, by MULLIN. 1999. Reprinted with permission of Delmar Learning, a division of Thomson Learning: www.thomsonrights.com. Fax 800-730-2215.

grounding ensures that **overcurrent protection devices** *operate fast when responding to ground faults.* Overcurrent protection devices include the main disconnect, circuit breakers, and fuses.

The service entrance neutral conductor must be grounded. This neutral conductor is bonded (discussed later) to the main panel board and a grounding electrode conductor is connected to a grounding electrode and all metal water pipes. Copper and stainless steel ground rods are commonly used as a grounding electrode. Metal underground gas pipe is not permitted as a grounding electrode. A

| FIGURE 9.6 | *Type SE service entrance cable.* |

This cable contains two insulated conductors and one "wrap-around" bare neutral conductor. There is reinforcement tape plus the final sunlight-resistant outer jacket.

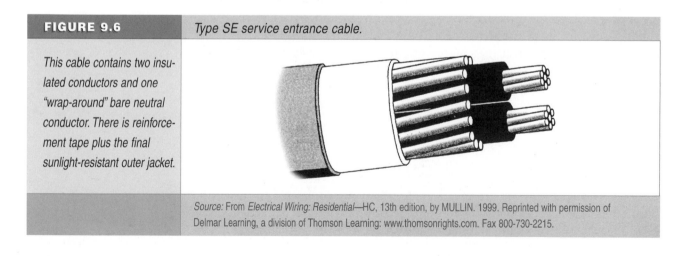

Source: From *Electrical Wiring: Residential*—HC, 13th edition, by MULLIN. 1999. Reprinted with permission of Delmar Learning, a division of Thomson Learning: www.thomsonrights.com. Fax 800-730-2215.

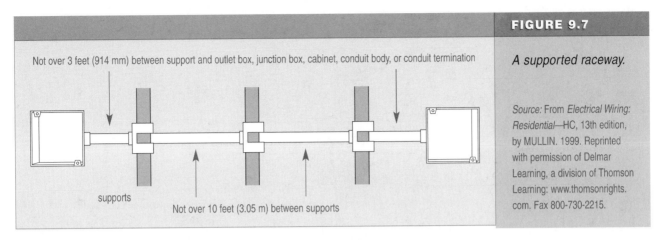

FIGURE 9.7

A supported raceway.

Source: From *Electrical Wiring: Residential—HC*, 13th edition, by MULLIN. 1999. Reprinted with permission of Delmar Learning, a division of Thomson Learning: www.thomsonrights. com. Fax 800-730-2215.

metal underground water piping system 10 feet or longer is an acceptable grounding electrode. It must be supplemented by at least one of the other grounding components mentioned previously. Figure 9.8 illustrates the grounding of a service drop system.

> **You Should Know**
>
> The ground rod is generally flush with or just below ground level. In some properties, inspectors can see the ground rod. If the upper end of the ground rod is exposed, the ground clamp and the grounding electrode conductors must be protected from physical damage. Electrical service must be grounded with a grounding rod when there is a private water system because well water supply pipes may not be used. If plastic pipe is not used, the water line generally serves as the ground when there is a municipal water supply.

Meter

A kilowatt-hour is equal to 1,000 watt-hours. Usage is measured by a kilowatt-hour meter. Three-wire meters (discussed later) are typically used for residential applications. Meters may be located either inside or outside the building.

Inspecting the incoming service. The incoming service is inspected as follows:

■ If the service is aboveground, check that the service entrance cable is the proper height above the ground and that it has the NEC-required minimum clearances. Refer back to Figure 9.5 for the various clearance requirements for service entrance conductors. Inspectors should become familiar with them.

■ Observe the condition of the outside cable that runs to the meter. Figure 9.9 illustrates a frayed exterior service cable exposing the wiring. If the cable deteriorates, the wires become exposed and can make contact with each other, causing a blowout or electrical fire. The service entrance cable or conduit should be firmly affixed to the structure beginning at the roof and traveling down the side of the house to the meter box. The service entrance cable is fastened to the building with cable clamps placed no more than 30 inches apart and within 12 inches of the meter box.

■ Inspect the condition of the electric meter. Make sure it is operational and is firmly secured to the exterior wall or ground.

■ Tree branches may be growing around and through the overhead cable. If so, record this on the inspection report. Advise your clients that the problem may

FIGURE 9.8

Service drop system grounding.

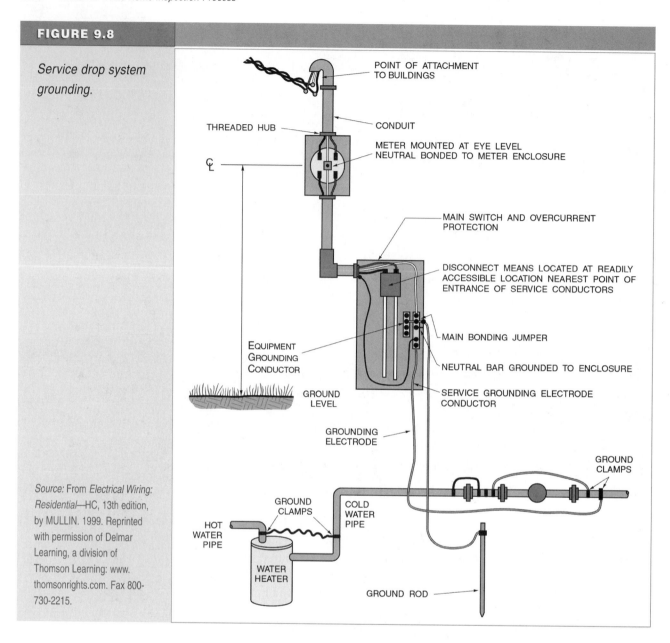

POINT OF ATTACHMENT TO BUILDINGS

THREADED HUB

CONDUIT

C̸L

METER MOUNTED AT EYE LEVEL
NEUTRAL BONDED TO METER ENCLOSURE

MAIN SWITCH AND OVERCURRENT PROTECTION

DISCONNECT MEANS LOCATED AT READILY ACCESSIBLE LOCATION NEAREST POINT OF ENTRANCE OF SERVICE CONDUCTORS

EQUIPMENT GROUNDING CONDUCTOR

MAIN BONDING JUMPER

NEUTRAL BAR GROUNDED TO ENCLOSURE

SERVICE GROUNDING ELECTRODE CONDUCTOR

GROUND LEVEL

GROUNDING ELECTRODE

GROUND CLAMPS

GROUND CLAMPS

HOT WATER PIPE

COLD WATER PIPE

WATER HEATER

GROUND ROD

Source: From *Electrical Wiring: Residential*—HC, 13th edition, by MULLIN. 1999. Reprinted with permission of Delmar Learning, a division of Thomson Learning: www. thomsonrights.com. Fax 800-730-2215.

be taken care of by the utility company in many cases. In some areas, tree trimming may be the responsibility of the home owner.

■ If there is a masthead on the roof to support the incoming cables, the masthead must be firmly attached to the house and in good condition. The masthead must extend three feet above the surface of the roof according to NEC requirements. In some cases, incoming cables are attached to the side of the building. A weather head may cover the incoming conductor to prevent water from dripping down the wires to the meter box. A weather head may appear on the top of the masthead as well.

MAIN PANEL BOARD

he *main panel board receives a large amount of electrical power from the public utility and distributes it in smaller amounts into the service panel and through a number of circuits.* The panel board is also called the main distribution board

FIGURE 9.9

A frayed service entrance cable.

Source: Anthony D'Agostino, Atlantic Inspection Service, Latham, New York.

or service entrance panel board. The incoming service entrance cable connects from the meter with one neutral wire to the neutral bus bar and two hot wires to screw terminals on the main disconnect switch. The **neutral bus bar** *is a conductor on the main panel board that is the connection for the neutral and ground wires.* All of the circuits are grounded by their connection to a conductor driven into the earth (discussed earlier). Panel boards should always have covers installed. If there is no cover, then the wiring is exposed. The main panel board contains *conductors called* **bus bars** *that provide electrical connections for fuses or circuit breakers.* Each circuit on the panel board is numbered and an identifying description is written next to the switch or on a chart; for example, #1 dryer. Figure 9.10 illustrates a diagram of a fused panel board. Figure 9.11 illustrates the circuit schedule (or labeling) of a panel board. Ideally, the panel board is located in a utility room, basement, or garage for ease of access. However, home inspectors may find the panel board in less ideal locations such as on the exterior wall of the property. The panel board may be in a location separate from the meter.

Main Disconnect

The main disconnect must be installed in a readily accessible location, either inside or outside of the house, to allow the service conductors inside the building to be as short as possible. The main disconnect can be found outside the house by the meter, as part of the main panel board inside or outside the structure, or in a separate box inside the structure. Disconnect switches are in the form of a number of circuit breakers or switches, a single pull-down lever, or a pull-out fuse box.

According to the NEC, the main disconnect switches on the panel board may not have more than six switches or six circuit breakers mounted in a single enclosure. This permits the disconnect of all electrical equipment in the house with no more than six hand movements. Some local codes may require a single main disconnect.

FIGURE 9.10

Fused panel board.

Source: Anthony D'Agostino, Atlantic Inspection Service, Latham, New York.

You Should Know
Main and Subpanels and Grounded Conductor Separation

Source: Michael Casey, Vice President & General Manager, Kaplan Professional Schools-Inspection Training Associates. www.lwarn2inspect.com

Subpanels are used to hook up and control the various electrical circuits and are connected to the main panel. The NEC requires that the grounded conductor be isolated from the grounding system except at the service panel. Subpanels are fed neutral and generally ground separately from the main panel. The word *neutral* means grounded conductor.

The grounding conductor picks up any fault current and provides a path back to the transformer to complete and clear the circuit by tripping the breaker. Therefore, equipment grounds are bonded (electrically continuous) with main and subpanels to protect the panels if they become energized.

If neutrals and grounds are bonded (connected), the return neutral current will split and run on parallel paths through the grounding and neutral system to the main panel and up the neutral to the transformer. These parallel paths may cause numerous problems.

Equipment grounds and neutrals should only connect together in service panels (the first panel with a disconnect after the meter). This is where the path to the transformer combines for both normal circuit flow and possible faults to ground through the service entrance neutral conductor. The main panel should be bonded to the neutral terminal bar providing a path for fault current should the enclosure become energized.

FIGURE 9.11

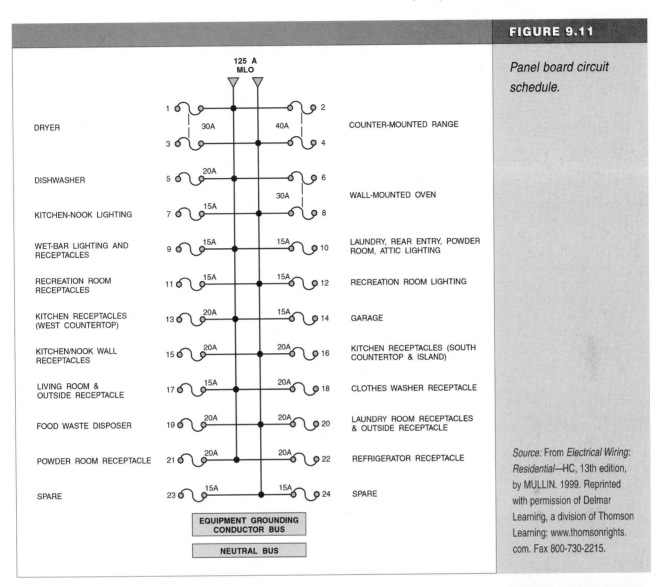

Panel board circuit schedule.

Source: From *Electrical Wiring: Residential—HC*, 13th edition, by MULLIN. 1999. Reprinted with permission of Delmar Learning, a division of Thomson Learning: www.thomsonrights.com. Fax 800-730-2215.

Home inspectors should not disconnect the electrical service to the structure during the course of the inspection.

Putting It to Work

Circuit Breakers and Fuses

An overcurrent may cause a fuse to melt or circuit breakers to trip, interrupting the electrical service. This is because the current on the circuit is greater than the fuse or circuit breaker's amperage rating. The fuse or circuit breaker rating for a particular wire size is determined by the ability of the wire to carry current at reasonably low (safe) temperatures. A **fuse** is *a device that has an internal metal link that melts and opens the circuit, causing electrical power to stop when overheating occurs.* Fuses are screwed into a fused panel board and the main disconnect is a pull-out fuse box generally containing cartridge fuses. Most melted fuses must be replaced with new ones because they are no longer usable. However, some types have replaceable links. Fuses can be mishandled, exposing individuals to high voltages. There are two types of fuses: cartridge and plug. Figure 9.12 illustrates commonly used fuses.

FIGURE 9.12   *Commonly used fuses.*

Threaded adapters are used to prevent someone from replacing a type S plug fuse of a specified amperage with a fuse of the wrong amperage.

Source: From *Construction Materials, Methods, and Techniques,* 1st edition, by SPENCE. 1998. Reprinted with permission of Delmar Learning, a division of Thomson Learning: www.thomsonrights.com. Fax 800-730-2215.

WINDOW TO VIEW LINK — FUSIBLE LINK

A TYPICAL PLUG FUSE

THE ADAPTER IS SCREWED INTO THE PLUG FUSE SOCKET ON THE PANELBOARD.

A TYPE S PLUG FUSE IS SCREWED INTO THE ADAPTER.

COPPER BLADE — 80 AMP

KNIFE — BLADE CARTRIDGE FUSE

COPPER RING — 30 AMP

FERRULE CARTRIDGE FUSE

The two types of cartridge fuses are knife blade and ferrule. The blades on the knife blade slip into metal clips on the panel board; the ferrule type clips into the copper rings on each end of the fuse holder. This connects the incoming power at the service entrance to the bus bars in the panel board. Ferrule fuses are rated from 10A to 60A and are generally used to protect currents to individual appliances such as an electric stove. Knife-blade fuses are used for service over 60A and are used at the service entrance between the incoming power line and the circuits in the panel board.

Plug fuses are available in 15A, 20A, 25A, and 30A sizes. They are used to protect individual circuits with small current requirements such as a series of lights. They are installed in a fuse box or panel board. When plug fuses are blown, they must be replaced. The standard plug fuse will blow when the fusible link is overheated. The time-delay fuse has a fusible link that melts immediately only when a short circuit occurs. If there is an overload, the link softens but does not break. If the overload is quickly removed, such as a momentary load when starting a large electric motor, it will not break.

A type S plug fuse (Figure 9.12) functions like a time-delay fuse; however, the threaded base is too small to be screwed into the fuse panel. An adapter base is required. The adapters are threaded for fuses of different ampere capacities. The adapter is screwed into the threaded fuse socket on the panel board. Because the adapter only accepts a plug fuse designed to fit it, a fuse of the wrong amperage cannot be screwed into place.

Putting It to Work

Fuse sizes are found stamped on the label, on the body of the fuse, or into one of the metal ferrules on either end of the fuse.

Circuit breakers *trip; that is, they switch the electrical power for a given circuit off if the current increases beyond the capacity of the system.* Circuit breakers are available in a molded case that inserts into the panel board. When a circuit breaker opens, the breaker is reset by moving the switch handle after the deficiency has

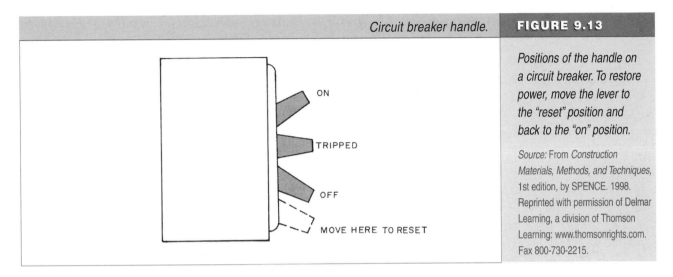

Circuit breaker handle.

FIGURE 9.13

Positions of the handle on a circuit breaker. To restore power, move the lever to the "reset" position and back to the "on" position.

Source: From *Construction Materials, Methods, and Techniques,* 1st edition, by SPENCE. 1998. Reprinted with permission of Delmar Learning, a division of Thomson Learning: www.thomsonrights.com. Fax 800-730-2215.

been corrected. Houses built since 1960 usually have circuit breakers rather than fuses. Figure 9.13 illustrates the handle positions of a circuit breaker.

You Should Know

Fuses and circuit breakers protect the electrical systems from overload and shorts in the circuit by stopping the flow of electrical current. Each circuit breaker or fuse must be identified as to its ampere rating; that is, the amount of amperage it can carry, as specified in the NEC. The ampere rating of a fuse or circuit breaker is indicated at the main panel board. Conductors of specific sizes must have a properly-sized fuse or circuit breaker to carry the electrical current.

Putting It to Work

Generally, while inspecting the electrical system, nothing should be opened except the cover on the main panel board. As with other electrical components, approach the main panel board with extreme caution. Before taking off the cover, check that the area surrounding and on top of the panel board is clear. All items that are stored on shelving above the panel board should be removed and there should be no clutter in front of it. Check that the floor in front of the board is not damp. Put your hand on the outside of the box prior to opening it to see if it feels warm. If it's warm, the panel is not safe to open. The warmth may be an indicator of a problem with the wiring that is causing sparks or arcing inside. This can only be addressed by an electrician. When you uncover the panel board, do not probe or touch inside the panel or point your fingers close to it to illustrate an item to your client. Remember, the wires are live. Caution your clients to stand clear of the panel while it is open and do not allow them to touch it.

Inspecting the Main Panel Board, Main Disconnect, Fuses, and Circuit Breakers

If the cover of the main panel board cannot be opened without shutting off the house power, indicate this on the inspection report and do not shut off the power.

■ Record the location of the main panel board and any sub panels in your report. A sub panel is an auxiliary panel that has its own set of circuit breakers and circuitry. An electrical system may have a number of sub panels, one for each specific appliance. Large-capacity circuit breakers found on a sub panel are for big appliances such as electric water heaters, dryers, or ovens.

■ Check the condition of the main panel board and any sub panels. If the equipment is outside, check that it is in a watertight box and is free of water, rust, and corrosion. The indoor main panel board is checked in the same manner. Note whether there is a cover on the panel and whether the wiring is exposed. Figure 9.14 illustrates a fused panel box with the cover off and the wiring exposed. This constitutes a safety hazard and is reported as such on the inspection report. Figure 9.15 illustrates a main panel board equipped with circuit breakers with many of the metal face plates missing. This is another safety hazard because it exposes the wiring underneath the circuit breakers. Figure 9.16 illustrates a main panel board with circuit breakers. Note that the main disconnect is positioned above the circuit breakers.

FIGURE 9.14

Fused panel box with exposed wiring.

Source: Anthony D'Agostino, Atlantic Inspection Service, Latham, New York.

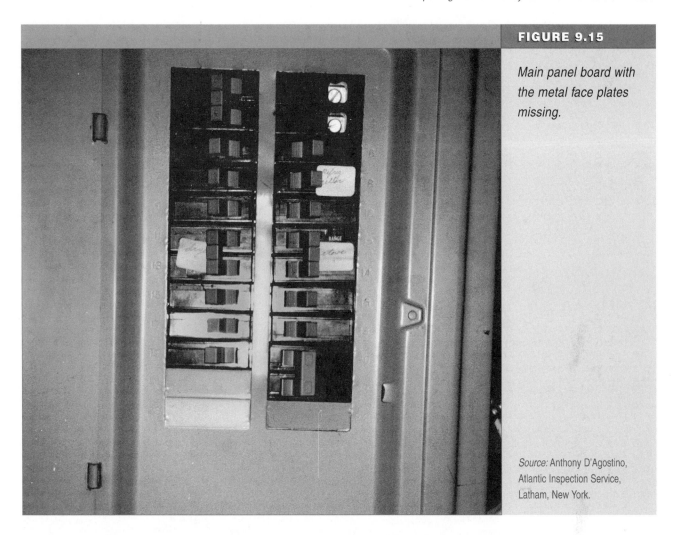

FIGURE 9.15

Main panel board with the metal face plates missing.

Source: Anthony D'Agostino, Atlantic Inspection Service, Latham, New York.

■ Attempt to locate the grounding conductor in the main panel board. Make sure that the main panel board is grounded to a ground rod or main water pipe. If it is grounded to a metal water pipe, it must be bonded. Bonding refers to the permanent joining of metallic parts to form an electrically conductive path that has the capacity to safely conduct current. Attempt to locate the grounding rod or the main water service coming into the building.

■ Note the amperage service. The main panel board may have an amperage rating written on it; however, the rating may be the same as or larger than the actual service. The only sure indicator of service size is found on the service entrance cables. Sometimes you may be able to read the size off the sheathing at the top of the service entrance conduit. Also, the size may be stamped on the outside of the drip loop (discussed earlier). Binoculars come in handy at this point. If the service entrance cable yields no information, a much less reliable possibility may be found at the main disconnect if it is a single disconnect switch. If the main disconnect is fused, there are two fuses in the service box. If each of these fuses is rated at 100 amp, then this is 100-amp service. A 200-amp service has two fuses rated at 200 amps each. Inspectors should exercise caution when examining these fuses. If you cannot read the labels, do not attempt to reach inside the service box. Even if the power is shut off, the service entrance conductors coming into the box are live. Inspectors who cannot ascertain the service should indicate this on the inspection report.

FIGURE 9.16

Main panel board with circuit breakers.

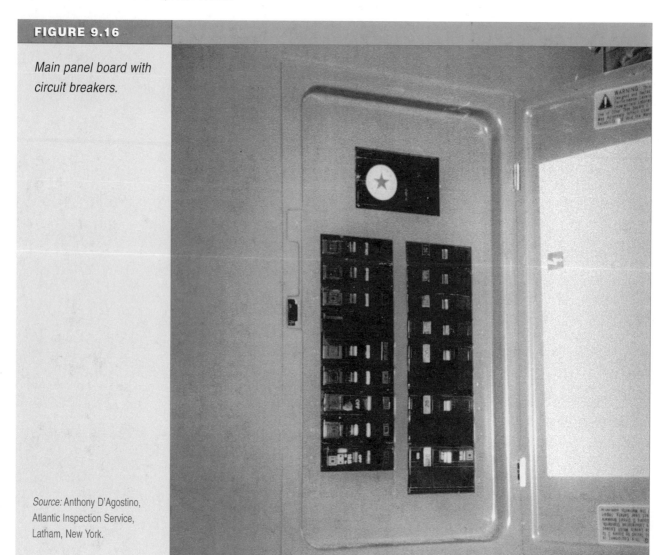

Source: Anthony D'Agostino, Atlantic Inspection Service, Latham, New York.

■ If feasible, determine whether the service entrance cable is compatible with the amperage rating of the panel board. Certain size conductors are compatible with amperage ratings. For example, a No. 2 aluminum and a No. 4 copper wire are compatible with an amperage rating of 100 amps, whereas a No. 4 aluminum wire and a No. 6 copper wire are compatible with an amperage rating of 60 amps. In some cases, the wiring size of the service entrance cable may be imprinted on the cable itself.

You Should Know

It is important to attempt to identify the service entrance wire size so that its compatibility with the fuses and circuit breakers can be ascertained. Fuses and circuit breakers and conductors should be compatible in terms of their current rating, although this is not always the case. Sometimes, inspectors may find that the amperage rating of the fuse or circuit breaker is more than the rating of the service entrance conductors. This condition is a safety hazard because the fuses or circuit breakers will not detect the overloading from the main service cable and will not shut off the current fast enough to keep the service entrance conductors from overheating.

■ If the main disconnect is located outside, check that it is in a watertight box. Check its condition for rust, corrosion, and adherence to the wall.

■ If there is no main disconnect, determine whether the power to the house can be turned off with no more than six hand movements.

■ Check that the proper sized fuse is inserted in the fuse holder and observe the condition of the fuse holders. Empty fuse holders must be properly covered.

WIRING MATERIALS

House wiring, simply put, travels from the circuit breaker or fuse panel through the walls of the building to the outlets where the current is used. This is known as branch circuit wiring which goes to the switches and outlets within the house. Wire that is on the outer surface of a wall must be enclosed in a conduit. Wire installed in the walls is threaded through drilled holes in the studs and other wood framing members, including the top and bottom plates and floor joists. The wire is also stapled or otherwise affixed to the wood frame. All rooms in the structure should have at least one outlet. Various types of wire and cable are used inside and outside the house.

Copper and aluminum are the two main residential wiring materials. These conductors are available in a number of diameters. Generally, the larger the diameter of the wire, the more current it can carry. Copper wire works better than aluminum. Copper is a stable medium that does not overheat and can carry large and small amperages. Most new construction uses copper wire except for wiring at the service entrance to the house, where aluminum works best. All cable design is regulated by the NEC.

Wire Size

The copper wire used in electrical installations is graded for size according to the American Wire Gauge (AWG) Standard. The wire diameter is expressed as a whole number. The higher the AWG number, the smaller the wire. AWG ranges from a very fine diameter to larger diameters for industrial applications. The wire may be a single strand (solid conductor) or may consist of many strands. Each strand of wire acts as a separate conducting unit. The wire used for a circuit depends on the maximum current to be carried. The minimum conduction size for branch circuit wiring is No. 14 AWG. Table 9.1 indicates the typical applications for different sized conductors.

Aluminum Wiring

Today aluminum wiring is used primarily where the current is heaviest. This is essentially at the point where the current is fed into the house; that is, the main service entry cable. It is also used for heavy appliances (240 volts) such as electric ranges or clothes dryers. If a house was built between 1965 and 1973, branch circuit aluminum wiring may have been used. Aluminum wiring used in conjunction with 15-amp circuit breakers or fuses can cause problems. Aluminum conductors have a higher resistance compared to a copper conductor for a given wire size, therefore causing a greater voltage drop. Another

TABLE 9.1		*Conductor applications chart.*
CONDUCTOR SIZE	**OVERCURRENT PROTECTION**	**TYPICAL APPLICATIONS**
No. 18 AWG	7 amperes. Class 2 circuit transformers provide overcurrent protection.	Low-voltage wiring for thermostats, chimes, security, remote control, home automation systems, etc. For these types of installations, No. 18 or 20 AWG can be used depending on the connected load and length of circuit.
No. 16 AWG	10 amperes. Class 2 circuit transformers provide overcurrent protection.	Same applications as above. Good for long runs to minimize voltage drop.
No. 14 AWG	15 amperes	Typical lighting branch-circuits.
No. 12 AWG	20 amperes	Small appliance branch-circuits for the receptacles in kitchens and dining rooms. Also laundry receptacles and workshop receptacles. Often used as the "home run" for lighting branch-circuits. Some water heaters.
No. 10 AWG	30 amperes	Most clothes dryers, built-in ovens, cooktops, central air conditioners, some water heaters, heat pumps.
No. 8 AWG	40 amperes	Ranges, ovens, heat pumps, some large clothes dryers, large central air conditioners, heat pumps.
No. 6 AWG	50 amperes	Electric furnaces, heat pumps.
No. 4 AWG	70 amperes	Electric furnaces, feeders to subpanels.
No. 3 AWG and larger	100 amperes	Main service entrance conductors, feeders to sub-panels, electric furnaces.

Source: From *Electrical Wiring: Residential—HC*, 13th edition, by MULLIN. 1999. Reprinted with permission of Delmar Learning, a division of Thomson Learning: www.thomsonrights.com. Fax 800-730-2215.

problem with aluminum is that the surface oxidizes when exposed to air, causing a poor connection. An inhibiter to prevent oxidation is now used in conjunction with aluminum wiring. Aluminum wire also expands and contracts to a greater degree than copper wire for an equal load. This can cause a poor connection because the wire can pull away from the terminal screws on a switch, fixture, and other outlet. The result of this poor connection is overheating at the switch or fixture.

In properties that have branch circuit aluminum wiring, inspectors may find that the wiring situation has been remediated. Remediation does not have to include the total replacement of the aluminum wiring. If inspectors find that the aluminum wiring situation has not been addressed, they should recommend that a qualified electrician review and remediate the problem.

Inspectors can observe the branch circuit wiring in the same places where piping is observed: the garage, basement, or attic. Wiring material is also observed at the main panel board. You can usually identify aluminum wiring because it has the word *aluminum* or the letters ALUM or AL written on the sheathing. The abbreviation for copper wiring is CU.

Low voltage can cause lights to dim or TV pictures to shrink. It may be caused   by a wire that is too small for the load being served, a circuit that is too long, or conductors operating at high temperatures having a higher resistance than when operating at lower temperatures.

BX Cable

This wiring is a type of armored electric cable. Armored cable is an assembly of insulated conductors (wires) and has a flexible metallic covering. An internal copper bonding strip provides a means of grounding. In some older BX cable, the sheathing itself is actually the ground. BX cable is used when the wires must be protected from physical damage.

Romex Cable

This cable is a nonmetallic sheath cable that is essentially the same as BX cable except that it is plastic coated and is, therefore, moisture resistant and flame retardant. Romex cable is less expensive than BX cable and is easier to install. However, many houses built before 1950 use BX cable.

Conduit

Conduit is a pipe-type enclosure used to house current-carrying conductors (wires). The wires are placed inside the conduit to protect them from damage if BX or Romex cable is not being used. Conduit is made of either galvanized steel or plastic and is a form of a closed raceway. It supports insulated electric wire and provides protection. Conduit can be run inside walls and ceilings, under floors, and in concrete slabs. Codes regulate the use and location of the various types. One type of conduit is a steel pipe available in three thicknesses. Rigid nonmetallic conduit is also available in polyvinyl chloride and high-density polyethylene.

Conduit made from aluminum is also available. It is lightweight and easy to work with; however, if embedded in concrete, it may crack. Conduit can be found at the service entrance to a house and is used both above and below ground. An important difference between conduit and BX and Romex cables is that BX and Romex cables are used only for branch circuit wiring, whereas conduit can be used in all house electrical applications.

Flexible metal conduit, called Greenfield, is used for short runs such as connecting a furnace to the power source. Greenfield is a type of conduit that looks like BX cable; however, there are no conductors inside until they are put in by an electrician. The distinguishing characteristic of Greenfield conductors is that they are made of flexible, rather than rigid, metal. Figure 9.17 illustrates flexible metal Greenfield conductors. Greenfield is used for connecting air conditioners, clothes dryers, and other large appliances when BX or Romex cable is not used. Although

FIGURE 9.17	Flexible metal conduit.

Source: From *Electrical Wiring: Residential*—HC, 13th edition, by MULLIN. 1999. Reprinted with permission of Delmar Learning, a division of Thomson Learning: www.thomsonrights.com. Fax 800-730-2215.

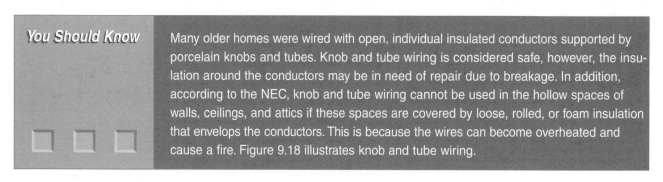

Greenfield conduit can be used only in dry interior places, it is useful in many applications because its flexibility allows it to withstand vibrations that can cause a rigid metal conduit to break.

Some codes do not permit the installation of any type of cable in residential buildings. These communities require the installation of a raceway system of wiring such as electrical metallic tubing, intermediate metal conduit, rigid metal conduit, or rigid nonmetallic conduit.

You Should Know	Many older homes were wired with open, individual insulated conductors supported by porcelain knobs and tubes. Knob and tube wiring is considered safe, however, the insulation around the conductors may be in need of repair due to breakage. In addition, according to the NEC, knob and tube wiring cannot be used in the hollow spaces of walls, ceilings, and attics if these spaces are covered by loose, rolled, or foam insulation that envelops the conductors. This is because the wires can become overheated and cause a fire. Figure 9.18 illustrates knob and tube wiring.

Inspecting the Wiring

■ Check that any observable wires or cables are affixed to the framing members and not hanging loose from a ceiling or other area.

■ Identify the type of branch circuit wiring on the inspection report. If the branch circuit wiring is aluminum and is connected to 15-amp breakers or fuses, it may constitute a safety hazard and should be so noted on the report.

FIGURE 9.18	Knob and tube wiring.

Knob and tube wiring is no longer installed, but it may be observed in older homes.

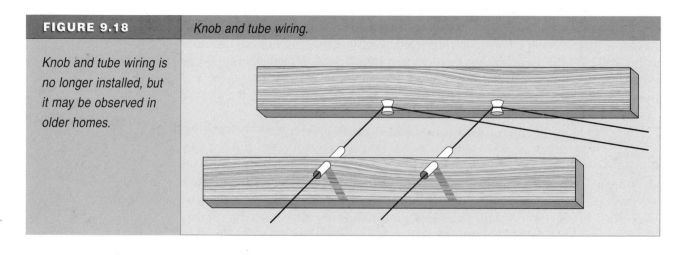

■ If you find a combination of knob and tube wiring embedded in insulation, note it as a safety hazard on your report.

■ In some structures, there are not enough outlets, especially in the kitchen. According to the NEC, extension cords may not take the place of permanent wiring.

■ While the main panel board cover is removed, examine the wiring: aluminum conductors, spliced wires inside the panel board, or more than one conductor in the main panel board connected to a circuit breaker. Problems may occur due to improper wiring practices. There may be a need to create a new circuit in the system, but there is not enough wiring inside the panel box to create the connection to the new circuit breaker. As a result, an existing wire is spliced. Also, another circuit breaker may be required because of a new appliance, but there is no room on the panel box. Instead of creating a sub panel board, the wire conductors are connected to an existing circuit breaker. These makeshift wiring practices constitute safety hazards.

■ Conductors of specific sizes must have the proper sized fuse or circuit breaker to carry the electrical current. Check that the wiring size (Table 9.1) matches the ampere rating of the circuit breaker or fuse.

■ Look for evidence of burnt wiring. This indicates that dangerous arcing might have occurred due to an improper wire size, splicing at the main panel board, or other hazardous occurrence.

Some inspectors use wire gauges to ascertain the size of a particular wire.   *Putting It to Work*

JUNCTION BOXES AND OUTLETS

Junction boxes *contain wiring and are used to provide the necessary space for making electrical connections.* Other boxes, serving the same purpose, are known as outlet boxes, device (switch) boxes, and conduit boxes. Figure 9.19 illustrates a junction box, switch device box, and nonmetallic box with a single knockout. A knockout is a space in a junction box through which wire or cable passes. Generally, this space is not visible to the inspector. According to the NEC, a box or other type of fitting must be installed wherever there are splices, outlets, switches, or other junction points. The box must be securely mounted and be large enough to hold the enclosed wiring. All cable or conduit must be affixed to a support, such as a wall stud, as it enters or leaves the box.

Boxes used for light fixtures must be designed so that a light fixture may be attached to it. Standard boxes may not be used as the sole support for ceiling fans unless they are listed for that purpose. In walls or ceilings constructed of wood or other combustible material, boxes must be installed so they are flush with the finished wall. In walls or ceiling constructed of concrete, tile, or other noncombustible material, the front edge of the box should not be set back more than one-quarter-inch from the finished surface. Boxes must be large enough for all of the enclosed conductors and wiring devices. Electrical boxes must be covered with a faceplate or other covering.

Many building codes require a fire-resistant rating of walls that may be jeopardized by the placement of junction boxes. To comply with certain fire code requirements, junction boxes may not be mounted back to back and if mounted on opposite sides of a stud, they must be at least 24 inches apart.

| FIGURE 9.19 | *Types of electrical boxes.* |

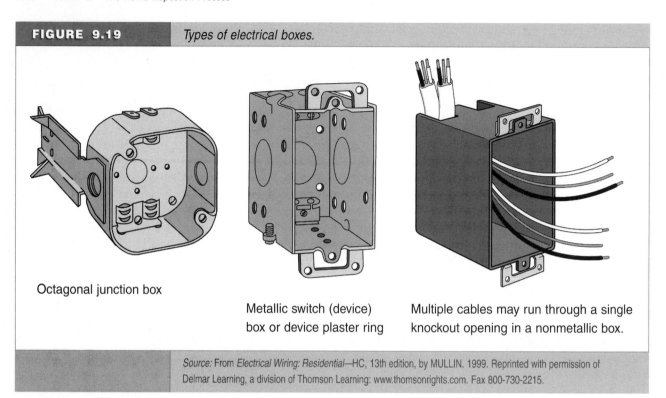

Octagonal junction box

Metallic switch (device) box or device plaster ring

Multiple cables may run through a single knockout opening in a nonmetallic box.

Source: From *Electrical Wiring: Residential—HC*, 13th edition, by MULLIN. 1999. Reprinted with permission of Delmar Learning, a division of Thomson Learning: www.thomsonrights.com. Fax 800-730-2215.

Outlets

An **outlet** *is a point on a wiring system where current is taken to supply equipment.* A **receptacle** *is connected to branch circuit wires that supply the current to equipment.* Outlets can be any type of opening—a plug, switch, or light fixture. Basically, there are three wires coming into a three-slot outlet: a neutral wire that is white and is connected to silver screws, a ground wire that is connected to a green screw near the bottom of the outlet (this ground wire is also connected to the house grounding system), and a black hot wire that is connected to the brass screws on the other side of the outlet from the neutral wire. Two-prong or slot outlets do not have a ground slot. Therefore, two-prong outlets may not be grounded. According to the NEC, all new construction must have outlets that contain ground slots. Circuits supplying wall receptacle outlets for lighting loads are generally 15-amp circuits; however, 20-amp circuits are also found in a typical residential branch wiring system.

Switches *are used to open and close electrical circuits and allow current to flow to appliances.* Switches have different actions that enable them to perform specific functions. For example, a single-pole, single-throw (SPST) switch makes or breaks a connection between two contact points. When the lever is on, the switch is turned up, the circuit is complete, and the appliance turns on. When the switch is turned down, the circuit is broken and the appliance goes off. This is the most commonly used switch. A single-pole, double-throw (SPDT) action is used to control a unit, such as a light, from two locations. This requires an SPDT switch at both locations.

In addition to traditional switches, inspectors may find switches that have dimmers, automatic timers, photoelectric eyes, and remote controls.

Ground Fault Circuit Interrupter

A **ground fault circuit interrupter (GFCI)** looks very much like a typical receptacle except that it has a test and reset button. *This device shuts off a circuit* *immediately if it senses a ground fault.* A GFCI monitors the current balance between the ungrounded "hot" conductor and the grounded "neutral" conductor. As soon as the current flowing through the "hot" conductor is in the range of four to six milliamperes or more than the current flowing through the "return" grounded conductor, the GFCI senses this unbalance and trips (opens) the circuit off. To protect against electric shock, the NEC requires that ground fault protection be provided for all 125-volt, 15- and 20-amp receptacle outlets:

- in bathrooms
- outdoors
- in kitchens for all receptacles that serve countertop surfaces including receptacles installed on islands and peninsulas
- within six feet from the edge of a wet bar sink
- in attached or detached garages
- in sheds, workshops, or storage buildings
- in crawl spaces that are at or below grade
- in unfinished basements
- by swimming pools

GFCIs are not required for receptacles that are not readily accessible, such as an overhead garage door opener, or in a place where an appliance is not easily moved. Ground fault circuit protection can be met in several ways. A GFCI circuit breaker installed on a branch circuit can shut off the entire circuit if a ground fault in the range of four to six milliamperes occurs. If a GFCI receptacle is installed, then only the receptacle is shut off when a ground fault greater than six milliamperes occurs.

Many inspectors choose to exceed the ASHI standards and check all accessible outlets.

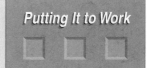

Putting It to Work

Inspecting Junction Boxes, Plugs, Switches, and Ground Fault Circuit Interrupters

- Visible junction and switch boxes must be checked. Make sure they have faceplates and that they are properly wired and secured.

- Plug in your circuit analyzer and check a representative number of accessible outlets in each room including the attic, garage, and basement as follows:

1. Determine that plugs have an adequate current reading. If not, the cause may be a loose connection at the receptacle or circuit breaker or that the circuit has switched off or that there is some other defect in the wiring.

2. Using the GFCI tester or circuit analyzer, test the GFCI button to see if it trips on all GFCIs. Determine whether there are GFCI receptacles at the required locations as discussed previously. Many homes do not have them.

3. Check that the receptacles are properly polarized. This means that the outlet has a neutral wire wired to the large slot and a hot wire wired to the smaller slot. Reverse polarity happens when the opposite occurs: the hot wire is wired to the large slot and the neutral wire is wired to the small slot.

Reversed polarity is a safety hazard because, although a plugged-in appliance works, the neutral wire is hot. Even if the switch is off, if the neutral wire is touched, a person could receive an electrical shock.

4. Check the receptacle for an open ground. This occurs when the outlet is not grounded with a ground wire. Inspectors can advise clients to install GFCIs to protect themselves from possible electric shock.

■ Test all wall switches to see that they are functional. Include alternative switches, such as dimmers, in your inspection. Both interior and exterior switches should be tested, as well as the doorbell.

■ If a light fixture fails to work and it does not seem to be from a burnt out bulb, the fixture may be defective or there may be a loose connection leading to the fixture. Note all nonworking light fixtures on the inspection report.

■ Check for the location of any electric heaters that may be in the house. Positioning electric baseboard heating below wall receptacles is a violation of the NEC. This is because a cord attached to a receptacle that lies over the baseboard creates a fire hazard (the cord might melt).

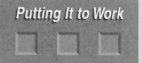

Putting It to Work

Before you check the GFCIs, inform the property owner that service to some appliances may be interrupted. Check that any computers in the house are turned off.

SMOKE DETECTORS

Many building codes require smoke detectors and even when not required by code, smoke detectors are commonly found in many houses. There are essentially two types: the photoelectronic and the ionization. Smoke detectors have an indicator light to show that the unit is functional. They also have a test button that simulates the presence of smoke. This button tests the detector's circuitry and alarm system. Smoke detectors sense smoke only—not heat, flames, or gas. The photoelectric smoke detector has a light sensor that measures the amount of light in a chamber. When smoke is present, an alarm is sounded as a result of a reduction in light due to the obstruction of the smoke. This type of sensor detects burning materials that produce great quantities of smoke and is less effective for gasoline and alcohol fires that do not produce heavy smoke.

The ionization detector contains a low-level radioactive source that supplies particles that ionize the air in the detector's smoke chamber. Plates in this chamber are oppositely charged. Because the air is ionized, an extremely small amount of current (millionths of an ampere) flows between the plates. Smoke entering the chamber impedes the movement of the ions, reducing the current flow and causing an alarm to sound. The ionization detector is effective for detecting the small amounts of smoke produced by gasoline and alcohol fires that are fast flaming. The detectors can be mounted on either the wall or ceiling but away from room corners if possible.

You Should Know

Most smoke detectors are battery powered. However, if they were installed during construction, it is possible to find some smoke detectors that are part of the house electrical system.

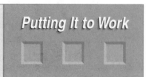

Inspectors who find that the smoke detector is not operational should first check the battery.

Inspecting the Smoke Detectors

Essentially, inspecting the smoke detectors means observing that there are the requisite number for the property and that they function properly. Smoke detectors should be installed on each floor of the house including the basement and attic. They should also be placed in an upstairs hallway if there are bedrooms. If the house is large, a detector should be installed outside each bedroom. A detector does not have to be closer than 25 feet to the kitchen because smoke from cooking often triggers the alarm.

Inspectors check the operability by pressing the reset button on each unit. Those units that are inoperable or missing from a prescribed area are noted on the inspection report. If the property does not have smoke detectors, it is acceptable for the home inspector to suggest the purchase of this equipment.

IMPORTANT POINTS

1. The electrical system inspection includes an examination of the service drop, service entrance conductors, cables, and raceways; the service equipment; the main disconnect; and system grounding. The inspection also includes the interior components: the main and sub panel boards, conductors, overcurrent protection devices, and a representative number of installed lighting fixtures, switches, and receptacles. Inspectors must describe the amperage and voltage rating of the service, identify the location of main disconnect(s) and sub panels, and note wiring methods. The presence and operability of smoke detectors must be checked.

2. Although inspectors are not responsible for code enforcement, familiarity with the sections of the NEC that pertain to the inspection is helpful. Older construction may not meet current code requirements and is, therefore, generally grandfathered in.

3. Electricity moves along wires called conductors. A good conductor has little resistance to the flow of electricity. Copper and aluminum are the two most commonly used wiring materials because they are good conductors of electricity.

4. Voltage is the electrical pressure that pushes through wires. A voltage service of 120/240 volts is standard; less voltage does not meet the requirements of a residential property.

5. Amperage is the amount of current or electricity flowing through a wire. The best indication of the service size is through the service entrance wires. Most residential service is 100 amperes. Service with less than 100 amps is generally substandard for the needs of a typical residential house.

6. Two types of entrance services exist. Aboveground cables that come from the nearest pole connecting to the service entrance conductors of the house or building are called a service drop. Electrical service that runs underground is called service lateral.

7. Grounding stabilizes the voltage, protecting the system. Proper grounding ensures that overcurrent protection devices operate quickly when responding to ground faults.

8. Inspectors should observe the condition of the outside cable that runs to the meter. Service entrance cable or conduit must be firmly affixed to the structure beginning at the roof and traveling down the side of the house to the meter box.

9. The main panel board receives a large amount of electrical power from the public utility and distributes it in smaller amounts into the service panel and through a number of circuits.

10. The main disconnect must be installed in a readily accessible location, either inside or outside of the house, to allow the service conductors inside the building to be as short as possible.

11. According to the NEC, the main disconnect switches on the panel board may not have more than six switches or six circuit breakers mounted in a single enclosure.

12. A fuse is a device that has an internal metal link that melts and opens the circuit, causing electrical power to stop when overheating occurs.

13. Circuit breakers are more convenient and safer than fuses. Circuit breakers trip; that is, they switch the electrical power for a given circuit off if the current increases beyond the capacity of the system.

14. Inspectors should check the condition of the main panel board and any sub panels. The cover should be removed to examine the components, but not if the removal must be preceded by a shutdown of the system.

15. Branch circuit wiring goes to the switches and outlets within the house. Wire that is on the outer surface of a wall must be enclosed in a conduit.

16. Aluminum branch circuit wiring causes a great deal of overheating in outlets and switches. Systems that have this type of wiring material for branch circuit application should be inspected by a qualified electrician to remediate the problem.

17. Armored cable is an assembly of insulated conductors in a flexible metallic enclosure and is found in branch circuit wiring that feeds the outlets.

18. Conduit is a pipe-type enclosure used to house current-carrying conductors (wires). Flexible metal conduit, called Greenfield, is used for short runs such as connecting a furnace to the power source.

19. Junction boxes contain wiring and are used to provide the necessary space for making electrical connections. The box must be securely mounted and large enough to hold the enclosed wiring.

20. GFCIs have a test and reset button. This device shuts off a circuit immediately if it senses a short circuit. Inspectors should test all GFCIs to see that they are functional.

21. Inspectors should check all wall switches to see that they are functional.

22. There are essentially two types of smoke detectors: the photoelectronic and the ionization. Smoke detectors should be installed on each floor of the house including the basement and attic.

CHAPTER REVIEW

Field Study Assignment 1

Using your practice property and a copy of the inspection checklist from Figure 4.4, inspect the electrical system. Note any problems you encounter for further exploration and discussion.

Field Study Assignment 2

To properly examine the electrical system, study sizes and types of wiring and cable. If possible, take an electrician or another person familiar with wiring systems through your practice property to show you the difference between the various conductors. Visit an electrical supply outlet, examine the type of cables and wires available, and purchase samples of each. Label these samples and take them with you when you inspect the property. A wire gauge may also help familiarize you with wire sizes.

REVIEW QUESTIONS   *Choose the letter that best answers the question.*

1. Electricity moves along wires that are known as:
   A. insulators
   B. resisters
   C. conductors
   D. raceways

2. Which of the following is NOT an overcurrent protection device?
   A. main disconnect
   B. fuse
   C. circuit breaker
   D. meter

3. Resistance to the flow of electricity is measured in:
   A. ohms
   B. kilowatts
   C. watts
   D. frequencies

4. The electrical pressure that pushes through the wires is known as the:
   A. amperage
   B. voltage
   C. ohm
   D. resistance

5. Aboveground cables coming from a utility pole to the service entrance conductors of a house are called the:
   A. service drop
   B. service lateral
   C. service entrance
   D. transformer

6. The utility company is responsible for the maintenance of which of the following?
   A. main panel board
   B. fuses and circuit breakers
   C. branch circuit wiring
   D. transformer

7. The aboveground service conductor must have a minimum of how many feet clearance from the top, sides, and fronts of windows that open?
   A. three feet
   B. four feet
   C. five feet
   D. six feet

8. All of the circuits in the house are grounded by their connection to:
   A. the service drop
   B. a conductor driven into the ground
   C. an exterior raceway
   D. the masthead on the roof

9. What is the maximum permitted number of hand movements to disconnect all house electrical equipment?
   A. three
   B. four
   C. five
   D. six

10. Which of the following is TRUE?
    A. Most fuses have to be replaced when melted.
    B. There is only one type of fuse.
    C. Fuses do not have an ampere rating.
    D. Handling fuses does not expose individuals to high voltages as do circuit breakers.

11. Circuit breakers are mostly found in houses built after:
    A. 1950
    B. 1960
    C. 1970
    D. 1980

12. Wire on the outer surface of a wall must be:
    A. aluminum
    B. type USE cable
    C. installed in a raceway
    D. used only for light fixtures

13. Besides aluminum, the most common residential wiring material is:
    A. iron
    B. steel
    C. lead
    D. copper

14. The larger the diameter of a conductor:
    A. the less current it can carry
    B. the more current it can safely carry
    C. the less it is used in residential applications
    D. the more it is used in residential applications

15. Aluminum wiring is used primarily for which of the following?
    A. light switches
    B. plugs
    C. electric ovens
    D. lamps

16. Which is the following is TRUE regarding BX cable? It:
    A. has a metallic covering
    B. is only used outdoors
    C. is no longer used in residential applications
    D. is never used in branch circuit wiring

17. The most important difference between conduit and BX or Romex cable is that:
    A. conduit is UL approved and BX and Romex cable are not
    B. conduit is used in branch circuit wiring and BX and Romex cable are not
    C. conduit is extensively used today and BX and Romex cable are not
    D. conduit is used in all house applications and BX or Romex cable are only used in branch circuit wiring

18. An older type of open, insulated wiring that was used in residential homes and that presents a fire hazard when covered with loose insulation is known as:
    A. Greenfield
    B. porcelain
    C. aluminum
    D. knob and tube

19. A type of box that holds splices, outlets, and switches is called a:
    A. panel box
    B. junction box
    C. receiver
    D. fuse box

20. According to the NEC, GFCIs need NOT be installed in which of the following places:
    A. bathroom
    B. unfinished basements
    C. by the overhead garage door opener
    D. in crawl spaces at or below grade

21. If a light fixture fails to work, the home inspector should do which of the following?

    A. Determine whether the bulb is dead.

    B. Examine all of the branch wiring leading to the light fixture.

    C. Attempt to repair the light fixture.

    D. Explain why the light fixture does not work on the home inspection report.

22. Which of the following is TRUE?

    A. All houses must have at least two smoke detectors.

    B. Smoke detectors sense fire and gas fumes.

    C. Photoelectric smoke detectors have a light sensor.

    D. Most smoke detectors are powered through the house electrical system.

23. If a property does not have any smoke detectors, the home inspector should:

    A. insist that the property owner or client purchase them immediately

    B. report the property owner to the code enforcement authority

    C. note the information on the home inspection report and suggest that the property owner or client purchase them

    D. offer to install the smoke detectors for the client

24. Smoke detectors should be located:

    A. in the kitchen and garage only

    B. on each floor of the house

    C. in the basement only

    D. in the attic only

25. The inspection of the electrical system should begin with which of the following locations on the property?

    A. basement

    B. exterior

    C. attic

    D. garage

ANSWER KEY

1. C	8. B	15. C	22. C
2. D	9. D	16. A	23. C
3. A	10. A	17. D	24. B
4. B	11. B	18. D	25. B
5. A	12. C	19. B	
6. D	13. D	20. C	
7. A	14. B	21. A	

CHAPTER 10

RECOGNIZING ENVIRONMENTAL ISSUES

Home inspectors are not required to perform environmental inspections. However, as these issues become increasingly problematic, inspectors may wish to offer certain environmental inspection services. This chapter explores environmental problems related to residential property and how they are identified and remediated.

LEARNING OBJECTIVES

1. Describe how a home inspector can protect himself from liability problems during the inspection of environmental concerns.
2. Describe the environmental concerns that may be tested by a home inspector.
3. Explain other environmental concerns that effect real property.

KEY TERMS

Asbestos

Carpenter ant

Carpenter bee

Electromagnetic field (EMF)

Formaldehyde

Friable

Lead

Powderpost beetle

Radon

Termite

Toxic substance

Underground storage tank

TABLE 10.1	TEST	EQUIPMENT	LAB ANALYSIS
Environmental tests that can be performed by home inspectors (subject to state regulation).	Radon	Charcoal canister	yes
	Water flow	Water gauge	no
	Water quality	Container for sampling	yes
	Electromagnetic fields	EMF tester	no
	Lead	Chemically loaded swab	no
	Mold	Sampling plate	yes

ENVIRONMENTAL TESTING LIABILITY ISSUES

As technology continues its advance into the new century, a variety of effective and user-friendly testing equipment has become available. This technology opens many possibilities for home inspectors to expand their roles and areas of expertise. At the same time, however, these services create more liability exposure. Review your errors and omissions policy with your insurance company to familiarize yourself with the limits of your coverage. If you don't feel comfortable performing a test because of a lack of procedural knowledge or for any other reason, you should not do it. Many environmental problems cannot be tested by the home inspector because they require special training, certification, or both. Table 10.1 summarizes the tests that can be performed by home inspectors.

Putting It to Work

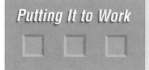

Most inspectors who perform an environmental observation or test charge an extra fee for this service.

You Should Know Environmental Testing

Environmental inspection and testing might not be covered by your home inspector license (should your state require one). Most states have regulations and licensing procedures for the inspection, testing, and remediation of environmental problems. Check your state and local government agencies to verify whether a license, certification, or registration is required for a certain environmental inspection or test. Many forms of testing may require an Environmental Protection Agency (EPA) certification. Refer to Figure 10.1 for an EPA office in your region.

AIR QUALITY

In the last several years, a growing body of scientific evidence has indicated that air within homes and other buildings can be more polluted than the outdoor air in even the largest and more industrialized cities. Other research indicates that people spend approximately 90 percent of their time indoors. The EPA estimates that 30 percent of all buildings and homes contain enough pollutants to affect people's health. Pollutants inside the home include:

EPA REGIONS		FIGURE 10.1
REGION 1 (Connecticut, Maine, Massachusetts, New Hampshire, Rhode Island, Vermont) EPA 1 Congress St., Suite 1100 Boston, MA 02114-2023 (617) 918-1111	REGION 6 (Arkansas, Louisiana, New Mexico, Oklahoma, Texas) EPA Fountain Place 12th Floor, Suite 1200 1445 Ross Avenue Dallas, TX 75202-2733 (214) 665-7220	*EPA regional offices.*
REGION 2 (New Jersey, New York, Puerto Rico, Virgin Islands) EPA 290 Broadway New York, NY 10007-1866 (212) 637-3000	REGION 7 (Iowa, Kansas, Missouri, Nebraska) EPA 901 North 5th Street Kansas City, KS 66101 (913) 551-7003	
REGION 3 (Delaware, DC, Maryland, Pennsylvania, Virginia, West Virginia) EPA 1650 Arch St. Philadelphia, PA 19103-2029 (215) 814-5000	REGION 8 (Colorado, Montana, North Dakota, South Dakota, Utah, Wyoming) EPA 999 18th Street, Suite 500 Denver, CO 80202-2466 (303) 312-6312	
REGION 4 (Alabama, Florida, Georgia, Kentucky, Mississippi, North Carolina, South Carolina, Tennessee) EPA Atlanta Federal Center 61 Forsythe Street, SW Atlanta, GA 30303-3104 (404) 562-9900	REGION 9 (Arizona, California, Hawaii, Nevada, American Samoa, Guam, Trust Territories of the Pacific) EPA 75 Hawthorne Street San Francisco, CA 94105 (415) 974-8000	
REGION 5 (Illinois, Indiana, Michigan, Minnesota, Ohio, Wisconsin) EPA 77 West Jackson Blvd. Chicago, IL 60604-3507 (312) 353-2200	REGION 10 (Alaska, Idaho, Oregon, Washington) EPA 1200 Sixth Avenue Seattle, WA 98101 (206) 553-1200 (800) 424-4372	

- bacteria
- formaldehyde
- oil, gas, kerosene, coal, or wood combustion sources
- building materials and furnishings that may contain formaldehyde, deteriorating asbestos, and other chemicals
- products for household cleaning and maintenance
- pressed-wood furniture
- central heating and cooling systems
- carpeting
- outside sources such as radon, pesticides, and outdoor air pollution

The relative importance of any single source depends on how much of a given pollutant it emits and how hazardous those emissions are. In some cases, factors such as the age of the source and whether or not it is properly maintained are significant. For example, an improperly adjusted gas stove can emit significantly more carbon monoxide than one that is properly adjusted. According to the EPA, half of all illnesses can be traced to indoor pollution. Many of the chemicals used in households have not been tested for their effect on human health. The following is a discussion of some of the main pollutants that find their way indoors.

Urea Formaldehyde Foam Insulation (UFFI)

Formaldehyde *is a colorless, gaseous chemical compound that is generally present at low, variable concentrations in indoor and outdoor air.* The use of formaldehyde compounds is fairly widespread in the manufacture of furniture, cabinets, and other building materials. These objects release the formaldehyde gas into the air. Moreover, formaldehyde is an ingredient in insulation foam that was formerly used in the home (see Chapter 7). Since 1985, the federal government, through HUD, has enforced regulations that sharply curtail the use of materials containing formaldehyde. Health hazards attributed to formaldehyde include skin rashes; watery eyes; burning sensations in the eyes, throat, and nasal passages; and breathing difficulties.

Testing and Remediation

Reducing formaldehyde levels in the home is a simple or complex task depending on the source of the gas. Initial procedures include steps to increase ventilation and improve the circulation of outside air through the home.

You Should Know
Propane or
Petroleum Gas

Some properties rely on liquified propane or petroleum gas as a fuel source. These chemically volatile tanks must be located outdoors. They must have a safe clearance from the house and not be located near an entryway or window. Piping for natural gas or from a tank can be copper, iron, or steel. Local code requirements delineate the piping material and placement of the tanks. Gas-fueled water heaters, furnaces, stoves, and other equipment should have shutoff valves in an accessible place.

Home inspectors can check gas emissions from furnaces, boilers, and in room air using a gas detector. Any significant emission is a safety hazard and the local utility company, as well as the property owner, must be alerted immediately.

Putting It to Work

Biological Agents and Allergens

Biological contaminants include bacteria, mold, mildew, viruses, mites, pollen, cockroaches, and animal dander. Contaminated central air handling (HVAC) systems can become breeding grounds for mold, mildew, and other biological contaminants and can distribute these contaminants through the residence. Mold and mildew growth is encouraged by damp conditions resulting from high humidity and water pipe leaks. Dust mites grow in a warm, damp environment, but are commonly found in carpets and upholstery. Respiratory illnesses are caused by inhaled viruses or bacteria. Allergic reactions to mold, mildew, and mites are also possible. Some biological contaminants trigger allergic reactions, including hypersensitivity, pneumonitis, and some types of asthma.

Testing and Remediation

By controlling the relative humidity level in a living space, the growth of biologicals can be minimized. A relative humidity of 30–50 percent is recommended to prevent water condensation on building materials. Standing water, water-damaged material, or wet surfaces serve as breeding grounds for molds, mildew, bacteria, and insects. To further remediate indoor air problems, home owners can install and use exhaust fans that are vented to the outdoors. Humidifiers should be kept clean because this equipment can become a breeding ground for biological contaminants.

Home inspectors can test for mold using culture-sampling plates that are taped to the supply vent of the air conditioner for about 10 minutes. The culture is sent to a lab for analysis (see Figure 10.2).

WATER QUALITY AND FLOW

lients generally want to know whether their water source is public or private. They are also concerned about the quality of the water. As a home inspector, you should have some knowledge about local water supplies. Although

---

FIGURE 10.2

The following are methods to help control or eliminate sources of pollution.

- increasing ventilation

- installing air-cleaning devices

- removing a source of pollution

- altering an activity

- unblocking an air supply vent

- opening a window to temporarily increase ventilation

General solutions to air quality problems.

federal, state, and local statutes protect our drinking water, its quality may be compromised all or some of the time. To learn more about the local water supply, home inspectors can refer their clients to local municipal water districts or other government bodies. These agencies regularly test the water supply and have reports on file that delineate the chemistry of the water supply. Although these reports are useful, they often require the assistance of a professional to interpret them.

Bacteria and toxins are two items that can compromise the safety of the water supply. Water is usually tested for the following:

■ *Bacteria.* These organisms are the most frequent contaminant in the water supply and cause the greatest amount of illness. A parasite known as *Giardia lamblia* that causes severe intestinal problems has shown up in some water supplies around the country. The public water supply in many municipalities is tested every day for bacterial contamination.

■ *Mineral content.* The goal is to have water that is not devoid of minerals, but does not have an over-abundance of minerals. One of the concerns with minerals in the water supply is dangerous amounts of lead.

Testing and Remediation

The only way to know whether the water from a municipal water supply is contaminated is to test it. If tests reveal that a state drinking water standard has been violated, the water supplier must move to correct the situation and then notify the state or local health department. If the home is supplied with water from its own private well, laboratory testing of a water sample is the only way to determine if the well water is contaminated. Generally, the well water quality for privately owned systems should meet the same standards as public water.

Testing for Well Water Quality and Flow

Home inspectors may be asked to test both well water quality and water flow. Water testing involves collecting samples of water and bringing them to a lab for analysis. Testing for lead in the water, for example, involves taking several samples. The first sample is taken directly from water that has been sitting in the pipes for several hours. If there is lead in the pipes or joints, this sample has the highest lead content. Another sample is taken after the water has run for a specified time. Inspectors who test well water quality should consult the lab where the water is tested to verify collecting procedures. Once the water is analyzed, the lab sends the results back to the inspector. The results should pinpoint any unacceptable levels of toxins found in the sample.

A water-flow test can be performed using a water gauge attached to a hose. Some devices check both the water pressure, which is measured in pounds per square inch (psi), and the water flow, which is measured in gallons per minute (gpm). An acceptable level for water pressure is a minimum of 3.5 psi. Water flow may be as high as 9 gpm.

TOXIC ELEMENTS AND REAL PROPERTY

The home inspector must have some knowledge of the various toxic elements found in the residential property. A **toxic substance** *is an element capable of causing adverse human health or environmental effects through*

exposure to even low levels. The average property may have many hidden, but dangerous, toxic substances including radon, asbestos, and lead.

Radon

Radon is *a colorless, odorless, tasteless, radioactive gas that is present worldwide in the environment as a byproduct of the natural decay of uranium in the earth.* Radon present in surrounding soil or in well water can be a source of radon in a home. Radon from the surrounding soil enters a home through small spaces and openings such as cracks in concrete, floor drains, sump pump openings, wall and floor joints in basements, and the pores in hollow block walls.

Radon can seep into groundwater and remain trapped there. Therefore, if a home is supplied with water taken from a groundwater source, there is a greater potential for a radon problem. The likelihood of radon in the water supply is greatly reduced in homes supplied with water from a municipal water supply. When radon gas and its decay products enter the home, they remain in circulation in the enclosed air. Outdoors, radon is not a problem because the surrounding air allows the gas to diffuse in the atmosphere. Figure 10.3 illustrates how radon can enter a house.

FIGURE 10.3

How radon enters a house.

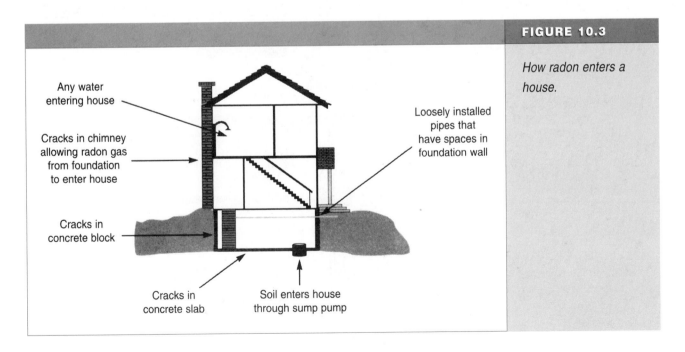

Any water entering house

Cracks in chimney allowing radon gas from foundation to enter house

Cracks in concrete block

Cracks in concrete slab

Soil enters house through sump pump

Loosely installed pipes that have spaces in foundation wall

The concentration of radon in air is measured in units of picocuries per liter (pCi/L) of air. Estimates suggest that many homes contain from one to two picocuries of radon per liter of air. If preliminary tests indicate radon levels greater than four pCi/L of air in livable areas of the home, the EPA recommends that a follow-up test be conducted. No level of radon is considered safe; there are risks even at very low levels. Radon gas breaks down into radioactive particles (called decay products) that remain in the air. As people breathe these particles, they become trapped in the lungs and cause damage that may lead to lung cancer.

Testing and Remediation

The only way to know whether a home has a radon problem is to test it. If radon is present in water supplies, it can be removed altogether or reduced by installing special filter systems. Normally, the cost of installing radon reduction equipment ranges from several hundred dollars to several thousand dollars. If the system chosen involves fans, pumps, or other appliances, the operating costs increase monthly utility bills. Figure 10.4 illustrates a radon reduction system.

Radon detection kits are available (in the form of charcoal canisters) and must be certified by the Environmental Laboratory Accreditation Program. Short- and long-term testing kits can be purchased from local or state departments of health, accredited laboratories, and hardware stores. The EPA recommends a short-term (two to seven days) charcoal test for initial testing. Short-term radon testing can be performed by home inspectors. After the canisters are placed in the house for the designated term, they are sent to an accredited laboratory to be analyzed. The lab notifies the home inspector of the results.

Other radon testing methods are available. They require longer testing periods and are more expensive, but they give a more accurate estimate of the long-term radon levels in a home. Alpha-track detectors measure radon on a seasonal or annual basis. An alpha-track detector comprises a filtered container with a small

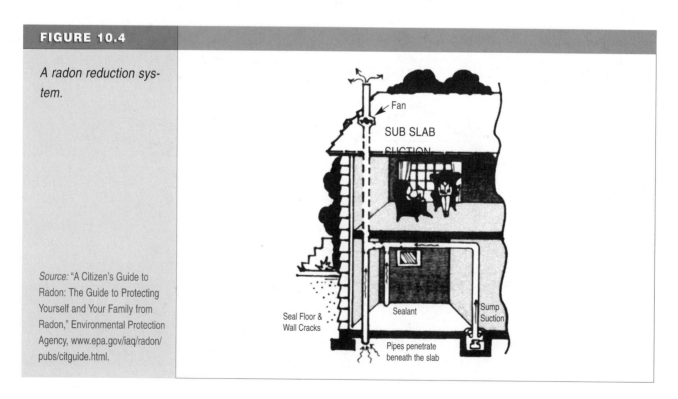

FIGURE 10.4

A radon reduction system.

Source: "A Citizen's Guide to Radon: The Guide to Protecting Yourself and Your Family from Radon," Environmental Protection Agency, www.epa.gov/iaq/radon/pubs/citguide.html.

piece of plastic inside. When radon decays in the air, the energy particles emitted strike the plastic and leave marks called "damage tracks." A laboratory then counts the number of tracks and that number corresponds to the concentration of radioactive substances in the test area. The alpha-track detectors are available from the Radon Hotline. Both testing methods can be used. Although an alpha-track detector is set up for several months to a year, the charcoal canister can provide an early warning of high radon levels. Tests that measure the amount of radon in water normally require a sample of tap water to undergo laboratory analysis. Figure 10.5 illustrates a letter from a home inspector advising clients of radon lab test results.

A letter advising clients of radon test results.	**FIGURE 10.5**

A T L A N T I C

INSPECTION SERVICE   COMMERCIAL & RESIDENTIAL

12 BELAIRE DRIVE   LATHAM, N.Y. 12110

(518) 783-1963

April 1, 2007
Alberto Pavel
133 Maple Hill Lane
Bear Creek, Montana 59007

Re: 29 Belfry Street
Bear Creek, Montana 59007

Dear Mr. Pavel:

The following is the test results of the Radon Analysis for the above mentioned property.

These test results are based on the placement of two (2) charcoal canisters No. 3276416 and No. 3276161 in the basement at the above mentioned location on March 1, 2007.

The test results are as follows:

A) Canister No: 3276416   Radon Concentration: 29.5 pci/liter
B) Canister No: 3276161   Radon Concentration: 28.8 pci/liter

The average radon concentration level is 29.15 pci/liter which is above E.P.A. guidelines of 4.0 pci/liter.

Recommended E.P.A. action:

( ) No action necessary - Screening measurements are below EPA action level.
(*) Mitigation necessary - Screening measurements are above EPA action level.

If you have any questions, do not hesitate to call at your earliest convenience.

Very truly yours,

Source: Anthony D'Agostino, Atlantic Inspection Service, Latham, New York.

Lead

Lead *is a toxic metallic element found worldwide in soil, water, and paint.* The toxic effects of lead have been known since ancient times. Lead can be found in the following:

- interior or exterior paint
- drinking water
- soil and dust around the home

The Consumer Product Safety Commission banned the use of lead-based paint in residential properties in 1978. According to the EPA, 75–80 percent of homes built prior to 1978 have lead-based paint. Lead can enter the air in a home when surfaces covered with lead-based paint are scraped, sanded, or heated with an open flame during paint-stripping procedures. Once released, lead particles circulate in the air and are inhaled or ingested through the mouth and nose.

Federal law has banned the use of materials containing lead in public water supplies and in residences connected to public water supplies. Also banned is the use of lead-based solder in plumbing applications, such as pipe connections, within homes and buildings. In older homes, lead can enter the drinking water as a byproduct when plumbing fixtures, pipes, and solder are corroded. In these instances, lead levels in water at the kitchen tap can be far higher than those found in water at treatment plants. If a house was built prior to 1950, there is a good chance that lead from exterior surface paint has accumulated in surrounding soils. The grounds surrounding the home should be well landscaped to minimize the likelihood of children being exposed to contaminated dust.

When ingested, lead accumulates in the blood, bones, and soft tissue of the body. High concentrations of lead in the body can cause death or permanent damage to the central nervous system, the brain, the kidneys, and red blood cells. Even low levels of lead may increase blood pressure in adults. Infants, children, pregnant women, and fetuses are more vulnerable to lead exposure than others because the lead is more easily absorbed into growing bodies.

Testing and Remediation

The only accurate way to determine whether paint contains lead is to remove a sample of the paint and have it tested in a qualified laboratory. To facilitate this, inspectors can remove a paint chip and take it for lab analysis. Again, the inspector should consult the lab for collection procedures. Lead-testing swabs are available to test for the presence of lead paint on certain objects. The inspector squeezes the swab shaft to release testing chemicals. The chemical is then rubbed on the object and if it turns a certain color, lead may be present. This test works for paint, solder, soil, and dust.

To remediate lead paint, it is best to leave it undisturbed if it is in good condition and there is little possibility that it will be eaten by children. Other procedures include covering the paint with wallpaper or some other building material or completely replacing the painted surface.

The only method to determine lead levels in water is to test a water sample.

Asbestos

Asbestos *is a fibrous mineral found in rocks and soil throughout the world.* Asbestos has been used in construction applications because it is strong, durable, fire retardant, and an efficient insulator. Alone or in combination with other materials, asbestos can be fashioned into a variety of products such as flooring, walls, ceiling tiles, exterior housing shingles, and insulation or fire retardant for heating and electrical systems. Between 1900 and 1980, some 30 million tons of asbestos were put in place. Since the 1970s, however, asbestos use has declined significantly. The United States now processes about 200,000 tons of asbestos every year into hundreds of different products. According to the EPA, however, many homes constructed in the past 20 years probably do not contain asbestos products.

Generally, if the material is in good condition and is in an area where it is not likely to be disturbed, the asbestos-containing material should be left in place. Although there are several types of asbestos, nearly 95 percent of all asbestos used in commercial products is a type called chrysotile. The potential of an asbestos-containing product to release fibers is dependent on several factors including its location and its degree of friability.

Friable *means that the asbestos-containing product can be crumbled easily and emit fibers.* The fibrous or fluffy spray-applied asbestos materials found in many buildings for fireproofing, insulating, or decorative purposes is generally considered friable. Some materials, such as vinyl floor tiles, are less likely to emit airborne fibers unless subject to sanding or cutting operations.

Over the years, the EPA and the Consumer Product Safety Commission (CPSC) have taken several steps to reduce the consumer's exposure to asbestos. These steps include label requirements for products containing asbestos and a ban of most asbestos products.

Home health risks arise when age, accidental damage, or normal cleaning, construction, or remodeling activities cause the asbestos-containing materials to crumble, flake, or deteriorate. Asbestos has been identified as a carcinogen (cancer-causing agent). Once ingested, asbestos fibers lodge in the lungs and can cause lung cancer. Experts are unable to provide assurance that any level of exposure to asbestos fibers is completely safe. Asbestosis is a chronic disease of the lungs that is directly caused by the inhalation of asbestos fibers. Mesothelioma is a cancer of the chest and abdominal membranes. This illness almost never occurs without exposure to asbestos. These diseases may not show up until 20 to 40 years after exposure.

Testing and Remediation

Testing for asbestos is generally performed by certified inspectors who have completed state-approved training. Information about becoming certified can be acquired by contacting the EPA regional office. Asbestos removal contractors are governed by federal regulations that specify training, protective clothing, and special respirators. Asbestos may be detected by air monitoring, bulk sampling of suspected materials, or wipe sampling of suspected materials or other objects in the area. Home inspectors may be able to recognize certain items that contain asbestos, such as pipe or water heater insulation, based on the age of the product.

The repair or removal of asbestos-containing products is generally a complicated process. Once asbestos is detected, there are several methods of response. In some cases, a special maintenance plan is developed to ensure that asbestos-containing materials are kept in good condition. If asbestos is found in a pipe or boiler covering, the covering is repaired. Other remedies include encapsulation, enclosure, and removal. Encapsulation is a process whereby the material is sprayed with a sealant to prevent fiber release. Enclosure consists of placing a barrier around the material. There are special procedures for removal. Total removal of even small amounts of asbestos-containing material is usually the last alternative.

Electromagnetic Fields

Anytime electricity flows through a wire, **electromagnetic fields** (EMFs) *are created.* There are actually *two separate fields: an electric field and a magnetic field.* The strength of the magnetic field results from the motion of the electricity. Electromagnetic fields are present where there are power lines. With power lines, there are generator and transmission lines; the longer the lines, the stronger the electricity. Small and large electrical appliances also emit EMFs. There are no federal laws that regulate EMF emissions. Some states have adopted a *prudent avoidance policy.* This means that people are advised to exercise caution and to avoid exposure to these fields when possible. In addition, for the protection of the public health, states may enact an acceptable limit of kilovolts for a given power line. Kilovolts are a measure of the voltage or *juice* flowing through a power line. An acceptable limit, for example, may be 345 kilovolts, as it is in New York. Magnetic field strength, measured in milligauss, is limited to a strength of 200 milligauss at the edge of a right-of-way. (The right-of-way is the strip of land on which a power line is built.)

Health Effects

Because of a congressional directive, the National Institute of Environmental Health Sciences, the National Institutes of Health, and the National Toxicology Program conducted a study to evaluate the health effects of exposure to very low-frequency EMFs. The majority of the panel of experts concluded that the fields, such as those that surround electric power lines, could be regarded as a possible human carcinogen. Earlier studies suggested that their presence causes a higher incidence of leukemia and brain cancer.

Testing and Remediation

Some power lines are stronger than others. Exposure decreases with distance. Electric fields can be shielded by walls, trees, or hills. Magnetic fields cannot be shielded. To reduce exposure, distance is the key. To reduce exposure in the home, electrical appliances should not be placed close to where people sleep, work, or sit. Because opposing magnetic fields can cancel each other out, a knowledgeable electrician can rewire a home to reduce magnetic fields. Home inspectors can use a digital field tester device to locate the source of EMFs.

Underground Storage Tanks

Underground storage tanks *are used for the bulk storage of chemicals and petroleum.* All underground storage tanks, large industrial or home based, can pose a hazard to surrounding soil and underground water. Any leakage may discharge petroleum products or other hazardous liquids into the soil and potentially contaminate groundwater resources. The EPA regulates the storage and maintenance of underground storage tanks used by business and industry.

Federal law does not require either the EPA or the states to regulate small above- or underground tanks containing 1,100 gallons or less of oil for on-premises heating use. Should home inspectors observe an underground storage tank on the property, they should find out if the tank is still in use. In some cases, the property owners may have converted to a different fuel source. The underground tank may be sitting there, possibly corroded, and leaking sediment into the surrounding soil. In other cases, although the tank may be in use, it may be old (20 years or more) and corroded to the point that it is leaking fuel into the soil.

Testing and Remediation

Should your clients, the purchasers, buy the property, the responsibility for cleaning up belongs to them. Home inspectors should find out the age of the tank from the property owners. Tests can be performed to determine leakage. Should there be a leak, the property owners may have to remediate the problem before title to the property is transferred. It is sometimes difficult to tell whether a tank is leaking, and this is usually beyond the scope of the home inspector's expertise. However, if it is determined that there is leakage, the owner must correct the leak. Cleanup is very expensive, even for the remediation of a small home heating oil storage tank. Depending on the scope of the cleanup, the cost can be several thousand dollars. Often, the product must be removed from the tank and the tank repaired or removed and replaced. In other cases, the sediment from empty unused tanks has to be removed and the tank filled in with sand or another product. Individual states generally have a specific agency that oversees and assists with the cleanup process.

WOOD-EATING PESTS

 n many states, only certified specialists can apply certain types of pesticides such as termiticide. However, the home inspector can learn to recognize the wood-eating pests that are found in the residential structure.

Putting It to Work

Should your client require a pest inspection as part of the home inspection process, the home inspector can bring a specialist at the time of the inspection and the pest inspection can be completed at the same time as the home inspection. Should a problem be found, remediation can be performed by the specialist at a later date.

Termites

There are several species of termites, but the eastern subterranean is the most common termite. **Termites** *eat wood* and can cause substantial structural damage. They most often eat wood that is close to or touching soil. These swarmer termites have wings that fall off easily. Termite infestation often can be detected from a pile of wings. Termites are pale-colored insects that are about one-quarter inch long and live in colonies. A mature queen can lay thousands of eggs each year and can survive 10 years. Eggs are tended by worker termites. The workers and soldiers do not have wings; the fertile males and females have long, thin wings.

Termite damage is usually first seen at or near the ground; however, damage can occur far above ground if the infestation has remained undetected for a long time. Termite-damaged wood is recognized by mud tubes that are lined with soil and are often found in wood next to heaters or fireplaces. This is because the soil in these areas is of a higher temperature during the winter. Termites multiply rapidly. The control of subterranean termites should be remediated by a professional. Termiticide may be applied in and around the home—around pipes, wells, and heating ducts.

To prevent infestation, moisture should not accumulate around the foundation because both ants and termites are attracted to moisture. Humidity should be controlled in the crawl space through proper ventilation.

Wood contact with the soil should be avoided. The soil should be graded away from the foundation. Wood posts and stairs embedded in concrete can be entry paths for termites. Wood mulch also attracts termites, especially when damp and moist, so it should be kept away from wood siding or doors and window frames.

Powderpost Beetles

A **powderpost beetle** *is a small, brownish red wood-eating insect.* Powderpost beetles infest softwoods (e.g., pine, spruce, fir) and hardwoods (e.g., oak, maple) and make small round holes in the wood. They are typically found in log houses and other wood components. Their presence is evidenced by small holes with fine sawdust streaming from them. The powderpost beetle takes many years to cause structural damage. Fumigation eradicates the infestation. Figure 10.6 depicts a powderpost beetle infestation.

Carpenter Ants

Carpenter ants *are black or red and black and range in size from one-quarter inch for a worker up to three-quarters of an inch for a queen.* Around the house, their nests are ordinarily found in porch pillars and roofs, windowsills, and any wood that is touching soil. Carpenter ant colonies live a very long time. Each colony is started by a single fertilized queen. Although carpenter ants do not generally cause structural damage, they can cause some damage over a period of years because they are so long lived. Recently, evidence has been collected that these ants can cause a great deal of damage to foam insulation. The control of carpenter ant infestations requires that the nest be found. To control the problem, any penetration of wood must be remediated. Wood that is infested with the ants must be chemically treated or removed. Home inspectors should identify areas of wood with water exposure as potential areas of carpenter ant infestation. If a nest is located, it is destroyed by the application of an appropriate pesticide.

Carpenter Bees

Carpenter bees *look like bumblebees. They are large metallic blue-black insects with bright yellow or orange hairs.* Carpenter bee nests are found in wood siding, the

FIGURE 10.6

A powderpost beetle infestation.

Source: Anthony D'Agostino, Atlantic Inspection Service, Latham, New York.

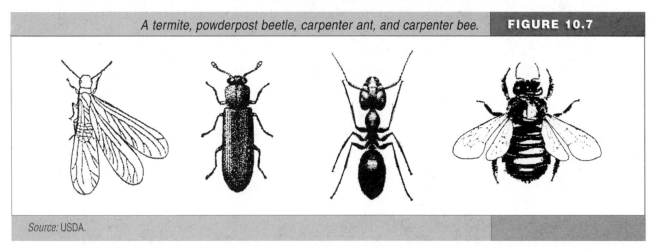

A termite, powderpost beetle, carpenter ant, and carpenter bee. **FIGURE 10.7**

Source: USDA.

ends of the logs in log houses, and other places where there is wood exposure. Both male and female bees work a one-half-inch circular hole into the wood, then work through a tunnel parallel to the surface of the wood. Carpenter bees are recognized by the cut or burrowed wood holes because they leave a residue of yellow sawdust and waste materials that stain the wood. These insects are controlled by spraying the entrance hole in the wood with an aerosol insecticide. Figure 10.7 illustrates a termite, powderpost beetle, carpenter ant, and carpenter bee.

IMPORTANT POINTS

1. Environmental services create more liability exposure. Review your errors and omissions policy with your insurance company to familiarize yourself with the limits of your coverage.

2. Check state and local government agencies to verify whether a license, certification, or registration is required to perform a certain environmental inspection or test.

3. The use of formaldehyde compounds is fairly widespread in the manufacture of furniture, cabinets, and other building materials.

4. Home inspectors can test for mold using culture sampling plates that are taped to the supply vent of the air conditioner. The culture is sent to the lab for analysis.

5. Bacteria and toxins are two items that can compromise the safety of the water supply. Another concern with the water supply is that it may contain dangerous amounts of lead.

6. Home inspectors may be asked to test both well water quality and water flow. Water testing involves collecting samples of water and bringing them to a lab for analysis.

7. A water-flow test can be performed using a water gauge attached to a hose. An acceptable level for water pressure is a minimum of 3.5 psi. Water flow may be as high as 9 gpm.

8. The EPA recommends a short-term charcoal test for the initial testing for radon. Alpha-track detectors measure radon on a seasonal or annual basis.

9. In older homes, lead can enter the drinking water as a byproduct when plumbing fixtures, pipes, and solder are corroded. Lead-testing swabs are available to test for the presence of lead paint on certain objects.

10. Generally, if the material is in good condition and in an area where it is not likely to be disturbed, asbestos-containing material should be left in place.

11. Anytime electricity flows through a wire, electromagnetic fields are created. Home inspectors can use a digital field tester device to find the source of EMFs.

12. The purchasers of a property are responsible for the cleanup of a leaking underground tank.

13. The eastern subterranean termite is the most common termite. Termites eat wood and can cause substantial structural damage.

CHAPTER REVIEW

Field Study Assignment 1

Using your practice property, investigate the areas that may pose an environmental problem. For example, is there moisture in any exposed wood in or around the structure, are there possible entryways for radon gas, are there high-tension transmitters nearby, or is there little or no ventilation?

Field Study Assignment 2

Examine a home inspection tool catalog and investigate the equipment that can assist with investigating environmental concerns.

1. Which of the following does NOT lessen liability exposure when performing environmental testing?
   A. using the proper standards for performing the test
   B. using the acceptable measurement range for the test results if the test does not go to a lab
   C. using a reputable or state-certified lab to analyze your samples
   D. carrying extra liability insurance

2. A colorless, odorless chemical found in many building materials, particularly insulation, is known as:
   A. radon
   B. freon
   C. formaldehyde
   D. lead

3. Mold and mildew found in the home fall into which category of pollutants?
   A. pesticides
   B. formaldehyde
   C. biological
   D. hazardous waste

4. A major way to remediate indoor pollutants is through:
   A. improving ventilation
   B. spraying with pesticides
   C. keeping all the windows tightly shut
   D. introducing moisture into the home

5. Which of the following substances is a danger to the public water supply?
   A. soil
   B. asbestos
   C. copper
   D. lead

6. A minimum acceptable water pressure is which of the following?
   A. 1.5 psi
   B. 2.5 psi
   C. 3.5 psi
   D. 9.5 psi

7. If water is taken from a groundwater source there is a possibility that the water may contain:
   A. asbestos
   B. radon
   C. formaldehyde
   D. magnetic fields

8. Radon is least likely to enter the house through the:
   A. attic
   B. floor drains
   C. sump pump openings
   D. joints in the basement

9. Radon is measured in units of:
   A. liters
   B. picocuries
   C. milligaus
   D. ounces

10. The home inspector can test for radon by using a:
    A. swab test
    B. charcoal canister
    C. wipe sampling
    D. gas meter

11. Alpha-tract detectors are used to measure:
    A. formaldehyde
    B. radon
    C. electromagnetic fields
    D. mold spores

12. Lead that has accumulated in soil surrounding a property most likely came from:
    A. acid rain
    B. the original soil composition
    C. exterior surface paint
    D. the water supply used to water the lawn

13. The segment of the population that is most likely to acquire lead poisoning from paint is:
    A. the elderly
    B. children
    C. teenagers
    D. all of the above groups are equally likely to be poisoned by lead-based paint

14. Which of the following is NOT a possible source of lead in and around the home?
    A. wood flooring
    B. soil
    C. paint
    D. drinking water

15. A fibrous mineral that is used in building products and is linked to lung disease is known as:
    A. asbestos
    B. radon
    C. lead
    D. UFFI

16. If a product containing asbestos is found in the home, is in good condition, and in an area where it is not likely to be disturbed, it should be:
    A. cut away and removed immediately
    B. left in place
    C. sprayed with paint
    D. burned and then removed

17. Encapsulation and enclosure are procedures used to remediate:
    A. radon
    B. asbestos
    C. leaking underground storage tanks
    D. formaldehyde

18. With regard to electromagnetic field emissions, which of the following is TRUE?
    A. Tests have shown that they cause lung disease.
    B. Distance is not a factor in protecting from emissions.
    C. They are not regulated by federal law.
    D. There are no suggested limits for kilovolts as to a given power line.

19. Which of the following is NOT generally tested or monitored by a home inspector?
    A. radon
    B. formaldehyde
    C. water flow
    D. leaky underground storage tanks

20. Electromagnetic fields are generally regulated by:
    A. federal law
    B. state law
    C. local laws
    D. no laws, only policy in some cases

21. Should a heating oil storage tank leak, the party responsible for cleanup is the:
    A. municipality
    B. EPA
    C. property owner
    D. heating oil company

22. The control of subterranean termites is remediated by:
    A. the home owner
    B. the home inspector
    C. a pest infestation professional
    D. the local health department

23. Which of the following is an insect that does NOT eat wood?
    A. carpenter ant
    B. termite
    C. powderpost beetle
    D. bumblebee

24. For the most part, termites begin to eat wood that:
    A. is painted
    B. found only in older homes
    C. is close to or touching soil
    D. is soft

25. Carpenter ants generally cause structural damage:
    A. over a period of years
    B. almost immediately on infestation
    C. only if the property has a great deal of wood rot
    D. only in properties that have a wood exterior

ANSWER KEY

1. D	8. A	15. A	22. C
2. C	9. B	16. B	23. D
3. C	10. B	17. B	24. C
4. A	11. B	18. C	25. A
5. D	12. C	19. D	
6. C	13. B	20. D	
7. B	14. A	21. C	

PART III

WORKBOOK AND

STUDY GUIDE

Workbook and Study Guide Contents

INSTRUCTIONS TO THE STUDENT

This Workbook and Study Guide reinforces what you have learned in the textbook. After you complete each chapter and the chapter activities, you are ready to reinforce your learning with the Workbook chapter that matches the one in the textbook. In each Workbook chapter, you will find a variety of exercises to help you understand and learn the material. Read over the following instructions before beginning the Workbook and Study Guide exercises to ensure an optimum learning experience.

1. Before beginning the Workbook exercises, review your textbook chapter and any notes. Focus on areas where you have had some difficulty.

2. Next, use the "Chapter Review" section in your textbook to review the important points contained in the chapter.

3. Now, turn to the Workbook. Study the list of course objectives. These objectives are identical to those listed in the textbook chapter. Answer the objectives in the space provided in the Workbook. Check your responses with those given in the Answer Key.

4. Now, refer to the key term definitions. The key terms in this Workbook are identical to the key terms that appear in the textbook. Learning the meaning of these key terms is essential because you will see them over and over again in exam questions. Complete the key term exercise later in the Workbook chapter. Remember, if you have questions regarding key terms or important points, refer back to your textbook for further clarification.

5. The next exercise consists of True–False questions. After completing these questions, check them with the Answer Key at the end of the Workbook.

6. The How Would You Respond? questions are based on situations you may encounter during your home inspection career and are designed to stimulate thinking. Although possible responses for these questions are provided in the Answer Key, no single response is the only "correct" answer. As you will see as you pursue your home inspection career, each particular situation can give rise to a variety of responses. Check any alternative answers with your instructor.

7. The key term fill-in questions appear next. Without referring back to the key terms at the beginning of the Workbook chapter, complete the exercise. Be sure to check your responses with the Answer Key.

8. Many of the workbook chapters include diagrams of various house system components. These diagrams appear in your textbook and each component of the diagram is labeled. In the Workbook, the labels are blank. You are asked to fill in the blanks. To check your responses, use the Answer Key.

All of the Workbook exercises are structured to help you learn and also to test your understanding of the material. Don't feel uncomfortable if at first you are not doing as well as you think you should. For some, this is new material and it will take some time to absorb it. Don't hesitate to do the activities more than once if you feel you need the practice. You will be gratified to see your proficiency level increase as you progress through the course!

Diagnostic Exam

After completing all of the Workbook chapters, take the practice 50-question exam. This sample exam is *diagnostic*; it will help you pinpoint areas in which you may need further study. Be sure to take the exam under exam conditions, giving yourself one hour to complete it. You should have no distractions or interruptions. The exam is divided into subject sections so that you can readily see where you need more review. You might find it helpful to review sections of the textbook to further clarify your answers. While taking the exam, make sure you know the meaning of each answer choice, even if it is not the correct answer. This alternate choice just may pop up on another exam.

If you don't pass this sample exam, further study is indicated. Check the areas where you are weak and re-study them. This sample exam is a good predictor of your performance on other home inspection exams that you may be required to pass, so you should not attempt another exam until you feel comfortable with the material presented in this review.

CHAPTER 1

AN INTRODUCTION TO THE PROFESSIONAL HOME INSPECTION

fter reading and reviewing Chapter 1 and answering the multiple-choice questions for that chapter, complete the following exercises. Refer back to your textbook to assist with your answers. Use the Answer Key at the end of the Workbook to check your responses.

Key Terms

The following key terms match those found in your textbook. Review the meaning of these terms and refer to the textbook for further clarification if needed.

- **Home inspection:** an examination and observation of the exterior and interior of residential property including the grounds, the structure, and the mechanical systems to determine structural defects, broken or obsolete components, and damage due to water, wear and tear, and other conditions.
- **Home inspection report:** a written itemization and detailed summation of the findings of the home inspector with regard to a subject property.
- **Home inspector:** a qualified professional who performs a home inspection.
- **Property condition disclosure form:** generally furnished to the seller by a real estate agent, the form asks the seller to disclose detailed information regarding the property.

Learning Objectives

The following objectives were discussed in your textbook. Write your responses to these objectives in the space provided.

1. Summarize the purpose of and define a home inspection.

2. Describe the reasons why home inspection is a profitable, satisfying career now and in the long term.

3. Explain the purpose of the property condition disclosure form.

_____

_____

_____

_____

_____

_____

4. Summarize the present and future status of state regulation of the home inspection industry.

_____

_____

_____

_____

_____

_____

5. List home inspection organizations that can provide more information relative to a career in home inspection.

_____

_____

_____

_____

_____

_____

True–False Questions

Indicate whether the statement is True or False.

_____ 1. In general, most buyers have first-hand knowledge of the various systems that make up the residential structure.

_____ 2. The most frequent request for home inspection is made by the parties offering to purchase a home.

_____ 3. Home inspectors may NOT participate in radon inspections.

_____ 4. A professional engineer license is required to perform home inspections.

_____ 5. Some states require that home inspectors be licensed, certified, or registered.

_____ 6. A home inspector must know how to repair defects found during an inspection.

_____ 7. Home inspectors who work part-time have very little chance of realizing income.

_____ 8. Very few home inspection organizations offer training of any kind.

_____ 9. A thorough home inspection can be completed in about one hour.

_____ 10. Home inspections may be performed for insurance purposes to assess property damage.

How Would You Respond?

Analyze the following situations and decide how the individuals should handle them in accordance with what you have learned.

1. Kyle is thinking about starting up a home inspection business. Although he feels confident about his abilities, he doesn't know how to set up a business. What are some of the most important things Kyle must do at the outset?

2. While Aviva is performing a home inspection, the home owner asks if she would closely examine the leak under the kitchen sink. In her former job, Aviva was a licensed plumber and she knows how to repair the leak. What should she do?

3. Evander's property is for sale and his real estate agent has asked him to complete a Seller's Property Condition Disclosure Form. The prospective buyers have hired Neil, a home inspector. When he arrives at the home, Evander hands him the disclosure form and tells Neil that he is extremely knowledgeable about his own property, that everything is on the form, and that the property does not need further inspection. How might Neil best handle the situation?

Key Term Review

Fill in the term that *best* completes each sentence.

1. An itemization and detailed summation of the findings of the home inspector with regard to the subject property is known as a(n) _____.

2. A form that asks the seller detailed information about his property is called a(n) _____.

3. A(n) _____ is a qualified professional who performs a home inspection.

4. A thorough examination of the exterior and interior of residential property including the grounds, the structure, and the mechanical systems that comprise the property to determine structural defects, broken or obsolete components, and damage due to water, wear and tear, and other conditions is known as a(n) _____.

CHAPTER 2

THE HOME INSPECTION BUSINESS

fter reading and reviewing Chapter 2 and answering the multiple-choice questions for that chapter, complete the following exercises. Refer back to your textbook to assist with your answers. Use the Answer Key at the end of the Workbook to check your responses.

Key Terms

The following key terms match those found in your textbook. Review the meaning of these terms and refer to the textbook for further clarification if needed.

- **Corporation:** a legal entity recognized by law with tax rates separate from individual income tax rates.

- **Doing business as (d/b/a):** a sole proprietorship that operates under a name other than the owner's.

- **Errors and omissions insurance:** a form of professional liability insurance that covers claims of negligence that occur while rendering a professional service.

- **Independent contractor:** an employment arrangement whereby the contractor does not receive a set salary on a regular basis, does not work set hours, and provides her own tools and equipment.

- **Latent defect:** a hidden or concealed defect that cannot be discovered by ordinary observation or inspection.

- **Limited liability company:** a form of business organization that combines the most favorable attributes of partnership and a corporation.

- **Partnership:** a form of business organization that is owned by two or more partners and is created by a contract between the partners.

- **Professional liability insurance:** covers individuals and business organizations for claims made by third parties.

- **Sole proprietorship:** the simplest form of business organization, it is owned by one individual and may use a name other than the owner's personal name.

Learning Objectives

The following objectives were discussed in your textbook. Write your responses to these objectives in the space provided.

1. List the advantages and disadvantages of opening a home inspection business.

_____

_____

_____

_____

_____

_____

2. Describe the various types of business organizations.

_____

_____

_____

_____

_____

_____

3. List what constitutes appropriate insurance coverage.

_____

_____

_____

_____

_____

_____

4. Differentiate between the employee and independent contractor employment arrangement and define the advantages and disadvantages of each.

_____

_____

_____

_____

_____

_____

5. List the items to consider when opening a home inspection business.

_____

_____

_____

_____

_____

_____

6. Summarize the issues that should be discussed with a prospective home
   inspection employer.

_____

_____

_____

_____

_____

True–False Questions

Indicate whether the statement is True or False.

_____ 1. A sole proprietorship is NOT a type of business organization.

_____ 2. Individuals who form a partnership must have an equal interest in the business.

_____ 3. The corporate form of business ownership protects a business owner from personal liability.

_____ 4. An example of a latent defect is a broken window.

_____ 5. An example of a latent defect is a cracked sewer drain under the foundation.

_____ 6. Home inspectors who work for themselves need NOT purchase professional liability insurance.

_____ 7. Professional liability insurance is commonly referred to as risk maintenance insurance.

_____ 8. Independent contractors receive a set salary on a weekly basis.

_____ 9. One advantage of the independent contractor arrangement for an employer is that the employer does not pay for benefits.

_____ 10. A business that hires independent contractors cannot also hire full- or part-time employees.

_____ 11. One of the first items to accomplish when setting up a home inspection business is to check state licensure requirements.

_____ 12. Home inspectors are prohibited by law from accepting credit cards.

_____ 13. It is a conflict of interest for self-employed home inspectors to work for other home inspection companies.

_____ 14. Home inspectors seeking employment need not investigate differences between home inspection firms because the differences are minimal.

_____ 15. Referral sources for home inspectors include other building contractors.

_____ 16. An advantage of part-time home inspection work is that part-time home inspectors are exempt from licensure in most instances.

How Would You Respond?

Analyze the following situations and decide how the individuals should handle them in accordance with what you have learned.

1. Soldana is ready to open a home inspection business but does not have the start-up money. Her brother offers to finance her operation, but he wants to know what's in it for him? What are Soldana's choices?

_____

_____

_____

_____

_____

2. The purchasers of a residential property recently sued Michael, a home inspector, because Michael did not discover a damp and crumbling foundation wall that was concealed behind wood paneling. Michael never purchased errors and omissions insurance. What are his options?

_____

_____

_____

_____

_____

_____

3. Theresa wants to work for EverRight Inspection Company as an independent contractor, but she also wants sick pay, health insurance, and paid vacation. Can she have it all?

_____

_____

_____

_____

_____

_____

Key Term Review

Fill in the term that *best* completes each sentence.

1. A form of business organization that is owned by two or more people is known as a(n) _____.

2. A(n) _____ is a hidden or concealed problem that is not easily observable.

3. A form of business organization owned by one individual is known as a(n) _____.

4. _____ is a type of insurance that covers individuals and business organizations for claims made by third parties.

5. A(n) _____ is a type of business organization with tax rates separate from individual income tax rates.

6. If Jamie Swan operates his home inspection business under the name of Swan Home Inspection Services, then Jamie Swan is _____ Swan Home Inspection Services.

7. If JayCee does work for Down Home Inspection, works her chosen hours, and does not receive benefits or salary, she is probably a(n) _____.

8. A type of business organization formed by two or more people that combines the most favorable attributes of a corporation and a partnership is known as a(n) _____.

CHAPTER 3

LAND USE REGULATIONS

 fter reading and reviewing Chapter 3 and answering the multiple-choice questions for that chapter, complete the following exercises. Refer back to your textbook to assist with your answers. Use the Answer Key at the end of the Workbook to check your responses.

Key Terms

The following key terms match those found in your textbook. Review the meaning of these terms and refer to the textbook for further clarification if needed.

- **Building permit:** permission from the appropriate local government authority to construct or renovate any type of property.

- **Certificate of occupancy:** a document issued by a local government agency, after a satisfactory inspection of a structure, that authorizes an owner or tenant to occupy a structure.

- **Condemnation:** the actual taking of property under the power of eminent domain.

- **Deed restrictions:** take the form of covenants or conditions and run with the land (move with the title in any subsequent deed).

- **Easement:** also known as a right-of-way; gives to someone the right to use or have access to, but not own or possess, land belonging to another.

- **Eminent domain:** the power of a government or its agencies to take private property for public use.

- **Escheat:** the power of the state to take title to property left by a person who has died and has no legal heirs.

- **Nonconforming use:** an authorized preexisting use of property in a zoned area that is different from the use specified by the zoning code.

- **Plat:** a recorded subdivision map that shows the lots, their sizes, and where they are situated in the subdivision.

- **Police power:** empowers government to fulfill its responsibility to provide for the public health, safety, and welfare of its citizens.

- **Setback requirements:** specified distances from the front and interior property lines to the building.

- **Special use permit:** allows use that is otherwise not permitted in a zone.

- **Spot zoning:** a specific property within a zoned area is rezoned to permit a use different from the zoning requirements for that area; it is illegal in many states.

- **Subdivision:** land that is divided into lots for development purposes.

- **Taxation:** one of the inherent burdens on private ownership of land; property taxes constitute a specific lien against the real estate.

- **Variance:** a permitted deviation from specific requirements of a zoning ordinance.

Learning Objectives

The following objectives were discussed in your textbook. Write your responses to these objectives in the space provided.

1. Distinguish between public and private control of land.

   _____

   _____

   _____

   _____

   _____

   _____

2. Define each type of public land control: police power, taxation, eminent domain, and escheat.

   _____

   _____

   _____

   _____

   _____

   _____

3. Describe how land use regulations, such as master plans that include zoning, affect a particular parcel, neighborhood, or community.

   _____

   _____

   _____

   _____

   _____

4. Explain how land use relates to building codes, building permits, and certificates of occupancy.

   _____

   _____

   _____

   _____

   _____

True–False Questions

Indicate whether the statement is True or False.

_____ 1. Deed restrictions only apply to the initial deed and do NOT appear on subsequent deeds.

_____ 2. Subdivision developers may NOT place deed restrictions on the properties they develop; only private residents can.

_____ 3. The exercise of police power need NOT be in the best interest of the public.

_____ 4. If there is no mortgage on a property, then property taxes need NOT be paid.

_____ 5. Taxes levied by a local government constitute a specific lien against the real estate.

_____ 6. Only the federal government, NOT state or local governments, may exercise the power of eminent domain.

_____ 7. State legislatures enact municipal zoning ordinances.

_____ 8. Public open space is a type of zoning classification.

_____ 9. The mayor's office decides the fair application of zoning ordinances.

_____ 10. Special use permits generally do NOT require that the property owner demonstrate undue hardship because of the current zoning.

_____ 11. If necessary, local ordinances regarding land use may oppose federal or state laws.

_____ 12. Building permits are NOT a form of land use control.

_____ 13. Some cities require a certificate of occupancy by a new tenant even though the structure is NOT new and has not been renovated.

How Would You Respond?

Analyze the following situations and decide how the individuals should handle them in accordance with what you have learned.

1. Justin is inspecting a home for buyers who have a boat that they wish to leave in the front driveway during the winter months. Because the homes in the neighborhood, including the subject property, are in the $300,000 range, Justin is curious to find out if there is a deed restriction prohibiting this practice. The sellers do not know if parking a boat in the front driveway is permissible in the subdivision. How might Justin find out?

_____

_____

_____

_____

_____

_____

2. Belinda is inspecting a residence with a home business. The current residents has operated a small beauty parlor in the basement for 50 years. This use has long been prohibited by the current zoning ordinance and no new businesses have been allowed in the zone for the past 20 years. The buyers of the property want to live in the home and convert the beauty parlor to a home-based craft store. Can the buyers do this and if so, how?

_____

_____

_____

_____

_____

_____

3. While performing an inspection on a 25-year-old home, Trevor notices several violations of local building codes. How should he handle this situation?

_____

_____

_____

_____

_____

_____

Key Term Review

Fill in the term that *best* completes each sentence.

1. An authorized deviation from the specific requirements of a zoning ordinance is known as a(n) _____.

2. A(n) _____ authorizes a use that is not otherwise permitted in a zone and is granted by the planning board or other legislative body.

3. A document called a(n) _____ is issued by a local government agency and authorizes occupancy of a structure.

4. _____ is the power of a government or its agencies to take private property for public use.

5. A preexisting use of property in a zoned area that is different from the use specified by the zoning code is known as a(n) _____.

6. A recorded subdivision map that shows the lots, their sizes, and where they are situated in the subdivision is called a(n) _____.

7. Specified distances from the front and interior property lines to the building are called _____.

8. Permission from the appropriate local government authority to construct or renovate any type of property is known as a(n) _____.

9. The power of a state to take property left by a person who has died without any legal heirs is called _____.

10. _____ is the actual taking of property under the power of eminent domain.

11. A(n) _____ is land that is divided into lots for development purposes.

12. The subdivision covenant filings for Happy Days Subdivision include a covenant that no RVs or boats can be parked in the front driveway of any home in the subdivision. This covenant is known as a(n) _____.

13. The _____ of real property creates a lien against the real estate.

14. A(n) _____ is usually required to lay underground telephone cable. The phone company that uses the land is said to have a(n) _____.

CHAPTER 4

HOME INSPECTION PROCEDURE AND REPORTING

After reading and reviewing Chapter 4 and answering the multiple-choice questions for that chapter, complete the following exercises. Refer back to your textbook to assist with your answers. Use the Answer Key at the end of the Workbook to check your responses.

Key Terms

The following key terms match those found in your textbook. Review the meaning of these terms and refer to the textbook for further clarification if needed.

- **Checklist report:** a systemized itemization of the various components of a property that is organized into sections that allow the inspector to check off inspected property components and comment on any specific problems.

- **Disclaimer:** is appended to the home inspection report and documents the scope of the inspection (what is included and what is not) and specifically indicates which items are omitted from the report, including opinions about the structure and design, building code compliance, and environmental problems.

- **Narrative report:** written in paragraph form and reflects the inspector's observation and opinion of the condition of a subject property.

- **Narrative report with checklist or rating system:** a narrative report combined with a checklist or rating system report that more fully explains the inspector's observations of the property.

- **Pre-inspection agreement:** a contract that protects both the home inspector and the client. It explains, in general terms, the scope of the inspection (what is included and what is not), the cost, and the procedures to address any dispute that may arise.

- **Rating system report:** uses a numerical evaluation on a scale, for example 1–5, to define the condition of each property component.

- **Statute of limitations:** varies from state to state and by the type of claim asserted. It sets the time frame for commencing a lawsuit and begins to run on the date the claim arose or the date on which the client knew or reasonably should have known of the claim.

Learning Objectives

The following objectives were discussed in your textbook. Write your responses to these objectives in the space provided.

1. Explain some of the ways to gain home inspection experience.

    _____

    _____

    _____

    _____

    _____

2. List the tools of the trade.

_____
_____
_____
_____
_____
_____

3. Describe communication strategies to use with clients (buyers) and owners (sellers) of the subject property.

_____
_____
_____
_____
_____
_____

4. Explain how to conduct the home inspection using the pre-inspection agreement and home inspection reports.

_____
_____
_____
_____
_____
_____

True–False Questions

Indicate whether the statement is True or False.

_____ 1. Many home inspectors have been a professional technician in one of the real estate fields.

_____ 2. Photos kept on file, whether used in the report or not, help protect the home inspector should a dispute with a client arise.

_____ 3. There is no need to use a thermometer when performing a home inspection.

_____ 4. Generally, a real estate closing is the reason for a home inspection.

_____ 5. A home inspection should not be performed if the home inspector and client have not signed a pre-inspection agreement.

_____ 6. The property's square footage is not important in determining the fee for the inspection.

——— 7. The clients should NOT be present during the home inspection.

——— 8. Home inspectors, if asked, should comment on the property's value.

——— 9. A home inspection should NOT be performed if the utilities are turned off.

——— 10. Generally, the inspection of the subject property should proceed from the outside in.

——— 11. Narrative reports should NOT be generated from a checklist report form.

——— 12. An attachment to the home inspection report may be a sketch of the property.

——— 13. Home inspectors may gather information for laboratory testing and analysis.

——— 14. The disclaimer appended to the home inspection report is optional.

——— 15. The home inspector should expect payment for services after the delivery of the home inspection report.

——— 16. Home inspectors should NOT discuss their findings with clients pending final delivery of the home inspection report.

——— 17. A home inspection report should NOT be delivered until all data from laboratory testing are available.

——— 18. Home inspection reports should NOT be faxed or e-mailed under any circumstances.

——— 19. A home inspector must have a professional engineer's license in order to comment on the condition of the roof shingles.

——— 20. A home inspector must have a professional engineer's license in order to comment on the load capabilities of the roof.

How Would You Respond?

Analyze the following situations and decide how the individuals should handle them in accordance with what you have learned.

1. Faisal generally charges $300 for an inspection of a typical three-bedroom home. The Basics tell Faisal that their home is much smaller than the typical midsize home, but it does have three bedrooms. They believe the $300 fee is too high. How can Faisal respond to the Basics?

_____

_____

_____

_____

_____

_____

2. Danny and Darcy Difficult refuse to sign a pre-inspection agreement. They tell Manny, their home inspector, that they have already signed one contract, the offer to purchase, and that it covers all contractual matters pertaining to the purchase of the property. How should Manny handle this?

_____

_____

_____

_____

_____

3. Rod, a home inspector, has quoted a fee thinking that he will be inspecting a midsize 2,500 square foot ranch home. His clients, the Blacklies, have been less than truthful. When he arrives at the subject property, he sees a ranch home with approximately 6,500 square feet of space. What should Rod do?

_____

_____

_____

_____

_____

_____

Key Term Review

Fill in the term that *best* completes each sentence.

1. A systemized itemization of the various components of a property that is organized into sections that allow the inspector to check off inspected property components is called a(n) _____.

2. A(n) _____ is a contract that protects both the home inspector and the client and explains, in general terms, the scope of the inspection.

3. Valerie, a professional home inspector, delivers a home inspection report written in paragraph form based on her observations and opinions of the condition of a subject property. This form of report is known as a(n) _____.

4. Because of the three-year limit on commencing a legal action as dictated by the _____, the clients were barred from pursuing a lawsuit against a home inspector who had performed a home inspection for them more than four years ago.

5. The fact that home inspectors need not uncover code violations is clearly stated in the _____ affixed to the home inspection report.

6. For a more complete picture of the property condition, Brett uses a narrative report with a(n) _____.

7. Nancy's home inspection report is based on numerical values assigned to each property condition and is known as a(n) _____.

CHAPTER 5

INSPECTING THE SITE

After reading and reviewing Chapter 5 and answering the multiple-choice questions for that chapter, complete the following exercises. Refer back to your textbook to assist with your answers. Use the Answer Key at the end of the Workbook to check your responses.

Key Terms

The following key terms match those found in your textbook. Review the meaning of these terms and refer to the textbook for further clarification if needed.

- **Appurtenance:** a right, privilege, or improvement belonging to, and passing with, the land.
- **Balusters:** poles or posts that run from the stair handrail vertically to the tread.
- **Drainage:** the land's ability to draw off surface water.
- **Grading:** the arrangement and preparation of the soil for construction.
- **Groundwater:** water beneath the surface of the earth that can be collected with wells, tunnels, or drainage galleries or that flows naturally to the earth's surface via seepage or springs.
- **Headroom:** the space between the stair and the overhang (or the ceiling inside the structure).
- **Hydrostatic pressure:** the push of water against a surface.
- **Percolation rate:** the speed at which standing water is absorbed by the soil.
- **Retaining walls:** structures made from a variety of materials, such as brick, stone, slate, poured concrete, concrete block, and pressure-treated wood, that are used to hold back areas of earth.
- **Riser:** the vertical area of the step that supports the tread.
- **Slope:** land surface that is graded on an angle.
- **Slope gradient:** the inclination of the soil surface from the horizontal.
- **Soil permeability:** the ability of the soil to absorb water.
- **Stringer:** also known as the carriage, it supports the stairway.
- **Surface runoff:** the loss of water from an area by its flow over the land's surface.
- **Topography:** includes types of soil; the location of water such as wetlands, springs, or floodplains; forest areas; and the location of rocks, trees, and other vegetation.
- **Tread:** the horizontal surface of the stair.
- **Water erosion:** the removal of soil material by flowing water; part of the process is the detachment of soil material by the impact of raindrops.
- **Water table:** the uppermost boundary of the groundwater.
- **Weepholes:** small perforations in retaining wall material that allow water drainage.

Learning Objectives

The following objectives were discussed in your textbook. Write your responses to these objectives in the space provided.

1. List the items included in a typical site inspection, according to industry standards.

_____
_____
_____
_____
_____
_____

2. Define drainage and explain how proper site grading eliminates drainage problems.

_____
_____
_____
_____
_____
_____

3. Describe what a water table is and its significance.

_____
_____
_____
_____
_____

4. Describe the problems that can occur with landscaping, walkways, driveways, other paved and masonry areas, steps and stoops, patios, porches, attached decks, and balconies.

_____
_____
_____
_____
_____

True–False Questions

Indicate whether the statement is True or False.

———— 1. A typical site inspection should always include an examination of the retaining walls (if they are a part of the site).

———— 2. Hydrology refers to the study of the earth's surface.

———— 3. Appurtenances are rights, privileges, and improvements belonging to, and passing with, the land.

———— 4. A site composed of slightly rolling hills and valleys provides more natural drainage than a very steep site.

———— 5. Proper drainage of a site does not deter wind erosion.

———— 6. Proper drainage of a site does little to prevent frost heaving problems.

———— 7. Sites that are located at the base of an incline are prone to less water erosion.

———— 8. Problems with soil percolation rates are one of the main sources of trouble that a home inspector may encounter on examination of the site.

———— 9. The length of a slope has considerable influence on runoff and potential water erosion.

———— 10. The texture of the soil has nothing to do with the permeability of water through the soil.

———— 11. The depth of the water table from the soil surface always remains the same.

———— 12. Footing drain tiles are seldom found in new construction.

———— 13. The Federal Emergency Management Agency (FEMA) produces floodplain maps.

———— 14. The biggest problem from tree branches growing toward the structure is pest infestation.

———— 15. Retaining walls without adequate drainage are subject to substantial hydrostatic pressure.

———— 16. Weepholes are used with gutter downspouts.

———— 17. Forces that cause driveway deterioration include the movement of underlying soil.

———— 18. The riser is the horizontal surface of the step.

———— 19. The construction of a patio does NOT lend itself to safety hazards.

———— 20. Negative moisture conditions are seldom, if ever, found in a porch crawl space.

How Would You Respond?

Analyze the following situations and decide how the individuals should handle them in accordance with what you have learned.

1. Darrell and Delancy Digital hire Marney to inspect a property that they are purchasing. On arrival, Marney finds that the property is completely computerized. There are computers that control the lights, the lawn sprinkler, the security system, and the appliances. Marney feels skeptical about proceeding with the inspection, but the Digitals urge her to proceed. What are her options?

_____

_____

_____

_____

_____

_____

_____

2. On inspection of a three-bedroom ranch, Naomi finds that the shrub beds are saturated with water even though it hasn't rained for a week. What are the possible causes of the problem?

_____

_____

_____

_____

_____

_____

_____

3. Trevor is inspecting a retaining wall made from railroad ties that appears to be on the verge of collapse. The wall seems to be heaving out from the embankment. The railroad ties themselves appear to be in good condition and the property is only one year old. What are the possible causes for the wall's deterioration?

_____

_____

_____

_____

_____

_____

_____

Key Term Review

Fill in the term that *best* completes each sentence.

1. Belinda has the right, for a fee, to cut timber from her neighbor's property. This right granted by the neighbor is known as a(n) _____.

2. A stairway is composed of the vertical area that supports the tread known as the _____, the horizontal surface of the stair known as the _____, the component that supports the stairway known as the _____, the airspace above the stairs under the overhang known as _____, and the vertical posts evenly spaced under the stair rail known as the _____.

3. The arrangement and preparation of the soil for construction by placing drainage areas where appropriate for water runoff is called _____.

4. Too much _____, that is the push of water, can cause a foundation wall to collapse.

5. A(n) _____ is land surface that is graded on an angle. Land that is nearly level has a(n) _____ of 1–3 percent.

6. The loss of water from an area by its flow over the land's surface is known as _____.

7. That portion of water beneath the surface of the earth that can be collected with wells, tunnels, or drainage galleries is called _____. Its uppermost surface is known as the _____.

8. The speed at which standing water is absorbed by the soil is known as the soil's _____.

9. _____ is the land's ability to draw off surface water.

10. _____ are structures used to hold back areas of earth.

11. The ability of soil to absorb water is known as its _____.

12. _____ is a study that includes soil types and the location of vegetation and water.

13. _____ are drainage holes often located in brick or concrete retaining walls.

14. When soil material is suspended in runoff water and carried away, this is known as _____.

Diagram Study

Identifying the components of a structure from a diagram helps you to learn them more quickly and helps you to complete the home inspection report. Fill in the numbered blanks on the diagram where indicated. Refer back to your textbook for a fuller explanation of these components.

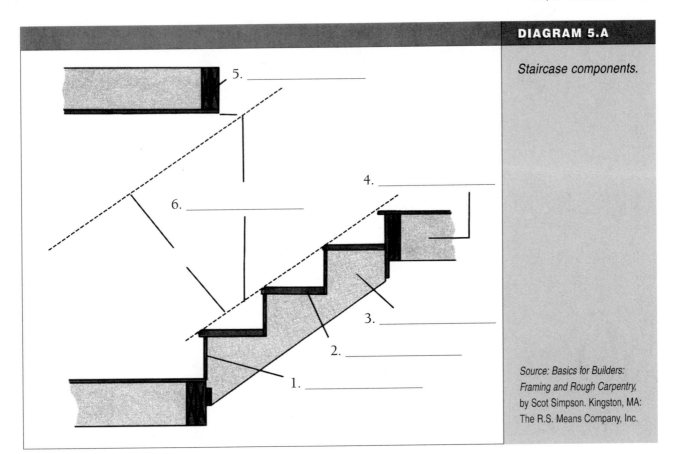

DIAGRAM 5.A

Staircase components.

5. _____

4. _____

6. _____

3. _____

2. _____

1. _____

Source: Basics for Builders: Framing and Rough Carpentry, by Scot Simpson. Kingston, MA: The R.S. Means Company, Inc.

CHAPTER 6

INSPECTING THE EXTERIOR

After reading and reviewing Chapter 6 and answering the multiple-choice questions for that chapter, complete the following exercises. Refer back to your textbook to assist with your answers. Use the Answer Key at the end of the Workbook to check your responses.

Key Terms

The following key terms match those found in your textbook. Review the meaning of these terms and refer to the textbook for further clarification if needed.

- **Balloon framing:** uses a single system of wall studs that run from the foundation through to the first and second floors to the ceiling support.
- **Casing:** the material that surrounds the window on the inside.
- **Control joints:** vertical spaces in the brick wall joints that allow for the expansion and contraction of the brick and mortar.
- **Cornice:** trim piece for the eave.
- **Counterflashing:** a second layer of flashing.
- **Creosote:** a black tar-like substance that builds up inside the chimney through normal use.
- **Cricket:** composed of metal flashing, it prevents snow and ice from building up against the chimney.
- **Double top plate:** used to tie the walls together and provide additional support for the ceiling and roof system.
- **Eave:** the lowest part of the roof that projects beyond the walls of the structure.
- **Fascia:** the area of material facing the outer edge of the soffit.
- **Felt paper:** exterior insulation material that is nailed over the sheathing.
- **Fixed-pane windows:** do not open or close (e.g., picture window or variations of the bay window).
- **Flashing:** a metallic material that is used in certain areas of the roof and walls to prevent water from seeping into the structure.
- **Floating slab:** constructed by pouring the footing first, then pouring the slab.
- **Floor joists:** framing members that span the distance between the foundation walls and the girder and provide support for the subfloor.
- **Floor truss:** a support member constructed in a factory by nailing a number of smaller members (2 × 4s or 2 × 6s) together in a number of triangular patterns to provide maximum strength.
- **Footing:** the concrete base below the frost line that supports the foundation of the structure.
- **Foundation wall:** generally composed of poured concrete, masonry (concrete) block, or brick; the height of the foundation wall determines whether the structure has a full basement or a crawl space.

- **Frieze board**: prevents wind and moisture from penetrating the junction of the soffit and sheathing.
- **Girder**: the main carrying beam, either steel or several wooden members fastened together (usually 2 × 10s, 2 × 12s, or larger), that spans the distance from one side of the foundation to the other.
- **Glazing**: the material inside the windowpane.
- **Headers**: beams that support the ceiling and the roof over the door and window openings.
- **House wrap**: exterior insulation material that is nailed over the sheathing.
- **Lally columns**: round steel columns filled with concrete that support the main carrying beam of the structure, they rest on a base plate, which is the column footing pad.
- **Light**: a layer of a glass window; windows may have one or more.
- **Monolithic slab**: the footing and slab are poured at the same time.
- **Muntins**: dividers that separate a window sash into smaller windows; may be a fake inset.
- **Pitch**: the slope of the roof.
- **Platform framing**: the structure's framing rests on a subfloor platform; the most common type of framing used in residential construction.
- **Plumb**: a position or measurement that is truly and exactly vertical, 90 degrees from a level surface.
- **Post-and-beam framing**: framing members are much larger than ordinary studs and may be four or six inches square; the larger posts are placed several feet apart instead of 16 or 24 inches on center.
- **Rafters**: the long wooden framing members that are fastened to the ends of the ceiling joists and form the gables of the roof.
- **Rails**: top and bottom pieces of the sash.
- **Rebars**: steel reinforcement embedded in the concrete foundation.
- **Ridge beam**: the highest part of the framing, it forms the apex, or top line, of the roof.
- **Roof truss system**: a roof frame made up of a number of smaller framing members; the truss carries the load-bearing function to the outer walls.
- **Sash**: the frame that surrounds and secures the glass.
- **Sheathing**: plywood covering placed over exterior framing members.
- **Sill plate**: the first wooden member of the house and is used as the nailing surface for the floor system.
- **Slab-on-grade construction**: the foundation is a concrete slab instead of a foundation wall; the concrete slab is poured directly on the ground, eliminating the crawl space or basement.
- **Soffit**: the perforated area under the roof extension that allows air to flow through the ridge vents to ventilate the attic.
- **Sole plate**: a horizontal base plate that serves as the foundation for the wall system.
- **Spalling**: the crumbling of brick.

- **Stile:** side framing member of the window sash.
- **Studs:** framing members, commonly 2 × 4s; 2 × 8s, 2 × 10s, or 2 × 12s, used vertically for wall construction.
- **Threshold:** the area on the ground in front of the door that keeps rain and snow from entering the structure.
- **Wood rot:** caused by a type of fungus that destroys wood; it is as damaging as termite or other insect infestation.

Learning Objectives

The following objectives were discussed in your textbook. Write your responses to these objectives in the space provided.

1. List the items that are included in the inspection of the property's exterior.

_____

_____

_____

_____

_____

_____

_____

2. Describe the structural components' interconnections.

_____

_____

_____

_____

_____

_____

_____

3. Briefly summarize the primary problem areas to examine during the exterior inspection.

_____

_____

_____

_____

_____

_____

_____

True–False Questions

Indicate whether the statement is True or False.

_____ 1. A typical exterior inspection includes an examination of the soffit.

_____ 2. A typical exterior inspection includes an examination of the shutters if they are part of the structure.

_____ 3. In heavy soils, the footing is wider to spread the weight of the load.

_____ 4. If the footing and slab are poured at the same time, it is called a floating slab.

_____ 5. Rebars embedded in the concrete foundation are rarely required by building codes.

_____ 6. A type of foundation crack is the shrinkage crack.

_____ 7. Squeaky floors may be caused by sheathing that is not properly butted together.

_____ 8. When a header spans more than one foot, double-length studs are constructed on either side of the header.

_____ 9. A plumb wall refers to a position or measurement 45 degrees from a level surface.

_____ 10. If an inspector observes a problem seemingly originating from behind the wallboard, he should cut out a small piece of the board to further examine the situation.

_____ 11. A sash is the frame that surrounds and secures the glass.

_____ 12. Wood rot is caused by moisture.

_____ 13. All exterior doors and windows containing glass must use tempered safety glass.

_____ 14. Factory-built roof truss systems are generally less functional than roof systems built on-site.

_____ 15. The cornice prevents wind and moisture from penetrating the junction of the soffit and sheathing.

_____ 16. Roofing shingles may buckle as a result of the expansion or contraction of the roof deck.

_____ 17. Many older chimneys do NOT have a tile liner.

_____ 18. Vinyl siding can expand and contract.

_____ 19. Brick veneer should be butted tightly against the sheathing, leaving no space.

_____ 20. The main problem with an exterior covering composed of stucco is that it tends to crack.

How Would You Respond?

Analyze the following situations and decide how the individuals should handle them in accordance with what you have learned.

1. Herbert inspects an older property. It is clear to him that the foundation is seriously compromised and must be replaced. His clients ask him to omit mentioning the serious condition of the foundation in his report. They explain that they intend to raise the house and move it to another location with a new foundation. What are Herbert's responsibilities in this situation?

_____

_____

_____

_____

_____

2. Sarah is inspecting a 50-year-old property with a slate roof. The roof is sloped and 20 feet off the ground. The roof also has a large stone chimney. Her clients are purchasing the house from the original owners who have never repaired the roof. What are Sarah's options and responsibilities regarding the roof inspection?

_____

_____

_____

_____

_____

3. Faith is inspecting a property that has a metal wood-burning stove in the family room. When Faith enters the room, there is a strong smell of smoke. How might Faith determine whether this is normal for a room with a wood-burning stove or if there might have been a chimney fire?

_____

_____

_____

_____

_____

Key Term Review

Fill in the term that *best* completes each sentence.

1. The _____ is the concrete base below the frost line that supports the foundation.

2. The _____ is the first wooden member of the house and is used as the nailing surface for the floor system.

3. _____ support the ceiling and the roof over the door and window openings.

4. The _____ is the highest part of the framing and forms the apex, or top line, of the roof.

5. The area of material on the roof facing the outer edge of the _____ is called the _____.

6. Steel reinforcements embedded in a concrete foundation are known as _____.

7. _____ prevents wind and moisture from penetrating the junction of the soffit and sheathing.

8. A metallic material that is used in certain areas of the roof and walls to prevent water from seeping into the structure is called _____. A second layer is known as _____. A type of flashing used to prevent snow and ice buildup is known as a(n) _____.

9. A framing member used to tie the walls together and provide additional support for the ceiling and roof system is known as a(n) _____.

10. _____ is a black tar-like substance that builds up inside the chimney through normal use.

11. A horizontal base plate that serves as the foundation for the wall system is called the _____.

12. The material that surrounds the window on the inside is known as the _____.

13. The lowest part of the roof that projects beyond the structure walls is known as the _____. Its trim piece is known as a(n) _____.

14. _____ are vertical spaces in the brick wall joints that allow for expansion and contraction of the brick and mortar.

15. The _____ is the area on the ground in front of the door that keeps rain and snow from entering the structure.

16. A type of foundation slab constructed by pouring the footing first and then pouring the slab is called a(n) _____. A footing and slab poured at the same time is called a(n) _____.

17. _____ is a material, such as glass, inside the windowpane. A layer of a glass window may have one or more _____.

18. Exterior insulation material nailed over the sheathing can be either _____ or _____.

19. Round steel columns filled with concrete that support the structure's main carrying beam are known as _____.

20. A picture window is an example of a(n) _____.

21. Framing members that span the distance between the foundation walls and the girder and provide support for the subfloor are called _____. If these framing members are factory constructed, they are known as _____. A factory-built roof frame is called a(n) _____.

22. The height of the _____ determines whether the structure has a full basement or a crawl space.

23. _____ is caused by a type of fungus that destroys wood.

24. Framing members used vertically for wall construction are called _____.

25. The _____ is the main carrying beam that spans the distance from one side of the foundation to the other.

26. Two _____ and two _____ are the four framing members of the window _____ that can be divided into smaller windows by _____.

27. The most common type of framing used in residential construction is called _____. A type of framing that uses a single system of wall studs that run from the foundation through the first and second floors to the ceiling support is called _____. A type of framing in which the framing members are much larger than ordinary studs and may be four or six inches square is called _____.

28. _____ is the slope of the roof.

29. _____ refers to a position or measurement that is truly and exactly vertical, 90 degrees from a level surface.

30. The crumbling of brick is known as _____.

Diagram Study

Identifying the components of a structure from a diagram helps you to learn them more quickly and helps you to complete the home inspection report. Fill in the numbered blanks on the diagrams where indicated. Refer back to your textbook for a fuller explanation of these components.

Residential structure components.   **DIAGRAM 6.A**

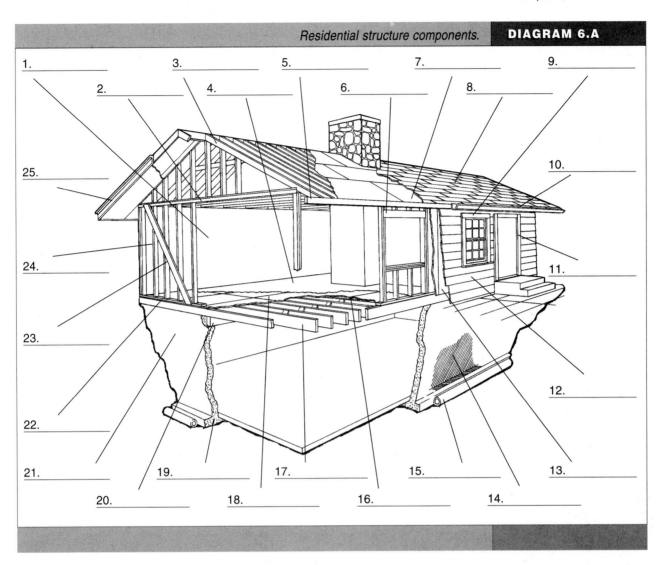

1. _____
2. _____
3. _____
4. _____
5. _____
6. _____
7. _____
8. _____
9. _____
10. _____
11. _____
12. _____
13. _____
14. _____
15. _____
16. _____
17. _____
18. _____
19. _____
20. _____
21. _____
22. _____
23. _____
24. _____
25. _____

DIAGRAM 6.B

Double-hung window components.

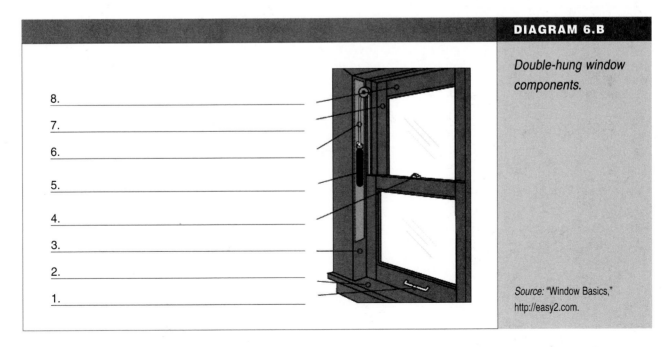

8. _____
7. _____
6. _____
5. _____
4. _____
3. _____
2. _____
1. _____

Source: "Window Basics,"
http://easy2.com.

DIAGRAM 6.C

Door components.

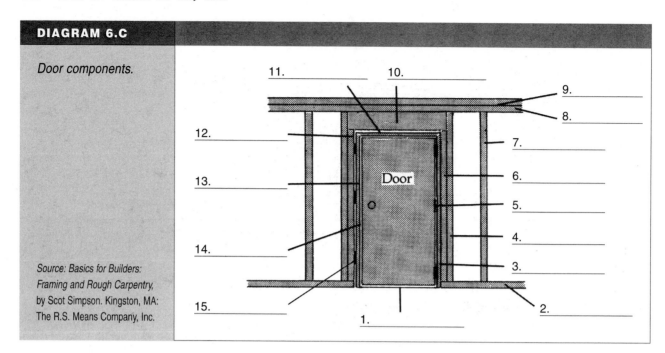

Source: Basics for Builders: Framing and Rough Carpentry, by Scot Simpson. Kingston, MA: The R.S. Means Company, Inc.

CHAPTER 7

INSPECTING THE INTERIOR

 fter reading and reviewing Chapter 7 and answering the multiple-choice questions for that chapter, complete the following exercises. Refer back to your textbook to assist with your answers. Use the Answer Key at the end of the Workbook to check your responses.

Key Terms

The following key terms match those found in your textbook. Review the meaning of these terms and refer to the textbook for further clarification if needed.

- **Ash dump door:** the metal door located in the inner hearth of some fireplaces that leads to an ash pit.

- **Ash pit:** a cavity underneath the firebox that is used as a receptacle for ashes and is accessible through a cleanout door.

- **Ash pit cleanout door:** a metal door located at the base of the chimney that leads to the ash pit.

- **Building envelope:** the materials that enclose the interior and through which heating, cooling, and fresh air pass.

- **Catalytic combustor:** a ceramic insert in a wood-burning stove that is round, square, or rectangular and has numerous small channels, or tubes, running through it that increase combustion activity.

- **Damper:** a plate or valve that closes the fireplace flue when the fireplace is not in use, preventing heat loss.

- **Efflorescence:** white stains often observed on the foundation wall or floor slab that are caused by masonry mineral salts combining with water as it penetrates through the floor or wall.

- **Extension springs:** generally mounted just above the horizontal track of the garage door, they provide lifting power by stretching (extending).

- **Flue:** the enclosed passageway in a chimney through which smoke and other gases move upward.

- **Flue collar:** the opening on the top, rear, or side of a wood-burning stove to which the stovepipe is connected.

- **Grout:** a mixture of Portland cement, lime, and sand that is mixed with water to fill and seal the spaces between tiles.

- **Gypsum board:** a type of wall panel composed of an inner core of noncombustible gypsum and paper surfacing on the front, back, and edges.

- **Internal reversing mechanism:** part of a garage door opener, it causes the door to reverse when it hits an obstruction.

- **Lift handle:** is affixed to the door (or is a pull rope attached to the bottom bracket in the lower corner) and is used with a door that is opened and closed manually.

- **Metal lath:** available in a variety of styles and resembling a mesh or honeycomb pattern, the lath supports the plaster that hardens around it.

- **Non-catalytic stove:** a wood-burning stove that maximizes combustion efficiency by providing a secondary combustion air system.

- **Photoelectric eye:** sensor mounted five to six inches off the floor on both sides of a garage door.
- **Resilient floor covering:** a manufactured interior floor covering in either sheet or tile form that returns to its original form after being bent, compressed, or stretched.
- **R-value:** the degree of resistance to heat transfer through the walls (heat is kept in or out); the larger the R-value, the greater the degree of insulation.
- **Section joint:** the space between garage door sections.
- **Subfloor:** a plywood surface nailed to the floor joists that serves as the surface for the floor finish.
- **Throat damper:** a damper located in the throat of the fireplace, just above the firebox.
- **Torsion springs:** usually mounted above the closed garage door, parallel and horizontal to the top section of the door, they provide lifting power by winding and unwinding while the door is opened or closed.
- **Trim:** made of either metal or wood and used to finish windows, doorways, cabinetry, shelving, and the areas where the floor meets the wall and the wall meets the ceiling.
- **Vapor barrier:** sheets of moisture-resistant material, such as polyethylene film, kraft paper, or aluminum foil, bonded to insulation that prevent warm interior air from mixing with cold exterior air and forming condensation within the wall.
- **Wythe:** a solid brick partition in a flue.

Learning Objectives

The following objectives were discussed in your textbook. Write your responses to these objectives in the space provided.

1. List the items that are included in the interior inspection of the subject property.

   _____

   _____

   _____

   _____

   _____

   _____

2. Describe the general procedure for performing the interior inspection.

   _____

   _____

   _____

   _____

   _____

   _____

3. Explain the significance of insulation and identify its locations within the structure.

_____

_____

_____

_____

_____

_____

4. Describe the importance of a vapor barrier.

_____

_____

_____

_____

_____

_____

5. Briefly summarize the main problems to look for during the interior inspection.

_____

_____

_____

_____

_____

_____

True–False Questions

Indicate whether the statement is True or False.

_____ 1. Building codes generally require that each room in a residential structure have one window.

_____ 2. Exterior doors are generally solid.

_____ 3. Gypsum board, or drywall, is generally found in homes built prior to 1950.

_____ 4. Metal laths are used in conjunction with drywall.

_____ 5. Dried out plaster can become powdery.

_____ 6. Suspended ceilings or ceiling tiles often conceal problem areas underneath.

_____ 7. A subfloor appears only in the basement.

_____ 8. An uneven floor surface may be caused by damaged floor joists.

_____ 9. The expansion and contraction of wood floorboards have no effect on the floor surface.

_____ 10. Home inspectors are NOT required to examine the trim.

_____ 11. Blanket insulation is no longer used in residential construction.

_____ 12. The R-value is to be considered when evaluating the pliability of resilient flooring.

_____ 13. The vapor barrier keeps moisture from entering the living space and becoming trapped in the attic.

_____ 14. Most homes built 15 or 20 years ago were constructed without vapor barriers.

_____ 15. Soffit vents provide an inflow of air into the attic.

_____ 16. Inadequate attic ventilation can compromise the roof system.

_____ 17. Furnaces located in garages or basements need little or no ventilation.

_____ 18. A dirt floor in a detached garage generally poses no problems.

_____ 19. Many garage doors do NOT have a safety cable installed inside the extension spring.

_____ 20. An indicator that a garage door is out of balance is that it does not stay open by itself.

How Would You Respond?

Analyze the following situations and decide how the individuals should handle them in accordance with what you have learned.

1. During an inspection, Dawn begins with the exterior including the roof, and then proceeds to the interior, beginning with the attic. She makes her way down to the second floor below the attic when she notices a water stain on a bedroom ceiling. Dawn had previously found no problems with either the roof or the attic. What is the correct protocol in analyzing the source of the water stain?

_____

_____

_____

_____

_____

2. Andy, a home inspector, pulls in his belt and sucks in his stomach, but he cannot make it through the opening that is the only access to the attic. What are his duties and options?

_____

_____

_____

_____

_____

3. Tyrone, a home inspector, walks into a one-story house he is inspecting and is surprised to find a suspended ceiling in the living room. On entering the kitchen, Tyrone finds that the kitchen ceiling is covered with ceiling tiles. Why should Tyrone further examine these two ceilings, and what information might he find?

_____

_____

_____

_____

_____

Key Term Review

Fill in the term that *best* completes each sentence.

1. The materials of a building that enclose the interior and through which heating, cooling, and fresh air pass are known as the _____.

2. A plate or valve that closes the fireplace flue when the fireplace is not in use is called the _____. A plate or valve located in the throat of the fireplace, just above the firebox is called a(n) _____.

3. _____ is a type of wall panel composed of an inner core of a noncombustible mineral with paper surfacing on the front, back, and edges.

4. A sensor that is mounted five to six inches off the floor on both sides of a garage door is known as a(n) _____.

5. _____ is a manufactured interior floor covering, in either sheet or tile form, that returns to its original form after being bent, compressed, or stretched.

6. _____ are usually mounted above the closed garage door and provide lifting power by winding and unwinding while the door is opened or closed.

7. A plywood surface nailed to the floor joists that serves as the surface for the floor finish is known as the _____.

8. The space between garage door sections is known as a _____.

9. Devices in wood-burning stoves that increase combustion activity are known as _____ stoves and _____ stoves.

10. The occurrence of white mineral stains on masonry is known as

_____.

11. The enclosed passageway in a chimney through which smoke and other gases move upward is called the _____. The _____ is the opening in the top, rear, or side of the stove to which the stovepipe is connected and through which exhaust is vented.

12. The _____ are generally mounted just above the horizontal track of the garage door and provide lifting power by stretching.

13. A mixture of Portland cement, lime, sand, and water that is used to fill and seal the spaces between tiles is called _____.

14. The degree of resistance to heat transfer is known as the _____.

15. _____ is either metal or wood and is used to finish windows, doorways, and the area where the floor meets the wall and the wall meets the ceiling.

16. A solid brick partition in the flue is called the _____.

17. Sheets of moisture-resistant material that prevent warm interior air from mixing with cold exterior air and forming condensation within the wall are known as the _____.

18. Resembling a mesh or honeycomb pattern, the _____ supports the plaster that hardens around it.

19. The _____ is affixed to a garage door to open and close the door manually.

20. The part of a garage door opener that causes the door to reverse when it hits an obstruction is called the _____.

21. The metal door located in the inner hearth of some fireplaces that leads to an ash pit is known as the _____. A cavity underneath the firebox that is used as a receptacle for ashes and is accessible by means of a cleanout door is known as the _____. A metal door located at the base of the chimney that leads to the ash pit is called the _____.

Diagram Study

Identifying the components of a structure from a diagram helps you to learn them more quickly and helps you to complete the home inspection report. Fill in the numbered blanks on the diagram where indicated. Refer back to your textbook for a fuller explanation of these components.

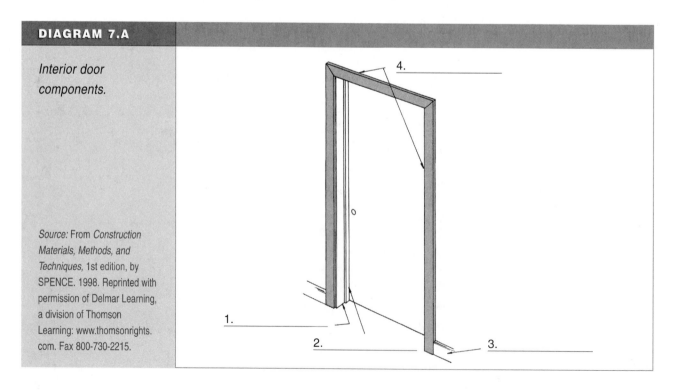

DIAGRAM 7.A

Interior door components.

Source: From Construction Materials, Methods, and Techniques, 1st edition, by SPENCE. 1998. Reprinted with permission of Delmar Learning, a division of Thomson Learning: www.thomsonrights.com. Fax 800-730-2215.

INSPECTING THE PLUMBING, HEATING, AND AIR-CONDITIONING SYSTEMS

After reading and reviewing Chapter 8 and answering the multiple-choice questions for that chapter, complete the following exercises. Refer back to your textbook to assist with your answers. Use the Answer Key at the end of the Workbook to check your responses.

Key Terms

The following key terms match those found in your textbook. Review the meaning of these terms and refer to the textbook for further clarification if needed.

- **Aquifer:** below ground-level rock bed over which water flows.
- **Backflow preventer:** keeps water from backing up in the water supply or drainage system.
- **Boilers:** used to transfer heat from a fuel source to a fluid, such as water, and are constructed from cast iron, steel, or copper.
- **BTU:** abbreviation for British thermal unit; a measure of heat energy, a BTU is the amount of heat required to raise the temperature of one pound of water by one degree Fahrenheit.
- **Cesspool:** a pit (sometimes lined with plastic) composed of stones and gravel through which raw sewage collects; it's a health and safety hazard and a code violation.
- **Cleanout:** a pipe fitted with a removable plug to assist in dislodging a pipe obstruction.
- **Compressor:** an air conditioner component that creates a flow of refrigerant from one part of the system to the other.
- **Condenser:** an air conditioner component that liquefies the refrigerant gas by cooling it.
- **Convector:** a heat-emitting unit in which heat is produced by the movement of air around a metal surface.
- **Evaporator:** an air conditioner component that takes heat from the air surrounding it and brings it to the refrigerant.
- **Float valve:** used to control water levels in tanks.
- **Forced warm air system:** a type of heating system that contains a fan or blower, a heat source such as gas or oil, a heat exchanger, and filters; works by extracting cool air from indoors and outdoors and passing this cool air through the heat sources.
- **Freon:** the most commonly used refrigerant in air conditioners.
- **Gate valve:** a type of valve generally used as the main water shutoff valve to the property.
- **Globe valve:** a type of valve that can either adjust or stop the flow of water; it is used at points where it is needed infrequently such as in bathrooms.
- **Heat exchanger:** the area where combustion or the burning of fuel for heat takes place in a furnace or hot water heater.

- **Hydronic system:** a type of system that heats and cools liquids such as water.

- **Main soil stack:** a drainage pipe that connects to the house drain where waste leaves the system.

- **Main vent stack:** is the top of the main soil stack and connects to all of the home's toilets.

- **Nonpotable water:** wastewater or recycled water used in plumbing fixtures that is not safe for consumption.

- **Plenum:** a large metal conduit box in the form of a duct located inside the heating system where hot air builds up pressure and is then forced out to room-heating elements.

- **Plumbing fixture:** an appliance requiring a water supply and drainage system.

- **Potable water:** water that is safe for drinking.

- **Pressure regulator valve (PRV):** also called a pressure-reducing valve, it is used to, limit, reduce, and automatically maintain the pressure of water within predetermined parameters.

- **Refrigerant:** any substance that produces a cooling effect by absorbing heat as it vaporizes (disperses into the air).

- **Septic system:** a household wastewater treatment system consisting of a house sewer, a septic tank, a distribution box, and an absorption field or a seepage pit.

- **Soil or waste stacks:** vertical pipes into which waste flows from waste pipes connected to each plumbing fixture.

- **Steam system:** a heating system that consists of a boiler, where steam is produced, and a system of pipes that conveys the steam to radiators, convectors, or other types of room-heating elements.

- **Temperature pressure relief valve:** used in hot water and steam systems, this valve allows hot water and steam to escape if the water temperature and pressure buildup are too high for the equipment.

- **Thermocouple:** a device that automatically closes the gas valve that controls the flow of gas and stops its flow if the pilot light goes out.

- **Thermostat:** a control device that automatically responds to temperature changes by opening and closing an electric circuit.

- **Trap:** a curved section of drainpipe that fills with water and provides a seal that prevents sewer gasses from entering a structure.

- **Valve:** a device used to regulate the flow of a liquid or gas; it may force the flow in a certain direction.

- **Vent system:** a system of pipes that provides a flow of air to and from a drainage system; it permits gases and odors to circulate up through the system and escape into the air.

- **Water hammer arrestor:** contains a hydraulic piston that absorbs the shock waves produced by sudden changes in water flow; it reduces the commonly heard banging in pipes.

Learning Objectives

The following objectives were discussed in your textbook. Write your responses to these objectives in the space provided.

1. List the items that are included in the inspection of the plumbing, heating, and cooling systems.

   _____

   _____

   _____

   _____

   _____

   _____

   _____

2. Describe the general procedure for the vent and pipe system inspection.

   _____

   _____

   _____

   _____

   _____

   _____

   _____

3. Describe the general procedure for inspecting the heating and cooling systems.

   _____

   _____

   _____

   _____

   _____

   _____

   _____

4. Explain how to examine the plumbing fixtures.

   _____

   _____

   _____

   _____

   _____

   _____

True–False Questions

Indicate whether the statement is True or False.

_____ 1. Nonpotable water is safe for consumption.

_____ 2. In most current applications, galvanized steel pipe is used to carry drinking water through the service supply line.

_____ 3. Home inspection standards generally require that the inspector test the drinking water quality.

_____ 4. Wells are generally situated near the wastewater disposal system.

_____ 5. The only plumbing fixture that must be connected to a vent pipe is the toilet.

_____ 6. When the inspector examines the septic system, he or she need not examine the absorption field.

_____ 7. A type of pipe fitting is a coupling.

_____ 8. To examine the pipe system, the inspector should always close the main water shutoff valve.

_____ 9. Pipe condensation can be avoided if the pipe is wrapped with insulation.

_____ 10. A disadvantage of copper pipe is that it can only be installed in warm weather climates.

_____ 11. A forced warm air heating system has circulator pumps that propel heated water to the convectors.

_____ 12. Steam heat uses a boiler and a system of pipes that conveys the heat to the radiators.

_____ 13. Radiant heat warms objects and people rather than the room itself.

_____ 14. Soot in and around the furnace may indicate that the vent pipe is clogged.

_____ 15. For inspection purposes, inspectors should turn on the heating and cooling systems in all kinds of weather.

_____ 16. When an air conditioner is combined with a furnace, pipes carry the refrigerant from the compressor to the evaporator coil inside the furnace.

_____ 17. Air-to-water heat pumps can heat both a living space and swimming pool.

_____ 18. If inspectors find ice buildup on the evaporator coil, they should first defrost the coil and then attempt to repair it.

_____ 19. A hot water tank requires a pipe extension attached to the temperature pressure relief valve for safety reasons.

_____ 20. When inspecting the faucets, inspectors should only check one or two and not every faucet in the house.

How Would You Respond?

Analyze the following situations and decide how the individuals should handle them in accordance with what you have learned.

1. David, a home inspector, has clients that are concerned about the water quality and functionality of the well and septic system located on the property they are buying. How might David handle their concerns?

_____

_____

_____

_____

_____

_____

2. While inspecting a toilet, Curtis gently grasps the toilet base to see if it is securely fastened to the floor. In doing so, a crack appears on the side of the toilet. What liability, if any, does Curtis have for the damage?

_____

_____

_____

_____

_____

_____

3. While inspecting a gas hot water heater, Diane detects a strong odor of gas and verifies the presence of gas with her gas meter. What are the steps she should take to handle this problem?

_____

_____

_____

_____

_____

_____

Key Term Review

Fill in the term that *best* completes each sentence.

1. Constructed from cast iron, steel, or copper, this heating vessel used to transfer heat from a fuel source, such as water, is called a(n) _____.

2. A type of valve that limits the water pressure on certain heating equipment is known as a(n) _____.

3. A(n) _____ is a substance that produces a cooling effect by absorbing heat as it vaporizes. The most commonly used substance for this purpose is called _____.

4. Water that is safe for drinking is known as _____. Water that is unsuitable for drinking is known as _____.

5. A(n) _____ is an appliance requiring water supply and drainage systems.

6. The _____ is the area in certain types of furnaces and hot water heaters where combustion, or the burning of fuel, takes place.

7. A type of system that requires that liquids, such as water, to be heated or cooled is called a(n) _____.

8. A type of valve generally used as the main water shutoff valve to the property is called a(n) _____. A(n) _____ is a type of valve that can either adjust or stop the flow of water and is installed where the valve is not frequently used.

9. A type of drainage pipe that connects to the house drain where the waste leaves the system is known as a(n) _____.

10. A large metal conduit box in the form of a duct located inside the heating system where hot air builds up pressure and is then forced out to the heat registers is known as the _____.

11. A type of heating system that is composed of a fan or blower and works by extracting cool air from indoors and outdoors is known as a(n) _____. A type of heating system that consists of a boiler and a system of pipes is known as a(n) _____.

12. A type of valve used to control the water level in tanks is called a(n) _____. A type of valve that keeps water from backing up in a water supply or drainage system is known as a(n) _____. A type of valve that allows hot water and steam to escape if the water temperature and pressure buildup are too high for the equipment is known as a(n) _____.

13. A(n) _____ is a measure of heat energy.

14. A drainpipe that is fitted with a removable plug to assist with dislodging a pipe obstruction is known as a(n) _____.

15. A heat-emitting unit where heat is produced by the movement of air around a metal surface is called a(n) _____.

16. A(n) _____ is an air-conditioning component that creates a flow of refrigerant from one part of the system to the other. The component in an air conditioner that liquefies the refrigerant gas by cooling it is called the _____. An air-conditioning component that takes heat from the air surrounding it and brings it to the refrigerant is known as the _____.

17. A pit that is a violation of plumbing codes and through which raw sewage collects is called a(n) _____.

18. A below ground-level rock bed over which water flows is called a(n) _____.

19. A(n) _____ is a private household waste treatment system.

20. Vertical pipes into which waste flows through drainage pipes from each plumbing fixture is called a(n) _____.

Diagram Study

Identifying the components of a structure from a diagram helps you to learn them more quickly and helps you to complete the home inspection report. Fill in the numbered blanks on the diagrams where indicated. Refer back to your textbook for a fuller explanation of these components.

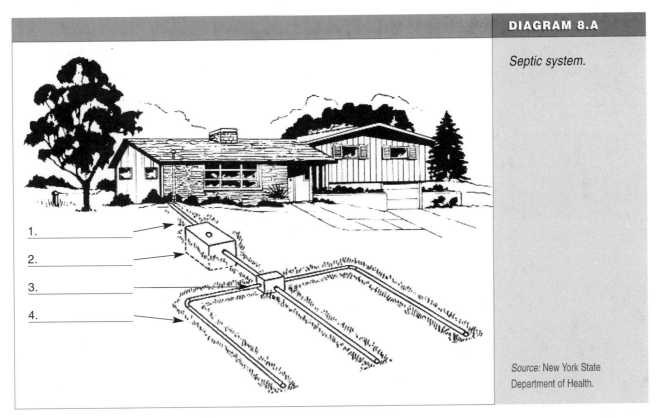

DIAGRAM 8.A

Septic system.

1. _____

2. _____

3. _____

4. _____

Source: New York State Department of Health.

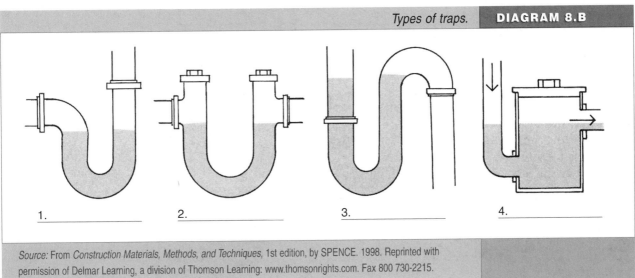

Types of traps. **DIAGRAM 8.B**

1. _____   2. _____   3. _____   4. _____

Source: From *Construction Materials, Methods, and Techniques,* 1st edition, by SPENCE. 1998. Reprinted with permission of Delmar Learning, a division of Thomson Learning: www.thomsonrights.com. Fax 800 730-2215.

DIAGRAM 8.C

Bathroom sink.

Source: From *Construction Materials, Methods, and Techniques,* 1st edition, by SPENCE. 1998. Reprinted with permission of Delmar Learning, a division of Thomson Learning: www.thomsonrights.com. Fax 800 730-2215.

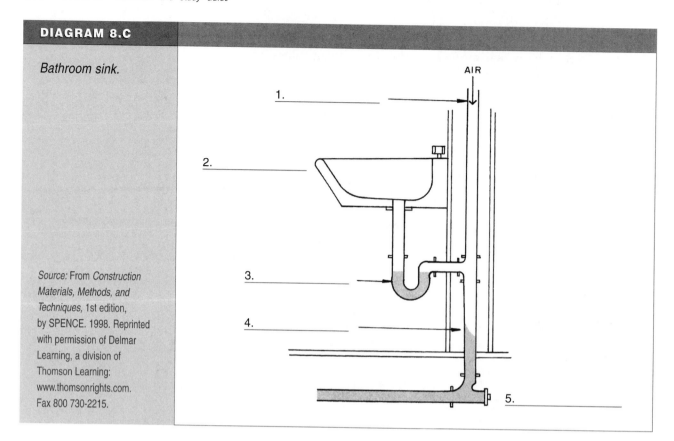

AIR

1.

2.

3.

4.

5.

CHAPTER 9

INSPECTING THE ELECTRICAL SYSTEM

A fter reading and reviewing Chapter 9 and answering the multiple-choice questions for that chapter, complete the following exercises. Refer back to your textbook to assist with your answers. Use the Answer Key at the end of the Workbook to check your responses.

Key Terms

The following key terms match those found in your textbook. Review the meaning of these terms and refer to the textbook for further clarification if needed.

- **Amperage:** the amount of current or electricity flowing through a wire.
- **Branch circuit wiring:** wiring that goes from the main panel board through the walls of the building to the switches and outlets.
- **Bus bars:** conductors on the main panel board that provide electrical connections for fuses or circuit breakers.
- **Circuit:** path that electricity travels.
- **Circuit breakers:** devices on the panel board that trip if the current increases beyond the capacity of the system and switch off the electrical power for a given circuit.
- **Conductors:** wires through which electricity flows; good conductors have little resistance to the flow of electricity.
- **Electric current:** the flow of electrons along a conductor such as a copper wire.
- **Fuse:** a device with an internal metal link that melts and opens the circuit, causing electrical power to stop when overheating occurs.
- **Ground fault circuit interrupter (GFCI):** a device that shuts off a circuit immediately if it senses a short circuit.
- **Insulators:** materials that are poor conductors of electricity and are, therefore, placed around wires to prevent electrical shock.
- **Junction boxes:** contain wiring and are used to provide the necessary space for making electrical connections.
- **Neutral bus bar:** a conductor on the main panel board that is the connection for the neutral and ground wires.
- **Ohm:** a unit of measurement for the resistance to the flow of electricity; a unit of electrical resistance of a conductor.
- **Outlet:** a point on a wiring system where current is taken to supply equipment.
- **Overcurrent protection devices:** respond quickly to ground faults; include the main disconnect, circuit breakers, and fuses.
- **Raceway:** used to support, enclose, and protect electrical wires.
- **Receptacle:** connected to branch circuit wires that supply the current to equipment.
- **Service drop:** aboveground cables that come from the nearest pole connecting to the service entrance conductors of the house or building.

- **Service entrance cable (SE cable):** a single conductor or several conductors, with or without covering, used for aboveground service entrance.
- **Service lateral:** electrical service that runs underground.
- **Service lateral conductors:** conductors installed between the transformers and the meters for underground service.
- **Switch:** used to open and close electrical circuits and allow current to flow to appliances.
- **Transformer:** used to change alternating current from one voltage to another.
- **Voltage:** the electrical pressure that pushes through wires.

Learning Objectives

The following objectives were discussed in your textbook. Write your responses to these objectives in the space provided.

1. List the items that are included in the electrical system inspection.

   _____

   _____

   _____

   _____

   _____

   _____

   _____

2. Define basic electrical system terminology.

   _____

   _____

   _____

   _____

   _____

   _____

   _____

3. Describe the general procedure for the electrical system inspection.

   _____

   _____

   _____

   _____

   _____

   _____

   _____

True–False Questions

Indicate whether the statement is True or False.

_____ 1. A unit of electric power is expressed in watts or kilowatts.

_____ 2. Transformers are used to reduce voltage levels coming into the building.

_____ 3. Home inspection standards require that the inspector note the amperage and voltage rating for the building.

_____ 4. Home inspection standards require that the inspector inspect the alarm system and components if they are part of the structure.

_____ 5. Aboveground incoming electrical service is known as service lateral.

_____ 6. Copper ground rods are commonly used as a grounding electrode.

_____ 7. Electrical meters are never located inside the structure.

_____ 8. The main disconnect is always located on the panel board.

_____ 9. Generally, when fuses are blown, they must be recharged and reinstalled in the fuse panel.

_____ 10. An aluminum conductor has a lower resistance to electrical current than a copper conductor.

_____ 11. Knob and tube wiring is currently being installed in residential properties.

_____ 12. According to the NEC, extension cords can take the place of permanent wiring.

_____ 13. Wiring should match the ampere rating of the circuit breaker or fuse.

_____ 14. To comply with certain building codes, junction boxes may not be mounted back-to-back.

_____ 15. Two-prong receptacles generally have a ground slot.

_____ 16. The most commonly used switch is the single-pole, single-throw switch.

_____ 17. According to the NEC, GFCIs must be installed within six feet of the edge of a wet bar sink.

_____ 18. Circuit analyzers are unreliable as a diagnostic tool.

_____ 19. Home inspectors should check that receptacles are properly polarized.

_____ 20. To inspect the electrical system, inspectors should turn off the power to the building.

How Would You Respond?

Analyze the following situations and decide how the individuals should handle them in accordance with what you have learned.

1. Vanessa, while inspecting a home, has a client who insists on touching the main panel board while Vanessa examines it. The client receives an electric shock, but is not injured. How could she have avoided this situation?

_____

_____

_____

_____

_____

_____

2. While examining the main panel board and the junction box, Craig is not sure, but thinks that aluminum branch circuit wiring might have been used. He doesn't want to alarm his client about a costly repair because he is not sure about his observations. How should he handle the situation?

_____

_____

_____

_____

_____

_____

3. LeGrand is performing his first inspection and does not feel confident about the electrical inspection. He is confused by all of the aboveground wires coming into the house and cannot tell them apart. He is also not happy about examining the main panel board. What should he do?

_____

_____

_____

_____

_____

_____

Key Term Review

Fill in the term that *best* completes each sentence.

1. Conductors on the main panel board that provide electrical connections for fuses or circuit breakers are known as _____.

2. The flow of electrons along a conductor, such as a copper wire, is defined as

   _____.

3. A device that melts and opens the circuit, causing electrical power to stop when overheating occurs, is called a(n) _____.

4. Wiring that travels from the main panel board through the walls of the building to the outlets where the current is used is known as _____.

5. _____ is the amount of current or electricity flowing through the wire.

6. _____ trip and switch off the electrical power for a given circuit if the current increases beyond the capacity of the system.

7. _____ respond quickly to ground faults and include the main disconnect, circuit breakers, and fuses.

8. A path that electricity travels is known as a(n) _____.

9. Electricity moves along wires that are known as _____.

10. Aboveground cables that come from the nearest pole connecting to the service entrance conductors of the house or building are known as a(n) _____.

11. _____ are used to change alternating current from one voltage to another.

12. A device that shuts off a circuit immediately if it senses a short circuit is called a(n) _____.

13. Materials that are poor conductors of electricity and are placed around wires to prevent electrical shock are known as _____.

14. A(n) _____ is a measurement of the resistance to the flow of electricity.

15. A(n) _____ is used to support, enclose, and protect electrical wires.

16. A single conductor or several conductors, with or without covering, that is used at the aboveground service entrance is known as _____.

17. _____ are used to open and close electrical circuits and allow current to flow to appliances. _____ are connected to branch circuit wires that supply the current to equipment. A(n) _____ is any type of opening including a plug, switch, or light fixture.

18. _____ are installed between the transformers and the meters for underground service.

19. Electrical service that runs from underground is called _____.

20. The electrical pressure that pushes through the wires is known as _____.

Diagram Study

Identifying the components of a structure from a diagram helps you to learn them more quickly and helps you to complete the home inspection report. Fill in the numbered blanks on the diagrams where indicated. Refer back to your textbook for a fuller explanation of these components.

DIAGRAM 9.A   *Service connection type.*

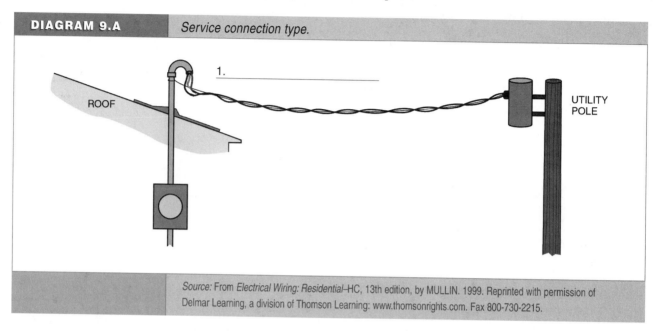

1. _____

ROOF

UTILITY POLE

Source: From *Electrical Wiring: Residential–HC*, 13th edition, by MULLIN. 1999. Reprinted with permission of Delmar Learning, a division of Thomson Learning: www.thomsonrights.com. Fax 800-730-2215.

DIAGRAM 9.B

Service connection type.

Source: From *Electrical Wiring: Residential–HC*, 13th edition, by MULLIN. 1999. Reprinted with permission of Delmar Learning, a division of Thomson Learning: www.thomsonrights.com. Fax 800-730-2215.

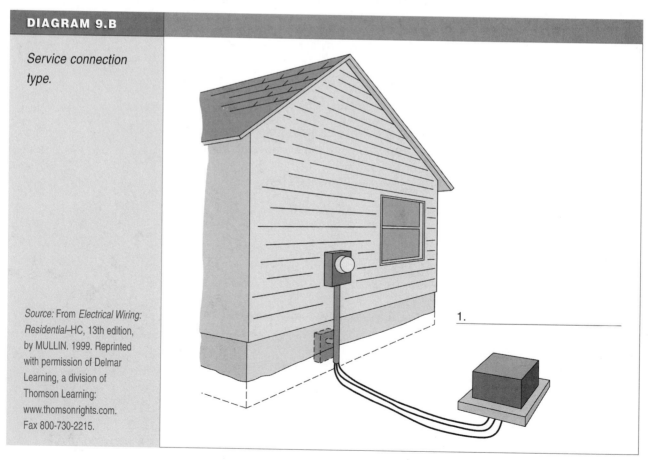

1. _____

CHAPTER 10

RECOGNIZING ENVIRONMENTAL ISSUES

 fter reading and reviewing Chapter 10 and answering the multiple-choice questions for that chapter, complete the following exercises. Refer back to your textbook to assist with your answers. Use the Answer Key at the end of the Workbook to check your responses.

Key Terms

The following key terms match those found in your textbook. Review the meaning of these terms and refer to the textbook for further clarification if needed.

- **Asbestos:** a fibrous material found in rocks and soil.
- **Carpenter ant:** a type of insect that eats wood.
- **Carpenter bee:** a type of insect that eats wood.
- **Electromagnetic field:** occurs anytime electricity flows through a wire; there are two separate fields: an electric field and a magnetic field.
- **Formaldehyde:** a colorless, gaseous chemical compound that is generally present at low, variable concentrations in indoor and outdoor air.
- **Friable:** the tendency of an asbestos-containing product to crumble easily and emit fibers.
- **Lead:** a toxic metallic element found in soil, water, and paint.
- **Powderpost beetle:** a type of insect that eats wood.
- **Radon:** a colorless, odorless, tasteless, radioactive gas that is present worldwide in the environment as a byproduct of the natural decay of uranium in the earth.
- **Termite:** a type of insect that eats wood.
- **Toxic substance:** an element capable of causing adverse human health or environmental effects through exposure to even low levels.
- **Underground storage tank:** used for the bulk storage of chemicals and petroleum.

Learning Objectives

The following objectives were discussed in your textbook. Write your responses to these objectives in the space provided.

1. Describe how a home inspector can protect himself from liability problems during the inspection of environmental concerns.

_____

_____

_____

_____

_____

_____

2. Describe the environmental concerns that may be tested by a home inspector.

_____

_____

_____

_____

_____

3. Explain other environmental concerns, not tested by a home inspector, that affect real property.

_____

_____

_____

_____

_____

True–False Questions

Indicate whether the statement is True or False.

_____ 1. Home inspectors require a special certification to perform any environmental test.

_____ 2. Pollutants inside a home may include pressed-wood furniture.

_____ 3. Formaldehyde poses no threat to the home environment.

_____ 4. Tests for water flow are measured according to pounds per square inch.

_____ 5. In public water supplies, the water is tested once a month for bacterial contamination.

_____ 6. Well water quality need not meet the same standards as the public water supply.

_____ 7. To test well water quality, only one water sample is generally taken to the lab.

_____ 8. If a home is supplied with water taken from a groundwater source, there is less potential for a radon problem than if the home is supplied with water from a municipal source.

_____ 9. No level of radon is considered safe.

_____ 10. The danger of radon is that it is radioactive.

_____ 11. An alpha-tract detector is a short-term measurement of radon in the home.

_____ 12. Home inspectors must be licensed to place charcoal radon test canisters in the home.

_____ 13. In some homes, plumbing systems can be a source of lead contamination.

_____ 14. Lead may be present in soil surrounding the property.

_____ 15. There is little or no lead present in paint in homes built before 1978.

_____ 16. The home inspector can use test swabs to determine the presence of lead in certain objects.

_____ 17. If found in the home, total removal of even small amounts of asbestos-containing material is the recommended procedure.

_____ 18. Electric fields can be shielded by walls, trees, or hills.

_____ 19. Should a property have a leak in an underground heating oil storage tank, the EPA will always assist in funding the cleanup.

_____ 20. Termite-damaged wood can be recognized by mud tubes that are lined with soil.

How Would You Respond?

Analyze the following situations and decide how the individuals should handle them in accordance with what you have learned.

1. Justin tests the water flow on the Desperate's well and finds it to be only 1.5 gpm, a substandard result. Justin's clients, the buyers, are not present during the test. The Desperate's ask Justin not to report this finding yet because they are going to complete a major overhaul of the well, including the installation of a new pump, prior to the sale. How should Justin handle this?

_____

_____

_____

_____

_____

2. Tracy and her clients are proceeding through the inspection of a property they want to buy when Tracy notices high-tension wires in a thicket of trees about 30 yards from the house. What are Tracy's duties here?

_____

_____

_____

_____

3. When Ari enters a subject property, he is overcome by a smell of must, mildew, and rot. The air is thick with unpleasant odors and there are no signs of ventilation. The carpet is worn and looks like a series of pets had made it their home. The major systems of the property are in working order. How does Ari communicate this to his clients?

_____

_____

_____

_____

Key Term Review

Fill in the term that *best* completes each sentence.

1. Tanks located underground and utilized for the bulk storage of chemicals and petroleum are known as _____.

2. A fibrous element used in many construction applications and capable of causing adverse health and environmental effects is known as _____. Because it has a tendency to crumble with hand pressure, it is described as _____.

3. _____, _____, _____, and _____ are all insects that eat wood.

4. Anytime electricity flows through a wire, a(n) _____ is created.

5. A colorless, gaseous chemical compound that is generally present at low concentrations in indoor and outdoor air and was used in foam insulation is known as _____.

6. An element capable of causing adverse human health or environmental effects under conditions of exposure to even low levels is known as a(n) _____.

7. A radioactive gas measured in picocuries is called _____.

8. A toxic element found in paint, soil, and water that is particularly dangerous to children when ingested is known as _____.

Diagram Study

Identifying items from a diagram helps you to learn them more quickly and helps you to complete the home inspection report. Fill in the numbered blanks on the diagram where indicated. Refer back to your textbook for a fuller explanation of the items.

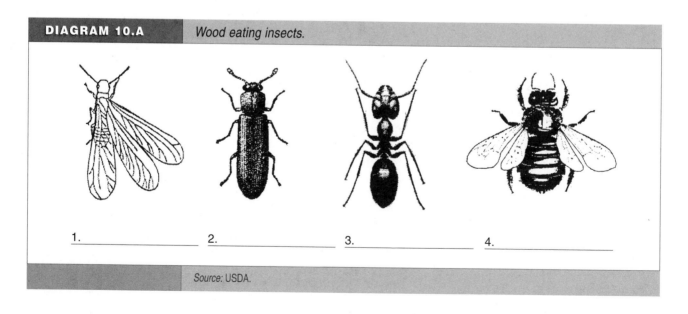

DIAGRAM 10.A   *Wood eating insects.*

1. _____   2. _____   3. _____   4. _____

Source: USDA.

50-QUESTION HOME INSPECTION DIAGNOSTIC EXAM

he following exam is diagnostic. It is divided into categories that match your textbook chapters. This format allows you to pinpoint those areas where you need further study. Pay attention to the wrong choices if you do not know them. Some of these wrong choices may appear on another exam!

Choose the letter that *best* answers the question. Each question is worth two points. The passing grade is 70 percent.

Chapter 1

An Introduction to the Professional Home Inspection

1. Which of the following is TRUE?
   A. The ability of a home inspector to work well with others is not important.
   B. Home inspectors do not have the option of being independent contractors.
   C. Home inspectors may review the property condition disclosure form.
   D. Home inspectors may not perform extra services unless specifically licensed to do so.

2. Credentials for home inspectors must include which of the following?
   A. engineering license
   B. college degree in building sciences
   C. electrical or plumbing license
   D. none of the above

3. To perform extra services such as a water quality evaluation, home inspectors must:
   A. have a special license
   B. bring samples to certified labs for analysis or recommend other professionals
   C. take special training classes prior to performing any extra services
   D. obtain the permission of the local building department

Chapter 2

The Home Inspection Business

4. Liability coverage is important to home inspectors because of the existence of:
   A. latent defects
   B. caveat emptor
   C. property condition disclosure
   D. states that do not have a licensure program for home inspectors

5. Danny is opening his own home inspection office. In preparation for opening, which of the following items is a task that he should NOT do?
   A. investigate licensure requirements
   B. create an income and expense projection
   C. think of a business name
   D. draft a pre-inspection agreement

6. One of the major advantages of being an independent contractor is:
   A. a guarantee of full-time work
   B. paid sick leave
   C. the freedom to work when one chooses
   D. a dependable fixed income

Chapter 3

Land Use Regulations

7. Which of the following is a public restriction on private property?
   A. setback requirements
   B. eminent domain
   C. deed restriction
   D. deed covenant

8. Which of the following is TRUE regarding building codes?
    A. Home inspectors must enforce the building code for their particular municipality.
    B. Home inspectors must report all code violations found in the properties they inspect.
    C. Home inspectors do not have a duty to enforce building codes.
    D. Only licensed home inspectors have a duty to enforce building codes.

9. If a utility company runs underground cables through a private property, the company's right to access the land is called:
    A. the power of eminent domain
    B. an easement
    C. escheat
    D. condemnation

Chapter 4

Home Inspection Procedure and Reporting

10. Which of the following tools would a home inspector be LEAST likely to need when performing a home inspection?
    A. circuit tester
    B. level
    C. hammer
    D. thermometer

11. Tom Trusting completes a home inspection for the Demerits and delivers the completed report to them. When he asks for payment, they tell him that, although they are satisfied with the inspection, they will not have the money to pay him for six months. Which of the following applies?
    A. Tom should not have delivered the report until he was paid in full for his services.
    B. Tom should have performed a credit check on his clients.
    C. Tom's situation is typical and there is no way around it.
    D. Tom should always collect his fee before he sets foot on the property.

12. The Wantmores tell Roger, a home inspector, that they had expected him to inspect the swimming pool on the property. Roger had not inspected the pool and tells the Wantmores that he had described the scope of his inspection in the:
    A. disclaimer
    B. errors and omissions policy
    C. checklist
    D. standards of practice

13. Why is the pre-inspection agreement important?
    A. It gives only the credentials of the inspector.
    B. It describes the parties' agreement about the scope of the inspection.
    C. It is required by law.
    D. It protects the property owner.

14. After an inspection of a property that the Nuliweds expect to purchase, their home inspector, Justine, informs them that the house needs $25,000 worth of work to make it habitable and that they should reconsider the purchase. Which of the following applies?
    A. Justine had every right to share her feelings.
    B. Justine can describe the problems with the property, but she should not advise the clients about the purchase of the property.
    C. Justine can only quote the property's value and nothing else.
    D. Justine should only state her feelings about the purchase of the property if asked by the clients.

15. Oliver, a home inspector and not a professional engineer, tells his clients that the property is structurally unsound and gives his reasons. Oliver's statement is:
    A. completely acceptable based on his information and expertise
    B. unacceptable because only engineers can comment on the structure of the house
    C. acceptable only if the home inspection report supports his comments in detail
    D. acceptable if Oliver is licensed or certified as a home inspector in his state

Chapter 5

Inspecting the Site

16. The land's ability to draw off surface water is called:
    A. grading
    B. slope
    C. erosion
    D. drainage

17. When the water table can be expected to extend beyond the top of the footing, the use of which of the following is indicated?
    A. drain tile
    B. weepholes
    C. control joints
    D. trusses

18. When retaining walls have inadequate drainage, they are subject to collapse due to which of the following?
    A. slope gradient
    B. surface runoff
    C. wind erosion
    D. hydrostatic pressure

19. The horizontal surface of the stair is known as the:
    A. riser
    B. stringer
    C. tread
    D. carriage

20. Decks are generally constructed from which of the following?
    A. brick
    B. pressure-treated wood
    C. concrete
    D. asphalt

21. Numerous soft spots in an asphalt driveway may most likely be an indicator of:
    A. overuse of salt
    B. drainage problems
    C. tree roots growing under the driveway
    D. soil movement

22. In concrete retaining walls, vertical cracks that appear open toward the top of the wall and then become narrow toward the bottom may indicate a problem with:
    A. settlement
    B. drainage
    C. hydrostatic pressure
    D. none of the above

Chapter 6

Inspecting the Exterior

23. A new type of wood foundation designed to keep moisture away from the foundation wall is known as:
    A. precast styrofoam block foundation
    B. permanent wood foundation
    C. exterior insulating finish system
    D. brick veneer foundation

24. When Nancy observes a bedroom wall in the house she is inspecting, she notices a large bulge in the drywall. The wall is not damp. What should she do?
    A. Cut through a small section of drywall to check the studs.
    B. Report her observations on the home inspection report and indicate that there may be a problem with the wall framing.
    C. Do and say nothing because the bulge is not significant.
    D. Peel back a small piece of wallpaper to check the bare drywall.

25. The material inside the window pane is known as:
    A. a light
    B. a stile
    C. a rail
    D. glazing

26. The main purpose of a roof shingle is:
    A. to decorate
    B. to provide waterproofing for the roof
    C. to insulate the roof
    D. to reflect the ultraviolet rays

27. Once all framing members are in, which of the following is placed directly over the frame?
   A. sheathing
   B. siding
   C. stucco
   D. felt paper

28. The main potential problem with an improperly installed exterior insulating finish system is:
   A. normal expansion cracks
   B. water penetration
   C. settlement
   D. hydrostatic pressure

Chapter 7

Inspecting the Interior

29. Evander has completed his inspection when his client notices a two-inch-diameter stain on the entrance way ceiling that he had missed. What should he do?
   A. Note the observation of the stain on the home inspection report.
   B. Go upstairs to ascertain the source of the stain, if possible.
   C. Tell his clients that they must pay him extra to investigate the stain because his inspection has been completed.
   D. Tell his clients that ceiling stains are generally not important and to forget about it.

30. Most walls are composed of which material?
   A. plaster
   B. metal
   C. gypsum
   D. wood

31. The first consideration when inspecting an interior floor is to:
   A. check its condition for aesthetic appearance
   B. find out if it is level
   C. measure it
   D. all of the above

32. Which of the following is TRUE with regard to the R-value?
   A. It is a measure of heat energy.
   B. It is rarely addressed in building codes.
   C. Home inspectors should not analyze or report on it.
   D. The larger the R-value, the smaller the degree of insulation.

33. Which of the following is NOT something that must be inspected in the attic?
   A. hidden wiring
   B. ventilation
   C. roof rafters
   D. building envelope

34. Which of the following statements regarding a detached garage is TRUE?
   A. Dirt floors are acceptable and pose no problem.
   B. Extension cord wiring to operate an overhead door is acceptable.
   C. Detached garages violate most building codes.
   D. The exterior of the detached garage should be examined using the same criteria as the main structure.

Chapter 8

Inspecting the Plumbing, Heating, and Air-Conditioning Systems

35. An efficient way to determine whether a water supply pipe is composed of lead is to:
   A. examine its color; lead in water has a darker color.
   B. use a small magnet; if it does not adhere to the pipe, it is not lead.
   C. taste the drinking water; lead has a gritty texture and metallic taste.
   D. check the building codes because they document the year that lead pipes used in the water supply was banned.

36. Wells should be built to a depth of more than:
   A. 5 feet
   B. 10 feet
   C. 15 feet
   D. 20 feet

37. The horizontal slope of the drainpipe is generally regulated by:
    A. the architect
    B. the builder
    C. plumbing codes
    D. the plumber

38. A type of valve that contains a hydraulic piston that absorbs the shock waves produced by sudden changes in water flow is called a:
    A. water hammer arrestor
    B. backflow preventer
    C. temperature pressure relief valve
    D. globe valve

39. Which of the following is NOT an example of a hydronic system?
    A. boilers
    B. steam furnaces
    C. gas hot water furnaces
    D. forced warm air furnaces

40. Which of the following is beyond the scope of a typical furnace inspection?
    A. locating the oil storage tank if the furnace is oil-fired
    B. checking the location and functionality of the thermostat
    C. determining that the heat supply is evenly balanced and distributed
    D. checking for ventilation around the furnace

41. Which component of the air-conditioning system is located outdoors?
    A. compressor
    B. condensate tray
    C. air filter
    D. fan

Chapter 9

Inspecting the Electrical System

42. Which of the following is TRUE regarding the National Electric Code (NEC)?
    A. It is a national standard for electrical installation.
    B. All properties must comply with current code requirements.
    C. Home inspectors must be familiar with all aspects of the code.
    D. The code is updated every year.

43. The minimum electrical service entering a property should be:
    A. 50 amps
    B. 100 amps
    C. 150 amps
    D. 200 amps

44. To protect cables from damage, which of the following is often installed to enclose, support, and protect them?
    A. an insulator
    B. a raceway
    C. an overcurrent protection device
    D. a junction box

45. Which of the following is FALSE?
    A. Conductors of specific sizes must have the proper size fuse or circuit breaker to carry the current.
    B. Fuses or circuit breakers must be identified as to their ampere rating.
    C. Fuses and circuit breakers protect the electrical system from overload and shorts.
    D. Most fuses are reusable.

46. A pipe-like enclosure used to house current-carrying conductors is called:
    A. conduit
    B. BX cable
    C. Romex cable
    D. Type USE cable

47. The path of electricity is known as a:
    A. cycle
    B. frequency
    C. circuit
    D. raceway

Chapter 10

Recognizing Environmental Issues

48. One of the most important considerations with certain types of environmental testing done by a home inspector is that:
    A. it may open the home inspector to certain liability issues
    B. inspectors cannot charge extra for these services
    C. most of the tests are costly to perform
    D. most of the tests are more time-consuming than they are worth

49. If liquefied propane is used as a fuel source, it should be located:
    A. outdoors directly next to the house
    B. in the basement in a well-ventilated space
    C. outdoors with a safe clearance from the house and away from entryways or windows
    D. anywhere on the property that is convenient for the property owner

50. Prudent avoidance policies pertain particularly to which of the following:
    A. radon
    B. electromagnetic fields
    C. asbestos
    D. lead

Chapter 1

Learning Objectives

1. A home inspection is a thorough examination of the exterior and interior of residential property including the grounds, the structure, and the mechanical systems that comprise the property to determine structural defects, broken or obsolete components, and damage due to water, wear and tear, and other conditions. The main purpose of most residential home inspections is to evaluate the property for potential buyers and other interested parties relative to the contact of sale.

2. The business of home inspection is directly related to the real estate industry; thus, home inspectors are needed as long as there are buyers and sellers of residential properties. Home inspectors can own and operate their own businesses with a comparatively small overhead and can work either full- or part-time.

3. The property condition disclosure form is furnished by the seller and offers details about the subject property. Home inspectors can review the form and compare it to the home inspection report for a fuller and more accurate picture of the property's condition.

4. Currently, several states require licensure, registration, or certification of home inspectors. Licensure is under consideration in many other state legislatures. Home inspectors must check licensure requirements prior to practicing home inspection.

5. Home inspection organizations offer accreditation, education, conferences, networking, and referrals.

True–False Questions

1. F	4. F	7. F	10. T
2. T	5. T	8. F	
3. F	6. F	9. F	

How Would You Respond?

1. Initially, Kyle might consult a competent accountant and attorney to discuss options for setting up and organizing his business. Interviews with local banks are also necessary to discuss loans, account set up, and charge card vendor arrangements. He might also contact other home inspectors, home inspection organizations, and the local chamber of commerce.

2. Although Aviva is competent to fix the leak, she is performing a home inspection and should complete the home inspection before rendering other services. Should she decide to complete repairs during the course of her home inspection work, Aviva should have proper licensure and insurance for the specific work she is doing.

3. Neil should thank the property owner for sharing the property condition disclosure form with him. He can explain to the home owner that he will compare and contrast the home owner's findings with his and will be glad to discuss any differences. The property condition disclosure form is not a substitute for a professional home inspection and under no circumstances should a home inspector use it as

such. Should the home owner refuse to allow Neil to complete a proper inspection, Neil must decline to perform the inspection and inform his client.

Key Term Review

1. home inspection report
2. property condition disclosure form
3. home inspector
4. home inspection

Chapter 2

Learning Objectives

1. Some advantages of owning your own business include the freedom to make your own decisions, personal satisfaction, and generating income when another job is not available. On the down side, you may not have a steady income to depend on, especially at first.

2. Types of business organizations include the sole proprietorship—owned by one individual; the partnership—owned by two or more individuals who do not necessarily have an equal ownership interest; the corporation—protects shareholders from personal liability and certain tax consequences; and limited liability companies—members are not personally liable for the LLCs acts and the LLC is taxed as a partnership.

3. Professional liability insurance covers individuals and business organizations for claims made by third parties. Professional liability insurance is referred to most commonly as errors and omissions (E&O) insurance.

4. According to the IRS code and state laws, an employee is one who receives a salary, benefits, works set hours, and is supervised by the employer. An independent contractor is one who works when he chooses, is not directly supervised by the employer, and is generally paid by the job on a fee or commission basis. The independent contractor does not receive a salary or benefits.

5. Some of the items to consider when opening a home inspection business include checking on licensure requirements, creating an income and expense projection, opening a bank account, deciding on a business name, assembling furniture and equipment, printing stationary and business cards, having required contracts drawn by an attorney, deciding on the location for the business, and investigating referral possibilities.

6. Certain issues that should be discussed with a prospective employer include the following: types of properties inspected, travel requirements, employee or independent contractor employment arrangement, reimbursement for out-of-pocket expenses, necessary tool or equipment purchases, transportation requirements, work space and clerical support availability, types of office systems, work availability and leads, and company support and assistance.

True–False Questions

1. F	5. T	9. T	13. F
2. F	6. F	10. F	14. F
3. T	7. F	11. T	15. T
4. F	8. F	12. F	16. F

How Would You Respond?

1. Soldana can offer a partnership to her brother. The partnership can be any percentage of ownership that Soldana and her brother agree on. Soldana is the working or general partner and her brother is a silent or limited partner who is not actively involved in the business. Soldana must check the licensure and certification laws in her state to determine whether this type of partnership arrangement for home inspectors is permissible.

2. Michael can hire an attorney to defend him against the allegations. Because he does not carry liability insurance, the cost of his defense and any award made to the plaintiffs are his responsibility.

3. Theresa probably cannot have it all. If she wants sick pay, health insurance, and paid vacations, she should work as a full-time employee. Although employers may offer independent contractors bonuses, compensation generally is limited to a fee or commission for services rendered.

Key Term Review

1. partnership
2. latent defect
3. sole proprietorship
4. professional liability insurance or errors and omissions insurance
5. corporation
6. doing business as (d/b/a)
7. independent contractor
8. limited liability company

Chapter 3

Learning Objectives

1. Private control of land is generally in the form of deed restrictions. These restrictions are imposed either by the developer of the original subdivision or by the original owner. These restrictions are in the form of covenants and conditions that run with the land; that is, they are conveyed through subsequent deeds. Public control of land is government control on federal, state, and local levels and exists for the benefit and welfare of the citizens.

2. The four types of public land use controls are police power (the authority of government to control or legislate for the welfare of the citizens), eminent domain (the authority of government to take land for public use), taxation (the authority to tax real property), and escheat (the authority of the state to take the real property of a person who dies without any legal heirs). These controls can be exercised only if the acts benefit the public.

3. Zoning ordinances are generally derived from a master plan. The community and its leaders create the master plan. The purpose of the plan is to avoid haphazard development and to create a community that benefits all residents. The zoning ordinances divide the community into sections that denote different uses. Some of these uses are residential, commercial, and industrial. Various uses can be mixed within a zone. The layout of the zones greatly impacts the quality and utility of the community and its properties.

4. Land is most often used for construction purposes. Building codes, permits, and certificates of occupancy offer a system of standards for building use

and construction. These standards address building materials and design, energy conservation, fire safety, disability issues, and many other areas.

True–False Questions

1. F	5. T	9. F	13. T
2. F	6. F	10. T	
3. F	7. F	11. F	
4. F	8. T	12. F	

How Would You Respond?

1. Justin might research the original subdivision filings that are recorded in the county clerk's office. Justin might ask to check the seller's deed to see if the restriction appears there. If he cannot access these documents, he could track down the subdivision developer.

2. The current beauty parlor–residence combination is an illustration of nonconforming use. This use is authorized until the current users sell the property. Generally, nonconforming uses do not run with the property. The new owners can apply for a special use permit.

3. Although Trevor should be familiar with federal, state, and local building codes, he is not a code inspector. These violations, however, may be noted on the inspection report and discussed with the party who hired him.

Key Term Review

1. variance
2. special use permit
3. certificate of occupancy
4. eminent domain
5. nonconforming use
6. plat
7. setback requirements
8. building permit
9. escheat
10. condemnation
11. subdivision
12. deed restriction
13. taxation
14. easement, right-of-way

Chapter 4

Learning Objectives

1. To gain on-the-job experience, seek out experienced inspectors and accompany them as they inspect homes. Another way to gain experience is to "practice" performing inspections on the homes of friends and family without compensation. Home inspectors can also seek the advice of other technicians working in real estate fields.

2. The basic tools necessary for home inspection include measuring tapes, binoculars, camera equipment, environmental testing equipment (optional), compass, face mask or respirator, electrical circuit tester, hand pick or awl, flashlights, ladders, level, maps, pliers, protective clothing, screwdrivers, hand mirror, thermometer, writing and business supplies, and office equipment and supplies.

3. The clients should be present at the inspection so the inspector can artic-ulate his findings about the subject property. Sellers are sources of information about the property. This information includes the location and age of certain property components. In addition, sellers may be a source of future business if they intend to purchase another home.

4. Prior to performing a home inspection, home inspectors must enter into a pre-inspection agreement with the client. This details the scope of the inspection and the responsibilities of both parties. The inspector has a choice of four differ-ent inspection report forms: the checklist, the rating system, the narrative, and the narrative with checklist or rating system. Whether or not the checklist report is the final form, it is generally used to perform the inspection. A fuller narrative report may be generated from it.

True–False Questions

1. T	6. F	11. F	16. F
2. T	7. F	12. T	17. F
3. F	8. F	13. T	18. F
4. T	9. F	14. F	19. F
5. T	10. T	15. F	20. T

How Would You Respond?

1. Faisal has a number of choices. He may refuse to perform the inspection because $275 is the minimum fee for any size home. He may agree to look at the property prior to the inspection and reassess the fee if warranted.

2. The offer to purchase contract has nothing to do with the contractual rela-tionship between Manny and his clients. Manny should refer the Difficults to their attorney for a further explanation. Manny should refuse to perform the inspection without a pre-inspection agreement.

3. Occasionally, clients are less than truthful about the scope of the inspection. A properly prepared pre-inspection agreement sets forth the particulars concern-ing the inspection's scope. In Rod's case, the contract specifies a 2,500-square-foot home. Rod is not contractually obligated to inspect the Blacklies' 6,500-square-foot home. Rod can renegotiate the contract or refuse to do the inspection. Some inspectors in this uncomfortable position, however, will perform the inspection at the agreed-upon price and chalk it up to experience.

Key Term Review

1. checklist report
2. pre-inspection agreement
3. narrative report
4. statute of limitations

5. disclaimer
6. rating system or checklist
7. rating system report

Chapter 5

Learning Objectives

1. A typical site inspection, according to industry standards, includes the inspection of the following: drainage and grading; landscaping, trees, shrubs, and

other vegetation; retaining walls; walkways, driveways, and other paved and masonry areas; steps and stoops; patios, porches, decks, and balconies; and all railings. Inspectors may perform other services as requested by the client if within the home inspector's scope of knowledge.

2. Drainage is the land's ability to draw off surface water. This can be accomplished naturally or artificially by pipes and other conduits such as drainage tiles. Proper grading ensures that surface water is directed away from the foundation. Water that is not directed away from the foundation will eventually penetrate the foundation wall, causing moisture problems including mold and mildew, heaving, cracking, and the total collapse of the foundation wall.

3. The water table is the uppermost boundary of the groundwater. The main problem with a high water table is that it can cause hydrostatic pressure on the floor slab. This hydrostatic pressure, in turn, causes the floor slab to buckle or heave upward. Should the water table drop with a corresponding decrease in pressure, the floor can sink. This floor movement can cause cracking and heaving of both the floor slab and the foundation wall. Footing drain tiles are regularly used to counteract problems associated with a high water table.

4. Landscaping concerns include overgrown trees and other vegetation that block sunlight from windows; overgrown and crowded shrubs promoting pest infestation; leaking and clogged gutter downspouts; and the drainage, strength, and stability of retaining walls. Inspection concerns for walkways, driveways, and other paved and masonry areas include material that is cracked, rutted, or crumbling and deterioration that presents a safety hazard. Steps and stoop concerns include the spacing of the balusters, deterioration of the step material, sinking or tilting of the stairway, and the absence of a stair rail. Concerns for patios, porches, attached decks, and balconies include the condition of the material, deterioration that poses a trip hazard, absence of a rail, stability, moisture conditions, and supports free from rot and decay.

True–False Questions

1. T	6. F	11. F	16. F
2. F	7. F	12. F	17. T
3. T	8. F	13. T	18. F
4. T	9. T	14. T	19. F
5. T	10. F	15. T	20. F

How Would You Respond?

1. A survey and examination of a computer system is not part of a typical inspection according to industry standards. If the clients agree, Marney can disregard those items that are controlled by the computer system and concentrate on components within the scope of the inspection. It would be advisable, however, for Marney to indicate that she is not responsible for inspecting any components related to the computer system in her disclaimer and again in the home inspection report.

2. Saturation of the shrub beds may have a number of causes, including a leaky gutter or a gutter downspout that is not angled away from the foundation wall. A related problem may be excess runoff from the roof that is not properly

disposed of by the gutters. Either the beds or the entire site may not be properly graded away from the foundation wall.

3. It is possible that the retaining wall is not properly anchored to the embankment and the pressure of earth and water is causing the wall to buckle. A wood retaining wall should be supported from the back with tiebacks that help secure the wall to the embankment. It is also possible that the drainage is poor behind the wall because it was not properly backfilled with porous material when constructed.

Key Term Review

1. appurtenance
2. riser, tread, stringer, headroom, balusters
3. grading
4. hydrostatic pressure
5. slope, slope gradient
6. surface runoff
7. groundwater, water table

8. percolation rate
9. drainage
10. retaining walls
11. permeability
12. topography
13. weepholes
14. water erosion

Diagram Study

Diagram 5.A: Stairway components.

1. riser
2. tread
3. stringer or carriage
4. floor joist

5. header
6. headroom

Chapter 6

Learning Objectives

1. Items included in an exterior inspection are the foundation and footings, including the crawl space; floor construction and wall framing, if visible; exterior wall covering, including flashing, siding, veneers, trim, paint, and caulking; exterior windows and doors and the corresponding framing and trim; the roof system, including the roof covering, drainage system, flashing, skylights, and other roof penetrations; eaves, soffits, and fascias, if accessible from the ground; and chimneys, flues, dampers, and associated components.

2. First, the footing is poured and the foundation wall is built. The house is then framed. The wooden sill is fastened to the foundation wall by anchor bolts. The sill plate is the first wooden member of the house and is used as the nailing surface for the floor system. The floor joists span the distance between the foundation walls and the girder and provide support for the subfloor. The main carrying beam, or girder, is either made of steel or several wooden members fastened together (usually with 2 × 10s, 2 × 12s, or larger) and spans the distance from one side of the foundation to the other. The joists rest on the girder for support. Various types of columns support the structure's main carrying beam. The

bearing walls are erected first and support the ceiling or the roof and include the outside wall frame. Nonbearing walls or partitions are walls that enclose interior space but do not support the structure. Openings in the wall for doors or windows must be reinforced to pick up the missing support of the vertical load. In the corners of the exterior walls, the top plate on one wall overlaps the top plate of the next and the walls are nailed together to bind the corner. Then, the interior walls fit into the top plates of the exterior walls. The ceiling joists rest on the wall's top plate. The ridge beam is the highest part of the framing and forms the apex, or top line, of the roof. Rafters are the long wooden members that are fastened to the ends of the ceiling joists and form the gables of the roof. A roof truss system may replace traditional rafters.

3. Here is a brief summary of primary problem areas to examine in the exterior inspection:

- Foundation—cracks, bulges, or undue settlement.
- Floors—improperly drilled holes that compromise the integrity of floor joists, and squeaky and sagging floors.
- Walls—bulges, water penetration, and rooms that are not plumb or square.
- Windows—operability, condition of cords and weights, wood rot, caulking, paint condition, broken glazing, and use of safety glass.
- Doors—caulking and paint, hinges, operability, and use of safety glass.
- Trim—condition, and missing or loose components.
- Roof—loose or missing shingles, stains on interior attic walls and ceilings, shingle condition, gutters filled with shingle granules, roof deck condition, missing or damaged flashing, proper penetration and adequate flashing of plumbing vents, clogged roof drains on flat roofs, missing or cracked pieces of slate, missing or cracked pieces of tile, substandard roof repair, condition of framing rafters, presence of wood rot, leakage around chimney penetrating the roof decking, other water stains, and damage to the integrity of the roof truss system.
- Chimney—warped damper, metal smoke chamber, connector pipe, or factory-built metal chimney; cracked or collapsed flue tiles or tiles with large chunks missing; discolored and distorted rain cap; creosote flakes and pieces found on the roof or ground; roofing material damaged from hot creosote; cracks in exterior masonry; evidence of smoke escaping through masonry mortar joints or tile liners; cracks in the chimney; whether the chimney structure is securely fastened to the roof; and damper operation.
- Exterior covering—cracked, warped, and missing pieces; spalling of the brick veneer; popping nails; wood rot.

True–False Questions

1. T	6. T	11. T	16. T
2. F	7. T	12. T	17. T
3. F	8. F	13. T	18. T
4. F	9. F	14. F	19. F
5. F	10. F	15. F	20. T

How Would You Respond?

1. Whatever the future intentions of the clients may be, Herbert has a duty to inspect and honestly report on all visible property components that are part of a standard home inspection. This includes the foundation. He can mention the proposed raising of the property in his home inspection report.

2. It is possible that both the roof and chimney of this home are compromised. However, a slate roof is extremely dangerous to physically investigate. Sarah should do the best she can with her binoculars and situate herself on the site or on a ladder to obtain the best possible observation point. If she suspects any problems at all, she should advise the clients to seek the services of a roofing specialist to further investigate. She notes this referral and all of her observations in the home inspection report.

3. Although Faith does not have a duty to inspect up through the chimney, there are certain signs that a chimney fire may have taken place, such as "puffy" creosote with rainbow-colored streaks that has expanded beyond the creosote's normal form; a warped damper, metal smoke chamber, connector pipe, or factory-built metal chimney; cracked or collapsed flue tiles, or tiles with large chunks missing; discolored and distorted rain cap; creosote flakes and pieces found on the roof or ground; roofing material damaged from hot creosote; cracks in exterior masonry; and evidence of smoke escaping through masonry mortar joints or tile liners.

Faith may not be able to observe all of these items; however, if she has reason to suspect that there is a problem with the chimney's functioning, she should advise her clients to seek the services of a professional chimney sweep. These professionals use telescopic devices and other tools that check the chimney's condition. She should include the fact that she made this referral and her own findings in the home inspection report.

Key Term Review

1. footing
2. sill plate
3. headers
4. ridge beam
5. soffit, fascia
6. rebars
7. frieze board
8. flashing, counterflashing, cricket
9. double top plate
10. creosote
11. sole plate
12. casing
13. eave, cornice
14. control joints
15. threshold
16. floating slab, monolithic slab
17. glazing, lights
18. felt paper, house wrap
19. lally columns
20. fixed-pane window
21. floor joists, floor trusses, roof truss system
22. foundation wall
23. wood rot
24. studs
25. girder
26. stiles, rails, sash, muntins
27. platform framing, balloon framing, post-and-beam framing
28. pitch
29. plumb
30. spalling

Diagram Study

Diagram 6.A: Residential structure components.

1. interior finish	14. damp-proofing
2. ceiling joist	15. drain tile
3. rafter	16. bridging
4. underlayment	17. floor joist
5. fascia	18. subfloor
6. header	19. footing
7. roof sheathing	20. floor girder
8. finish roof	21. foundation wall
9. window casing	22. plate
10. metal gutter	23. corner brace
11. door jamb	24. stud
12. siding	25. soffit
13. wall sheathing	

Diagram 6.B: Double-hung window components.

1. lift	5. sash weight
2. sill	6. sash cord
3. interior stop	7. stile
4. sash lock	8. rail

Diagram 6.C: Door components.

1. threshold	9. double plate
2. bottom plate	10. header
3. hinge jamb	11. header jamb
4. stud	12. space for shimming
5. door hinge	13. latch jamb
6. trimmer	14. door stop
7. stud	15. shims
8. top plate	

Chapter 7

Learning Objectives

1. The interior inspection includes all interior rooms; accessible doors and locking mechanisms; walls, ceilings, floors, and stairways; the garage, garage doors, and garage door openers; the attic including opening(s), accessibility, framing, sheathing, insulation, ventilation, and exposed wiring; and flues, dampers, associated components, fireplaces including manufactured solid fuel or gas-burning appliances, and mechanical ventilation systems.

2. The interior inspection proceeds in an orderly, systematic fashion using the home inspection checklist. The interior inspection encompasses many of the same

components in each room: the walls, ceilings, floors, windows, and doors. Examine the stairways, and the counters and cabinets in the kitchen and bathroom. The fireplace or other fuel-burning appliance, attic, basement, and garage are also included, if these are part of the house. Some inspectors like to start at the top floor and work their way down. Others prefer to begin with the front entrance.

3. The primary purpose of insulation is to resist the flow of heat from one area to another. It provides the double benefit of preventing heat loss in the winter and protecting against heat overload in the summer. Generally, all areas that are exposed to exterior temperatures require insulation. The structure's ceilings, walls, roof, foundation walls, and slab edge must be insulated. Insulation is rated according to an R-value. Because the R-value means the degree of resistance to heat transfer, the larger the R-value, the greater the degree of insulation. Insulation combined with a vapor barrier prevents condensation inside the walls and eliminates the potential for wood rot and other types of damage.

4. Codes may require that all building envelope materials that absorb moisture be protected by a vapor barrier on the insulation applied to the warm (inside) wall of exterior walls. Water vapor is generated from the activities inside the structure, such as cooking and bathing, as well as moisture conditions generated on the exterior. As warm air rises in the structure, so does the moisture. The vapor barrier is composed of sheets of moisture-resistant material such as polyethylene film, kraft paper, or aluminum foil bonded to the insulation. The vapor barrier prevents the warm interior air from mixing with the cold exterior air and forming condensation within the wall. Should condensation occur, the structure, in effect, "sweats" and can cause the wood framing members to rot and damage other components.

5. The main problems to look for during the interior inspection include walls, ceilings, and floors that sag or have cracks or water stains; doors, windows, and locks that are broken or warping; tearing, cracking, or heaving of the floor material; stairways that are not secure and that violate safety codes; fire hazards such as unventilated furnaces and garages that allow gas vapors into the house; fireplace and fuel-burning stoves that show evidence of malfunction such as a broken damper; garage doors that do not stay open; and garage openers with a malfunctioning reverse mechanism. In addition, the basement is checked for water penetration and dampness. The attic is examined for accessibility, the presence of insulation and ventilation, and the condition of the roof system that can be observed from the inside.

True–False Questions

1. T	6. T	11. F	16. T
2. T	7. F	12. F	17. F
3. F	8. T	13. T	18. F
4. F	9. F	14. T	19. T
5. T	10. F	15. T	20. T

How Would You Respond?

1. First, Dawn should stop to analyze the problem. What is the location of the bedroom in relation to other parts of the structure? Dawn must carefully examine the bedroom and adjacent areas to identify the source. What is above the ceiling, for instance? Does the portion of the roof and attic above this bedroom have

dormers or other finished spaces? Are air-conditioning ducts or plumbing pipes hidden in the ceiling? Through analysis and process of elimination, Dawn may or may not have an answer. The possible answers might be verified during a return trip to the component of the structure where she suspects the problem originates.

2. If the attic is inaccessible, Andy is under no duty to jeopardize his safety by trying to squeeze through the opening. The problem should be so noted on the home inspection report. If Andy, however, can move up somewhat through the opening with a flashlight, opportunities exist for some observation and examination. For example, Andy can observe the presence or absence of insulation. He can also possibly observe the condition of the inside roof deck and the roof rafters. Is there an attic fan? He may even be able to note any moisture problems in the attic space.

3. Because it is rather unusual to find a suspended ceiling in the living room, Tyrone should find out if the ceiling was constructed to cover up a problem with the original ceiling. Tyrone can remove one or more of the suspended ceiling tiles and carefully examine the ceiling underneath for water penetration, sagging, dampness, and missing pieces. The kitchen tiles are glued to the ceiling and should not be touched; however, if there are loose or missing tiles, Tyrone may be able to gain a further look at the kitchen ceiling. Because this is a one-story structure, water penetration or moisture may indicate a problem with the roof.

Key Term Review

1. building envelope
2. damper, throat damper
3. gypsum board
4. photoelectric eye
5. resilient floor covering
6. torsion springs
7. subfloor
8. section joint
9. catalytic combustor, non-catalytic
10. efflorescence
11. flue, flue collar
12. extension springs
13. grout
14. R-value
15. trim
16. wythe
17. vapor barrier
18. metal lath
19. lift handle
20. internal reversing mechanism
21. ash dump door, ash pit, ash pit cleanout door

Diagram Study

Diagram 7.A: Interior door components.

1. door jamb
2. door stop
3. base
4. door casing

Chapter 8

Learning Objectives

1. In general, the plumbing, heating, and air-conditioning inspection includes the water supply and distribution systems, water and fuel shutoff valves, wastewater and drainage systems, any accessible pipes used for water supply and drainage, pipe vent systems, hot water heaters, heating equipment, air-conditioning system, and all

plumbing fixtures. Inspectors may include other items, such as well and septic system inspections, if their expertise allows and there is client demand.

2. The first item to determine when inspecting the vent pipes is whether there is a plumbing vent stack venting through the roof. The absence of the vent stack is a violation of plumbing codes. The inspector should check every fixture for foul smells. All accessible pipes are examined for leakage, rust, corrosion, pipe size, and noise. Check that all cold water pipes are insulated properly and that condensation is not visible. If possible, feel the insulation to see if it is dry.

3. Each room must have at least one heating vent, convector, radiator, or other means of heating. Attempt to find out the age of the heating system. Examine the furnace for leaks and corrosion. Check for an abnormal amount of soot in and around the furnace. Determine whether the heater has a safety switch, and whether there is adequate ventilation if it is enclosed in a furnace room. If the property has an oil-fired furnace, locate the oil storage tank. Examine aboveground oil storage tanks for leaks, rust, and corrosion. Check the location of the thermostat and that it is registering. In gas-fired systems, check the pilot light. Observe the gas burners inside the heat exchanger. With gas-fired furnaces, a black solid iron pipe should carry the gas from its source (the metered gas line) to the furnace. There should also be a drip leg attached to the pipe just before the pipe enters the furnace. With a hot water system, make sure the circulator pumps go on. Check to see that the heated water is circulating through the pipes in the system. Observe the temperature pressure gauge. To check the hot air system, turn on the thermostat and let it cycle. Make sure the blowers are functioning. Check that the outside air-conditioning unit is on level ground and that the unit is not covered by trees, bushes, or other vegetation. The unit should have adequate clearance on all sides and be situated on the shady side of the structure if possible. Make sure the fan is operational. Check that the condensation from the evaporator coil is not leaking out of the evaporator coil pan. Verify that the air filter is installed. If possible, check for ice buildup.

4. The kitchen sink is tested for water flow, proper drainage, and whether the hot and cold water supply lines are hooked up correctly. Check the pipe connection between the dishwasher and the water supply lines for leakage. Check that the drain and water source are hooked up correctly. Verify that the sink has a P-trap to block any sewer gases from escaping through the pipe. All sinks should be securely fastened to the counter or to the wall if the sink is a wall mount. In the bathroom, check that the water supply pipes and the drainpipe are hooked up correctly. Look for cracks in the sink bowl. Flush the toilet and observe that the water drains properly. Determine that the bowl is tightly secured to the floor. Remove the tank top and observe the toilet as it flushes to verify that the moving parts are functioning properly. Check that the toilet has a separate shutoff valve. Check the faucets in the shower, tub, and sinks. Using a moisture meter, check behind the bathroom tile for moisture problems.

True–False Questions

1. F	6. F	11. F	16. T
2. T	7. T	12. T	17. T
3. F	8. F	13. T	18. F
4. F	9. T	14. T	19. T
5. F	10. F	15. F	20. F

How Would You Respond?

1. Most standards of practice do not require that a home inspector comment on water quality, whether from a municipal system or a well, or the functionality of a private wastewater system. Many homes, however, do rely on private water supply and wastewater systems. If the home inspector feels qualified to perform a basic inspection as discussed in the textbook, he can do this. The disclaimer in the home inspection agreement should cover the scope of this and other types of inspections. Should a problem be observed during the well or septic inspection, the inspector should advise the clients to consult with a qualified professional.

Water quality must be tested by a certified lab. As an extra service, home inspectors can bring samples of water to the lab for testing. If this service is performed, the inspector must collect and package the sample according to guidelines furnished by the lab. The inspector also has the right to refuse to perform these services.

2. Any damages that occur during the performance of professional services is generally covered by liability or errors and omissions insurance. After the accident, Curtis should thoroughly investigate the chain of events to determine whether he was the cause of the damage to the toilet. Whether Curtis believes that the accident was his fault or not, he must report the events, to the best of his knowledge, to his insurance company. They will also investigate the incident. Curtis should also immediately report the accident to the property owners.

3. A gas leak is a safety hazard and must be remedied immediately. Although hand-held gas analyzers are very accurate, a qualified professional should be called in to further analyze the source of the leak and repair it. If the leak is on or near a gas hot water heater or furnace, Diane should ask the home owners, if they are available, if she can turn off the gas. She can also open a window to provide ventilation until help arrives. The local power company should be called immediately. They will come to the house and give advice as to what to do. The client should be told to notify the real estate broker handling the transaction.

Key Term Review

1. boiler
2. pressure regulator valve
3. refrigerant, freon
4. potable water, nonpotable water
5. plumbing fixture
6. heat exchanger
7. hydronic system
8. gate valve, globe valve
9. main soil stack
10. plenum
11. forced warm air system, steam system
12. float valve, backflow preventer, temperature pressure relief valve
13. BTU/British thermal unit
14. cleanout
15. convector
16. compressor, condenser, evaporator
17. cesspool
18. aquifer
19. septic system
20. soil stack

Diagram Study

Diagram 8.A: Septic system.

1. house sewer
2. septic tank
3. distribution box
4. absorption trench

Diagram 8.B: Types of traps.

1. P-trap
2. U-trap
3. S-trap
4. drum trap

Diagram 8.C: Bathroom sink.

1. fixture vent
2. sink or lavatory
3. trap
4. stud wall
5. cleanout

Chapter 9

Learning Objectives

1. The electrical system inspection includes an examination of the service drop, service entrance conductors, cables, and raceways; the service equipment; the main disconnect; and the system grounding. The inspection also includes the interior components: the main and sub panel boards; conductors; overcurrent protection devices; and a representative number of installed lighting fixtures, switches, and receptacles. Inspectors must identify the amperage and voltage rating for the building, the location of main disconnect(s) and sub panels, and note wiring methods. The presence of aluminum branch circuit wiring and the absence of smoke detectors must be noted. Smoke detectors must be checked for functionality.

2. The basic electric terminology includes the following: Electric current is the flow of electrons along a conductor, such as a copper wire. The current travels in a path known as the circuit. The amount of current or electricity flowing through the wire is called the amperage. Voltage is the electrical pressure that pushes through a wire. The electricity moves along wires that are known as conductors. A good conductor has little resistance to the flow of electricity. Some conductors or wires have more resistance than others. An ohm is a unit of electrical resistance of a conductor. The resistance to the flow of electricity is measured in ohms.

3. The inspection begins with the exterior where the service enters the house. The home inspector should define the type of incoming service: service drop if aboveground or service lateral if underground. The condition of the service entrance cables is examined. If the electric meter and the main panel board or main disconnect are located outdoors, inspect this equipment at this time. Proceed to the interior and locate the main panel board if not found outside. After an examination of the main disconnect and panel board, move through the structure. Check the garage and attic for wires, cables, conduit, and junction boxes. Next, examine the operation of light switches, light fixtures, receptacles, and GFCIs. Outdoor light fixtures should also be checked. Finally, check the location of smoke detectors and ascertain their functionality.

True–False Questions

1. T	6. T	11. F	16. T
2. T	7. F	12. F	17. T
3. T	8. F	13. T	18. F
4. F	9. F	14. T	19. T
5. F	10. F	15. F	20. F

How Would You Respond?

1. Vanessa could have avoided this dangerous situation by explaining the "ground rules" prior to the inspection. Inspectors naturally want clients with them during an inspection to see both the good and problematic aspects of the property. However, the inspection must be accomplished with safety as a primary goal. Prior to opening the panel board, Vanessa should have placed her client at a safe distance from the board and explained that he cannot approach or touch the board and why. Her instructions should include the fact that live conductors and other components that can cause dangerous and sometimes fatal electric shock are situated on the panel board. Based on this information, most people will cooperate with the inspector's instructions. However, if Vanessa senses that safety precautions will be ignored by the client, she should skip that part of the inspection for the time being. Vanessa has the option of returning to the panel board once the client has left.

2. Craig is doing the right thing if he shares his suspicions with the client. Aluminum branch circuit wiring is a safety hazard and should be examined by a professional electrician. Craig can candidly explain that he is not sure about the wiring problem and recommend that the client seek the advice of a professional electrician. Craig's observations and suggestions to the client are noted in the inspection report.

3. It is not unusual for novice, and sometimes more experienced, home inspectors to be accompanied by another professional from a specific field. It actually may be necessary for the novice home inspector. Some new inspectors may have trouble with the plumbing system, or the structure, or another system. Until LeGrand feels confident about the electrical system, he should bring another home inspector or an electrician who can assist him with that part of the inspection. He may have to share a portion of his fee with this individual. LeGrand should carefully observe the inspection so that he can gain the knowledge and confidence to eventually perform this aspect of the inspection without assistance.

Key Term Review

1. bus bars
2. electric current
3. fuse
4. branch circuit wiring
5. amperage
6. circuit breakers
7. overcurrent protection devices
8. circuit
9. conductors
10. service drop
11. transformers
12. ground fault circuit interrupter (GFCI)
13. insulators
14. ohm
15. raceway
16. service entrance cable (SE cable)
17. switches, receptacles, outlet
18. service lateral conductors
19. service lateral
20. voltage

Diagram Study

Diagram 9.A: Service connection type.

1. service drop

Diagram 9.B: Service connection type.

1. service lateral

Chapter 10

Learning Objectives

1. The following are some considerations that may lessen a home inspector's liability during the performance of environmental testing:

- Learn the proper standards for performing the test.
- Learn the acceptable measurement range for the test results should the test not go to a lab.
- Use a reputable or state-certified lab to analyze samples.
- Use state-of-the-art equipment that is appropriate for the test performed.
- Wear protective clothing if necessary and avoid areas that pose a danger.
- Receive training on how to perform the test and obtain certification when required.
- Refuse to perform a test if you do not have appropriate knowledge and training.

2. Although the home inspector may test for a variety of environmental issues, some of the test procedures involve the collection of samples that must be brought to a lab for analysis and verification. A home inspector may place charcoal canisters in a home to test for radon. Alpha-track detectors may be used for long-term testing. A home inspector may test for the presence of formaldehyde, electromagnetic fields, lead, mold, and the water-flow capability of a well. The home inspector may also collect samples for well water testing and paint chip testing (for lead); however, proper collection procedures must be observed.

3. Other issues that affect real property include leaking underground storage tanks, wood-eating pest infestation, asbestos products that may be breaking apart and emitting fibers into the air, other indoor allergens in building materials and carpets, and other biological contaminants such as animal dander, pollen, and dust mites.

True–False Questions

1. F	6. F	11. F	16. T
2. T	7. F	12. F	17. F
3. F	8. F	13. T	18. T
4. F	9. T	14. T	19. F
5. F	10. T	15. F	20. T

How Would You Respond?

1. It is obvious that the well system is in need of repair or overhaul. Justin must report all observations fairly and honestly to all parties. To omit this part of the report is just as dishonest as giving a false statement. Justin should report his findings to the clients and suggest that they contact the Desperates and the real estate agent. Often, monetary adjustments are made for equipment that is in need of repair or overhaul at the real estate closing and the sale can take place despite certain defects.

2. After Tracy observes the power lines, she should point out the observation to her clients. Should they express concern about safety issues regarding

electromagnetic fields, Tracy should refer her clients to the EMF hotline (1-800-363-2383) for further information.

3. Ari should point out to the clients that the air quality in the home seems to be less than healthy. Ari should emphasize, however, that his conclusions are not based on scientific tests. If Ari has found that there is no ventilation system on the property, he should let his clients know this. If Ari performs environmental testing, he could offer to perform a mold test. He could also suggest that the carpets be removed. In addition, he should suggest that his clients have a specialist perform a complete air quality test on the property prior to closing.

Key Term Review

1. underground storage tanks
2. asbestos, friable
3. termites, carpenter ants, powderpost beetles, carpenter bees
4. electromagnetic field
5. formaldehyde
6. toxic substance
7. radon
8. lead

Diagram Study

Diagram 10.A: Wood-eating insects.

1. termite
2. powderpost beetle
3. carpenter ant
4. carpenter bee

Diagnostic Exam Answer Key

1. C	14. B	27. A	40. C
2. D	15. B	28. B	41. A
3. B	16. D	29. B	42. A
4. A	17. A	30. C	43. B
5. D	18. D	31. B	44. B
6. C	19. C	32. C	45. D
7. B	20. B	33. D	46. A
8. C	21. B	34. D	47. C
9. B	22. A	35. B	48. A
10. C	23. B	36. D	49. C
11. A	24. B	37. C	50. B
12. A	25. D	38. A	
13. B	26. B	39. D	

The Standards of Practice and Code of Ethics of
THE AMERICAN SOCIETY OF HOME INSPECTORS®

www.ashi.org

TABLE OF CONTENTS

Distribution of this material is not an indication of ASHI® Membership. For a free listing of the Membership go to "Find an Inspector" at www.ashi.org. To obtain additional copies or request permission to reprint The ASHI® Standards of Practice and Code of Ethics, contact:

The American Society of Home Inspectors, Inc.®
932 Lee Street, Suite 101
Des Plaines, IL 60016

800-743-ASHI/2744

HOME INSPECTION

Home inspections were being performed in the mid 1950s, and by the early 1970s were considered by many consumers to be essential to the real estate transaction. The escalating demand was due to a growing desire by homebuyers to learn about the condition of a house prior to purchase. Meeting the expectations of consumers required a unique discipline, distinct from construction, engineering, architecture, or municipal building inspection. As such, home inspection requires its own set of professional guidelines and qualifications. The American Society of Home Inspectors (ASHI) formed in 1976 and established the ASHI Standards of Practice and Code of Ethics to help buyers and sellers make real estate transaction decisions based on accurate, objective information.

American Society of Home Inspectors

As the oldest, largest and highest profile organization of home inspectors in North America, ASHI takes pride in its position of leadership. Its Membership works to build public awareness of home inspection and to enhance the technical and ethical performance of home inspectors.

Standards of Practice

The ASHI Standards of Practice guide home inspectors in the performance of their inspections. Subject to regular review, the Standards of Practice reflect information gained through surveys of conditions in the field and of the consumers' interests and concerns. Vigilance has elevated ASHI's Standards of Practice so that today they are the most widely-accepted home inspection guidelines in use and are recognized by many government and professional groups as the definitive standard for professional performance.

Code of Ethics

ASHI's Code of Ethics stresses the home inspector's responsibility to report the results of the inspection in a strictly fair, impartial, and professional manner, avoiding conflicts of interest.

ASHI Membership

Selecting the right home inspector can be as important as finding the right home. ASHI Members have performed no fewer than 250 fee-paid inspections in accordance with the ASHI Standards of Practice. They have passed written examinations testing their knowledge of residential construction, defect recognition, inspection techniques, and report-writing, as well as ASHI's Standards of Practice and Code of Ethics. Membership in the American Society of Home Inspectors is well-earned and maintained only through meeting requirements for continuing education.

Find local ASHI Members by calling 1-800-743-2744 or visiting the ASHI Web site at www.ashi.org.

ASHI STANDARDS OF PRACTICE

1. INTRODUCTION

The American Society of Home Inspectors®, Inc. (ASHI®) is a not-for-profit professional society established in 1976. Membership in ASHI is voluntary and its members are private home *inspectors*. ASHI's objectives include promotion of excellence within the profession and continual improvement of its members' inspection services to the public.

2. PURPOSE AND SCOPE

2.1   The purpose of the Standards of Practice is to establish a minimum and uniform standard for home *inspectors* who subscribe to these Standards of Practice. *Home inspections* performed to these Standards of Practice are intended to provide the client with objective information regarding the condition of the *systems* and *components* of the home as *inspected* at the time of the *home inspection*. Redundancy in the description of the requirements, limitations, and exclusions regarding the scope of the *home inspection* is provided for emphasis only.

2.2   ***Inspectors* shall:**

   A. adhere to the Code of Ethics of the American Society of Home Inspectors.

   B. inspect *readily accessible*, visually observable, *installed systems* and *components* listed in these Standards of Practice.

   C. *report*:

     1. those *systems* and *components inspected* that, in the professional judgment of the *inspector*, are not functioning properly, significantly deficient, *unsafe*, or are near the end of their service lives.

     2. recommendations to correct, or monitor for future correction, the deficiencies *reported* in 2.2.C.1, or items needing *further evaluation*. (Per Exclusion 13.2.A.5 *inspectors* are NOT required to determine methods, materials, or costs of corrections.)

     3. reasoning or explanation as to the nature of the deficiencies *reported* in 2.2.C.1, that are not self-evident.

     4. *systems* and *components* designated for inspection in these Standards of Practice that were present at the time of the *home inspection* but were not *inspected* and the reason(s) they were not *inspected*.

2.3   **These Standards of Practice are not intended to limit *inspectors* from:**

   A. including other inspection services or *systems* and *components* in addition to those required in Section 2.2.B.

   B. designing or specifying repairs, provided the *inspector* is appropriately qualified and willing to do so.

   C. excluding *systems* and *components* from the inspection if requested by the client.

3.   STRUCTURAL COMPONENTS

3.1   **The *inspector* shall:**

   A. *inspect:*

     1. *structural components* including the foundation and framing.

     2. by probing a *representative number* of *structural components* where deterioration is suspected or where clear indications of possible deterioration exist. Probing is NOT required when probing would damage any finished surface or where no deterioration is visible or presumed to exist.

   B. *describe:*

     1. the methods used to *inspect under-floor crawl spaces* and attics.

     2. the foundation.

     3. the floor structure.

     4. the wall structure.

     5. the ceiling structure.

     6. the roof structure.

3.2   **The *inspector* is NOT required to:**

   A. provide any *engineering* or architectural services or analysis.

   B. offer an opinion as to the adequacy of any *structural system* or *component*.

4.   EXTERIOR

4.1   **The *inspector* shall:**

   A. *inspect*:

     1. *siding*, flashing and trim.

     2. all exterior doors.

     3. attached or adjacent decks, balconies, stoops, steps, porches, and their associated railings.

     4. eaves, soffits, and fascias where accessible from the ground level.

     5. vegetation, grading, surface drainage, and retaining walls that are likely to adversely affect the building.

     6. adjacent or entryway walkways, patios, and driveways.

   B. *describe*:

     1. *siding*.

EXTERIOR 4.2, Continued

4.2   The *inspector* is NOT required to *inspect*:

A. screening, shutters, awnings, and similar seasonal accessories.

B. fences.

C. geological and/or soil conditions.

D. *recreational facilities*.

E. outbuildings other than garages and carports.

F. seawalls, break-walls, and docks.

G. erosion control and earth stabilization measures.

5. ROOFING

5.1   The *inspector* shall:

A. *inspect*:

1. roofing materials.
2. *roof drainage systems*.
3. flashing.
4. skylights, chimneys, and roof penetrations.

B. *describe*:

1. roofing materials.
2. methods used to *inspect* the roofing.

5.2   The *inspector* is NOT required to *inspect*:

A. antennae.

B. interiors of flues or chimneys that are not *readily accessible*.

C. other *installed* accessories.

6.   PLUMBING

6.1   The *inspector* shall:

A. *inspect*:

1. interior water supply and distribution *systems* including all fixtures and faucets.
2. drain, waste, and vent *systems* including all fixtures.
3. water heating equipment and hot water supply *system*.
4. vent *systems*, flues, and chimneys.
5. fuel storage and fuel distribution *systems*.
6. drainage sumps, sump pumps, and related piping.

B. *describe*:

1. water supply, drain, waste, and vent piping materials.
2. water heating equipment including energy source(s).
3. location of main water and fuel shut-off valves.

6.2   The *inspector* is NOT required to:

A. *inspect*:

1. clothes washing machine connections.
2. interiors of flues or chimneys that are not *readily accessible*.
3. wells, well pumps, or water storage related equipment.
4. water conditioning *systems*.
5. solar water heating *systems*.
6. fire and lawn sprinkler *systems*.
7. private waste disposal *systems*.

B. determine:

1. whether water supply and waste disposal *systems* are public or private.
2. water supply quantity or quality.

C. operate *automatic safety controls* or manual stop valves.

7.   ELECTRICAL

7.1   The *inspector* shall:

A. *inspect*:

1. service drop.
2. service entrance conductors, cables, and raceways.
3. service equipment and main disconnects.
4. service grounding.
5. interior *components* of service panels and sub panels.
6. conductors.
7. overcurrent protection devices.
8. a *representative number* of *installed* lighting fixtures, switches, and receptacles.
9. ground fault circuit interrupters.

B. *describe*:

1. amperage and voltage rating of the service.
2. location of main disconnect(s) and sub panels.
3. presence of solid conductor aluminum branch circuit wiring.
4. presence or absence of smoke detectors.
5. *wiring methods*.

7.2   The *inspector* is NOT required to:

A. *inspect*:

1. remote control devices.
2. *alarm systems* and *components*.
3. low voltage wiring *systems* and *components*.
4. ancillary wiring *systems* and *components*. not a part of the primary electrical power distribution *system*.

B. measure amperage, voltage, or impedance.

Continued

8. HEATING

8.1 **The** *inspector* **shall:**

A. open *readily openable access panels.*

B. *inspect*:

1. *installed* heating equipment.
2. vent *systems*, flues, and chimneys.

C. *describe*:

1. energy source(s).
2. heating *systems*.

8.2 **The** *inspector* **is NOT required to:**

A. *inspect*:

1. interiors of flues or chimneys that are not *readily accessible*.
2. heat exchangers.
3. humidifiers or dehumidifiers.
4. electronic air filters.
5. solar space heating *systems*.

B. determine heat supply adequacy or distribution balance.

9. AIR CONDITIONING

9.1 **The** *inspector* **shall:**

A. open *readily openable access panels.*

B. *inspect*:

1. central and through-wall equipment.
2. distribution *systems*.

C. *describe*:

1. energy source(s).
2. cooling *systems*.

9.2 **The** *inspector* **is NOT required to:**

A. *inspect* electronic air filters.

B. determine cooling supply adequacy or distribution balance.

C. *inspect* window air conditioning units.

10. INTERIORS

10.1 **The** *inspector* **shall** *inspect*:

A. walls, ceilings, and floors.

B. steps, stairways, and railings.

C. countertops and a *representative number* of *installed* cabinets.

D. a *representative number* of doors and windows.

E. garage doors and garage door operators.

10.2 **The** *inspector* **is NOT required to** *inspect*:

A. paint, wallpaper, and other finish treatments.

B. carpeting.

C. window treatments.

D. central vacuum *systems*.

E. *household appliances*.

F. *recreational facilities*.

11. INSULATION & VENTILATION

11.1 **The** *inspector* **shall:**

A. *inspect*:

1. insulation and vapor retarders in unfinished spaces.
2. ventilation of attics and foundation areas.
3. mechanical ventilation *systems*.

B. *describe*:

1. insulation and vapor retarders in unfinished spaces.
2. absence of insulation in unfinished spaces at conditioned surfaces.

11.2 **The** *inspector* **is NOT required to disturb insulation.** See 13.2.A.11 and 13.2.A.12.

12. FIREPLACES AND SOLID FUEL BURNING APPLIANCES

12.1 **The** *inspector* **shall:**

A. *inspect*:

1. *system components*.
2. chimney and vents.

B. *describe*:

1. fireplaces and *solid fuel burning appliances*.
2. chimneys.

12.2 **The** *inspector* **is NOT required to:**

A. *inspect*:

1. interiors of flues or chimneys.
2. firescreens and doors.
3. seals and gaskets.
4. automatic fuel feed devices.
5. mantles and fireplace surrounds.
6. combustion make-up air devices.
7. heat distribution assists (gravity fed and fan assisted).

B. ignite or extinguish fires.

C. determine draft characteristics.

D. move fireplace inserts and stoves or firebox contents.

Continued

13.   GENERAL LIMITATIONS AND EXCLUSIONS

13.1   General limitations:

A. The *inspector* is NOT required to perform any action or make any determination not specifically stated in these Standards of Practice.

B. Inspections performed in accordance with these Standards of Practice:

1. are not *technically exhaustive.*

2. are not required to identify concealed. conditions, latent defects, or consequential damage(s).

C. These Standards of Practice are applicable to buildings with four or fewer dwelling units and their garages or carports.

13.2   General exclusions:

A. *Inspectors* **are NOT required to determine:**

1. conditions of *systems* or *components* that are not *readily accessible.*

2. remaining life expectancy of any *system* or *component.*

3. strength, adequacy, effectiveness, or efficiency of any *system* or *component.*

4. the causes of any condition or deficiency.

5. methods, materials, or costs of corrections.

6. future conditions including but not limited to failure of *systems* and *components.*

7. the suitability of the property for any specialized use.

8. compliance with regulatory requirements (codes, regulations, laws, ordinances, etc.).

9. market value of the property or its marketability.

10. the advisability of purchase of the property.

11. the presence of potentially hazardous plants or animals including, but not limited to, wood destroying organisms or diseases harmful to humans including molds or mold-like substances.

12. the presence of any environmental hazards including, but not limited to, toxins, carcinogens, noise, and contaminants in soil, water, and air.

13. the effectiveness of any *system installed* or method utilized to control or remove suspected hazardous substances.

14. operating costs of *systems* or *components.*

15. acoustical properties of any *system* or *component.*

16. soil conditions relating to geotechnical or hydrologic specialties.

B. *Inspectors* **are NOT required to offer:**

1. or perform any act or service contrary to law.

2. or perform *engineering* services.

3. or perform any trade or any professional. service other than *home inspection.*

4. warranties or guarantees of any kind.

C. *Inspectors* **are NOT required to operate:**

1. any *system* or *component* that is *shut down* or otherwise inoperable.

2. any *system* or *component* that does not respond to *normal operating controls.*

3. shut-off valves or manual stop valves.

D. *Inspectors* **are NOT required to enter:**

1. any area that will, in the opinion of the *inspector*, likely be dangerous to the *inspector* or other persons or damage the property or its *systems* or *components.*

2. *under-floor crawl spaces* or attics that are not *readily accessible.*

E. *Inspectors* **are NOT required to inspect:**

1. underground items including but not limited to underground storage tanks or other underground indications of their presence, whether abandoned or active.

2. items that are not *installed.*

3. *installed decorative* items.

4. items in areas that are not entered in accordance with 13.2.D.

5. detached structures other than garages and carports.

6. common elements or common areas in multi-unit housing, such as condominium properties or cooperative housing.

F. *Inspectors* **are NOT required to:**

1. perform any procedure or operation that will, in the opinion of the *inspector*, likely be dangerous to the *inspector* or other persons or damage the property or its *systems* or *components.*

2. describe or report on any *system* or *component* that is not included in these Standards and was not *inspected.*

3. move personal property, furniture, equipment, plants, soil, snow, ice, or debris.

4. *dismantle* any *system* or *component*, except as explicitly required by these Standards of Practice.

ASHI STANDARDS OF PRACTICE GLOSSARY OF ITALICIZED TERMS

Alarm Systems
Warning devices *installed* or free-standing including but not limited to smoke detectors, carbon monoxide detectors, flue gas, and other spillage detectors, and security equipment

Automatic Safety Controls
Devices designed and *installed* to protect *systems* and *components* from unsafe conditions

Component
A part of a *system*

Decorative
Ornamental; not required for the proper operation of the essential *systems* and *components* of a home

Describe
To identify (in writing) a *system* or *component* by its type or other distinguishing characteristics

Dismantle
To take apart or remove any *component*, device, or piece of equipment that would not be taken apart or removed by a homeowner in the course of normal maintenance

Engineering
The application of scientific knowledge for the design, control, or use of building structures, equipment, or apparatus

Further Evaluation
Examination and analysis by a qualified professional, tradesman, or service technician beyond that provided by the *home inspection*

Home Inspection
The process by which an *inspector* visually examines the *readily accessible systems* and *components* of a home and which *describes* those *systems* and *components* in accordance with these Standards of Practice

Household Appliances
Kitchen, laundry, and similar appliances, whether *installed* or free-standing

Inspect
To examine any *system* or *component* of a building in accordance with these Standards of Practice, using *normal operating controls* and opening *readily openable access panels*

Inspector
A person hired to examine any *system* or *component* of a building in accordance with these Standards of Practice

Installed
Attached such that removal requires tools

Normal Operating Controls
Devices such as thermostats, switches, or valves intended to be operated by the homeowner

Readily Accessible
Available for visual inspection without requiring moving of personal property, *dismantling*, destructive measures, or any action that will likely involve risk to persons or property

Readily Openable Access Panel
A panel provided for homeowner inspection and maintenance that is *readily accessible*, within normal reach, can be removed by one person, and is not sealed in place

Recreational Facilities
Spas, saunas, steam baths, swimming pools, exercise, entertainment, athletic, playground or other similar equipment, and associated accessories

Report
Communicate in writing

Representative Number
One *component* per room for multiple similar interior *components* such as windows, and electric receptacles; one *component* on each side of the building for multiple similar exterior *components*

Roof Drainage Systems
Components used to carry water off a roof and away from a building

Shut Down
A state in which a *system* or *component* cannot be operated by *normal operating controls*

Siding
Exterior wall covering and cladding; such as: aluminum, asphalt, brick, cement/asbestos, EIFS, stone, stucco, veneer, vinyl, wood, etc.

Solid Fuel Burning Appliances
A hearth and fire chamber or similar prepared place in which a fire may be built and that is built in conjunction with a chimney; or a listed assembly of a fire chamber, its chimney, and related factory-made parts designed for unit assembly without requiring field construction

Structural Component
A *component* that supports non-variable forces or weights (dead loads) and variable forces or weights (live loads)

System
A combination of interacting or interdependent *components*, assembled to carry out one or more functions.

Technically Exhaustive
An investigation that involves *dismantling*, the extensive use of advanced techniques, measurements, instruments, testing, calculations, or other means

Under-floor Crawl Space
The area within the confines of the foundation and between the ground and the underside of the floor

Unsafe
A condition in a *readily accessible*, *installed system* or *component* that is judged to be a significant risk of bodily injury during normal, day-to-day use; the risk may be due to damage, deterioration, improper installation, or a change in accepted residential construction standards

Wiring Methods
Identification of electrical conductors or wires by their general type, such as non-metallic sheathed cable, armored cable, or knob and tube, etc.

ASHI® CODE OF ETHICS
For the Home Inspection Profession

Integrity, honesty, and objectivity are fundamental principles embodied by this Code, which sets forth obligations of ethical conduct for the home inspection profession. The Membership of ASHI has adopted this Code to provide high ethical standards to safeguard the public and the profession.

Inspectors shall comply with this Code, shall avoid association with any enterprise whose practices violate this Code, and shall strive to uphold, maintain, and improve the integrity, reputation, and practice of the home inspection profession.

1. Inspectors shall avoid conflicts of interest or activities that compromise, or appear to compromise, professional independence, objectivity, or inspection integrity.

A. Inspectors shall not inspect properties for compensation in which they have, or expect to have, a financial interest.

B. Inspectors shall not inspect properties under contingent arrangements whereby any compensation or future referrals are dependent on reported findings or on the sale of a property.

C. Inspectors shall not directly or indirectly compensate realty agents, or other parties having a financial interest in closing or settlement of real estate transactions, for the referral of inspections or for inclusion on a list of recommended inspectors, preferred providers, or similar arrangements.

D. Inspectors shall not receive compensation for an inspection from more than one party unless agreed to by the client(s).

E. Inspectors shall not accept compensation, directly or indirectly, for recommending contractors, services, or products to inspection clients or other parties having an interest in inspected properties.

F. Inspectors shall not repair, replace, or upgrade, for compensation, systems or components covered by ASHI Standards of Practice, for one year after the inspection.

2. Inspectors shall act in good faith toward each client and other interested parties.

A. Inspectors shall perform services and express opinions based on genuine conviction and only within their areas of education, training, or experience.

B. Inspectors shall be objective in their reporting and not knowingly understate or overstate the significance of reported conditions.

C. Inspectors shall not disclose inspection results or client information without client approval. Inspectors, at their discretion, may disclose observed immediate safety hazards to occupants exposed to such hazards, when feasible.

3. Inspectors shall avoid activities that may harm the public, discredit themselves, or reduce public confidence in the profession.

A. Advertising, marketing, and promotion of inspectors' services or qualifications shall not be fraudulent, false, deceptive, or misleading.

B. Inspectors shall report substantive and willful violations of this Code to the Society.

STANDARDS OF PRACTICE

NAHI™

NATIONAL ASSOCIATION OF HOME INSPECTORS, INC.

i

STANDARDS OF PRACTICE

National Association of Home Inspectors, Inc.

These Standards may not be reproduced without written permission from the National Association of Home Inspectors, Inc.

© 1990 - 4.2006 edition.

4248 Park Glen Road
Minneapolis, Minnesota 55416
PHONE 952–928–4641 • FAX 952–929–1318

NATIONAL ASSOCIATION OF HOME INSPECTORS, INC.

TABLE OF CONTENTS

2

1. PURPOSE, SCOPE AND GENERAL STATEMENTS

1.1   The Standards of Practice (Standards) provide the minimum standards of performance for a written report on a residential home inspection performed by and for the exclusive use of members of the National Association of Home Inspectors, Inc. (NAHI™). Use of the NAHI logo and name is limited to those persons holding the designation of Regular Member. Associate, NAHI CRI and Affiliate Members may use specifically designated logos in advertising.

1.2   The Standards define and clarify the purpose, conditions, limitations, exclusions, and certain terms relating to an inspection.

1.3   The Standards describe those items, components, and systems included in the scope of an inspection.

1.4   The Standards apply only to the inspection of buildings with one (1) to four (4) dwelling units.

1.5   The Standards apply to a visual inspection of the readily accessible areas of the included items, components, and systems to determine if, at the time of the inspection, they are performing their intended function without regard to life expectancy.

1.6   The purpose of the inspection is to identify visible defects and/or conditions that, in the judgement of the inspector, adversely affect the function and/or integrity of the items, components, and systems.

1.7   Inspections performed under the Standards are basically visual and rely upon the opinion, judgement, and experience of the inspector, and are not intended to be technically exhaustive.

1.8   Inspections shall be performed in a time period sufficient to allow compliance with the provisions of the Standards.

1.9   Inspections performed under the Standards shall not be construed as a compliance inspection of any code, governmental regulation, or manufacturer's installation instructions or procedures. In the event a law, statute, or ordinance prohibits a procedure recommended in the Standards, the inspector is relieved of the obligation to adhere to the prohibited part of the Standards.

1.10   Inspections performed under the Standards are not an expressed or implied warranty or a guarantee of the adequacy, performance, or useful life of any item, component, or system in, on, or about the inspected property.

3

1.11 Detached building(s) and detached garage(s) located on the property will be inspected under these Standards only if specifically listed in the inspection report.

1.12 The National Association of Home Inspectors, Inc. recommends that its members perform inspections in accordance with these Standards, the Code of Ethics, and applicable law(s). The Standards are not intended to limit members from performing "additional inspection services."

1.13 The inspector shall report on any system and component included in these standards of practice which were present at the time of the home inspection but were not inspected and provide the reason they were not inspected.

2. GENERAL LIMITATIONS AND EXCLUSIONS

2.1 Inspections performed under the Standards exclude any item(s) concealed or not readily accessible to the inspector. The inspector is not required to move furniture, personal, or stored items; lift floor coverings; move attached wall, ceiling coverings, or panels; or perform any test(s) or procedures(s) which could damage or destroy the item(s) being evaluated.

2.2 The following are excluded and not limited to: appliances, recreational facilities, alarms, intercoms, speaker systems, radio controlled devices, security devices and lawn irrigation systems.

2.3 The determination of the presence of or damage caused by termites or any other wood-damaging insects or organism is excluded.

2.4 Also excluded from a standard home inspection is the determination of the indoor air quality or sickness of any building including, but not limited to, the presence or absence of all manner of biological activity, such as molds, insects, birds, pets, mammals, and other flora and fauna, and their consequent physical damage, toxicity, odors, waste products, and noxiousness.

2.5 Use of special instruments or testing devices, such as amp meters, pressure gauges, moisture meters, gas detectors and similar equipment is not required.

2.6 The inspection is not required to include information from any source concerning previous property, geological, environmental or hazardous waste conditions, manufacturer recalls or conformance of proper manufacturer's installation of any component or system, or information contained in Consumer Protection Bulletin.

STANDARDS OF PRACTICE

4

The inspection is not required to include information from any source concerning past or present violations of codes, ordinances, or regulations.

2.7 The inspection and report are opinions only, based upon visual observation of existing conditions of the inspected property at the time of the inspection. **THE REPORT IS NOT INTENDED TO BE, OR TO BE CONSTRUED AS, A GUARANTEE, WARRANTY, OR ANY FORM OF INSURANCE.** The inspector will not be responsible for any repairs or replacements with regard to the property or the contents thereof.

2.8 The inspector is not required to determine property boundary lines or encroachments.

2.9 The inspector is not required to provide an inspection of any condominium common component, system or evaluate condominium reserve accounts.

2.10 The inspector is not required to enter any premises that visibly shows a physical threat to the safety of the home inspector or others nor inspect any area or component that poses a danger to the inspector or others.

3. SITE

3.1 Components for Inspection.

3.1.1 Building perimeter, land grade, and water drainage directly adjacent to the foundation.

3.1.2 Trees and vegetation that adversely affect the structure.

3.1.3 Walks, grade steps, driveways, patios, and retaining walls contiguous with the structure.

3.2 Procedures for Inspection.

The inspector will:

3.2.1 Describe the type of material and inspect the condition of the driveways, walkways, grade steps, patios, and other items contiguous with the inspected structure.

3.2.2 Observe the drainage, grading, and vegetation for conditions that adversely affect the structure.

3.3 Limitations.

The inspector is NOT required to:

3.3.1 Inspect fences or privacy walls.

3.3.2 Evaluate the condition of trees, shrubs, and or other vegetation.

3.3.3 Evaluate or determine soil or geological conditions, site engineering, or property boundaries.

STANDARDS OF PRACTICE

5

4. FOUNDATIONS

4.1 Components for Inspection.

4.1.1 Foundation walls, first-floor systems, other support and sub-structure components, stairs.

4.1.2 Ventilation (when applicable).

4.1.3 Grade slab and/or floor slab.

4.2 Procedures for Inspection.

The inspector will:

4.2.1 Describe the type of structure and material comprising the structure and other items inspected.

4.2.2 Observe the condition and serviceability of visible, exposed areas of foundation walls, grade slab, bearing walls, posts, piers, beams, joists, trusses, subfloors, chimney foundations, stairs, and other similar structural components.

4.2.3 Inspect foundations for indications of flooding, moisture, or water penetration.

4.2.4 Observe subfloor crawl space ventilation and vapor barriers.

4.2.5 Operate the sump pump when present.

4.2.6 Inspect the visible and accessible wooden members.

4.2.7 Observe the visible condition of floor slab when present.

4.3 Limitations.

The inspector is NOT required to:

4.3.1 Enter subfloor crawl spaces with headroom of less than 3 feet, obstructions, or other detrimental conditions.

4.3.2 Move stored items or debris or perform excavation to gain access.

4.3.3 Enter areas which, in the inspector's opinion, may contain conditions or materials hazardous to the health and safety of the inspector.

4.3.4 Operate sump pumps equipped with internal/water dependent switches.

5. EXTERIOR

5.1 Components for Inspection.

5.1.1 Visible structural components.

5.1.2 Wall covering, trim, and protective coating.

5.1.3 Windows and doors.

6

5.1.4 Attached porches, decks, steps, balconies, handrails, guardrails, and carports.

5.1.5 Visible exterior portions of chimneys.

5.2 Procedures for Inspection.

The inspector will:

5.2.1 Describe the type and material comprising the exterior components inspected.

5.2.2 Observe the condition of the components from the ground level.

5.2.3 Observe the condition of a representative number of visible windows and doors.

5.2.4 Inspect attached porches, decks, steps, balconies, handrails, and guardrails.

5.3 Limitations.

The inspector is NOT required to:

5.3.1 Inspect buildings, decks, patios, retaining walls, and other structures detached from the house.

5.3.2 Evaluate function of shutters, awnings, storm doors, storm windows and similar accessories.

5.3.3 Inspect or test the operation of security locks, devices, or systems.

5.3.4 Evaluate the presence, extent, and type of insulation and vapor barriers in the exterior walls.

5.3.5 Examine the interior of the chimney flues or determine the presence or absence of flue liners.

5.3.6 Inspect for safety type glass or the integrity of thermal window seals or damaged glass.

6. ROOF COVERINGS, FLASHINGS, GUTTERS, DOWNSPOUTS AND ROOF VENTILATION

6.1 Components for Inspection.

6.1.1 Roof covering material.

6.1.2 Rain gutter and downspout system.

6.1.3 Visible portions of roof flashings.

6.1.4 Roof ventilation.

6.1.5 Roof soffits and fascias.

6.1.6 Roof skylights and other roof accessories.

7

6.2 Procedures for Inspection.

The inspector will:

6.2.1 Describe the type of roofing and gutters.

6.2.2 Observe the condition of visible roof material, rain gutter and downspout systems, visible portions of roof flashings, roof soffits and fascias, roof vents, skylights and other roof accessories visible from the exterior.

6.2.3 If possible, inspect the roof surface and components from arms-length distance or with binoculars from the ground.

6.2.4 Inspect flat roofs where internal accessibility is readily and safely available.

6.2.5 Report presence of roof ventilation.

6.3 Limitations.

The inspector is NOT required to:

6.3.1 Walk on or access a roof where it could damage the roof or roofing material or be unsafe for the inspector.

6.3.2 Remove snow, ice, debris or other conditions that prohibit the observation of the roof surfaces.

6.3.3 Inspect internal gutter and downspout systems and related underground drainage piping.

6.3.4 Inspect antennas, lightning arresters, or similar attachments.

6.3.5 Operate powered roof ventilators.

6.3.6 Determine remaining life expectancy of roof coverings, presence or absence of hail damage; manufacturers' defects, exceptions, installation methods or recalls; or number of layers.

6.3.7 Determine adequacy of roof ventilation.

7. ROOF STRUCTURE, ATTIC AND INSULATION

7.1 Components for Inspection.

7.1.1 Roof framing, sheathing and decking.

7.1.2 Attic insulation.

7.2 Procedures for Inspection.

The inspector will:

7.2.1 Describe the type of material comprising the roof structure in the visible attic area.

7.2.2 Observe the condition of the visible roof structure and attic components where readily and safely accessible.

7.2.3 Investigate evidence of the presence of water penetration.

STANDARDS OF PRACTICE

8

7.2.4 Determine the presence of attic insulation and its approximate thickness.

7.3 Limitations.

The inspector is NOT required to:

7.3.1 Enter attic spaces with headroom of less than 5 feet, with insulation covering the ceiling joists, or bottom truss chord, or if there are obstructions, trusses, or other detrimental conditions.

7.3.2 Break or otherwise damage the surface finish or weather seal on or around access panels and covers.

8. ATTACHED GARAGE(S)/CARPORT(S)

8.1 Components for Inspection.

8.1.1 Exterior and interior walls and ceilings, floors, windows, doors, roof, and foundation.

8.1.2 Electrical system and components.

8.1.3 Plumbing system and components.

8.1.4 Heating systems or units.

8.2 Procedures for Inspection.

The inspector will:

8.2.1 Describe the type and material of door(s), exterior walls, roof (if applicable), and other items to be inspected.

8.2.2 Observe the condition and function of listed components; electric, plumbing, heating and similar systems.

8.2.3 Inspect vehicle doors for type, general condition, and intended function by manual operation or by the use of permanently affixed opener(s).

8.3 Limitations.

The inspector is NOT required to:

8.3.1 Inspect or operate equipment housed in the garage area except as otherwise addressed in the Standards.

8.3.2 Verify or certify safe operation of any auto reverse or related safety function(s) of a vehicle door.

9. ELECTRICAL

9.1 Components for Inspection.

9.1.1 Entrance of the primary service from masthead to main panel.

9.1.2 Main and sub-panels including feeders.

STANDARDS OF PRACTICE

9.1.3 Branch circuits, connected devices, and lighting fixtures.

9.2 Procedures for Inspection.

The inspector will:

9.2.1 Describe the type and location of primary service (overhead or underground), voltage, amperage, and over-current protection devices (fuses or breakers).

9.2.2 Observe the existence of a connected grounding conductor when readily accessible.

9.2.3 Inspect the main and branch circuit conductors for proper over-current protection and condition by visual observation after removal of the readily accessible main and sub electric panel cover(s).

9.2.4 Report the presence of aluminum branch circuit wiring at the main and sub-panels.

9.2.5 Verify operation of a representative number of accessible switches, receptacles and light fixtures.

9.2.6 Verify grounding and polarity of a representative number of receptacles in proximity to plumbing fixtures or on the exterior.

9.2.7 Verify operation of ground fault circuit interrupters (GFCI), if present.

9.2.8 Observe the general condition of visible branch circuit conductors that may constitute a hazard to the occupant or the structure by reason of improper use or installation of electrical components.

9.3 Limitations.

The inspector is NOT required to:

9.3.1 Insert any tool, probe or testing device into the main or sub-panels.

9.3.2 Activate electrical systems or branch circuits which are not energized.

9.3.3 Operate overload protection devices.

9.3.4 Inspect ancillary systems, including but not limited to: burglar alarms, home protection systems, low voltage relays, smoke/heat detectors, antennas, electrical de-icing tapes, lawn sprinkler wiring, swimming pool wiring, or any systems controlled by timers.

9.3.5 Move any objects, furniture, or appliances to gain access to any electrical component.

9.3.6 Test every switch, receptacle, and fixture.

9.3.7 Remove switch and outlet cover plates.

9.3.8 Inspect electrical equipment not readily accessible or dismantle any electrical device or control.

9.3.9 Verify continuity of connected service ground(s).

10. PLUMBING

10.1 Components for Inspection.

10.1.1 Visible water supply lines.

10.1.2 Visible waste/soil and vent lines.

10.1.3 Fixtures and faucets.

10.1.4 Domestic hot water system and fuel source.

10.2 Procedures for Inspection.

The inspector will:

10.2.1   Describe the material of the main line and water supply lines.

10.2.2   Verify the presence of a main water supply valve.

10.2.3   Describe the type of sanitary waste piping.

10.2.4   Describe the type and capacity of domestic water heating unit(s).

10.2.5   Inspect the condition of accessible and visible water and waste lines.

10.2.6   Inspect and operate fixtures and faucets.

10.2.7   Inspect and operate the domestic hot water system.

10.2.8   Inspect and operate drain pumps and waste ejector pumps when possible.

10.2.9   Test the water supply for functional flow.

10.2.10 Test waste lines from sinks, tubs and showers for functional drainage.

10.3 Limitations.

The inspector is NOT required to:

10.3.1   Operate any main, branch or fixture valve, except faucets, or determine water temperature.

10.3.2   Inspect any system that is shut-down or secured.

10.3.3   Inspect any plumbing components not readily accessible.

10.3.4   Inspect any exterior plumbing components or interior or exterior drain systems.

10.3.5   Inspect interior fire sprinkler systems.

10.3.6   Evaluate the potability of any water supply.

11

10.3.7   Inspect water conditioning equipment, including softener and filter systems.

10.3.8   Operate freestanding or built-in appliances.

10.3.9   Inspect private water supply systems.

10.3.10 Test shower pans, tub and shower surrounds, or enclosures for leakage.

10.3.11 Inspect gas supply system for materials, installation or leakage.

10.3.12 Evaluate the condition and operation of water wells and related pressure tanks and pumps; the quality or quantity of water from on-site water supplies; or the condition and operation of on-site sewage disposal systems such as cesspools, septic tanks, drain fields, related underground piping, conduit, cisterns, and equipment.

10.3.13 Inspect and operate fixtures and faucets if the flow end of the faucet is connected to an appliance.

10.3.14 Record location of any on-site visible fuel tanks within or directly adjacent to structure.

11. CENTRAL HEATING

11.1 Components for Inspection.

11.1.1   Fuel source.

11.1.2   Heating equipment.

11.1.3   Heating distribution.

11.1.4   Operating controls.

11.1.5   Flue pipes, chimneys and venting.

11.1.6   Auxiliary heating units.

11.2 Procedures for Inspection.

The inspector will:

11.2.1   Describe the type of fuel, heating equipment, and heating distribution system.

11.2.2   Operate the system using normal readily accessible control devices.

11.2.3   Open readily accessible access panels or covers provided by the manufacturer or installer, if readily detachable.

11.2.4   Observe the condition of normally operated controls and components of the systems.

11.2.5   Observe visible flue pipes, dampers and related components for functional operation.

12

11.2.6   Observe the condition of a representative number of heat sources in each habitable space of the house.

11.2.7   Inspect the operation of fixed supplementary heat units. See 2.6 for more information.

11.3 Limitations.

*The inspector is **NOT** required to:*

11.3.1   Activate or operate heating or other systems that do not respond to normal controls or have been shut-down.

11.3.2   To inspect or evaluate a heat exchanger.

11.3.3   Inspect equipment or remove covers or panels that are not readily accessible.

11.3.4   Dismantle any equipment, controls, or gauges.

11.3.5   Inspect the interior of chimney flues.

11.3.6   Inspect heating system accessories, such as humidifiers, air purifiers, motorized dampers, heat reclaimers, etc.

11.3.7   Inspect solar heating systems.

11.3.8   Activate heating, heat pump systems, or other systems when ambient temperatures or other circumstances are not conducive to safe operation or may damage the equipment.

11.3.9   Evaluate the type of material contained in insulation and/or wrapping of pipes, ducts, jackets and boilers.

11.3.10 Operate digital-type thermostats or controls.

11.3.11 Evaluate the capacity, adequacy, or efficiency of a heating or cooling system.

11.3.12 Test or operate gas logs, built-in gas burning appliances, grills, stoves, space heaters, or solar heating devices.

11.3.13 Determine clearance to combustibles or adequacy of combustion air.

12. CENTRAL AIR CONDITIONING

12.1 Components for Inspection.

12.1.1   Cooling equipment.

12.1.2   Cooling distribution.

12.1.3   Operating controls.

13

12.2 Procedures for Inspection.

The inspector will:

12.2.1   Describe the type of central air conditioning system and energy sources.

12.2.2   Operate the system using normal control devices.

12.2.3   Open readily accessible access panels or covers provided by the manufacturer or installer, if readily accessible.

12.2.4   Observe the condition of controls and operative components of the complete system, conditions permitting.

12.2.5   Observe the condition of a representative number of the central air cooling outlets in each habitable space of the house.

12.3 Limitations.

*The inspector is **NOT** required to:*

12.3.1   Activate or operate cooling or other systems that have been shut-down.

12.3.2   Inspect gas-fired refrigeration systems, evaporative coolers, or wall or window-mounted air conditioning units.

12.3.3   Check the pressure of the system coolant or determine the presence of leakage.

12.3.4   Evaluate the capacity, efficiency, or adequacy of the system.

12.3.5   Operate equipment or systems if exterior temperature is below 60° Fahrenheit or when other circumstances are not conducive to safe operation or may damage the equipment.

12.3.6   Remove covers or panels that are not readily accessible.

12.3.7   Dismantle any equipment, controls, or gauges.

12.3.8   Check the electrical current drawn by the unit.

12.3.9   Operate digital-type thermostats or controls.

13. INTERIOR

13.1 Components for Inspection.

13.1.1   Walls, ceilings, floors, windows, and doors.

13.1.2   Steps, stairways, balconies, railings.

13.1.3   Fireplaces.

14

13.1.4   Electric outlets and fixtures.

13.1.5   Plumbing fixtures and components.

13.1.6   Heating and cooling distribution.

13.2 Procedures for Inspection.

The inspector will:

13.2.1   Observe the visible condition of the surfaces of walls, ceilings, and floors relative to structural integrity and evidence of water penetration.

13.2.2   Verify the presence of steps, stairways, balconies, handrails and guardrails and observe their condition.

13.2.3   Describe type, material, condition and operation of a representative number of windows, doors and their hardware.

13.2.4   Inspect the exterior condition of the kitchen cabinets and countertops.

13.2.5   Observe the condition of fireplaces, dampers, fire boxes and hearths readily visible.

13.2.6   Locate and observe a representative number of electrical outlets/fixtures and wiring in each room as described in Section 9.

13.2.7   Comment on presence or absence of smoke detectors.

13.2.8   Observe condition and operation of plumbing fixtures and components in each room as described in Section 10.

13.3 Limitations.

*The inspector is **NOT** required to:*

13.3.1   Ignite fires in a fireplace or stove to determine the adequacy of draft, perform a chimney smoke test, or inspect any solid fuel device in use.

13.3.2   Evaluate the installation or adequacy of inserts, wood burning stoves, or other modifications in a fireplace, stove, or chimney.

13.3.3   Determine clearance to combustibles in concealed areas.

13.3.4   Determine cosmetic condition of ceilings, walls, floor coverings, and components.

13.3.5   Determine if the bath and/or kitchen vent fan ducting exhausts air to exterior of house.

15

GLOSSARY OF TERMS

Activate: To turn on, supply power, or enable systems, equipment, or devices to become active by normal control means. Examples include turning on the gas or water supply valves to the fixtures and appliances and activating electrical breakers or fuses.

Additional Inspection Services: Those services offered in addition to the home inspection as defined in these standards, including but not limited to the following examples; wood destroying insect-organism and environmental testing.

Adversely Affect: Constitute, or potentially constitute, a negative or destructive impact.

Appliance: A household device operated by use of electricity or gas. Not included in this definition are components covered under central heating, central cooling, or plumbing.

Detrimental Conditions: Any conditions that, in the opinion of the inspector, may likely be unsafe, unhealthy, or in any way harmful to the inspector or to components of the property.

Describe: To distinguish from another system or component.

Evaluate: To ascertain, judge, or form an opinion about an item or condition.

Foundation: The base upon which the structure or a wall rests; usually masonry, concrete, or stone, and generally partially underground.

Function: The action for which an item, component or system is specially fitted or used or for which an item, component or system exists; to be in action or perform a task.

Functional: Performing, or able to perform, a function.

Functional Drainage: A drain is functional when it empties in a reasonable amount of time and is not subject to overflow when one of its supply faucets is left on.

Functional Flow: Sufficient water flow to provide uninterrupted supply to the highest, unrestricted tap (faucet furthest from the source) when a single intermediate, unrestricted tap is operated simultaneously with uninterrupted flow.

Habitable: In a condition suitable for human habitation.

Habitable Spaces: Rooms or spaces used for sitting, sleeping, bathing, toilets, eating or cooking. Not considered habitable spaces by these Standards are closets, halls, storage spaces and utility areas.

16

Heat Source: A heat source may be a radiator, convector unit, radiant panel, heat pipe, ductwork, grille, register, or other device(s) from which heat is intended to be emitted.

Home Inspection: The process by which an inspector visually examines the readily accessible systems and components of a home and operates those systems and components utilizing the Standards of Practice as a guideline.

Inspect: To evaluate carefully without use of technically exhaustive methods.

Inspected Property: The readily accessible areas of the buildings, site, items, components, and systems included in the inspection.

Intended Function: Performing or able to perform the usual function for which an item is designed, or fitted; and be in a condition (state of repair) appropriate to this function, its age and location. [See Function]

Observe: To see through visual directed attention.

Operate: To cause equipment or systems that have been activated to perform their intended function(s), such as turning on a water faucet or turning up the thermostat on an activated heating system.

Readily Accessible: An item or component is readily accessible if, in the judgement of the inspector, it is capable of being safely observed without movement of obstacles, detachment or disengagement of connecting or securing devices, or other unsafe or difficult procedures to gain access.

Representative Number: A sufficient number to serve as a typical or characteristic example of the item(s) inspected.

Shut-down: A system or equipment is considered to be shut-down when its normal control device(s) will not cause it to become activated or operational. The inspector is not required to activate or operate safety devices (fuses, breakers, etc.) in the "off" position. It is not the responsibility of the inspector to put these controls in the "on" mode, nor to ensure that the equipment or systems to be tested are operable at the time of the inspection.

Slab on Grade: Structures that have no crawl space and are in direct contact with the soil. Slabs may or may not have supporting piers or pads.

Technically exhaustive: An inspection is technically exhaustive when it involves the use of measurements, instruments, testing calculations and other means to develop scientific or engineering findings, conclusions, and recommendations.

Verify: To confirm or substantiate.

PURPOSE STATEMENT

To maintain the integrity and high standard of skill and practice in the home inspection profession, the following rules of conduct and ethics shall be binding upon the NAHI inspector.

CODE OF ETHICS #1

Home inspection services that the inspector provides to the client(s) shall conform to the National Association of Home Inspectors, Inc.™ Standards of Practice.

CODE OF ETHICS #2

The inspector will act as an unbiased third party to the real estate transaction and will discharge the inspector's duties with integrity and fidelity to the client.

CODE OF ETHICS #3

The inspector will only express an opinion on any aspect of an inspected property when it is based on the experience, training, education and professional opinion of the inspector.

CODE OF ETHICS #4

The inspector shall not provide services that constitute the unauthorized practice of any profession that requires a special license if the inspector does not hold that license.

CODE OF ETHICS #5

The inspector shall not accept compensation for a home inspection from more than one party without written disclosure to the inspector's client(s).

CODE OF ETHICS #6

The inspector may recommend or offer products or additional services to the client consistent with the provisions of this Code of Ethics. If the services or products recommended or offered by the inspector are:

(a) to be purchased from or provided by the inspector, their agents or employees;

(b) to be purchased from or provided by any entity, organization, or venture in which the inspector has an interest; or

(c) will result in any compensation or benefit to the inspector, financial or otherwise,

then the products or services may only be recommended or offered after a written disclosure to the client of the inspector's interest in the transaction and advising the client to obtain competitive bids.

CODE OF ETHICS #7

The inspector will not provide any compensation, inducement, or reward directly or indirectly, to any person or entity other than a client, for the referral of business to the inspector. (The purchase and/or use of advertising or marketing services or products are not considered compensation, inducement, or reward.)

CODE OF ETHICS #8

The inspector will not conduct a home inspection or prepare a home inspection report for which the inspector's fee is contingent upon the conclusions in the report.

CODE OF ETHICS #9

The inspector will not disclose any information concerning the results of the inspection without the approval of the client for whom the inspection was performed, unless compelled by court order.

CODE OF ETHICS #10

Home inspectors, while providing professional services, or in their employment practices, shall not discriminate against any person on the basis of age, race, color, religion, sex, handicap, family status, national origin or any other status protected by law.

CODE OF ETHICS #11

The inspector shall make every effort to uphold, maintain and improve the professional practice, integrity, and reputation of NAHI. The inspector will report violations of this Code by other members, and any other relevant information to NAHI for possible remedial action.

CODE OF ETHICS #12

While this Code of Ethics establishes obligations that may be higher than those mandated by law, in any instance where the Code of Ethics and the law conflict, the obligations of the law must take precedence.

NACHI STANDARDS OF PRACTICE

Standards of Practice of the National Association of Certified Home Inspectors

(Last revised: 12/7/04)

Table of Contents

1. Definitions and Scope

1.1. A Home inspection is a non-invasive visual examination of a residential dwelling, performed for a fee, which is designed to identify observed material defects within specific components of said dwelling. Components may include any combination of mechanical, structural, electrical, plumbing, or other essential systems or portions of the home, as identified and agreed to by the Client and Inspector, prior to the inspection process.

   I. A home inspection is intended to assist in evaluation of the overall condition of the dwelling. The inspection is based on observation of the visible and apparent condition of the structure and its components on the date of the inspection and not the prediction of future conditions.

   II. A home inspection will not reveal every concern that exists or ever could exist, but only those material defects observed on the day of the inspection.

1.2. A Material defect is a condition with a residential real property or any portion of it that would have a significant adverse impact on the value of the real property or that involves an unreasonable risk to people on the property. The fact that a structural element, system or subsystem is near, at or beyond the end of the normal useful life of such a structural element, system or subsystem is not by itself a material defect.

1.3. An Inspection report shall describe and identify in written format the inspected systems, structures, and components of the dwelling and shall identify material defects observed. Inspection reports may contain recommendations regarding conditions reported or recommendations for correction, monitoring or further evaluation by professionals, but this is not required.

2. Standards of Practice

2.1. Roof

I. The inspector shall inspect from ground level or eaves:

  A. The roof covering.
  B. The gutters.
  C. The downspouts.
  D. The vents, flashings, skylights, chimney and other roof penetrations.
  E. The general structure of the roof from the readily accessible panels, doors or stairs.

II. The inspector is not required to:

  A. Walk on any roof surface.
  B. Predict the service life expectancy.
  C. Inspect underground downspout diverter drainage pipes.
  D. Remove snow, ice, debris or other conditions that prohibit the observation of the roof surfaces.
  E. Inspect antennae, lightning arresters, or similar attachments.

2.2. Exterior

I. The inspector shall inspect:

  A. The siding, flashing and trim.
  B. All exterior doors, decks, stoops, steps, stairs, porches, railings, eaves, soffits and fascias.
  C. And report as in need of repair any spacings between intermediate balusters, spindles, or rails for steps, stairways, balconies, and railings that permit the passage of an object greater than four inches in diameter.
  D. A representative number of windows.
  E. The vegetation, surface drainage and retaining walls when these are likely to adversely affect the structure.
  F. And describe the exterior wall covering.

II. The inspector is not required to:

  A. Inspect or operate screens, storm windows, shutters, awnings, fences, outbuildings, or exterior accent lighting.
  B. Inspect items, including window and door flashings, which are not visible or readily accessible from the ground.
  C. Inspect geological, geotechnical, hydrological and/or soil conditions.
  D. Inspect recreational facilities.
  E. Inspect seawalls, break-walls and docks.
  F. Inspect erosion control and earth stabilization measures.
  G. Inspect for safety type glass.
  H. Inspect underground utilities.
  I. Inspect underground items.
  J. Inspect wells or springs.
  K. Inspect solar systems.
  L. Inspect swimming pools or spas.
  M. Inspect septic systems or cesspools.
  N. Inspect playground equipment.
  O. Inspect sprinkler systems.
  P. Inspect drain fields or drywells.
  Q. Determine the integrity of the thermal window seals or damaged glass.

2.3. Basement, Foundation & Crawlspace

I. The inspector shall inspect:

  A. The basement.
  B. The foundation.
  C. The crawlspace.
  D. The visible structural components.
  E. Any present conditions or clear indications of active water penetration observed by the inspector.
  F. And report any general indications of foundation movement that are observed by the inspector, such as but not limited to sheetrock cracks, brick cracks, out-of-square door frames or floor slopes.

II. The inspector is not required to:

  A. Enter any crawlspaces that are not readily accessible or where entry could cause damage or pose a hazard to the inspector.
  B. Move stored items or debris.
  C. Operate sump pumps with inaccessible floats.
  D. Identify size, spacing, span, location or determine adequacy of foundation bolting, bracing, joists, joist spans or support systems.
  E. Provide any engineering or architectural service.
  F. Report on the adequacy of any structural system or component.

2.4. Heating

I. The inspector shall inspect:

  A. The heating system and describe the energy source and heating method using normal operating controls.
  B. And report as in need of repair electric furnaces which do not operate.

C. And report if inspector deemed the furnace inaccessible.

II. The inspector is not required to:

A. Inspect or evaluate interiors of flues or chimneys, fire chambers, heat exchangers, humidifiers, dehumidifiers, electronic air filters, solar heating systems, solar heating systems or fuel tanks.

B. Inspect underground fuel tanks.

C. Determine the uniformity, temperature, flow, balance, distribution, size, capacity, BTU, or supply adequacy of the heating system.

D. Light or ignite pilot flames.

E. Activate heating, heat pump systems, or other heating systems when ambient temperatures or when other circumstances are not conducive to safe operation or may damage the equipment.

F. Override electronic thermostats.

G. Evaluate fuel quality.

H. Verify thermostat calibration, heat anticipation or automatic setbacks, timers, programs or clocks.

2.5. Cooling

I. The inspector shall inspect:

A. The central cooling equipment using normal operating controls.

II. The inspector is not required to:

A. Determine the uniformity, temperature, flow, balance, distribution, size, capacity, BTU, or supply adequacy of the cooling system.

B. Inspect window units, through-wall units, or electronic air filters.

C. Operate equipment or systems if exterior temperature is below 60 degrees Fahrenheit or when other circumstances are not conducive to safe operation or may damage the equipment.

D. Inspect or determine thermostat calibration, heat anticipation or automatic setbacks or clocks.
E. Examine electrical current, coolant fluids or gasses, or coolant leakage.

2.6. Plumbing

I. The inspector shall:

A. Verify the presence of and identify the location of the main water shutoff valve.

B. Inspect the water heating equipment, including combustion air, venting, connections, energy sources, seismic bracing, and verify the presence or absence of temperature-pressure relief valves and/or Watts 210 valves.

C. Flush toilets.

D. Run water in sinks, tubs, and showers.

E. Inspect the interior water supply including all fixtures and faucets.

F. Inspect the drain, waste and vent systems, including all fixtures.

G. Describe any visible fuel storage systems.

H. Inspect the drainage sump pumps testing sumps with accessible floats.

I. Inspect and describe the water supply, drain, waste and main fuel shut-off valves, as well as the location of the water main and main fuel shut-off valves.

J. Inspect and determine if the water supply is public or private.

K. Inspect and report as in need of repair deficiencies in the water supply by viewing the functional flow in two fixtures operated simultaneously.

L. Inspect and report as in need of repair deficiencies in installation and identification of hot and cold faucets.

M. Inspect and report as in need of repair mechanical drain-stops that are missing or do not operate if installed in sinks, lavatories and tubs.

N. Inspect and report as in need of repair commodes that have cracks in the ceramic material, are improperly mounted on the floor, leak, or have tank components which do not operate.

II. The inspector is not required to:

A. Light or ignite pilot flames.

B. Determine the size, temperature, age, life expectancy or adequacy of the water heater.

C. Inspect interiors of flues or chimneys, water softening or filtering systems, well pumps or tanks, safety or shut-of valves, floor drains, lawn sprinkler systems or fire sprinkler systems.

D. Determine the exact flow rate, volume, pressure, temperature, or adequacy of the water supply.

E. Determine the water quality or potability or the reliability of the water supply or source.

F. Open sealed plumbing access panels.

G. Inspect clothes washing machines or their connections.

H. Operate any main, branch or fixture valve.

I. Test shower pans, tub and shower surrounds or enclosures for leakage.

J. Evaluate the compliance with local or state conservation or energy standards, or the proper design or sizing of any water, waste or venting components, fixtures or piping.

K. Determine the effectiveness of anti-siphon, back-flow prevention or drain-stop devices.

L. Determine whether there are sufficient clean-outs for effective cleaning of drains.

M. Evaluate gas, liquid propane or oil storage tanks.

N. Inspect any private sewage waste disposal system or component of.

O. Inspect water treatment systems or water filters.

P. Inspect water storage tanks, pressure pumps or bladder tanks.

Q. Evaluate time to obtain hot water at fixtures, or perform testing of any kind to water heater elements.

R. Evaluate or determine the adequacy of combustion air.

S. Test, operate, open or close safety controls, manual stop valves and/or temperature or pressure relief valves.

T. Examine ancillary systems or components, such as, but not limited to, those relating to solar water heating, hot water circulation.

2.7. Electrical

I. The inspector shall inspect:

A. The service line.

B. The meter box.

C. The main disconnect.

D. And determine the rating of the service amperage.

E. Panels, breakers and fuses.

F. The service grounding and bonding.

H. A representative sampling of switches, receptacles, light fixtures, AFCI receptacles

I. And test all GFCI receptacles and GFCI circuit breakers observed and deemed to be GFCI's during the inspection.

I. And report the presence of solid conductor aluminum branch circuit wiring if readily visible.

J. And report on any GFCI-tested receptacles in which power is not present, polarity is incorrect, the receptacle is not grounded, is not secured to the wall, the cover is not in place, the ground fault circuit interrupter devices are not properly installed or do not operate properly, or evidence of arcing or excessive heat is present.

K. The service entrance conductors and the condition of their sheathing.

L. The ground fault circuit interrupters observed and deemed to be GFCI's during the inspection with a GFCI tester.

M. And describe the amperage rating of the service.

N. And report the absence of smoke detectors.

O. Service entrance cables and report as in need of repair deficiencies in the integrity of the insulation, drip loop, or separation of conductors at weatherheads and clearances.

II. The inspector is not required to:

A. Insert any tool, probe or device into the main panel, sub-panels, downstream panels, or electrical fixtures.

B. Operate electrical systems that are shut down.

C. Remove panel covers or dead front covers if not readily accessible.

D. Operate over current protection devices.

E. Operate non-accessible smoke detectors.

F. Measure or determine the amperage or voltage of the main service if not visibly labeled.

G. Inspect the alarm system and components.

H. Inspect the ancillary wiring or remote control devices.

I. Activate any electrical systems or branch circuits which are not energized.

J. Operate overload devices.

K. Inspect low voltage systems, electrical de-icing tapes, swimming pool wiring or any time-controlled devices.

L. Verify the continuity of the connected service ground.

M. Inspect private or emergency electrical supply sources, including but not limited to generators, windmills, photovoltaic solar collectors, or battery or electrical storage facility.

  N. Inspect spark or lightning arrestors.

  O. Conduct voltage drop calculations.

  P. Determine the accuracy of breaker labeling.

2.8. Fireplace

  I. The inspector shall inspect:

    A. The fireplace, and open and close the damper door if readily accessible and operable.

    B. Hearth extensions and other permanently installed components.

    C. And report as in need of repair deficiencies in the lintel, hearth and material surrounding the fireplace, including clearance from combustible materials

  II. The inspector is not required to:

    A. Inspect the flue or vent system.

    B. Inspect the interior of chimneys or flues, fire doors or screens, seals or gaskets, or mantels.

    C. Determine the need for a chimney sweep.

    D. Operate gas fireplace inserts.

    E. Light pilot flames.

    F. Determine the appropriateness of such installation.

    G. Inspect automatic fuel feed devices.

    H. Inspect combustion and/or make-up air devices.

    I. Inspect heat distribution assists whether gravity controlled or fan assisted.

    J. Ignite or extinguish fires.

    K. Determine draft characteristics.

    L. Move fireplace inserts, stoves, or firebox contents.

    M. Determine adequacy of draft, perform a smoke test or dismantle or remove any component.

    N. Perform an NFPA inspection.

2.9. Attic, Ventilation & Insulation

  I. The inspector shall inspect:

    A. The insulation in unfinished spaces.

    B. The ventilation of attic spaces.

    C. Mechanical ventilation systems.

    D. And report on the general absence or lack of insulation.

  II. The inspector is not required to:

    A. Enter the attic or unfinished spaces that are not readily accessible or where entry could cause damage or pose a safety hazard to the inspector in his or her opinion.

    B. To move, touch, or disturb insulation.

    C. To move, touch or disturb vapor retarders.

    D. Break or otherwise damage the surface finish or weather seal on or around access panels and covers.

    E. Identify the composition of or the exact R-value of insulation material.

    F. Activate thermostatically operated fans.

    G. Determine the types of materials used in insulation/wrapping of pipes, ducts, jackets, boilers, and wiring.

    H. Determine adequacy of ventilation.

2.10. Doors, Windows & Interior

  I. The inspector shall:

    A. Open and close a representative number of doors and windows.

    B. Inspect the walls, ceilings, steps, stairways, and railings.

    C. Inspect garage doors and garage door openers by operating first by remote (if available) and then by the installed automatic door control.

    D. And report as in need of repair any installed electronic sensors that are not operable or not installed at proper heights above the garage door.

    E. And report as in need of repair any door locks or side ropes that have not been removed or disabled when garage door opener is in use.

    F. And report as in need of repair any windows that are obviously fogged or display other evidence of broken seals.

  II. The inspector is not required to:

    A. Inspect paint, wallpaper, window treatments or finish treatments.

    B. Inspect central vacuum systems.

    C. Inspect safety glazing.

    D. Inspect security systems or components.

    E. Evaluate the fastening of countertops, cabinets, sink tops and fixtures, or firewall compromises.

    F. Move furniture, stored items, or any coverings like carpets or rugs in order to inspect the concealed floor structure.

    G. Move drop ceiling tiles.

    H. Inspect or move any household appliances.

I. Inspect or operate equipment housed in the garage except as otherwise noted.

J. Verify or certify safe operation of any auto reverse or related safety function of a garage door.

K. Operate or evaluate security bar release and opening mechanisms, whether interior or exterior, including compliance with local, state, or federal standards.

L. Operate any system, appliance or component that requires the use of special keys, codes, combinations, or devices.

M. Operate or evaluate self-cleaning oven cycles, tilt guards/latches or signal lights.

N. Inspect microwave ovens or test leakage from microwave ovens.

O. Operate or examine any sauna, steam-jenny, kiln, toaster, ice-maker, coffee-maker, can-opener, bread-warmer, blender, instant hot water dispenser, or other small, ancillary devices.

P. Inspect elevators.

Q. Inspect remote controls.

R. Inspect appliances.

S. Inspect items not permanently installed.

T. Examine or operate any above-ground, movable, freestanding, or otherwise non-permanently installed pool/spa, recreational equipment or self-contained equipment.

U. Come into contact with any pool or spa water in order to determine the system structure or components.

V. Determine the adequacy of spa jet water force or bubble effect.

W. Determine the structural integrity or leakage of a pool or spa.

3. Limitations, Exceptions & Exclusions

3.1. Limitations:

I. An inspection is not technically exhaustive.

II. An inspection will not identify concealed or latent defects.

III. An inspection will not deal with aesthetic concerns or what could be deemed matters of taste, cosmetic, etc.

IV. An inspection will not determine the suitability of the property for any use.

V. An inspection does not determine the market value of the property or its marketability.

VI. An inspection does not determine the advisability or inadvisability of the purchase of the inspected property.

VII. An inspection does not determine the life expectancy of the property or any components or systems therein.

VIII. An inspection does not include items not permanently installed.

IX. These Standards of Practice apply only to homes with four or fewer dwelling units.

3.2. Exclusions:

I. The inspectors are not required to determine:

A. Property boundary lines or encroachments.

B. The condition of any component or system that is not readily accessible.

C. The service life expectancy of any component or system.

D. The size, capacity, BTU, performance, or efficiency of any component or system.

E. The cause or reason of any condition.

F. The cause for the need of repair or replacement of any system or component.

G. Future conditions.

H. The compliance with codes or regulations.

I. The presence of evidence of rodents, animals or insects.

J. The presence of mold, mildew or fungus.

K. The presence of air-borne hazards.

L. The presence of birds.

M. The presence of other flora or fauna.

N. The air quality.

O. The existence of asbestos.

P. The existence of environmental hazards.

Q. The existence of electro-magnetic fields.

R. The presence of hazardous materials including, but not limited to, the presence of lead in paint.

S. Any hazardous waste conditions.

T. Any manufacturer recalls or conformance with manufacturer installation or any information included in the consumer protection bulletin.

U. Operating costs of systems.

V. Replacement or repair cost estimates.

W. The acoustical properties of any systems.

X. Estimates of how much it will cost to run any given system.

II. The inspectors are not required to operate:

A. Any system that is shut down.

B. Any system that does not function properly.

C. Or evaluate low voltage electrical systems such as, but not limited to:

1. Phone lines.
2. Cable lines.
3. Antennae.
4. Lights.
5. Remote controls.

D. Any system that does not turn on with the use of normal operating controls.

E. Any shut off valves or manual stop valves.

F. Any electrical disconnect or over current protection devices.

G. Any alarm systems.

H. Moisture meters, gas detectors or similar equipment.

III. The inspectors are not required to:

A. Move any personal items or other obstructions, such as, but not limited to:

1. Throw rugs.
2. Furniture.
3. Floor or wall coverings.
4. Ceiling tiles.
5. Window coverings.
6. Equipment.
7. Plants.
8. Ice.
9. Debris.
10. Snow.
11. Water.
12. Dirt.
13. Foliage.
14. Pets

B. Dismantle, open, or uncover any system or component.

C. Enter or access any area which may, in the opinion of the inspector, to be unsafe or risk personal safety.

D. Enter crawlspaces or other areas that are unsafe or not readily accessible.

E. Inspect underground items such as, but not limited to, underground storage tanks or other indications of their presence, whether abandoned or actively used.

F. Do anything which, in the inspector's opinion, is likely to be unsafe or dangerous to the inspector or others or damage property, such as, but not limited to, walking on roof surfaces, climbing ladders, entering attic spaces or negotiating with dogs.

G. Inspect decorative items.

H. Inspect common elements or areas in multi-unit housing.

I. Inspect intercoms, speaker systems, radio-controlled, security devices or lawn irrigation systems.

J. Offer guarantees or warranties.

K. Offer or perform any engineering services.

L. Offer or perform any trade or professional service other than home inspection.

M. Research the history of the property, report on its potential for alteration, modification, extendibility, or its suitability for a specific or proposed use for occupancy.

N. Determine the age of construction or installation of any system structure, or component of a building, or differentiate between original construction or subsequent additions, improvements, renovations or replacements thereto.

O. Determine the insurability of a property.

P. Perform or offer Phase 1 environmental audits.

Q. Inspect on any system or component which is not included in these standards.

4. Glossary of Terms

4.1. Accessible: Can be approached or entered by the inspector safely, without difficulty, fear or danger.

4.2. Activate: To turn on, supply power, or enable systems, equipment, or devices to become active by normal operating controls. Examples include turning on the gas or water supply valves to the fixtures and appliances and activating electrical breakers or fuses.

4.3. Adversely Affect: Constitute, or potentially constitute, a negative or destructive impact.

4.4. Alarm System: Warning devices, installed or free-standing, including but not limited to: Carbon monoxide detectors, flue gas and other spillage detectors, security equipment, ejector pumps and smoke alarms.

4.5. Appliance: A household device operated by use of electricity or gas. Not included in this definition are components covered under central heating, central cooling or plumbing.

4.6. Architectural Service: Any practice involving the art and science of building design for construction of any structure or grouping of structures and the use of space within and surrounding the structures or the design, design development, preparation of construction contract documents, and administration of the construction contract.

4.7. Component: A permanently installed or attached fixture, element or part of a system.

4.8. Condition: The visible and conspicuous state of being of an object.

4.9. Crawlspace: The area within the confines of the foundation and between the ground and the underside of the lowest floor structural component.

4.10. Decorative: Ornamental; not required for the operation of essential systems and components of a home.

4.11. Describe: Report in writing a system or component by its type, or other observed characteristics, to distinguish it from other components used for the same purpose.

4.12. Determine: To arrive at an opinion or conclusion pursuant to examination.

4.13. Dismantle: To open, take apart or remove any component, device or piece that would not typically be opened, taken apart or removed by an ordinary occupant.

4.14. Engineering Service: Any professional service or creative work requiring engineering education, training, and experience and the application of special knowledge of the mathematical, physical and engineering sciences to such professional service or creative work as consultation, investigation, evaluation, planning, design and supervision of construction for the purpose of assuring compliance with the specifications and design, in conjunction with structures, buildings, machines, equipment, works or processes.

4.15. Enter: To go into an area to observe visible components.

4.16. Evaluate: To assess the systems, structures or components of a dwelling.

4.17. Examine: To visually look. See Inspect.

4.18. Foundation: The base upon which the structure or wall rests; usually masonry, concrete, or stone, and generally partially underground.

4.19. Function: The action for which an item, component, or system is specially fitted or used

or for which an item, component or system exists; to be in action or perform a task.

4.20. Functional: Performing, or able to perform, a function.

4.21. Home Inspection: The process by which an inspector visually examines the readily accessible systems and components of a home and operates those systems and components utilizing these Standards of Practice as a guideline.

4.22. Household Appliances: Kitchen and laundry appliances, room air conditioners, and similar appliances.

4.23. Inspect: To visually look at readily accessible systems and components safely, using normal operating controls and accessing readily accessible panels and areas in accordance with these Standards of Practice.

4.24. Inspected Property: The readily accessible areas of the buildings, site, items, components, and systems included in the inspection.

4.25. Inspector: One who performs a real estate inspection.

4.26. Installed: Attached or connected such that the installed item requires tool for removal.

4.27. Material Defect: Refer to section 1.2.

4.28. Normal Operating Controls: Devices such as thermostats that would be operated by ordinary occupants which require no specialized skill or knowledge.

4.29. Observe: To see through visually directed attention.

4.30. Operate: To cause systems to function or turn on with normal operating controls.

4.31. Readily Accessible: An item or component is readily accessible if, in the judgment of the inspector, it is capable of being safely observed without movement of obstacles, detachment or disengagement of connecting or securing devices, or other unsafe or difficult procedures to gain access.

4.32. Recreational Facilities: Spas, saunas, steam baths, swimming pools, tennis courts, playground equipment, and other exercise, entertainment or athletic facilities.

4.33. Report: A written communication (possibly including digital images) of any material defects seen during the inspection.

4.34. Representative Number: A sufficient number to serve as a typical or characteristic example of the item(s) inspected.

4.35. Safety Glazing: Tempered glass, laminated glass, or rigid plastic.

4.36. Shut Down: Turned off, unplugged, inactive, not in service, not operational, etc.

4.37. Structural Component: A component which supports non-variable forces or weights (dead loads) and variable forces or weights (live loads).

4.38. System: An assembly of various components to function as a whole.

4.39. Technically Exhaustive: A comprehensive and detailed examination beyond the scope of a real estate home inspection which would involve or include, but would not be limited to: dismantling, specialized knowledge or training, special equipment, measurements, calculations, testing, research, analysis or other means.

4.40. Unsafe: A condition in a readily accessible, installed system or component which is judged to be a significant risk of personal injury during normal, day-to-day use. The risk may be due to damage, deterioration, improper installation or a change in accepted residential construction standards.

4.41. Verify: To confirm or substantiate.

Code of Ethics

The National Association of Certified Home Inspectors (NACHI) promotes a high standard of professionalism, business ethics and inspection procedures. NACHI members subscribe to the following Code of Ethics in the course of their business.

1. Duty to the Public

1. The NACHI member shall abide by the Code of Ethics and substantially follow the NACHI Standards of Practice.

2. The NACHI member shall not engage in any practices that could be damaging to the public or bring discredit to the home inspection industry.

3. The NACHI member shall be fair, honest, impartial, and act in good faith in dealing with the public.

4. The NACHI member shall not discriminate in any business activities on the basis of race, color, religion, sex, national origin, familial status, sexual orientation, or handicap and shall comply with all federal, state and local laws concerning discrimination.

5. The NACHI member shall be truthful regarding his/her services & qualifications.

6. The NACHI member shall have no undisclosed conflict of interest with the client, nor shall the NACHI member accept or offer any undisclosed commissions, rebates, profits or other benefit, nor shall the NACHI member accept or offer any disclosed or undisclosed commissions, rebates, profits or other benefit from from real estate agents, brokers or any third parties having financial interest in the sale of the property nor shall the NACHI member offer or provide any disclosed or undisclosed financial compensation directly or indirectly to any real estate agent, real estate broker or real estate company for referrals or for inclusion on lists of preferred and/or affiliated inspectors or inspection companies.

7. The NACHI member shall not communicate any information about an inspection to anyone except the client without the prior written consent of the client, except where it may affect the safety of others or violates a law or statute.

8. The NACHI member shall always act in the interest of the client, unless doing so violates a law, statute or this Code of Ethics.

9. The NACHI member shall use a written contract that specifies the services to be performed, limitations of services and fees.

10. The NACHI member shall comply with all government rules and licensing requirements of the jurisdiction where he/she conducts business.

11. The NACHI member shall not perform or offer to perform, for an additional fee, any repairs or associated services to structure on which the member or member's company has prepared a home inspection report, for a period of 12 months. This provision shall not include services to components and/or systems which are not included in the NACHI standards of practice.

2. Duty to Continue Education

1. The NACHI member shall comply with NACHI's current Continuing Education Requirements.

2. The NACHI member shall pass the NACHI's Online Inspector Exam once every calendar year.

3. Duty to the Profession and NACHI

1. The NACHI member shall strive to improve the Home Inspection Industry by sharing his/her lessons and/or experiences for the benefit of all. This does not preclude the member from copyrighting or marketing his/her expertise to other Inspectors or the public in any manner permitted by law.

2. The NACHI member shall assist the NACHI leadership in disseminating and publicizing the benefits of NACHI membership.

3. The NACHI member shall not engage in any act or practice that could be deemed damaging, seditious or destructive to NACHI, fellow NACHI members, NACHI employees, leadership or directors. Member(s) accused of acting or deemed in violation of such rules shall be reviewed by the Ethics committee for possible sanctions and/or expulsion from NACHI.

4. The NACHI member shall abide by NACHI's current membership requirements.

5. The NACHI member shall abide by NACHI's current message board rules.

HOME INSPECTION ORGANIZATIONS

The following data are subject to change. Refer to the respective Web sites for current information and details.

Organization	Internet Contact	Designations	Standards of Practice/ Code of Ethics	Continuing Education/ Training/ Seminars	Application Fees and Dues
American Association of Home Inspectors (AAHI) 5147-D 69th Street P.O. Box 64309 Lubbock, TX 79464 806-794-1190/Fax: 806-794-8901	aahi@aahi.com www.aahi.com	Certified Home Inspector Member Company Member Affiliate Member (Non-active member)	✔	✔	$200
American Inspectors Society (AIS) P.O. Box 702 Stone Mountain, GA 30086 706-219-7680	www.homeinspector training.com	Certified Home Inspector	✔	✔	based on training
American Society of Home Inspectors®, Inc. (ASHI) 932 Lee Street, Suite 101 Des Plaines, IL 60016 847-759-2820 or 800-743-ASHI (2744)/Fax: 847-759-1620	www.ashi.org	Members (M) Candidates w/Logo (CL) Candidates (CN)	✔	✔	Application fee–$80 Dues–$375
Housing Inspection Foundation (HIF) 1224 North Nokomis NE Alexandria, MN 56308 320-763-6350 Fax: 320-763-9290	www.iami.org	Registered Home Inspector (RHI) Certified Housing Consultant (CHC) Certified Home Inspector (CHI)	✔	✔	Dues–$195

Organization	Internet Contact	Designations	Standards of Practice/ Code of Ethics	Continuing Education/ Training/ Seminars	Application Fees and Dues
National Association of Building Inspection Engineers (NABIE) P.O. Box 522158 Salt Lake City, UT 84152 800-294-7729 Fax 801-583-1531	www.nabie.org	Intern Member Professional Member Executive Member Diplomate of the Academy Fellow of the Academy	✔	Membership open only to professional engineers and architects	Application fee–$25; Intern member–$175 Professional Member–$175; Executive Member–$225; Diplomate and Fellow–$275
National Association of Home Inspectors (NAHI) 4248 Park Glen Road Minneapolis, MN 55416 952-928-4641, 800-448-3942 Fax 952-929-1318	www.nahi.org	Associate and Regular Membership Certified Real Estate Inspector (NAHI CRI)	✔	✔	Application fee–$50 Associate and regular member–$295 NAHI CRI–$345
The Foundation of Real Estate Appraisers (FREA) 4907 Morena Blvd., Suite 1415 San Diego, CA 92117 800-882-4410 Fax: 858-273-8026	info@frea.com www.frea.com	Residential Real Estate Inspector (RREI); Commercial Real Estate Inspector (CREI)	✔	✔	Dues–$245
Society of Professional Real Estate Inspectors (SPREI) 993 Summer St. Lynnfield, MA 01940 781-334-4500	sprei@sprei.org www.sprei.org	Candidate Member; Registered Senior Member	✔	✔	Dues–$195

Absorption field A system of narrow trenches through which the discharge from a septic tank infiltrates into the surrounding soil.

Americans with Disabilities Act Federal legislation that protects the rights of individuals with physical or mental impairments.

Amperage The amount of current or electricity flowing through a wire.

Anchor post Component of a tieback used to support a wood retaining wall; the anchor post is attached perpendicularly to the back of the wall.

Appurtenance A right, privilege, or improvement belonging to, and passing with, the land.

Aquifer Below ground-level rock bed over which water flows.

Asbestos A fibrous material found in rocks and soil.

Ash dump door The metal door located in the inner hearth of some fireplaces that leads to an ash pit.

Ash pit A cavity underneath the firebox that is used as a receptacle for ashes and is accessible through a cleanout door.

Ash pit cleanout door A metal door located at the base of the chimney that leads to the ash pit.

Avulsion Sudden loss or gain of land because of water or a shift in a riverbed that has been used as a boundary.

Backflow preventer Keeps water from backing up in a water supply or drainage system.

Balloon framing Uses a single system of wall studs that run from the foundation through to the first and second floors to the ceiling support.

Baluster Pole or post that runs from the stair handrail vertically to the tread.

Bearing wall Supports the ceiling or the roof and includes the outside wall frame.

Boilers Used to transfer heat from a fuel source to a fluid, such as water, and are constructed from cast iron, steel, or copper.

Branch circuit wiring Wiring that goes from the main panel board through the walls of the building to the switches and outlets.

BTU Abbreviation for British thermal unit; a measure of heat energy, a BTU is the amount of heat required to raise the temperature of one pound of water by one degree Fahrenheit.

Building codes Public land use controls regulating construction.

Building envelope The materials that enclose the interior and through which heating, cooling, and fresh air passes.

Building permit Permission from the appropriate local government authority to construct or renovate any type of property.

Bus bars Conductors on the main panel board that provide electrical connections for fuses or circuit breakers.

Carpenter ant A type of insect that eats wood.

Carpenter bee A type of insect that eats wood.

Casing The material that surrounds the window on the inside.

Catalytic combustor A ceramic, round, square, or rectangular insert with numerous small channels, or tubes, running through it that increase combustion activity.

Certificate of occupancy A document issued by a local government agency, after a satisfactory inspection of a structure, that authorizes an owner or tenant to occupy the structure.

Cesspool A pit (sometimes lined with plastic) composed of stones and gravel through which raw sewage collects; it's a health and safety hazard and a code violation.

Checklist report A systemized itemization of the various components of a property that is organized into sections that allow the inspector to check off inspected property components and comment on any specific problems.

Circuit Path that electricity travels.

Circuit breakers Trip and switch off the electrical power for a given circuit if the current increases beyond the capacity of the system.

Cleanout A pipe fitted with a removable plug to assist in dislodging a pipe obstruction.

Compressor An air conditioner component that creates a flow of refrigerant from one part of the system to the other.

Condemnation The actual taking of property under the power of eminent domain.

Condenser An air conditioner component that liquefies the refrigerant gas by cooling it.

Conductors Wires that electricity moves through; good conductors have little resistance to the flow of electricity.

Control joints Vertical spaces in the brick wall joints that allow for the expansion and contraction of the brick and mortar.

Convector A heat-emitting unit in which heat is produced by the movement of air around a metal surface.

Cornice Trim piece for the eave.

Corporation A legal entity recognized by law with tax rates separate from individual income tax rates.

Counterflashing A second layer of flashing.

Creosote A black tar-like substance that builds up inside the chimney through normal use.

Cricket Composed of metal flashing, it prevents snow and ice from building up against the chimney.

Damper A plate or valve that closes the fireplace flue when the fireplace is not in use, preventing heat loss.

Deadman Component of a tieback used to support a wood retaining wall; the deadman is positioned parallel to the wall and perpendicular to the anchor post.

Deed restrictions Take the form of covenants or conditions and run with the land (move with the title in any subsequent deed).

Disclaimer Is appended to the home inspection report and documents the scope of the inspection and specifically indicates which items are omitted from the report, including opinions about the structure and design, building code compliance, and environmental problems.

Distribution box A part of a septic system that distributes the flow from the septic tank evenly to the absorption field or seepage pits.

Doing business as (d/b/a) A sole proprietorship that operates under a name other than the owner's.

Double top plate Used to tie the walls together and provide additional support for the ceiling and roof system.

Drainage The land's ability to draw off surface water.

Easement The right of another to use or have access to land belonging to another; also called right-of-way.

Eave The lowest part of the roof that projects beyond the walls of the structure.

Efflorescence White stains often observed on the foundation wall or floor slab that are caused by masonry mineral salts combining with water as it penetrates through the floor or wall.

Electric current The flow of electrons along a conductor such as a copper wire.

Electromagnetic field Occurs anytime electricity flows through a wire; there are two separate fields: an electric field and a magnetic field.

Eminent domain Power of a government or its agencies to take private property for public use.

Encroachment Trespass on the land of another as a result of an intrusion by some structure or other object.

Erosion The wearing away of land by water, wind, or other processes of nature.

Errors and omissions insurance A form of professional liability insurance that covers claims of negligence that occur while rendering a professional service.

Escheat The power of the state to take title to property left by a person who has died and has no legal heirs.

Evaporator An air conditioner component that takes heat from the air surrounding it and brings it to the refrigerant.

Extension springs Generally mounted just above the horizontal track of the garage door, they provide lifting power by stretching (extending).

Fascia The area of material facing the outer edge of the soffit.

Felt paper Exterior insulation material that is nailed over the sheathing.

Fixed-pane windows Do not open or close (e.g., picture window or variations of the bay window).

Flashing A metallic material that is used in certain areas of the roof and walls to prevent water from seeping into the structure.

Floating slab A type of foundation slab constructed by pouring the footing first, then pouring the slab.

Float valve Used to control water levels in tanks.

Floor joists Framing members that span the distance between the foundation walls and the girder and provide support for the subfloor.

Floor truss A support member constructed in a factory by nailing a number of smaller members (2 × 4s or 2 × 6s) together in a number of triangular patterns to provide maximum strength.

Flue The enclosed passageway in a chimney through which smoke and other gases move upward.

Flue collar The opening on the top, rear, or side of a wood-burning stove to which the stovepipe is connected.

Footing The concrete base below the frost line that supports the foundation of the structure.

Forced warm air system A type of heating system that contains a fan or blower, a heat source such as gas or oil, a heat exchanger, and filters; works by extracting cool air from indoors and outdoors and passing this cool air through the heat sources.

Formaldehyde A colorless, gaseous chemical compound that is generally present at low, variable concentrations in both indoor and outdoor air.

Foundation wall Generally composed of poured concrete, masonry (concrete) block, or brick; the height of the foundation wall determines whether the structure has a full basement or a crawl space.

Freon The most commonly used refrigerant in air conditioners.

Friable The ability of an asbestos-containing product to crumble easily and emit fibers.

Frieze board Prevents wind and moisture from penetrating the junction of the soffit and sheathing.

Fuse A device with an internal metal link that melts and opens the circuit, causing electrical power to stop when overheating occurs.

Gate valve A type of valve generally used as the main water shutoff valve to the property.

Girder The main carrying beam, either steel or several wooden members fastened together (usually 2 × 10s, 2 × 12s, or larger), that spans the distance from one side of the foundation to the other.

Glazing The material inside the windowpane.

Globe valve A type of valve that can adjust or stop the flow of water; it is used at points where it is needed infrequently such as in bathrooms.

Grading The arrangement and preparation of the soil for construction.

Ground fault circuit interrupter (GFCI) A device that shuts off a circuit immediately if it senses a short circuit.

Groundwater Water beneath the surface of the earth that can be collected with wells, tunnels, or drainage galleries or that flows naturally to the earth's surface via seeps or springs.

Grout A mixture of Portland cement, lime, and sand that is mixed with water to fill and seal the spaces between tiles.

Gypsum board A type of wall panel composed of an inner core of noncombustible gypsum and paper surfacing on the front, back, and edges.

Headers Beams that support the ceiling and the roof over the door and window openings.

Headroom The space between the stair and the overhang (or the ceiling inside the structure).

Heat exchanger The area where combustion or the burning of fuel for heat takes place in a furnace or hot water heater.

Hectare Metric system equivalent to the U.S. measurement of 2.47 acres.

Home inspection An examination of the exterior and interior of residential property including the grounds, the structure, and the mechanical systems to determine structural defects; broken or obsolete components; and damage due to water, wear and tear, and other conditions.

Home inspection report A written itemization and detailed summation of the findings of the home inspector with regard to a subject property.

Home inspector A qualified professional who performs a home inspection.

House wrap Exterior insulation material that is nailed over the sheathing.

Hydronic system A type of system that heats and cools liquids such as water.

Hydrostatic pressure The push of water against a surface.

Improvements Changes or additions made to a property, such as walls or roads, that generally increase the value of a property.

Independent contractor A worker who does not receive a set salary, does not work set hours, and provides his own tools and equipment.

Insulators Materials that are poor conductors of electricity and are, therefore, placed around wires to prevent electrical shock.

Internal reversing mechanism Part of a garage door opener, it causes the door to reverse when it hits an obstruction.

Joists Wooden framing members used to construct floors and ceilings.

Junction boxes Contain wiring and are used to provide the necessary space for making electrical connections.

Lally columns Round steel columns filled with concrete that support the main carrying beam of the structure, they rest on a base plate, which is the column footing pad.

Latent defect A hidden or concealed defect that cannot be discovered by ordinary observation or inspection.

Lead A toxic metallic element found in soil, water, and paint.

Lift handle Affixed to a garage overhead door (or a pull rope attached to the bottom bracket in the lower corner of the door) and used with a door that is opened and closed manually.

Light A layer of a glass window; windows may have one or more.

Limited liability company A form of business organization that combines the most favorable attributes of a partnership and a corporation.

Main soil stack A drainage pipe that connects to the house drain where waste leaves the system.

Main vent stack The top of the main soil stack that connects to all of the home's toilets.

Metal lath Available in a variety of styles and resembling a mesh or honeycomb pattern, the lath supports the plaster that hardens around it.

Monolithic slab A type of foundation slab where the footing and slab are poured at the same time.

Muntins Dividers that separate a window sash into smaller windows; may be a fake inset.

Narrative report Is written in paragraph form and reflects the inspector's observation and opinion of the condition of a subject property.

Narrative report with checklist or rating system A narrative report combined with a checklist or rating system report that more fully explains the inspector's observations of the subject property.

National Electric Code National standard for electrical installation and service.

Neutral bus bar A conductor on the main panel board that is the connection for the neutral and ground wires.

Non-catalytic stove A wood-burning stove that maximizes combustion efficiency by providing a secondary combustion air system.

Nonconforming use An authorized preexisting use of property in a zoned area that is different from the use specified by the zoning code.

Nonpotable water Wastewater or recycled water used in plumbing fixtures that is not safe for consumption.

Ohm A unit of measurement for resistance to the flow of electricity; a unit of electrical resistance of a conductor.

Outlet A point on a wiring system where current is taken to supply equipment.

Overcurrent protection device Responds quickly to ground faults; includes the main disconnect, circuit breakers, and fuses.

Partnership A form of business organization that is owned by two or more partners and is created by a contract between the partners.

Percolation rate The speed at which standing water is absorbed by the soil.

Photoelectric eye Sensor mounted five to six inches off the floor on both sides of a garage door.

Pitch The slope of the roof.

Plat A recorded subdivision map that shows the lots, their sizes, and where they are situated in the subdivision.

Platform framing The structure's framing rests on a subfloor platform; the most common type of framing used in residential construction.

Plenum A large metal conduit box in the form of a duct located inside the heating system where hot air builds up pressure and is then forced out to room heating elements.

Plumb A position or measurement that is truly and exactly vertical, 90 degrees from a level surface.

Plumbing fixture An appliance requiring a water supply and drainage system.

Police power Empowers government to fulfill its responsibility to provide for the public health, safety, and welfare of its citizens.

Post-and-beam framing Framing members are much larger than ordinary studs and may be four or six inches square; the larger posts are placed several feet apart instead of 16 or 24 inches on center.

Potable water Water that is safe for drinking.

Powderpost beetle A type of insect that eats wood.

Pre-inspection agreement A contract that protects both the home inspector and the client. It explains, in general terms, the scope of the inspection (what is included and what is not), the cost, and the procedures to address any dispute that may arise.

Pressure regulator valve (PRV) Also called a pressure-reducing valve; a type of valve that limits the water pressure, it reduces and automatically maintains the pressure of water within predetermined parameters.

Professional liability insurance Covers individuals and business organizations for claims made by third parties.

Property condition disclosure form Generally furnished to the seller by a real estate agent, the form asks the seller to disclose detailed information regarding the property.

Raceway Used to support, enclose, and protect electrical wires.

Radon A colorless, odorless, tasteless, radioactive gas that is present in the environment as a byproduct of the natural decay of uranium in the earth.

Rafters The long wooden framing members that are fastened to the ends of the ceiling joists and form the gables of the roof.

Rails Top and bottom pieces of the window sash.

Rating system report Uses a numerical evaluation on a scale, for example 1–5, to define the condition of each property component.

Rebars Steel reinforcement embedded in the concrete foundation.

Receptacle Connected to branch circuit wires that supply the current to equipment.

Refrigerant Any substance that produces a cooling effect by absorbing heat as it vaporizes (disperses into the air).

Residential Lead-Based Paint Hazard Reduction Act Sets forth the procedures for disclosing the presence of lead-based paint in properties built prior to 1978.

Resilient floor covering A manufactured interior floor covering in either sheet or tile form that returns to its original form after being bent, compressed, or stretched.

Retaining walls Structures made from a variety of materials, such as brick, stone, slate, poured concrete, concrete block, and pressure-treated wood, that are used to hold back areas of earth.

Ridge beam The highest part of the framing, it forms the apex, or top line, of the roof.

Right-of-way An easement allowing someone to use the land of another.

Riparian rights The right of a property owner whose land adjoins a watercourse, such as a river, to access and use the water.

Riser The vertical area of the step that supports the tread.

Roof truss system A roof frame made up of a number of smaller framing members; it carries the load-bearing function to the outer walls.

R-value The degree of resistance to heat transfer through the walls (heat is kept in or out); the larger the R-value, the greater the degree of insulation.

Sash The frame that surrounds and secures the glass.

Section joint The area between garage door sections.

Seepage pit A covered pit through which the discharge from the septic tank infiltrates into the surrounding soil.

Septic system A household wastewater treatment system consisting of a house sewer, septic tank, distribution box, and an absorption field or seepage pit.

Service drop Aboveground cables that come from the nearest pole connecting to the service entrance conductors of the house or building.

Service entrance cable (SE cable) A single conductor or several conductors, with or without covering, used for aboveground service entrance.

Service lateral Electric service that runs underground.

Service lateral conductors Conductors installed between the transformers and the meters for underground service.

Setback requirements Specified distances from the front and interior property lines to the building.

Sheathing Plywood covering placed over exterior framing members.

Sick building syndrome A chemical illness that may be caused by the air quality inside a commercial building.

Sill plate The first wooden member of the house and is used as the nailing surface for the floor system.

Slab-on-grade construction The foundation is a concrete slab instead of a foundation wall; the concrete slab is poured directly on the ground, eliminating the crawl space or basement.

Slope Land surface that is graded on an angle.

Slope gradient The inclination of the soil surface from the horizontal.

Soffit The perforated area under the roof extension that allows air to flow through the ridge vents to ventilate the attic.

Soil permeability The ability of the soil to absorb water.

Soil stacks Vertical pipes into which waste flows from waste pipes connected to each plumbing fixture.

Sole plate A horizontal base plate that serves as the foundation for the wall system.

Sole proprietorship The simplest form of business organization that is owned by one individual and may use a name other than the owner's personal name.

Spalling The crumbling of brick.

Special use permit Allows use that is otherwise not permitted in a zone.

Spot zoning A specific property within a zoned area is rezoned to permit a use different from the zoning requirements for that area; it is illegal in many states.

Statute of limitations Varies from state to state and by the type of claim asserted. It sets the time frame for commencing a lawsuit and begins to run on the date the claim arose or the date on which the client knew or reasonably should have known of the claim.

Steam system A heating system that consists of a boiler, where steam is produced, and a system of pipes that conveys the steam to radiators, convectors, or other types of room-heating elements.

Stile Side framing member of the window sash.

Stringer Also known as the carriage, it supports the stairway.

Studs Framing members, commonly 2 × 4s, 2 × 8s, 2 × 10s, or 2 × 12s, used vertically for wall construction.

Subdivision Land that is divided into lots for development purposes.

Subfloor A plywood surface nailed to the floor joists that serves as the surface for the floor finish.

Surface runoff The loss of water from an area by its flow over the land's surface.

Switch Used to open and close electrical circuits and allow current to flow to appliances.

Taxation One of the inherent burdens on private ownership of land; property taxes constitute a specific lien against the real estate.

Temperature pressure relief valve Used in hot water and steam systems, it allows hot water and steam to escape if the water temperature and pressure buildup are too high for the equipment.

Termite A type of insect that eats wood.

Thermocouple A device that automatically closes the gas valve that controls the flow of gas and stops its flow if the pilot light goes out.

Thermostat A control device that automatically responds to temperature changes by opening and closing an electric circuit.

Threshold The area on the ground in front of the door that keeps rain and snow from entering the structure.

Throat damper A damper located in the throat of the fireplace, just above the firebox.

Tiebacks Component of a wood retaining wall; must be anchored to the soil to prevent collapse of the wall.

Topography Includes types of soil; the location of water such as wetlands, springs, or floodplains; forest areas; and the location of rocks, trees, and other vegetation.

Torsion springs Usually mounted above the closed garage door, parallel and horizontal to the top section of the door, they provide lifting power by winding and unwinding while the door is opened or closed.

Toxic substance An element capable of causing adverse human health or environmental effects through exposure to even low levels.

Transformer Used to change alternating current from one voltage to another.

Trap A curved section of drainpipe that fills with water and provides a seal that prevents sewer gasses from entering a structure.

Tread The horizontal surface of the stair.

Trim Made of either metal or wood and used to finish windows, doorways, cabinetry, shelving, and the areas where the floor meets the wall and the wall meets the ceiling.

Underground storage tanks Used for the bulk storage of chemicals and petroleum.

Urea formaldehyde foam insulation (UFFI) A type of foam containing formaldehyde used as home insulation until the early 1980s.

U.S. Department of Housing and Urban Development (HUD) A federal agency that administers funding for projects related to housing.

Valve A device used to regulate the flow of a liquid or gas; it may force the flow in a certain direction.

Vapor barrier Sheets of moisture-resistant material, such as polyethylene film, kraft paper, or aluminum foil, bonded to insulation that prevent warm interior air from mixing with cold exterior air and forming condensation within the wall.

Variance A permitted deviation from specific requirements of a zoning ordinance.

Vent system A system of pipes that provides a flow of air to and from a drainage system; it permits gases and odors to circulate up through the system and escape into the air.

Voltage The electrical pressure that pushes through wires.

Water erosion The removal of soil material by flowing water.

Water hammer arrestor A type of valve that contains a hydraulic piston that absorbs the shock waves produced by sudden changes in water flow; it reduces the commonly heard banging in pipes.

Water table The uppermost boundary of the groundwater.

Weepholes Small perforations in retaining wall material that allow water drainage.

Wetlands Federal- and state-protected transition areas between uplands and aquatic habitats that provide flood and storm water control, surface and groundwater protection, erosion control, and pollution treatment.

Wood rot Caused by a type of fungus that destroys wood; it is as damaging as termite or other insect infestation.

Wythe A solid brick partition in the flue.

Zoning ordinance A statement setting forth the type of use permitted under each zoning classification and the specific requirements for compliance.

INDEX